The Handbook of

Logistics and Distribution Management

Second Edition

The Handbook of
Logistics and Distribution Management

Alan Rushton John Oxley Phil Croucher

The Institute of
Logistics and Transport

KOGAN
PAGE

First edition 1989
This edition 2000
Reprinted 2004

Kogan Page Limited
120 Pentonville Road
London N1 9JN
UK

Kogan Page US
22883 Quicksilver Drive
Sterling VA 20166-2012
USA

www.kogan-page.co.uk
© Rushton, Oxley and Croucher, 1989, 2000

British Library Cataloguing in Publication Data

A CIP record for this book is available from the British Library.

ISBN 0 7494 3365 5

Typeset by JS Typesetting, Wellingborough, Northants
Printed in Great Britain by Bell & Bain Ltd, Glasgow

Contents

List of figures

List of tables

Preface

In the preface to the first edition of this book, I wrote that a prime objective for writing the book was to provide an up-to-date text at a reasonable cost. We also felt that there was a significant gap in the literature for a book that offered a broad framework as well as a clear and straightforward description of the basic functions and elements related to logistics and distribution. The feedback that we received indicated that we had met these goals, and that the book was the core text for its subject area. Indeed, as we enter the new millennium, the original book is still selling – although the rate of change in business and logistics is such there is much in the original edition that is now outdated.

Hence this new and heavily revised edition has similar objectives to the first – those of simplicity of style and relevance of context.

The scope of logistics has grown rapidly in the past few years and this is reflected in the content of the book. We have included key aspects of supply chain philosophy and practice, but have tried to retain the focus on distribution and logistics that was a feature of the first edition of the book.

As with the first edition, it has not been possible to cover in depth all of the associated functions that we might have liked. Shortage of space necessitated this compromise. Thus, such elements as manufacturing and procurement are featured but only at a fairly superficial level and only in-depth when there are relevant interfaces with distribution and logistics.

John Oxley and I have welcomed Phil Croucher as a co-author of the new book. Phil has a practical strategic and operational background in distribution and logistics.

As well as his enthusiasm, he has provided a pragmatic and very experienced input to the writing of the book.

Once again, much of the context of the book has been drawn together from material that has been developed for the various Masters courses in Logistics and Supply Chain Management run at the Cranfield Centre for Logistics and Transportation, Cranfield School of Management. Work at Cranfield has included basic coursework, many company-based student projects and more traditional areas of research. In addition we continue to be involved in undertaking company training courses and consultancy assignments. Thus we undoubtedly owe our colleagues and our graduates many thanks – and apologies where we have included any of their ideas in the book without directly acknowledging them.

The logistics industry continues to change radically and to grow in importance. The quality of logistics managers and staff has also developed with the growth in responsibility and scope that a job in logistics entails. We hope that this book will help in the logistics managers' quest to improve service and reduce cost, as well as keeping them aware of the many different facets of logistics and the supply chain. It should be of interest to practising managers and supervisors, to those candidates undertaking examinations for the various professional institutes, and to undergraduate and graduate students who are reading for degrees in logistics, distribution and supply chain management, or where these subjects are an integral part of their course. It should also provide strong support for those participating in Web-based training in logistics.

The book is divided into seven distinct sections, each covering a key subject area in logistics. These are:

1. Concepts of Logistics and Distribution.
2. Planning for Logistics.
3. Procurement and Inventory Decisions.
4. Warehousing and Storage.
5. Freight Transport.
6. Information and Supply Chain Management.
7. Associated Factors.

Part 1 considers the key concepts of logistics and distribution. The first chapter of the book provides an introduction to the subject area and some definitions are given. The main elements and functions are reviewed, together with a brief look at the historical development of distribution and logistics up to the present day. Some statistics are introduced that indicate the importance of logistics to both companies and economies. Chapter 2 concentrates on the integrated nature of logistics and the supply chain. The traditional, but still very relevant, Total Logistics Concept is explained and typical trade-offs are considered. A planning hierarchy for distribution and logistics is outlined. Finally, in this chapter, some of the main moves towards integration are discussed.

Customer service is a major aspect within logistics, and this is considered in Chapter 3. The components of customer service are described and an approach to developing a customer service policy is outlined. Customer service measurement is reviewed. Chapter 4 concentrates on channels of distribution - the different types and different structures. A method of channel selection is considered. Also, the all-important question of whether to contract out logistics is assessed. Alternative types of third party operation are reviewed, together with the many services that are offered. The key drivers for contracting out are described. The final chapter of this first part of the book reviews some of the main issues and challenges for logistics, from external influences to consumer-related developments.

Part 2 covers the ways and means of planning for logistics. Chapter 6 begins with an overview of the strategic planning process and then considers a specific logistics design framework. The next chapter concentrates on one of the main aspects of this design framework – the planning of logistics processes. The key logistics processes are described and then an approach to process design or re-design is proposed. Some of the main tools and techniques are explained. Chapter 8 considers the planning of physical distribution activities – the more traditional pastures of depot location decisions. A discussion on the role of depots and warehouses is followed by a detailed assessment of the different cost relationships that are fundamental to the physical distribution planning process. A planned approach to designing an appropriate strategy is included.

Chapter 9 is concerned with the way in which logistics and distribution is organized within the company. The relationship with other corporate functions is considered. The need to develop more process-oriented organizational structures, rather than maintaining the traditional functional perspective is proposed. The specific role of the logistics and distribution manager is described. Some payment schemes and mechanisms that are common to the industry are outlined. The next chapter provides a very practical view of some of the common tactical and operational decisions that are made in distribution.

The final chapter in this section of the book is concerned with manufacturing and materials management. Manufacturing is rarely a function that is found directly within the auspices of logistics. It is, however, a major factor within the broader context of the supply chain and is a principal interface with logistics. Thus, some of the key elements in manufacturing and materials management are introduced in this chapter.

Part 3 concentrates on those issues that are involved with procurement and inventory decisions. Chapter 12 covers basic inventory planning and management. The reasons for holding stock are considered and the different types of stock are outlined. The implications of stockholding on other logistics functions are described, and the use of different inventory replenishment systems is explained. Re-order quantity decisions are discussed and the EOQ method is outlined. Simple demand forecasting is introduced. Chapter 13 describes some of the recent developments in inventory planning, particularly the way that inventory is viewed across the supply chain as a whole. The important relationship of inventory and time is explored. Key advances in inventory planning for manufacturing and for retailing are outlined. The final chapter in this section covers some of the main principles concerned with procurement. This is another area within the supply chain that has a significant interface with logistics, so a broad overview of key elements is described.

In Part 4, consideration is given to those factors that are concerned with warehousing and storage. Chapter 15 introduces the main warehousing principles and also provides an outline of the main warehouse operations. Storage systems and storage equipment are considered in Chapter 16. Included here are the principles of storage as well as descriptions of the various types of storage systems and storage equipment that are available. Chapter 17 concentrates on the many different handling systems and equipment types that are used from fork lift trucks through to conveyors. In Chapter 18, some of the main warehouse operations are described. The first, and particularly important function, is that of order picking. The main principles of order picking are explained, and the various order picking methods are outlined.

Chapter 19 considers some of the more advanced types of warehouse system. These are particularly relevant in the light of some of the recent changes in customer requirements and in the new developments in supply chain strategies and structures. An approach to warehouse and depot design and layout is described in Chapter 20. The methods described here are an essential guide to ensuring that a warehouse or depot is designed to be effective in the light of the logistics operation as a whole. Various warehouse management and information systems are outlined in Chapter 21

Part 5 concentrates on those areas of logistics and distribution specifically related to freight transport. Chapter 22 considers international logistics and the choice of transport mode. Initially, the relative importance of the different modes is reviewed and various operational factors for modal choice are described. The main attributes of the key modes of transport are outlined. Finally, a simple approach for modal choice selection is proposed, together with a brief review of some key aspects of international trade. In Chapter 23 the important developments in inter-modal transport are discussed.

The remaining chapters in this section of the book are concerned with aspects of road freight transport. Vehicle selection factors are described in Chapter 24. Included here are the main types of vehicle and vehicle body, different operational aspects, and load types and characteristics. In Chapter 25, vehicle and fleet costing is considered. The main transport costs are indicated and whole life costing is described. Various elements concerning road freight transport legislation and the implications for fleet operations are outlined in Chapter 26. The final part of section 5, Chapter 27, concentrates on the planning and resourcing of road freight transport operations. This includes the need for planning, and the important use of vehicle routing and scheduling to aid this process. The main objectives of routing and scheduling are indicated, and the different types of problem are described. The basic characteristics of road transport delivery are discussed, and they are related to broad data requirements. Examples of both manual and computer routing and scheduling methods are outlined.

Section 6 covers the important subject of information and supply chain management. This begins in Chapter 28, the monitoring and control of logistics and distribution, with an assessment of the need for effective monitoring. A description of a formal approach to logistics monitoring and control is then outlined. Several different means of measurement are introduced and a number of areas of best practice are considered. Examples of detailed key performance and cost indicators are given. Chapter 29 describes the use of benchmarking as a major technique for identifying best practice in logistics. As well as an overview of benchmarking procedures, a detailed approach to benchmarking distribution activities is outlined. Chapter 30 looks at information technology in the supply chain. There have been, and continue to be, many major advances in I.T. and information systems. This chapter serves to provide an overview of some of those elements that are particularly important to logistics and the main components of distribution.

The final section of the book pulls together a number of elements that don't fit easily into previous sections. The question of whether or not to contract out logistics was assessed in an early chapter. The actual process of selection is described in Chapter 31. A step by step guide is given from the initial need to identify the type of service that is required through to the need to manage the contract once it has been implemented. Chapter 32 considers a very important area of responsibility in logistics – that of security and safety. Many aspects that are relevant to logistics planning and operations are discussed. Another important consideration is the impact of logistics operations on the environment. This is reviewed in Chapter 33. The final chapter of the book provides a summary of some of the new concepts and developments that already impact on the way that logistics is planned and managed, and which will continue to influence logistics in the future. Included in Chapter 34 are some of the influences of the Internet and e-logistics, as well as the idea of the agile supply chain.

Alan Rushton

Abbreviations

NB: This section is designed to demystify many of the more common abbreviations of the industry. The fact that many may also appear in the text is not relevant – students may consult this section quite independently.

3D	Three dimensional
3PL	Third Party Logistics
4D	Four directional
4PL	Fourth Party Logistics
ABC curve	Pareto or ABC analysis
ADR	Accord Dangereuse Routier
AGV	Automated Guided Vehicle
APR	Adjustable Pallet Racking
Artic	Articulated
AS/RS	Automated Storage and Retrieval system
ASEAN	Association of South East Asian Nations
ASME	American Society of Mechanical Engineers
ATP	Accord Transport Perisable
B2B	Business to Business
B2C	Business to Consumer
BOM	Bill of Materials
BS	British Standard

BSI	British Standards Institution
CB trucks	Counterbalanced fork-lift trucks
CCLT	Cranfield Centre for Logistics and Transportation
CCTV	Closed Circuit Television
CFR	Cost and freight
CIF	Cost, Insurance, Freight
CIM	Computer Integrated Manufacturing
CIPS	Chartered Institute of Purchasing and Supply
CMI	Co-Managed Inventory
CMR	Convention Relative au Transport Internationale de Merchandises par Route
CNG	Compressed Natural Gas
CPT	Carriage paid to
CRP	Continuous Replenishment
CT	Community Transit
dB (a)	Decibel
DAF	Delivered at frontier
DC	Distribution Centre
DCF	Discounted Cash Flow
DDP	Delivered duty paid
DDU	Delivered duty unpaid
DEQ	Delivered ex-quay duty paid
DERV	Diesel Engined Road Vehicle
DES	Delivered ex-ship
DHL	An Airfreight Company
DoT	Department of Transport
DPP	Direct Product Profitability
DRP	Distribution Requirements Planning
EAN	European Article Number
EBQ	Economic Batch Quantity
ECR	Efficient Consumer Response
EDI	Electronic Data Interchange
EFTA	European Free Trade Area
EOQ	Economic Order Quantity
EPOS	Electronic Point of Sale
ERP	Enterprise Resource Planning
ES	Exponential smoothing
EU	European Union
Ex Works	From the supplier's factory

FAS	Free alongside ship
FCA	Free carrier
FEM	Federation European de la Manutention
FEU	Forty Feet Equivalent Unit
FIBC	Flexible Intermediate Bulk Container
FIFO	First in First out
FILO	First in Last out
FMCG	Fast moving consumer goods
FMS	Flexible Manufacturing Systems
FOB	Free on Board
FOC	Fire Officer's Committee
FRES	Federation of Recruitment & Employment Services
FTA	Freight Transport Association
GDP	Gross Domestic Product
GPS	Global Positioning System
GTIN	Global Trade Item Number
GVW	Gross Vehicle Weight
HGV	Heavy Goods Vehicle
HSE	Health and Safety Executive
HSWA	Health and Safety at Work Act
IBC	Intermediate Bulk Container
IJPDLM	*International Journal of Physical Distribution and Logistics Management*
ISO	International Standards Organisation
IT	Information Technology
ITT	Invitation to Tender
JDE	J D Edwards
JIT	Just-in-Time
LCL	Less than container load
LED	Light-emitting diode
LGV	Large Goods Vehicle
LIFO	Last in First out
LNG	Liquid Natural Gas
LOLO	Lift on/Lift off
LPG	Liquified Petroleum Gas
LTL	Less than truck load
MAM	Maximum authorized mass
MIS	Management Information Systems
MRP	Materials Requirements Planning

MRPII	Manufacturing Resource Planning
NAFTA	North American Free Trade Association
NCPDM	National Council of Physical Distribution Management
NDC	National Distribution Centre
NPV	Net Present Value
OCR	Optical character recognition
OTIF	On time in full
P & D	Pick up and Deposit
PCs	Personal computers
PEST analysis	Political, Economic, Socio-cultural, Technological
PLC	Product Life Cycle
POD	Proof of Delivery
PM	Particulate Matter
QA	Quality Assurance
QC	Quality Control
QFD	Quality Function Deployment
QR	Quick Response
R & D	Research and Development
RDC	Regional Distribution Centre (sometimes also Radio Data Communication)
RF	Radio Frequency
RFI	Request for Information
RFP	Request for Proposal
RFQ	Request for Quotation
RFS	Road-friendly suspension
ROCE	Return on Capital Employed
ROL	Re-order Level
RORO	Roll on Roll off
SAD	Single Administration Document
SEM	Single European Market
SEMA	Storage Equipment Manufacturers Association
SKU	Stock Keeping Unit
SSAP 21	Statements of Standard Accounting Practice 21
STGO	Special Types General Order
SWL	Safe Working Load
SWOT	Strengths, weaknesses, opportunities and threats
TEU	Twenty Feet Equivalent Unit
TIR	Transport International Routier
TLC	Total Logistics Concept

TQM	Total Quality Management
TUPE	Transfer of Undertakings: Protection of Employees
UN/EDIFACT	United Nations/Electronic Data Interchange for Administration, Commerce & Transport
VMI	Vendor Managed Inventory
VNA	Very Narrow Aisle
WIP	Work in Progress

Part 1

Concepts of logistics and distribution

1

Introduction to logistics and distribution

INTRODUCTION

Distribution has been an important feature of industrial and economic life for many years, but it is only in the relatively recent past that it has been recognized as a major function in its own right. The main reason for this lapse has probably been the nature of distribution itself. It is a function made up of many sub-functions and sub-systems each of which has been, and may still be, treated as a distinct management operation.

Both the academic and the business world now accept that there is a need to adopt a more global view of these different operations in order to take into account how they interrelate and interact with one another.

The appreciation of the scope and importance of distribution and logistics has led to a more scientific approach being adopted towards the subject. This approach has been aimed at the overall concept of the logistics function as a whole and also at the individual sub-systems. Much of this approach has addressed the need for, and means of, planning distribution and logistics, but has also considered some of the major operational issues.

DEFINITIONS

Parallel to the growth in the importance of distribution and logistics has been the growth in the number of associated names and different definitions that are used. Some of the different names that have been applied to distribution and logistics include:

- physical distribution;
- logistics;
- business logistics;
- materials management;
- procurement and supply;
- product flow;
- marketing logistics;
- supply chain management;

and there are several more.

There is, realistically, no 'true' name or 'true' definition that should be pedantically applied, because products differ, companies differ and systems differ. Logistics is a diverse and dynamic function that has to be flexible and has to change according to the various constraints and demands imposed upon it and with respect to the environment in which it works.

So these many terms are used, often interchangeably, in literature and in the business world. One quite widely accepted view shows the relationship as follows:

Logistics = Supply + Materials management + Distribution

As well as this, logistics is concerned with *physical* and *information* flows from raw material through to the final distribution of the finished product. Thus supply and materials management represents those flows into and through the production process, while distribution represents those flows from the final production point through to the customer or end user. Major emphasis is now placed on the importance of information as well as physical flows, and an additional and very relevant factor is that of reverse logistics – the flow of products and packaging back through the system. Figure 1.1 illustrates these different elements.

The question of the most appropriate definition of logistics and its associated namesakes is always an interesting one. Here, the textbooks provide some fascinating reading. Some of the better-known definitions include:

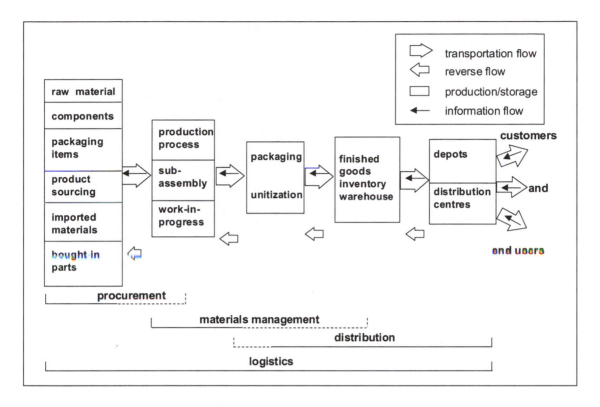

Figure 1.1 A logistics configuration showing the key components of logistics and the importance of physical flows and information flows

Logistics is the Art and Science of Determining Requirements; Acquiring them; Distributing them and finally, Maintaining them in an operational ready condition for their entire life.

(Stone, 1968)

... the management of all activities which facilitate movement and the co-ordination of supply and demand in the creation of time and place utility.

(Hesket, Glaskowsky and Ivie, 1973)

Logistics is the strategic management of movement, storage and information relating to materials, parts and finished goods in supply chains, through the stages of procurement, work-in-progress and final distribution. Its overall goal is to contribute to maximum current and future profitability through the cost effective fulfilment of customer orders.

(Cooper, ed, 1994)

Logistics is... the positioning of resource at the right time, in the right place, at the right cost, at the right quality.

(UK Institute of Logistics and Transport, 1998)

... the efficient movement of finished product from the end of the production line to the consumer, and in some cases includes the movement of raw materials from the source of supply to the beginning of the production line. These activities include freight transportation, warehousing, material handling, protective packaging, inventory control, plant and warehouse site selection, order processing, marketing forecasting and customer service.

(US National Council of Physical Distribution Management (NCPDM))

It is interesting to detect the different biases – military, economic, etc. It is not easy to determine which of the many definitions is most suitable. An appropriate modern definition that applies to most industry might be that logistics concerns the efficient transfer of goods from the source of supply through the place of manufacture to the place of consumption in a cost-effective way whilst providing an acceptable service to the customer. This focus on cost-effectiveness and customer service will be a point of emphasis throughout this book.

ELEMENTS OF LOGISTICS AND DISTRIBUTION

The NCPDM definition gives a useful list of some of the most important elements within distribution. This is a clear indication of the scope of distribution and its many facets.

This list can be 'exploded' once again to reveal the detailed aspects within the different elements. All of these functions and sub-functions need to be planned in a systematic way, in terms both of their own local environment and of the wider scope of the distribution system as a whole. A number of questions need to be asked and decisions made. The different ways of answering these questions and making these decisions will be addressed in the chapters of this book as consideration is given to how to plan and operate the distribution and logistics function.

Some examples include the following categories:

- storage, warehousing and materials handling
  - location of warehouses
  - number and size of distribution depots
  - type of operation
  - etc;

- transport
  - mode of transport
  - type of delivery operation
  - load planning
  - route schedule
  - etc;
- inventory
  - what to stock
  - where to stock
  - how much to stock
  - etc;
- information and control
  - design of systems
  - control procedures
  - forecasting
  - etc;
- packaging and unitization
  - unit load
  - protective packaging
  - handling systems
  - etc.

In addition, the total system interrelationships need to be considered and planned within the constraints of appropriate costs and service levels.

HISTORICAL PERSPECTIVE

The elements of distribution and logistics have, of course, always been fundamental to the manufacturing, storage and movement of goods and products. It is only relatively recently however that distribution and logistics have come to be recognized as vital functions within the business and economic environment. The role of logistics has changed in that it now plays a major part in the success of many different operations and organizations. In essence, the underlying concepts and rationale for logistics are not new. They have evolved through several stages of development, but still use the basic ideas such as trade-off analysis, value chains and systems theory together with their associated techniques.

There have been several distinct stages in the development of distribution and logistics.

1950s and early 1960s

In this period, distribution systems were unplanned and unformulated. Manufacturers manufactured, retailers retailed, and in some way or other the goods reached the shops. Distribution was broadly represented by the haulage industry and manufacturers' own-account fleets. There was little positive control and no real liaison between the various distribution-related functions.

1960s and early 1970s

In the 1960s and 1970s the concept of *physical distribution* was developed with the gradual realization that the 'dark continent' was indeed a valid area for managerial involvement. This consisted of the recognition that there was a series of interrelated physical activities such as transport, storage, materials handling and packaging that could be linked together and managed more effectively. In particular there was recognition of a relationship between the various functions, which enabled a systems approach and total cost perspective to be used. Under the auspices of a physical distribution manager, a number of distribution trade-offs could be planned and managed to provide both improved service and reduced cost. Initially the benefits were recognized by manufacturers who developed distribution operations to reflect the flow of their product through the supply chain.

1970s

This was an important decade in the development of the distribution concept. One major change was the recognition by some companies of the need to include distribution in the functional management structure of an organization. The decade also saw a change in the structure and control of the distribution chain. There was a decline in the power of the manufacturers and suppliers, and a marked increase in that of the major retailers. The larger retail chains developed their own distribution structures, based initially on the concept of regional or local distribution depots to supply their stores.

1980s

Fairly rapid cost increases and the clearer definition of the true costs of distribution contributed to a significant increase in professionalism within distribution. With this professionalism came a move towards longer-term planning and attempts to identify and pursue cost-saving measures. These measures included centralized distribution, severe reductions in stock-holding and the use of the computer to provide improved information and control. The growth of the third-party distribution service industry was also of major significance, with these companies spearheading developments in information and equipment technology. The concept of and need for *integrated* logistics systems were recognized by forward-looking companies that participated in distribution activities.

Late 1980s and early 1990s

In the late 1980s and early 1990s, and linked very much to advances in information technology, organizations began to broaden their perspectives in terms of the functions that could be integrated. In short, this covered the combining of materials management (the inbound side) with physical distribution (the outbound side). The term 'logistics' was used to describe this concept (see Figure 1.1). Once again this led to additional opportunities to improve customer service and reduce the associated costs. One major emphasis recognized during this period was the importance of the informational aspects as well as the physical aspects of logistics.

1990s

In the 1990s the process was developed even further to encompass not only the key functions within an organization's own boundaries, but also those functions outside that also contribute to the provision of a product to a final customer. This is known as *supply chain management* (see Figure 1.2). The supply chain concept thus recognizes that there may be several different organizations involved in getting a product to the market-place. Thus, for example, manufacturers and retailers should act together in partnership to help create a logistics pipeline that enables an efficient and effective flow of the right products through to the final customer. These partnerships or alliances should also include other intermediaries within the supply chain, such as third-party contractors.

2000 and beyond

Business organizations face many challenges as they endeavour to maintain or improve their position against their competitors, bring new products to market and increase the profitability of their operations. This has led to the development of many new ideas for improvement, specifically recognized in the redefinition of business goals and the re-engineering of entire systems.

One business area where this has been of particular significance is that of logistics. Indeed, for many organizations, changes in logistics have provided the catalyst for major enhancements to their business. Leading organizations have recognized

Figure 1.2 The concept of the supply chain – this refers to the idea of the development of a logistics pipeline approach for products to flow through the supply chain to the end customer

that there is a positive 'value added' role that logistics can offer, rather than the traditional view that the various functions within logistics are merely a cost burden that must be minimized regardless of any other implications.

Thus, the role and importance of logistics has, once again, been recognized as a key enabler for business improvement.

IMPORTANCE OF LOGISTICS AND DISTRIBUTION

It is useful, at this point, to consider logistics in the context of business and the economy as a whole. Logistics is an important activity making extensive use of the human and material resources that affect a national economy. Several investigations have been undertaken to try to estimate the extent of the impact of logistics on the economy.

One such study indicated that about 30 per cent of the working population in the UK are associated with work that is related to logistics. A recent study undertaken by Michigan State University in the USA, and reported in the *Financial Times* in December 1998, indicated that logistics alone represented between 10 and 15 per cent of the gross domestic product of most major North American, European and Asia/Pacific economies. This is summarized in Table 1.1.

These numbers represent some very substantial costs, and serve to illustrate how important it is to understand the nature of logistics costs and to identify means of keeping these costs to a minimum.

The breakdown of the costs of the different elements within logistics has also been included in a number of surveys. A survey of US logistics costs indicated that transport was the most important element at 46 per cent, followed by storage/warehousing (22 per cent), inventory carrying cost (22 per cent) and administration (10 per cent).

Table 1.1 Logistics costs for key countries

GDP	Logistics ($m)	Logistics ($m)	GDP %
North America			
Canada	585,105	70,191	12.00
Mexico	334,726	49,753	14.86
US	7,576,100	795,265	10.50
Subtotal	8,495,931	915,209	10.77
Europe			
Belgium/Luxembourg	286,383	32,573	11.37
Denmark	174,237	22,440	12.88
France	1,537,582	171,230	11.14
Germany	2,352,472	306,264	13.02
Greece	122,870	15,269	12.43
Ireland	67,392	9,611	14.26
Italy	1,214,272	137,027	11.28
Netherlands	392,550	44,495	11.33
Portugal	101,182	12,871	12.72
Spain	581,565	67,022	11.52
UK	1,151,348	122,344	10.63
Subtotal	7,981,853	941,146	11.79
Asia/Pacific			
Hong Kong	153,068	20,992	13.71
Japan	4,599,706	522,982	11.37
Korea	484,777	59,764	12.33
Singapore	94,063	13,074	13.90
Taiwan	273,440	35,686	13.05
Subtotal	5,605,054	652,498	11.64
Remaining other countries	7,080,122	916,168	12.94
1996 global size	29,162,960	3,425,021	11.74

Source: Financial Times, December 1998

These broad figures are supported by a European logistics productivity survey, produced by A T Kearney. These results, covering the major EU economies, placed transport at 41 per cent, inventory carrying cost at 23 per cent, warehousing at 21 per cent and administration at 15 per cent of overall costs. In both studies, therefore, the transport cost element of distribution was the major constituent part.

It is interesting to see how the relative make-up of these costs varies from one company to another and, particularly, from one industry to another. Listed in Table 1.2 are some examples of logistics costs from different companies. These are taken from a recent industry cost audit undertaken in the UK by Dialog Consultants Ltd. They are roughly comparable, but reflect the difficulty some companies have in directly categorizing their costs.

Table 1.2 Cost as a percentage of sales turnover

Cost as Percentage of Sales Turnover	Transport Cost	Warehouse/ Depot Cost	Inventory Investment/ Holding Cost	Admin- istration Cost	Overall Distribution Cost
Main company business	%	%	%	%	%
Office Equipment	3.20	10.70	0.87		14.77
Health Supplies	1.36	9.77	0.66	0.19	11.98
Soft Drinks	2.53	2.71	0.44		5.68
Beer (Food and Drink)	8.16	2.82	0.56	2.19	13.74
Spirits Distribution	0.37	0.27	0.07	0.10	0.81
Cement	25.20	9.10	7.10	4.60	46.00
Automotive Parts	2.07	6.35	1.53		9.96
Gas Supply (non-bulk)	9.41	2.45	0.02		11.98
Computer Maintenance	0.45	0.10	0.29	0.05	0.88
Computer Supply	0.65	0.78	0.09		1.52
Healthcare	0.96	1.08	1.21		3.25
Specialist Chemicals	7.23	1.95	0.20	0.49	9.87
Fashion	0.38	1.31	0.33		2.02
Food Packaging	3.14	3.73	0.85		7.72

Source: Benchmark survey of UK companies by Dialog Consultants Ltd

One of the main reasons for these cost differences is that logistics structures can and do differ quite dramatically between one company and another, and one industry and another. Channels can be short (ie very direct) or long (ie have many intermediate stocking points). Also, channels may be operated by manufacturers, retailers or, as is now becoming increasingly common, by specialist third-party distribution companies. In the examples shown above, the relative importance of logistics is, of course, measured in relationship to the overall value of the particular products in question. Cement is a low-cost product (as well as being a very bulky one!), so the relative costs of its logistics are very high. Spirits (whisky, gin, etc) are very high-value products, so the relative logistics costs appear very low. These and other associated aspects are discussed in subsequent chapters.

LOGISTICS AND DISTRIBUTION STRUCTURE

The discussion in the previous sections of this chapter has illustrated the major components to be found within a logistics or distribution system. The fundamental characteristics of a physical distribution structure could be considered as the flow of material or product, interspersed at various points by periods when the material or product is stationary. This flow is usually some form of transportation of the product. The stationary periods are usually for storage, or to allow some change to the product to take place – manufacture, assembly, packing, break bulk, etc.

A simple distribution flow is illustrated in Figure 1.3. The different types of transport (primary, local delivery, etc) and stationary functions (production, finished goods inventory, etc) are shown. It should be noted that to support these physical flows and functions, there is a complementary flow of information, which allows the physical flow to occur.

There is also, of course, a cost incurred to enable the distribution operation to take place. The importance of this distribution or logistical cost to the final cost of the product has already been highlighted. As has been noted, it can vary according to the sophistication of the distribution system used and the intrinsic value of the product itself. One idea that has been put forward in recent years is that these different elements of logistics are providing an 'added value' to a product as it is made available to the final user – rather than just imposing an additional cost. This is a more positive view of logistics, and is a useful way of assessing the real contribution and importance of logistics and distribution services. Figure 1.4 provides an example of this cost or added value for a typical low-cost product. The added value element varies considerably from one product to another.

THE INDUSTRY AND EDUCATION

Logistics and distribution are now recognized as being vital and integral parts of the business and economy of a country. In recent years, in many different countries,

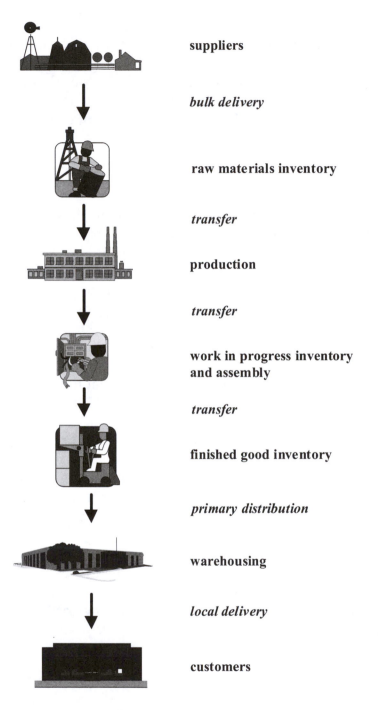

Figure 1.3 A typical physical distribution flow of material from suppliers through to customers, showing stationary functions and movement functions

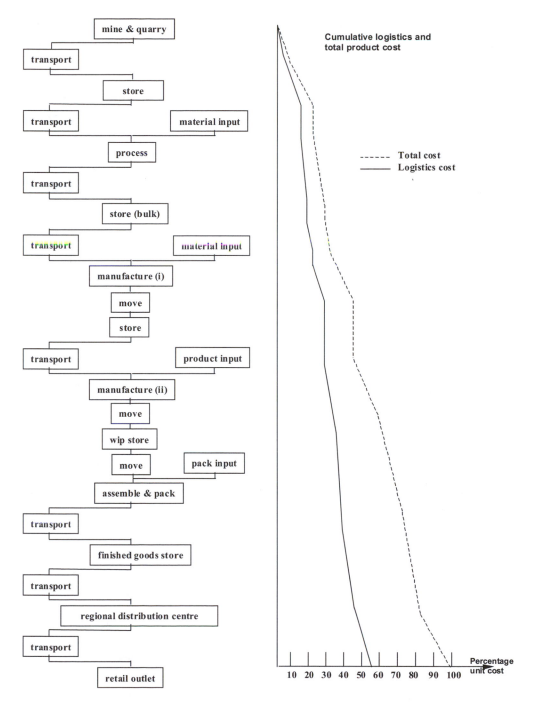

Figure 1.4 The cost make-up of a consumer product, showing the 'added value' of the logistics element as a unit cost through the logistics chain

the logistics industry has set out to develop a distinct professionalism to reflect this increasing growth in importance.

In the UK, for example, the industry is served by the Institute of Logistics and Transportation, recently formed from the Institute of Logistics and the Chartered Institute of Transport. The Institute plays a leading role in promoting logistics and distribution as a recognized profession. Membership has increased dramatically over the past few years and it continues to rise. The Institute provides a full programme of conferences and seminars in order to promote the industry.

The Chartered Institute of Purchasing and Supply (CIPS) is the largest professional purchasing and supply organization in Europe. The role of distribution and logistics is fundamental to the Institute's areas of interest. Membership to the Institute is by examination, and logistics is a major element within all of the Institute's activities, including the professional examination syllabus, and the public courses and conference programmes.

In terms of education, there are now a number of opportunities open to the individual who chooses to make his or her career in logistics and distribution. The Cranfield Centre for Logistics and Transportation (CCLT) is located within the Cranfield School of Management, at Cranfield University in the UK. The Centre offers both a full-time (one-year) and part-time (two-year) Masters programme in logistics and supply chain management. Participants from across the world have attended these programmes. From the outset, these postgraduate courses have been designed specifically for the logistics and distribution industry.

Other educational developments have also taken place. The University of Huddersfield, for example, offers an undergraduate course in transport and distribution, while many business studies and transport courses provide options related to distribution and logistics. In addition, various institutes, the Cranfield Centre for Logistics and Transportation and others, offer one- to five-day short courses on various distribution, logistics and supply-chain-related topics.

SUMMARY

In this initial chapter, a number of subjects have been introduced. These will be expanded in subsequent chapters of the book.

The rather confusing number of associated names and different definitions were indicated and a few of the very many definitions were considered. No 'true' or definitive definition was offered, because logistics and distribution can and do differ dramatically from one industry, company or product to another.

The recent history of distribution was outlined, and a series of statistics served to illustrate how important logistics and distribution are to the economy in general and to individual companies. The breakdown between the constituent parts of distribution was given.

The basic structure of distribution and logistics was described, and the concepts of material and information flow and the added value of logistics were introduced. Finally, some of the opportunities for education and training were outlined.

2

Integrated logistics and the supply chain

INTRODUCTION

In the first chapter, different definitions of logistics were introduced, and the main components of distribution were outlined. It was shown that the major distribution functions were part of a flow process within the broad logistics operation. In this chapter, the emphasis is on the need to integrate the various distribution and logistics components into a complete working structure that enables the overall system to run at the optimum. Thus the concept of 'total logistics' is described and the importance of recognizing the opportunities for appropriate trade-offs is discussed. Some key aspects of planning for logistics are reviewed. Finally, a number of recent developments in logistics thinking are put forward, including the globalization of many companies, integrated planning systems, supply chain management and the use of logistics to help create competitive advantage.

THE TOTAL LOGISTICS CONCEPT

The total logistics concept (TLC) aims to treat the many different elements that come under the broad category of distribution and logistics as one single integrated system. It is a recognition that the interrelationships between different elements, for example, delivery transport and storage, need to be considered within the context of the broader supply chain. Thus, the total system should be considered and not just an individual element or sub-system in isolation.

An understanding of the concept is especially important when planning for any aspect of distribution and logistics. A simple, practical example helps to emphasize the point:

> A company produces plastic toys that are packaged in cardboard boxes. These boxes are packed on to wooden pallets that are used as the basic unit load in the warehouse and in the transport vehicles for delivery to customers.
>
> A study indicates that the cardboard box is an unnecessary cost because it does not provide any significant additional protection to the quite robust plastic toys, and it does not appear to offer any significant marketing advantage. Thus, the box is discarded, lowering the unit cost of the toy, and so providing a potential advantage in the market-place.
>
> One unforeseen result, however, is that the toys, without their boxes, cannot be stacked on to wooden pallets because they are unstable, but must be stored and moved instead in special trays. These trays are totally different to the unit load that is currently used in the warehouse and on the vehicles (ie the wooden pallet). The additional cost penalty in providing special trays and catering for another type of unit load for storage and delivery is a high one – much higher than the savings made on the product packaging.

This example illustrates a classic case of *sub-optimization* in a distribution system. It shows how the concept of total logistics can be ignored at some significant cost. As the product packaging costs have been reduced, those concerned with this company function will feel that they have done their job well. The overall effect on the total logistics cost is, in fact, a negative one. The company is better served by disregarding this potential saving on packaging because the additional warehouse and transport costs mean that total costs increase.

This simple example of sub-optimization emphasizes the point concerning the interrelationships of the different logistics elements. A more positive viewpoint is to interpret these and other interrelationships in a planned approach to identifying and determining *cost trade-offs*. These will provide a positive benefit to the logistics system as a whole. Such a trade-off may entail additional cost in one function but will provide a greater cost saving in another. The overall achievement will be a net gain to the system.

This type of trade-off analysis is an important part of planning for logistics. Four different levels of trade-off have been identified:

1. *Within distribution components*: those trade-offs that occur within single functions. One example would be the decision to use random storage locations compared to fixed storage locations in a depot. The first of these provides better storage utilization but is more difficult for picking; the second is easier for picking but does not provide such good storage utilization.

2. *Between distribution components*: those trade-offs between the different elements in distribution. To reverse the previous packaging example, a company might increase the strength and thus the cost of packaging but find greater savings through improvements in the warehousing and storage of the product (ie block stacking rather than a requirement for racking).

3. *Between company functions*: there are a number of areas of interface between company functions where trade-offs can be made. These are illustrated in Figure 2.1, which lists many of the different logistics activities and indicates which company function each one might affect. An example is the trade-off between optimizing production run lengths and the associated warehousing costs of storing the finished product. Long production runs produce lower unit costs (and thus more cost-effective production), but mean that more product must be stored for a longer period (which is less cost-effective for warehousing).

4. *Between the company and external organizations*: where a trade-off may be beneficial for two companies that are associated with each other. For example, a change from a manufacturer's products being delivered direct to a retailer's stores to delivery via the retailer's distribution system might lead to mutual savings for the two companies.

These types of trade-offs are thus at the heart of the total logistics concept. For the planning of distribution and logistics, it is important that this overall view of a logistics system and its costs is taken. The other side of the equation is, of course, the need to provide the service level that is required by the customer. This balance of total logistics cost and customer service level is essential to successful logistics.

PLANNING FOR DISTRIBUTION AND LOGISTICS

In order to ensure that the concept of total logistics is put into practice, and that suitable trade-offs are achieved, it is essential that a positive planning approach is adopted. In this section, the various planning horizons with their associated logistics decisions are discussed. In Chapter 6 a more formalized planning framework will be discussed. This will be developed in subsequent chapters into a more practical and detailed approach to logistics planning.

Activity \ Function	Finance	Production	Distribution	Marketing
MH Equipment	✓		✓	
Storage Systems	✓		✓	
Depot Building	✓		✓	
Delivery Transport	✓		✓	✓
Distribution Information Systems		✓	✓	
Inventory Control				
Production Control	✓	✓	✓	
Customer Service		✓	✓	
Depot Location		✓	✓	✓
Order Processing	✓		✓	✓
Finished Goods Warehouse	✓	✓	✓	
Packaging	✓	✓	✓	✓
Unit Load		✓	✓	✓
etc				

Figure 2.1 Interfaces between different company functions where trade-offs can be made

Planning should be undertaken according to a certain hierarchy that reflects different planning time horizons. These are generally classified as strategic, tactical and operational. They are represented in Figure 2.2. There is an overlap between the main planning stages, which emphasizes that there are many planning factors that can be covered by different stages in this planning hierarchy. The relative importance of these various aspects of logistics may differ between one company and another. The choice of transport mode could, for example, be an initial strategic decision and a subsequent tactical decision for the same company. It might also be a strategic decision for a company that is setting up a new global logistics operation, but might be a tactical decision for another company that is principally a supplier to a locally based market and only occasionally exports over long distances.

Figure 2.2 also indicates the interrelationship of planning and control within this hierarchy. Both of these different elements are essential to the running of an effective and efficient logistics operation. One way to envisage the difference between these two concepts is as follows: planning is about ensuring that the operation is set up to run properly – it is 'doing the right thing' or preparing for and planning the operation 'effectively'; control is about managing the operation in the right way – it is 'doing the thing right' or making sure that the operation is being run 'efficiently'.

Once again it is not relevant to define exactly which strategic, tactical and operational decisions or tasks within a company should be classified as either planning or control. Most elements need to be planned correctly in the first place, and then subsequently they need to be monitored and controlled to ensure that the operation is running as well as it should be. The practical means of monitoring and controlling logistics are described in Chapter 28.

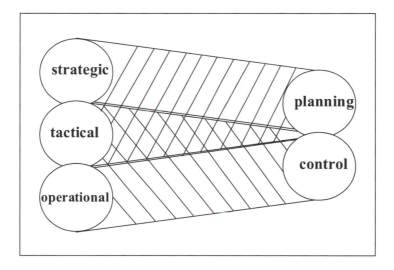

Figure 2.2 Logistics planning hierarchy

Some of the major aspects and differences between the three time horizons can be summarized as follows:

● strategic
 – a medium- to long-term horizon
 – one to five years (plus) time span

- overall 'structural' decisions are made, generally balancing and trading off between company functions or other organizations
- corporate financial plans and policies provide the financial basis for strategic planning
- policy decisions are developed into a strategic plan;
- tactical
  - a short- to medium-term horizon
  - six months to one year (plus) time span
  - decisions that involve sub-systems only – generally not expected to impose on other logistics components
  - annual budgets provide the financial/cost basis
  - the detail of the strategic plan is being put into effect;
- operational
  - this is really day-to-day decision making
  - operations are controlled against expected standards and rules
  - weekly and monthly reports are provided for control purposes
  - this concerns the implementation of the detail of regular operations.

The importance and relevance of these different aspects will, of course, vary according to the type and scale of business, product, etc. It is helpful to be aware of the planning horizon and the associated implications for each major decision that is made.

It is possible to identify many different elements within distribution and logistics that can be broadly categorized within this planning hierarchy. As already indicated, these may vary from one company to another, and from one operation to another. Some of these – in no particular order – are as follows:

- strategic
  - customer service
  - channels of distribution
  - supply points
  - production locations
  - types of depot/depot configuration
  - number of depots
  - location and size of depots
  - transport modal choice
  - third party or own account
  - direct delivery
  - stock levels
  - etc;

- tactical (for example at depot level)
    - transport
      vehicle types
      vehicle size
      vehicle numbers
      contract hire
      trunking routes
      delivery schedules
      driver resources
      support facilities
      etc
    - depot storage
      design
      layout
      space allocation
      storage media
      handling methods
      fork-lift truck numbers
      fork-lift truck types
      unit loads
      etc
    - administration/information
      information support systems
      monitoring procedures
      stock control
      stock location system
      order processing
      documentation
      etc;
- operational
    - goods receipt and checking
    - bulk storage
    - order picking
    - stock replenishment
    - order marshalling
    - load scheduling
    - returns
    - personnel availability
    - stock update

- documentation completion
- vehicle maintenance
- vehicle workshop activity
- etc.

These examples serve to emphasize the complexity of distribution and logistics. In addition, they underline the need for appropriate planning and control. Distribution and logistics are not merely the transportation of goods from one point to another. There are many and varied elements that go together to produce an effective distribution and logistics operation. These elements interrelate, and they need to be planned over suitable time horizons.

The planning and control of an operation can also be described within the context of a broader planning cycle. This emphasizes the need for a systematic approach, where continual review takes place. This is an important idea in logistics because most operations need to be highly dynamic – they are subject to continual change as both demand and supply of goods and products regularly varies according to changes in customer requirements for new products and better availability. One example of a fairly common framework is shown as the planning and control cycle in Figure 2.3.

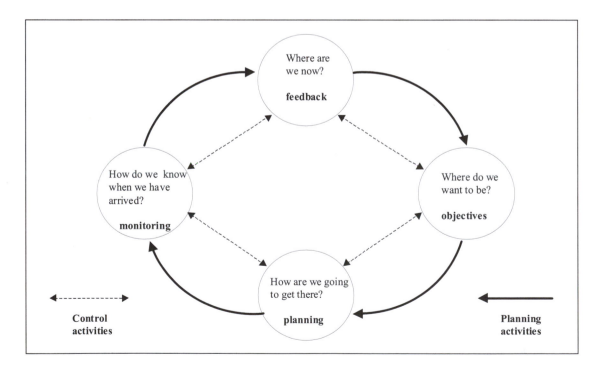

Figure 2.3   The planning and control cycle

The cycle begins with the question 'Where are we now?' Here the aim is to provide a picture of the current position. This might be through an information feedback procedure or through the use of a specific logistics or distribution audit. The second stage is to determine the objectives of the logistics process, to identify what the operation should be trying to achieve. These need to be related to such elements as customer service requirements, marketing decisions, etc.

The third stage in the cycle is the planning process that spans the strategic and operational levels previously discussed. Finally, there is a need for monitoring and control procedures to measure the effectiveness of the distribution operation compared to the plan. The cycle has then turned full circle and the process is ready to begin again. This allows for the dynamic nature of logistics, the need for continual review and revision of plans, policies and operations. This must be undertaken within a positive planning framework in order to ensure that continuity and progress are maintained.

GLOBALIZATION AND INTEGRATION

One area of significant change in recent years has been the increase in the number of companies operating in the global market-place. This necessitates a broader perspective than when operating as an international company. In the latter, although companies may have a presence across a wide geographic area, this is supported on a local or regional basis through local or regional sourcing, manufacturing, storage and distribution. In the former, the company is truly global, with a structure and policy that represents a global business. Typical attributes will include:

- global branding;
- global sourcing;
- global production;
- centralization of inventories;
- centralization of information;

but with the ability to provide for local requirements, be this electronic standards for electrical goods, language on packaging or left-/right-hand drive alternatives in the automotive industry.

To service global markets, logistics networks become, necessarily, far more expansive and far more complex. Once again, the need is to plan and manage logistics as a complete system. As well as the attributes already mentioned, companies operating in a global market are often involved with the outsourcing of some manufacturing and the use of 'focused' factories that specialize in a limited number of products.

The major logistics implications of globalization are:

- extended supply lead times;
- extended and unreliable transit times;
- multiple break bulk and consolidation options;
- multiple freight mode and cost options;
- production postponement with local added value.

It is obvious from this that there is a direct conflict between globalization and the move to the just-in-time operations that are being sought by many companies. In global companies there is a tendency to see order lead times increase and inventory levels rise because of the distances involved and the complexity of logistics. In companies moving to the just-in-time philosophy there is a desire to reduce lead times and to eliminate unnecessary stock and waste within their operations. For those companies trying to achieve both goals, there is a clear challenge for logistics.

INTEGRATED SYSTEMS

To support the need to develop more integrated operations there have been a number of recent developments in logistics and distribution systems that have the concept of total logistics as their basis. Thus, quite revolutionary 'trade-offs' are now being practised. The major reason for this explosion of new ideas is twofold. The first is the realization of the importance and cost of logistics. The second is the progress made in the field of information technology, which has enabled the type of detailed analysis to be undertaken that was previously impossible. Some of these alternative approaches to integrated physical and information systems are described in the following three sections.

Direct product profitability (DPP)

DPP is a technique of allocating all of the appropriate costs and allowances to a given product. All distribution costs (storage, transport, etc) are therefore assigned to a specific product rather than taking an average over a whole product range. Thus, in the same way that a budgetary system operates, the actual costs of distributing a product are monitored and compared to a standard cost determined using DPP. In this way, areas of inefficiency can be identified. DPP techniques can identify the costs of specific products to individual customers and so provide invaluable information for effective marketing strategies.

Materials requirements planning (MRP) and distribution requirements planning (DRP)

MRP/DRP systems have been developed as sophisticated, computerized planning tools that aim to make the necessary materials or inventory available when needed. The concept originated with materials requirements planning (MRP), an inventory control technique for determining dependent demand for manufacturing supply. Subsequently, manufacturing resource planning (MRP II) was developed with the objective of improving productivity through the detailed planning and control of production resources. MRP II systems are based on an integrated approach to the whole manufacturing process from orders through production planning and control techniques to the purchasing and supply of materials. Distribution requirements planning (DRP) is the application of MRP II techniques to the management of inventory and material flow – effective warehousing and transportation support.

DRP systems operate by breaking down the flow of material from the source of supply through the distribution network of depots and transportation modes. This is undertaken on a time-phased basis to ensure that the required goods 'flow' through the system and are available as and when required – at the right place, at the right time, one of the classic distribution definitions. Integrated systems of this nature require sophisticated, computerized information systems as their basis. The benefits of an effective system can be readily seen in terms of reduced freight, storage and inventory holding costs and improved customer service.

Just-in-time (JIT)

JIT originated as a new approach to manufacturing and has been successfully applied in many industries such as the automotive industry. It has significant implications for distribution and logistics. The overall concept of JIT is to provide a production system that eliminates all activities that neither add value to the final product nor allow for the continuous flow of material – in simple terms, that eliminates the costly and wasteful elements within a production process. The objectives of JIT are vitally linked to distribution and logistics, including as they do:

- the production of goods the customer wants;
- the production of goods when the customer wants them;
- the production of perfect quality goods; and
- the elimination of waste (labour, inventory, movement, space, etc).

There are a number of JIT techniques used to a greater or lesser extent by the generally large companies that have adopted the JIT philosophy. These techniques include:

- pull scheduling – whereby production is linked to 'demand pull' rather than 'schedule push' control systems (thus throughout the production and supply process only the precise material requirements are drawn, serving to eliminate the need for inventory);
- mixed production – this means that only the required goods need to be produced as processes can be easily switched to other products;
- fast set-up times – enabling almost continuous production of different products;
- preventative maintenance – to ensure unbroken production;
- revised plant layout – to minimize handling and movement;
- total quality control – identifying errors and defects at source;
- supplier liaison – extending JIT principles to suppliers.

An effective JIT system must be integrated throughout the manufacturing operation and must also include the supply and demand aspects of the business. It demands an effective and efficient information and physical distribution system to ensure that the major benefits can be realized.

As with all such approaches, JIT has some negative points as well as the more positive ones listed above. It can, for example, lead to increased traffic flows due to the need for smaller but more frequent deliveries of goods to the customer.

LOGISTICS AND SUPPLY CHAIN MANAGEMENT

Much of the previous content of this chapter has led us towards the more recent concept of supply chain management. This is, in reality, an extension of the ideas that have been developed concerning the integrated nature of logistics. We have considered the total logistics concept that advocates the benefits of viewing the various elements of logistics as an integrated whole. Supply chain management is similar, but also includes the supplier and the end user in the process. Figure 2.4 illustrates this within a typical pipeline approach (the same as the pipeline described in the previous chapter). This is the major difference between supply chain management and traditional logistics.

There are four distinct differences claimed for supply chain management over the more classic view of logistics, although some of these elements have also been recognized as key to the successful planning of logistics operations. These four are:

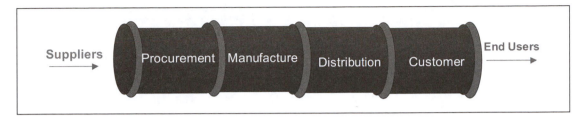

Figure 2.4 A simple supply chain pipeline that emphasizes the flow of product through the system

1. The supply chain is viewed as a single entity rather than a series of fragmented elements such as procurement, manufacturing, distribution, etc. This is also how logistics is viewed in most forward-looking companies. The real change is that both the suppliers and the end users are included in the planning process, thus going outside the boundaries of a single organization in an attempt to plan for the supply chain as a whole.
2. Supply chain management is very much a strategic planning process, with a particular emphasis on strategic decision making rather than on the operational systems.
3. Supply chain management provides for a very different approach to dealing with inventory throughout the pipeline process. Traditionally, inventory has been used as a safety-valve between the separate components within the pipeline – thus leading to large and expensive stocks of products. Supply chain management aims to alter this perspective so that inventory is used as a last resort to balance the integrated flow of product through the pipeline.
4. Central to the success of effective supply chain management is the use of integrated information systems that are a part of the whole supply chain rather than merely acting in isolation for each of the separate components. These enable visibility of product demand and stock levels through the full length of the pipeline. This has only become a possibility with the recent advances in information systems technology.

The move towards integration within different supply chains has been relatively slow; indeed, most companies have fairly limited integration within their own organizations. Full external integration is thus still a 'Holy Grail' that many organizations are striving to achieve. Many companies have moved to functional integration with some achieving an element of full internal integration. Figure 2.5 illustrates the different levels of integration a company might reach. The need to hold large inventories where integration is poor is demonstrated by this diagram.

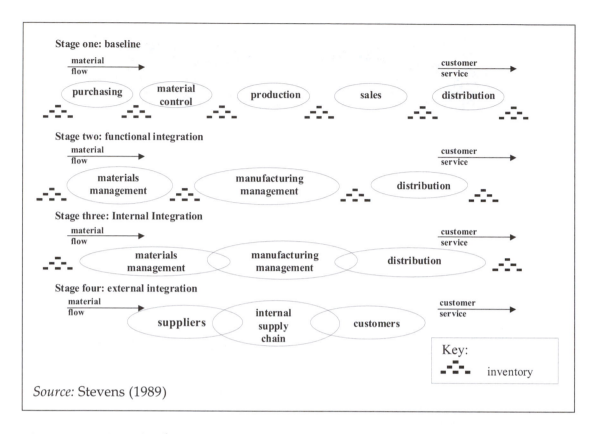

Figure 2.5 Supply chain integration

COMPETITIVE ADVANTAGE THROUGH LOGISTICS

Attitudes towards distribution and logistics have changed quite dramatically in recent years. It has been a long-held view that the various elements within logistics have merely created additional cost for those companies trying to sell products in the market-place. Although there is, of course, a cost associated with the movement and storage of goods, it is now recognized that distribution and logistics also provide a very positive contribution to the value of a product. This is because logistics operations provide the means by which the product can reach the customer or end user in the appropriate condition and required location.

It is therefore possible for companies to compete on the basis of providing a product either at the lowest possible cost (so that the customer will buy it because it is the least expensive) or at the highest possible value to the customer (eg if it is exactly where and how the customer wants it). Some companies may, indeed, try to achieve both of these objectives. This is particularly important these days as there are many products that are not sold on the basis of their brand name alone but that are, in fact, like commodities sold on the basis of availability or price. This applies to many food products as well as technical products, such as mobile phones and personal computers.

These ideas are illustrated in Figure 2.6. This simple quadrant shows that a company may compete as a *service leader*, where it is trying to gain an advantage over its competitors by providing a number of key service elements to differentiate itself. Or it may compete as a *cost leader* where it is trying to utilize its resources so that it offers the product at the lowest possible cost, thus gaining a productivity advantage. Examples of how this might be achieved are given in Figure 2.6. For a value/differential advantage, this might include the provision of a specially tailored service or the use of several different channels of distribution so that the product is available in the market-place in a number of different ways. It might include a guaranteed service level or a regular update on the status of orders. For a cost/productivity advantage, this will include a number of different means of cost minimization, such as maintaining very low levels of inventory and ensuring that all manufacturing and distribution assets are kept at a high utilization.

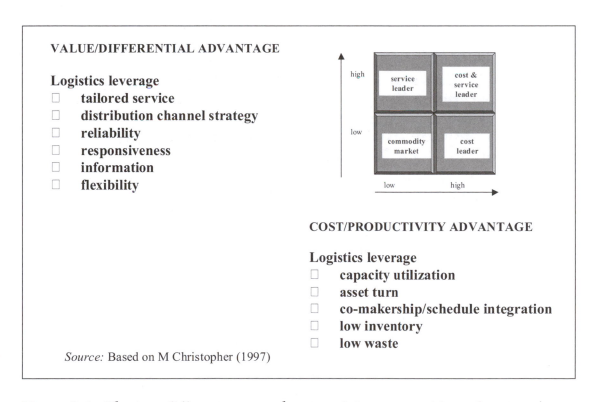

Figure 2.6   The two different approaches to gaining competitive advantage

SUMMARY

The realization of the need for the effective planning and control of distribution, coupled with the obvious interrelationships within distribution and logistics systems, have led to the development of several new approaches towards integrated systems. The recent advances in information technology have made the practical application of these new approaches feasible. All in all, there has been a very positive move towards an integrated approach to logistics although for many companies, both large and small, there is still considerable scope for improvement.

The more complex and sophisticated systems and concepts such as DPP, MRP, DRP and JIT have been adopted by a number of large, generally multinational companies. Smaller companies have been slower to adopt these concepts, despite the clear benefits to be gained. The main reasons for this are:

- a lack of organizational integration that reflects the role and importance of logistics and distribution;
- a failure to develop adequate long-term plans for logistics strategy; and
- insufficiently developed information structures and support systems to provide the appropriate databases for good logistics planning and management.

For many small and medium-sized companies, there is also the very pertinent factor that they need to learn to walk the distribution/logistics path before they attempt to run on it. But even for companies such as these, there is a great deal to be gained from taking those first few steps towards recognizing that logistics should be viewed as an integrated system and that there is a strong interrelationship between the different elements of transportation, storage, information, etc. In addition, there is the need to adopt a positive approach to the planning and control of those systems.

Fortunately, in the past few years, companies have, to a greater or lesser extent, realized the importance and relevance of distribution and logistics to their business as a whole. Thus, organizational structures and planning policies are now beginning to reflect this integrated approach.

In this chapter, the 'total logistics concept' has been introduced and the need to recognize the opportunities for logistics trade-offs has been emphasized. The importance of the need to integrate the various distribution and logistics components into a complete working structure that enables the overall system to run at the optimum has been identified. Some key aspects of planning for logistics have been reviewed. Finally, a number of recent developments in logistics thinking have been put forward, including the globalization of companies, integrated planning systems, supply chain management and the use of logistics to help create competitive advantage.

3

Customer service and logistics

INTRODUCTION

The vast majority of companies consider customer service to be an important aspect of their business. When pressed, however, there are many companies that find it difficult to describe exactly what they mean by customer service or provide a precise definition of customer service measures. Traditionally, service provisions have been based on very broad assumptions of what customers want, rather than taking into account the real requirements of customers or at least customers' perceptions of what they require.

There are several major points that need to be considered. One is the definition of customer service, and another is its measurement. It is also important to understand that customer service and customer service requirements can and will differ not just between industries and companies, but additionally between the market segments a business might serve.

Another relevant factor is the recognition of the complexity of customer service provision. Customer service is inextricably linked to the process of distribution and logistics. Within this process, there are many influences that may be relevant to customer service. These range from the ease of ordering to stock availability to delivery reliability. Finally, there is the need to balance the level of service provided with the cost of that provision. The downfall of many a service offering is often the unrealistic and unrecognized high cost of providing a service that may, in the event, be greater than is required by the customer.

The key to achieving a successful customer service policy is to develop appropriate objectives through a proper framework that includes liaison with the customer, and then to measure, monitor and control the procedures that have been set up.

THE COMPONENTS OF CUSTOMER SERVICE

The logistics components of customer service can be classified in different ways. They may be seen as transaction-related elements, where the emphasis is on the specific service provided, such as on-time delivery, or they may be seen as functional attributes that are related to overall aspects of order fulfilment, such as the ease of order taking.

Transaction elements are usually divided into three categories, to reflect the nature and timing of the particular service requirements:

1. *Pre-transaction elements*: these are customer service factors that arise prior to the actual transaction taking place. They include
    -   written customer service policy
    -   accessibility of order personnel
    -   single order contact point
    -   organizational structure
    -   method of ordering
    -   order size constraints
    -   system flexibility
    -   transaction elements.
2. *Transaction elements*: these are the elements directly related to the physical transaction and are those that are most commonly concerned with distribution and logistics. Under this heading would be included
    -   order cycle time
    -   order preparation
    -   inventory availability
    -   delivery alternatives
    -   delivery time
    -   delivery reliability
    -   delivery of complete order
    -   condition of goods
    -   order status information.

3. *Post-transaction elements*: these involve those elements that occur after the delivery has taken place, such as
    - availability of spares
    - call-out time
    - invoicing procedures
    - invoicing accuracy
    - product tracing / warranty
    - returns policy
    - customer complaints and procedures
    - claims procedures.

Customer service elements can also be classified by multifunctional dimensions. The intention is to assess the different components of customer service across the whole range of company functions, to try to enable a seamless service provision. Time, for example, constitutes a single requirement that covers the entire span from order placement to the actual delivery of the order – the order cycle time. One of the main consequences of this approach is that it enables some very relevant overall logistics measures to be derived. These will be considered later in this chapter. The four main multifunctional dimensions are:

1. time – usually order cycle time;
2. dependability – guaranteed fixed delivery times of accurate, undamaged orders;
3. communications – ease of order taking;
4. flexibility – the ability to recognize and respond to a customer's changing needs.

There are many different elements of customer service, and their relevance and relative importance will vary according to the product, company and market concerned.

A CUSTOMER SERVICE POLICY

The fact that there are so many different elements of customer service as indicated in the previous section underlines the need for a company to have a clearly defined customer service policy. Also, there are many different types of customer even for the same product. A can of cola, for example, may be bought in a supermarket, a corner shop, a petrol station or from a self-service dispensing unit. It is unlikely that a manufacturer of cola would wish to provide exactly the same level and style of service to all these very different customer types – an additional argument for the need for a clearly defined customer service policy.

Many studies have been undertaken to measure the effects of poor customer service. These studies conclude, quite categorically, that where stock is not available or where delivery is unreliable, many buyers will readily turn to an alternative supplier's products to fulfil their requirements.

Once the positive need for a customer service policy has been recognized and accepted, it is necessary to determine the basic requirements and format of this policy. These might include:

- an understanding of the different market segments that exist;
- an awareness of the customers' needs or perceived needs within this segmentation;
- the determination of clearly defined and quantifiable standards of customer service in relation to the different market segments;
- an understanding of the trade-off between the costs and levels of customer service;
- measurement of the service provided; and
- liaison with customers to ensure an understanding and appreciation of the service provided.

It is also important to understand what minimum requirements are necessary when identifying any particular service policy. A supplier is really working towards meeting customers' minimum requirements to cross the threshold of customer satisfaction. If these minimum requirements are not met, the supplier cannot even expect to be considered as a feasible supplier. Once these requirements are met and the supplier begins to exceed them, it then becomes possible to achieve customer satisfaction and begin to add value to the supply relationship.

The next stage is to set about defining this customer service policy. In the following section such an approach is described.

AN APPROACH FOR DEVELOPING A CUSTOMER SERVICE POLICY

It is possible to develop a logical approach to facilitate the establishment of a suitable customer service policy. One such approach is shown in Figure 3.1. This is a six-step plan to identify key customer service components and then to design a suitable customer service package.

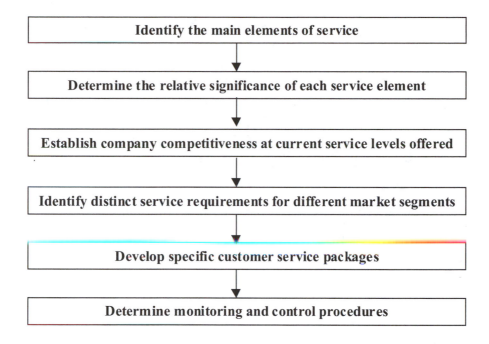

Figure 3.1 An approach to establishing a customer service policy

The main steps are as follows:

1. *Identify the main elements of service.* As already discussed, it is important to identify those elements of service that are most highly rated by the customer. Only then can the company's resources be concentrated on these key factors. The main means of determining these key components are by market research techniques. These processes might include
   – the identification of the main decision-maker or buyer of the product
   – the use of personal interviews to determine the importance of customer service and the different elements within customer service
   – the use of group interviews to determine the same.
   The importance of this stage is to identify relevant measures of service that are generated by customers themselves and not imposed arbitrarily by 'best guesses' from outside.
2. *Determine the relative significance of each service element.* Once again, there are various research techniques that can be used to measure the relative importance of the service components identified. For a fairly small list of components, some form of order ranking ('most' to 'least' important) or rating scale (one to six

according to importance) can be used. One relatively recent technique is that of trade-off analysis. This provides a more sophisticated format for considering and measuring the *relative* importance of different combinations of service components, rather than just scoring them on an individual basis. Straightforward rating of the key elements is often sufficient. A simple example of such a rating table is shown in Figure 3.2. It is also possible at this stage to identify what the minimum requirements are for customer service – that threshold below which it is unlikely that a customer will consider a company as a feasible supplier.

How would you rate these different elements of customer service?						
(Score from 1–6; 1 = not at all important, 6 = extremely important)						
	Please circle					
Frequency of delivery	1	2	3	4	5	6
Reliability of delivery	1	2	3	4	5	6
Stock availability and continuity of supply	1	2	3	4	5	6
Orders filled completely	1	2	3	4	5	6
Accuracy of invoices	1	2	3	4	5	6
Customer query handling	1	2	3	4	5	6

Figure 3.2 Rating table for selected customer service factors

3. *Establish company competitiveness at current service levels offered.* Having identified the key service components and their relative importance to the customer, the next step is to measure how well the company is performing for each of these key components. This can be undertaken by means of a questionnaire that lists the key components that have been identified and asks for a rating on perceived performance. This will provide an indication of where the company is both underperforming and overperforming, and where it has got it about right. See Figure 3.3. This shows that there is a target area for service in which the company should be operating. It will highlight those areas where there is room for improvement, and those areas where too much effort is being spent. There is little benefit in performing extremely well in those areas that are of little consequence to the customer.

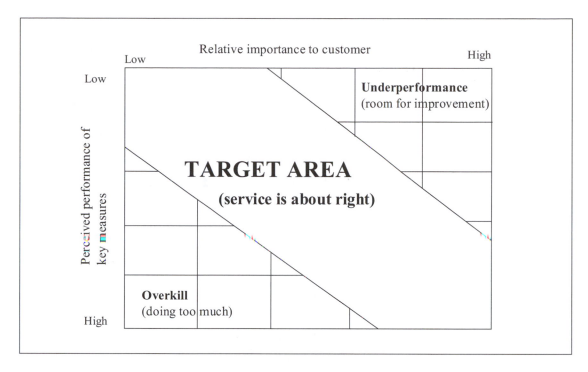

Figure 3.3 Customer service targets

It is also important to be aware of the company's own position compared to that of its major competitors. Respondents can be asked to rate each competing company in a similar way on a separate questionnaire. The results will indicate how each competitor performs according to the key service components. The company's performance can then be compared to the competition's and also to the most important service elements as identified in the previous stage of the study. This will provide some very useful information on how well the company is performing compared to its competitors, but importantly this can be related directly to the customers' key customer service requirements. Figure 3.4 gives an example of this. Here it can be seen that our company is performing reasonably well *overall* compared to our key competitor (the right-hand side of the figure), but that our competitor is actually performing much better than our company *in those elements that are most important to the customer* (the left-hand side of the figure). The usefulness of such an approach is clearly demonstrated by this simple example. This is often known as competitive benchmarking. From this type of information, an appropriate customer service strategy can be developed.

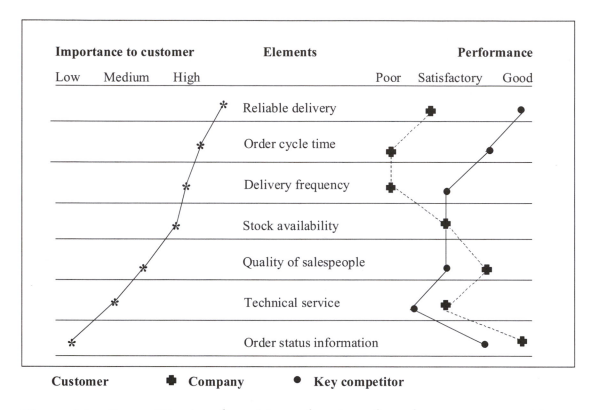

Figure 3.4 Competitive benchmarking – showing where there are opportunities to improve service when comparing with customer requirements and key competitors

4. *Identify distinct service requirements for different market segments.* It is now recognized that the needs of different customers can vary quite substantially. This may be true in terms of product quality, method of ordering, level of service or any other of the many different service elements that can be identified. Within a total market, it is possible to identify distinct submarkets or segments. A typical example might be the supply of stationery items. These might be supplied to retailers for sale to the public, to wholesalers for further distribution or direct to public service bodies or private companies for their own consumption. Each segment of the overall market may require a distinctly different level of service, or may react differently to certain deficiencies of service. The cola example discussed earlier in this chapter provides another example of different types of service requirement. Once different market segments have been identified, a number of specific customer service policies can be developed, each of which should suit the relevant groups or segments.

5. *Develop specific customer service packages.* These will depend on the results obtained from the stages that have been described. Having identified alternative packages for the different market segments, these need to be costed out accordingly. By doing so, appropriate costs can be compared and the most suitable packages determined, not just by the service element but also by the costs involved in the presentation of each package.

6. *Determine monitoring and control procedures.* It is vital to ensure that any service policy implemented is also monitored. This requires an effective focus on the measurement of the service provided, involving a systematic and continuous concentration on monitoring and control. In practice, it is rare for this to be adequately carried out: firstly, because companies do not have a recognized customer service policy, and secondly, because companies find it difficult to construct quantifiable standards that are capable of measurement. The first task, then, is to identify the factors that need to be measured. These should be based on the major elements identified in the customer service packages that are developed. The second task is to produce a measure or series of measures. This can be undertaken in different ways for different elements, but must be fair and appropriate for the task in hand. The development of such measures, together with relevant examples, is described later in this chapter. One final point concerns the need to ensure that any service measures are periodically reviewed. Businesses change fairly rapidly, with new products and new customers appearing continually. A regular updating of service measures is relevant, so that old measures are discarded as they become redundant, and new measures are created as they become necessary. Some large companies carry out regular customer service studies designed to identify such changes in service requirements.

LEVELS OF CUSTOMER SERVICE

It has already been stressed that there is a need to balance the level of customer service with the cost of providing that service. This balance is not easy to define, although it can be described quite easily as the point where the additional revenue for each increment of service is equal to the extra cost of providing that increment.

It is seldom possible to devise a policy that is absolutely optimal in terms of the cost/service balance. Some companies adopt a cost minimization approach where specific service objectives are laid down and met at a minimum cost. Others choose a service maximization approach where a distribution budget is fixed, and the 'best' service supplied within this cost constraint. The most appropriate approach to adopt will depend on particular product, business or market situations.

One factor that is clear, however, is the relationship between cost and service. This is shown in Figure 3.5. The cost of providing a given service is markedly higher the nearer it reaches the 'perfect service' – that is, the 100 per cent mark. Thus, an increase of 2 per cent in service levels will cost far more between 95 and 97 per cent than between 70 and 72 per cent. It should also be noted that a service increase from, say, 95 to 97 per cent may well have little, if any, noticeable impact on the customer's perception of the service being provided, even though it is a costly improvement.

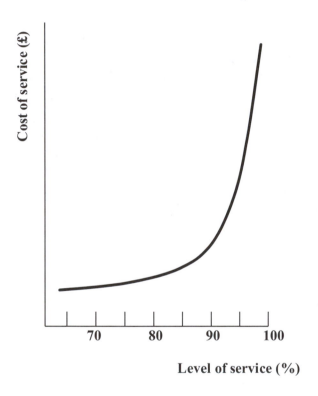

Figure 3.5 Relationship between cost and service level

MEASURING CUSTOMER SERVICE

It is probably quite clear from reading this chapter that there are many different measures of customer service that might be used. The most important message is that whatever measures are used, they must reflect the key service requirements for the customer in question. This is not always as obvious as it might seem. One particular example is that of order fulfilment. It is possible to measure this in a number of different ways:

- the number of orders completely satisfied, say 18 out of 20, over a period (90%);
- the number of lines delivered from a single order, say 75 out of the 80 lines requested (94%);
- the number of line items or cases delivered from a single order, say 75 out of the 80 lines requested, but only 1,400 of the 1,800 total line items (78%);
- the value of the order completed, say £750 of the £900 order (83%).

Any or all of these might be used and there is no right or wrong one. The most appropriate is the one that best suits the operation in question. As will be shown later, it may also be relevant to use a combination of these measures.

There are other measures that can be made. These measures might, for example, be aimed at assessing the timeliness of delivery operations. Many express parcels companies set great store by the speed of their delivery operations, and calculate in detail the time taken from receipt of order or parcel collection to final delivery. This idea is also used for conventional operations. Thus, order fulfilment can also be measured with respect to the order cycle time or the actual lead time from the receipt of the order to its final delivery to the customer. For a typical stock order this will be made up of the following discrete times:

- order receipt to order entry;
- order entry to allocation for picking;
- allocation to dispatch;
- dispatch to delivery.

Some companies now recognize what is known as 'the perfect order'. This is a measure that attempts to take into account all of the main attributes that go towards the completion of an order that absolutely satisfies customer requirements. This is known as 'on time in full' or OTIF. The key components are:

- delivered complete to the quantities ordered;
- delivered exactly to the customer's requested date and time;
- no delivery problems (damage, shortage, refusal);
- accurate and complete delivery documentation.

Thus perfect order fulfilment, in this context, can be measured as:

$$\text{order fulfilment} = \frac{\text{number of perfect orders}}{\text{total number of orders}} \times 100\%$$

Organizations must therefore set clear, customer-service-driven measures of performance that reflect the real standards they are aiming to achieve. These, typically, ask severe questions of many logistics operations. For realistic measurement, any discrepancies should be assessed cumulatively. Thus, if they include

orders received on time	98%
orders received complete	97%
orders received damage-free	99%
orders filled accurately	99%
orders invoiced accurately	96%

the actual customer service measure achieved is (98 × 97 × 99 × 99 × 96) = 89 per cent. This is not as good as it first looks when considering each measure individually.

In the United States, a study by A T Kearney concentrating on the food industry identified five key customer service elements, all of which are very pertinent and provide a challenge for logistics operations. This study indicated what performance expectations were expected in 2000 (see Table 3.1). For many operations, particularly in the grocery industry, the measures are still relevant, but the expectations have already been surpassed.

Table 3.1 Customer service elements for the food industry

Element	1995	2000
Product Availability	98%	99%
Order Cycle Time	9 days	7 days
Complete Orders Shipped	90%	94%
Accurate Invoices Provided	90% of invoices	93%
Damaged Products	1%	0.5%

Sources: Grocery Manufacturers of America and A T Kearney (1995) Customer service data for food industry

THE CUSTOMER SERVICE EXPLOSION

The importance of customer service as a critical success factor for most companies has been emphasized in recent years. There are, perhaps, many different reasons for this resurgence in importance, but the major change stems from a growing realization that satisfying the customer is the key to achieving competitive success. Companies that fail to appreciate this do so at their peril because they may lose significant market share. Service, nowadays, is the key factor of differentiation in a customer's decision to buy one brand rather than another. In other words, good customer service can provide the distinctive difference between one company's offer and its competitors'. Thus, customer service strategy must play a major role in the determination of company strategy.

One key factor that comes through all this is the important role that logistics has to play in providing good customer service. The ability to improve service levels and to maintain this improvement is a challenge that faces many companies. What has led to this change? The major factors are:

- The growth in customer expectations – thus service fulfilment has become a priority for any successful strategy.
- The growing professionalism of buyers – many buyers now recognize the importance of service as well as price in the product offering.
- Markets have become increasingly service-sensitive – there is little else to differentiate between products.
- The diminution of brand loyalty, particularly with respect to FMCG, where immediate product availability is the vital factor.
- The development of new ideas such as relationship marketing where fulfilling service expectations is the key and customer retention is a priority.

SUMMARY

This chapter has considered some of the key aspects of customer service and logistics. The major components of customer service were described. They were summarized as:

1. *Pre-transaction elements*: these are customer service factors that arise prior to the actual transaction taking place.
2. *Transaction elements*: these are the elements directly related to the physical transaction and are those that are most commonly concerned with distribution and logistics.

3. *Post-transaction elements*: these involve those elements that occur after the delivery has taken place.

The need for an appropriate customer service policy was emphasized. An approach for developing such a policy was outlined. This included six main steps:

1. Identify the main elements of service.
2. Determine the relative significance of each service element.
3. Establish company competitiveness at the current service levels that are being offered.
4. Identify distinct service requirements for different market segments.
5. Develop specific customer service packages.
6. Determine monitoring and control procedures.

The importance of accurate customer service measurement was explained. Different measures of order fulfilment were described and the concept of 'the perfect order' was put forward – 'on time in full' or OTIF.

Achieving appropriate and effective customer service has become a critical factor for success for most companies operating in today's competitive environment. This chapter has considered some of the key requirements for successful customer service in logistics.

4

Channels of distribution

INTRODUCTION

This chapter looks at the alternative ways in which products can reach their market. Different types of distribution channel are discussed and an approach to channel selection is described. Finally, the very important question of whether to run an own-account distribution operation or whether to use a third party is reviewed.

Physical distribution channel is the term used to describe the method and means by which a product or a group of products are physically transferred, or distributed, from their point of production to the point at which they are made available to the final customer. In general, this end point is a retail outlet, shop or factory, but it may also be the customer's house, because some channels bypass the shop and go direct to the consumer.

In addition to the physical distribution channel, another type of channel exists. This is known as the *trading or transaction channel*. The trading channel is also concerned with the product, and with the fact that it is being transferred from the point of production to the point of consumption. The trading channel, however, is concerned with the non-physical aspects of this transfer. These aspects concern the sequence of negotiation, the buying and selling of the product, and the ownership of the goods as they are transferred through the various distribution systems.

One of the more fundamental issues of distribution planning is regarding the choice and selection of these channels. The question that arises, for both physical and trading channels, is whether the producer should transfer the product directly to the consumer, or whether intermediaries should be used. These intermediaries are, at the final stage, very likely to be retailers, but for some of the other links in the supply chain it is now very usual to consider a third-party operator to undertake the operation.

CHANNEL TYPES AND STRUCTURE

There are several alternative channels of distribution that can be used, and a combination of these may be incorporated within a channel structure. The diagram in Figure 4.1 indicates the main alternative channels for a single consumer product being transferred from a manufacturer's production point to a retail store or shop. Channels from industrial suppliers to industrial customers are, of course, equally important. Many of the alternatives described here are relevant for movements such as these.

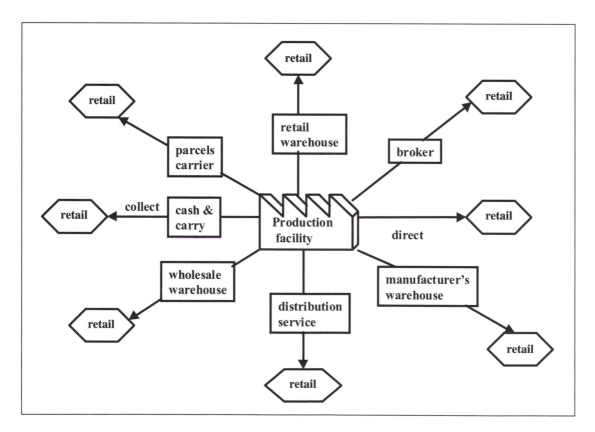

Figure 4.1 Alternative distribution channels for consumer products

The alternative channels are described below.

Manufacturer direct to retail store

The manufacturer or supplier delivers direct from the production point to the retail store. As a general rule, this channel is only used when full vehicle loads are being delivered.

Manufacturer via manufacturer's distribution operation to retail store

This was one of the classic physical distribution channels and the most common channel for many years. Here, the manufacturer or supplier holds its products either in a finished goods warehouse, a central depot or a series of regional depots. The products are trunked in large vehicles to the depots, where they are stored and then broken down into individual orders that are delivered to retail stores on the supplier's retail delivery vehicles. Since the 1970s, the use of this type of physical distribution channel has decreased in importance due to a number of developments in alternative channels of physical distribution. This type of channel is still commonly used by the brewing industry.

Manufacturer via retailer depot to retail store

This channel consists of manufacturers supplying their products to national distribution centres (NDCs) or regional distribution centres (RDCs), which are depots run by the retail organizations. These centres act as consolidation depots, as goods from the various manufacturers and suppliers are consolidated at the depot. The retailers then use their own delivery vehicles to deliver full vehicle loads of all the different manufacturers' products to their own stores. This type of distribution channel grew in importance during the 1970s and 1980s as a direct result of the growth of the large multiple retail organizations that are now a feature of the high street and of the large retail parks. Many retailers now use third parties to run these final delivery operations.

Manufacturer to wholesaler to retail shop

Wholesalers have acted as the intermediaries in distribution chains for many years, providing the link between the manufacturer and the small retailers' shops. However, this physical distribution channel has altered in recent years with the development of wholesale organizations or voluntary chains. These wholesaler organizations are known as 'symbol' groups in the grocery trade. They were generally begun on the basis of securing a price advantage by buying in bulk from manufacturers or suppliers. One consequence of this has been the development of an important physical distribution channel because the wholesalers use their own depots and vehicle fleets.

Manufacturer to cash-and-carry wholesaler to retail shop

Another important development in wholesaling has been the introduction of cash-and-carry businesses. These are usually built around a wholesale organization and consist of small independent shops collecting their orders from regional wholesalers, rather than having them delivered. The increase in cash-and-carry facilities has arisen because many suppliers will not deliver direct to small shops because the order quantities are very small.

Manufacturer via third-party distribution service to retail shop

Third-party distribution or the distribution service industry has grown very rapidly indeed in recent years. The industry has grown for a number of reasons, the main ones being the extensive rise in distribution costs and the constantly changing and more restrictive distribution legislation that has occurred. Thus, a number of companies have developed a particular expertise in warehousing and distribution. These companies consist of those offering general distribution services as well as those that concentrate on providing a 'specialist' service for one type of product (eg china and glass, hanging garments), or for one client company. Developments in third-party distribution are considered at the end of this chapter.

Manufacturer via small parcels carrier to retail shop

Very similar to the previous physical distribution channel, these companies provide a 'specialist' distribution service where the 'product' is any small parcel. There has been an explosion in the 1980s and 90s of small parcels companies, specializing particularly in 'next day' delivery. The competition generated by these companies has been quite fierce.

Manufacturer via broker to retail shop

This is a relatively rare type of channel, and may sometimes be a trading channel and *not* a physical distribution channel. A broker is similar to a wholesaler in that it acts as intermediary between manufacturer and retailer. Its role is different, however, because it is often more concerned with the marketing of a series of products, and not really with their physical distribution. Thus a broker may use third-party distributors, or it may have its own warehouse and delivery system. The broker can provide an alternative physical distribution channel.

The main alternative physical distribution channels described above refer to those consumer products where the movement is from the manufacturer to the retail store. There are additional channels for industrial products and for the delivery of some consumer products that do not fit within the structure of the diagram because they bypass the retail store. They necessitate the consideration of different types of distribution channel.

Mail order

The use of mail order or catalogue shopping has become very popular. Goods are ordered by catalogue, and delivered to the home by post or parcels carrier. The physical distribution channel is thus from manufacturer to mail order house as a conventional trunking operation, and then to the consumer's home by post or parcels carrier, bypassing the retail store.

Factory direct to home

The direct factory-to-home channel is a relatively rare alternative. It can occur by direct selling methods often as a result of newspaper advertising. It is also commonly used for 'one-off' special products that are specially made and do not need to be stocked in a warehouse to provide a particular level of service to the customer.

Internet and shopping from home

There is now an important development in shopping from home via the Internet. Initial physical distribution channels were similar to those used by mail order operations – by post and parcels carrier. The move to Internet shopping for grocery products has led to the introduction of specialist home delivery distribution operations. These are run either by the retailers themselves or by third-party companies. In addition, it is now possible to distribute some products, such as music, software and films, directly, computer to computer.

Factory to factory

The factory-to-factory channel is an extremely important one, as it includes all of the movement of industrial products, of which there are very many. This may cover raw materials, components, part-assembled products, etc. Options vary according to the type and size of product and order, and may range from full loads to small parcels.

It can be seen from the list of alternative channels that the channel structures can differ very markedly from one company to another. The main differences are:

- the types of intermediaries (as shown above);
- the number of levels of intermediaries (how many companies handle the product); and
- the intensity of distribution at each level (ie are all or just selective intermediaries used at the different levels?).

An individual company may have many different products and many different types of customer. Such a company will therefore use a number of different channels within its distribution operation. This, together with the large number of variable factors and elements possible within a channel structure, makes it difficult to summarize effectively. The diagram of Figure 4.2, however, gives a fair representation of a typical single-channel structure. Note the different physical and trading channels.

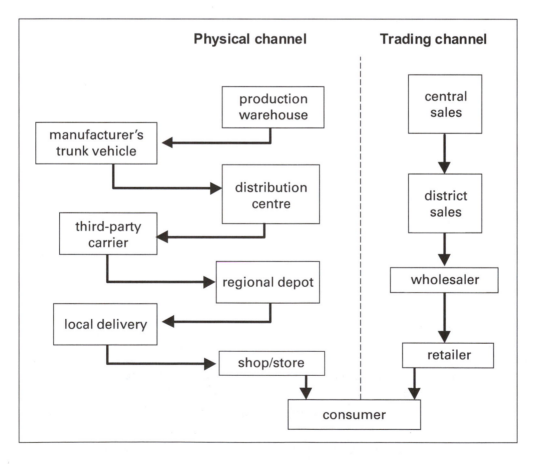

Figure 4.2 Typical channel of distribution, showing the different physical and trading routes to the consumer

CHANNEL SELECTION

Channel objectives will necessarily differ from one company to another, but it is possible to define a number of general points that are likely to be relevant. These should normally be considered by a company in the course of its distribution planning process to ensure that the most appropriate channel structure is developed. The main points that need to be addressed are as follows:

- *To make the product readily available to the market consumers at which it is aimed.* Perhaps the most important factor here is to ensure that the product is represented in the right type of outlet or retail store. Having identified the correct market-place for the goods, the company must make certain that the appropriate physical distribution channel is selected to achieve this objective.
- *To enhance the prospect of sales being made.* This can be achieved in a number of ways. The most appropriate factors for each product or type of retail store will be reflected in the choice of channel. The general aims are to get good positions and displays in the store, and to gain the active support of the retail salesperson, if necessary. The product should be 'visible, accessible and attractively displayed'. Channel choice is affected by this objective in a number of ways:
  - Does the deliverer arrange the merchandise in the shop?
  - Are special displays used?
  - Does the product need to be demonstrated or explained?
  - Is there a special promotion of the product?
- *To achieve co-operation with regard to any relevant distribution factors.* These factors may be from the supplier's *or* the receiver's point of view, and include minimum order sizes, unit load types, product handling characteristics, materials handling aids, delivery access (eg vehicle size) and delivery time constraints, etc.
- *To achieve a given level of service.* Once again, from both the supplier's and the customer's viewpoints, a specified level of service should be established, measured and maintained. The customer normally sees this as crucial, and relative performance in achieving service level requirements is often used to compare suppliers and may be the basis for subsequent buying decisions.
- *To minimize logistics and total costs.* Clearly, costs are very important, as they are reflected in the final price of the product. The selected channel will reflect a certain cost and this cost must be assessed in relation to the type of product offered and the level of service required.
- *To receive fast and accurate feedback of information.* A good flow of relevant information is essential for the provision and maintenance of an efficient distribution service. It will include sales trends, inventory levels, damage reports, service levels, cost monitoring, etc.

The main objectives that a company needs to clarify when determining the most appropriate physical distribution channels to use have been outlined above. A number of important associated factors also need to be considered. These factors clearly affect the decisions that need to be made when designing a channel or channels used in a distribution system. They can be summarized with respect to the following general characteristics.

Market characteristics

The important consideration here is to use the channels and types of outlet most appropriate for the eventual end user. The size and spread of the market is also important. If a market is a very large one that is widely spread from a geographic point of view, then it is usual to use 'long' channels. A long channel is one where there are several different storage points and a number of different movements for the product as it goes from production to the final customer. Where a market has only a very few buyers in a limited geographical area, then 'short' channels are used. Examples of these channels are illustrated in Figure 4.3.

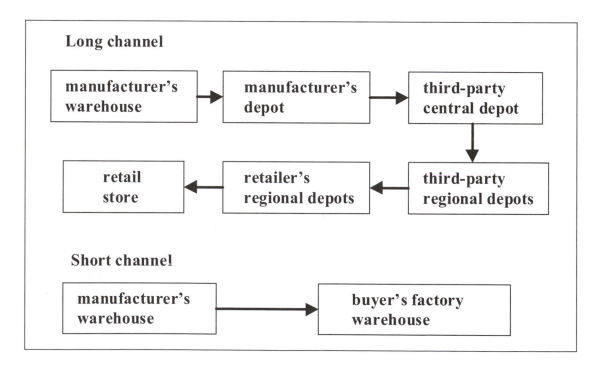

Figure 4.3 'Long' and 'short' distribution channels

Product characteristics

The importance of the product itself when determining channel choice should not be underestimated. This is because the product may well impose constraints on the number of channels that can be considered. For example:

- High-priced items are more likely to be sold direct via a short channel, because the high gross profit margins can more easily cover the higher sales and distribution costs that are usual from short channels. In addition, the security aspects of highly priced items (eg jewellery, watches, CDs, etc) makes a short channel much more attractive because there is less opportunity for loss and theft than with a long channel.
- Complex products often require direct selling because any intermediary may not be able to explain the product (ie how it works) to potential customers.
- New products may have to be marketed directly or by mail order because traditional outlets may be reluctant to stock the product.
- Products with a time constraint need a 'fast' channel, for obvious reasons, eg bread, cakes, newspapers, etc.
- Products with a handling constraint may require a specialist physical distribution channel, eg frozen food, china and glass, hanging garments.

Channel characteristics

As well as taking account of market and product characteristics, another aspect to be considered concerns the characteristics of the channel itself. There are two different factors that are important. Firstly, does the channel being considered serve or supply the customer in the way required? A simple example might be a new grocery product that needs to be demonstrated or tested in the shop. There would be no point in distributing this product through a small self-service store where no facilities can be provided for a demonstration. Secondly, how efficient is the channel being considered? Efficiency may include a number of different features related to sales or distribution. These might include the sales potential in the outlets served, the size of orders placed, the frequency of delivery required, etc.

Competitive characteristics

Competitive characteristics that need to be considered concern the activities of any competitors selling a similar product. Typical decisions are whether to sell the product alongside these similar products, or whether to try for different, exclusive outlets for the product to avoid the competition. It may well be that the consumer preference for a wide choice necessitates the same outlets being supplied. Good examples include confectionery and most grocery items.

Also of very real significance is the service level being offered by the competition. It is essential that channel selection is undertaken with a view to ensuring that the level of service that can be offered is as good as, or better than, that which is being provided by key competitors. This may well be the main area for competitive advantage, especially for those products where it is very difficult to differentiate on quality and price.

Company resources

In the final analysis, it is often the size and the financial strength of the company that is most important in determining channel strategy. Only a fairly large and cash-rich company can afford to set up a distribution structure that includes all of its own warehousing and transport facilities. With these, the company has more control and can provide the service it thinks its customers require. Smaller and less financially secure companies may have to use intermediaries or third-party organizations to perform their distribution function. In these instances, it may be less easy to ensure provision of the service they feel their customers would like.

These factors will all need to be taken into account when designing a channel structure and selecting the appropriate channel members. A formalized approach that might be adopted when undertaking the design of a channel structure is set out in Figure 4.4.

Third-party or own-account distribution and logistics

The most common channel decision for those operating in physical distribution is whether to use a third-party distribution service, or whether to run an own-account (in-house) distribution operation. Third-party distribution has been an important alternative in the UK for many years. Across most of continental Europe and also North America, the use of third-party distribution service providers has also now grown significantly. Table 4.1 indicates the breakdown of contract logistics for the main European countries. It shows that the average for all of Europe is over 25 per cent. The UK, at 37.5 per cent, has the highest proportion of contracted-out operations.

The own-account/third-party decision is rarely a straightforward one, especially as there are a number of different types of third-party distribution operation available. The main ones include the following:

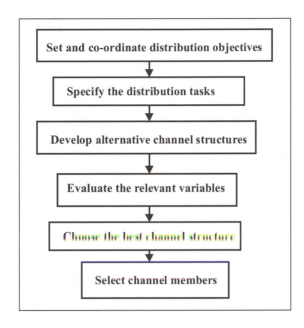

Figure 4.4 Designing a channel structure – a formalized approach

Table 4.1 Breakdown between contracted-out and in-house logistics for the main European countries (estimated, 1998)

Country	Contracted-out $	In-house $	Total $	Contracted-out %
Germany	10,417	30,167	40,584	25.7%
France	8,470	20,509	28,979	29.2%
UK	9,537	15,923	25,460	37.5%
Italy	2,249	13,838	16,087	14.0%
Spain	1,570	6,306	7,876	19.9%
Netherlands	1,879	5,239	7,118	26.4%
Belgium	1,165	3,297	4,462	26.1%
Austria	776	2,999	3,775	20.6%
Sweden	840	2,693	3,533	23.8%
Denmark	675	2,433	3,108	21.7%
Finland	486	1,786	2,272	21.4%
Ireland	260	756	1,016	25.6%
Portugal	161	719	880	18.3%
Greece	96	705	801	12.0%
Total	38,581	107,370	145,951	26.4%

Source: Datamonitor, 1999

- *Dedicated (or exclusive) distribution operation.* This is where a complete distribution operation is provided by a third-party company. The third party undertakes to provide the customer with all its distribution requirements, exclusively, on a national or regional basis. The resources used will include warehouses, depots, transport fleets, managers, etc. These are obviously confined to very large companies. Typical examples are BOC Transhield, Transcare, Salserve and Fashionflow, which provide exclusive services for the Marks and Spencer range of products. This type of service is very common in the UK and has now been developed across the rest of Europe and North America.

- *Multi-user (or shared-user) distribution operation.* Multi-user distribution operations are similar to dedicated operations, the principal difference being that a small group of client companies is catered for, rather than just a single client. One of the characteristics of this type of service is that ideally the clients are all manufacturers or suppliers of goods and their products are all delivered to the same or similar customers, for example grocery products to grocery stores, supermarkets, catering establishments, etc. These are also known as shared-user operations. The advantage of this approach is that expensive distribution costs are shared between the clients so all parties enjoy the benefits.

- *Specialist distribution operation.* These distribution operations are used for the storage and movement of products that require special facilities or services, and the distribution operation run by the third-party company is especially tailored to suit these needs. There are several examples. One is the frozen-food distribution service run by companies such as Christian Salvesen. Other examples are Tibbet and Britten (hanging garments).

- *Regional multi-client distribution operation.* These operations are provided for any number of clients, and for most product types. They are usually provided by a 'general' third-party distributor that has probably started as a very small operation and grown into a regional operation concentrated in a specific small geographic area (eg in the UK – East Anglia, north of Scotland).

- *National multi-client distribution operation.* This category is very similar to the previous one, a service being provided for any number of clients and product types. The main difference relates to the size of the operation. This is nationwide, and would include a trunking operation between the companies' depots, so that if necessary a client company can have a delivery service to anywhere in the country.

- *Transit operation.* These are operations where the operator is not involved in the storage of any products for a manufacturer, but is only providing a collect, break bulk and delivery service. Thus, no unordered stocks are held, although some minor stock-holding may occur for a limited number of product lines.

- *Joint venture.* A limited number of operations have been set up whereby a third-party operator and a client company form a separate distribution company called a joint venture. This may occur where a company with its own distribution operation has some underutilized resources. It will then link up with a third-party operator and offer the services on a wider basis. This has occurred in the hanging goods and the high-tech sectors.
- *Occasional use.* Many companies use third-party services on an occasional basis or as an aid to support their own-account operations. There are a number of reasons why a company might do this: to cover seasonal peaks in demand; to cover weekly demand peaks; for non-standard products that don't fit easily into their own operation (very small or very large products); to deliver to peripheral geographic areas where there is only limited demand for their products; for non-standard operations (returns, collections, etc).

Third-party distribution has developed rapidly over the past few decades and has become a very competitive and dynamic industry. There has been a significant growth in both the number and the size of companies. In recent years a number of major players have come to the fore, from a variety of different backgrounds, as companies from different sectors bid to cut themselves a slice of the distribution service market. This has been particularly true for those companies trying to develop pan-European operations. In Europe, for example, key players have evolved from:

- Logistics companies with a tradition of operating in the field, albeit initially on a national basis only. These include Exel Logistics, Christian Salvesen, Danzas, Tibbet and Britten, TNT Logistics, Hays, Zust Ambrosetti, Schneider, and Ryder.
- Freight forwarders looking to expand their operations away from the traditional area of shipping. Included here are Kuehne and Nagel, P and O Nedlloyd, and Thyssen Logistics.
- General hauliers and carriers such as Frans Maas, Schenker, Danzas, and Westerman.
- Air freight companies, including DHL, UPS, and Fedex.

The result of this fast growth and robust competition has meant that third-party companies now offer many distribution and distribution-related services. The basic types of service can vary from contract hire to the provision of single vehicles or a fleet of vehicles to fully dedicated operations, including storage, primary and secondary transport, management services, order processing and stock control. A list of the most common services includes:

- trunking;
- collection;
- break bulk;
- fleet management;
- telesales;
- management information;
- local delivery;
- stock-holding warehouse;
- transhipment;
- cross-docking;
- order picking;
- inventory management;
- general management;
- contract hire;
- home delivery;
- production inspection;
- packing;
- returns; and
- merchandising.

But there are also many other services offered. Some of these are known as 'value added' services because they reflect, in particular, those items or services that add a lot of additional value to the product being distributed. Examples of these are:

- *Specialist or niche services*, where the operation is specifically designed for a particular product. The development of hanging garment distribution is typical – here the entire distribution operation, from production point through finished goods warehouse, primary transport, depot, delivery transport and into the retail store, is all provided on hanging rails. Products are thus stored and moved as 'sets' of garments on hangers. Some of the storage operations are very sophisticated automated systems.
- *Time reliable services*, which are set up to support the just-in-time operations of major manufacturers. Typical here are the sequencing centres that have been developed in the automotive industry to support line-side production. TNT, Hays, and Ryder provide these for Rover, General Motors, and Nissan, whereby line-ready production modules are supplied direct to the production line so that the relevant components can be introduced into the manufacturing process at exactly the appropriate time.

- *Assembly*: the computer industry offers a number of examples where basic products, such as PC monitors or processing units are initially distributed to the relevant market before being finally made ready for the final customer. This is likely to include the 'badging' of the equipment with the appropriate name and the installation of the final language software. This is often undertaken by the third-party distributor.
- *Repacking* is another area of value added development. A typical example might be the need to blister-pack two different items that are to go out as a distinct retail product – a torch together with a battery. This is another niche operation favoured by a few specialist distribution companies.
- *Refurbishment*: in the light of current environmental legislation many manufacturing companies have endeavoured to re-engineer their products so that parts from some used products can be reused in new products. It is necessary to return these parts through the supply chain – not an easy task as most distribution operations tend to be geared to moving products out to the customer and not back from the customer to the manufacturer. This has provided an opportunity for third-party companies to offer this return-and-refurbishment operation.
- *Packaging returns*: again linked to environmental legislation, there is a need to collect packaging for reuse or disposal. A number of third-party operators have set up reverse logistics operations for the large grocery multiples. Examples include the development of recycling centres for the disposal of waste and the repair and washing of reusable containers.

A summary of the traditional breakdown of broad service types is given in Table 4.2. This considers the different types of service or operation against four of the main attributes – asset dedication, speed of delivery, size of consignment and contractual basis. The key question of cost is negotiable as and when the service is required.

KEY DRIVERS FOR THIRD-PARTY DISTRIBUTION

There are a large number of advantages and disadvantages claimed for and against both third-party and own-account distribution. Some of these can be objectively assessed. Others are subjective, relating more to historical convention and personal preference than to anything else. The major drivers for and against the use of a third party can be split into three broad categories covering cost, organizational and physical factors.

Table 4.2 Breakdown of broad service types by attribute

Broad Service Type	Asset Dedication	Speed of Delivery	Size of Consignment	Contractual Basis
Express	shared	next day	small	transaction
Groupage	shared	slower than express	larger than express	transaction
General Haulage	shared	slower than express	as required	transaction or contract
Shared or Multi-user Distribution	shared	slower than dedicated	as required	contract
Dedicated Contract Distribution	dedicated	as required	as required	contract

Cost factors include the following:

- There are *capital cost* advantages claimed for third-party distribution because clients do not have to invest in facilities and resources such as depots and vehicles as they might for their own operation. Thus, the capital can be invested in other areas of the business, such as new production machinery, retail stores, etc.
- There are day-to-day or *operating cost* savings because the operation is more efficient. Both third-party and own-account users often claim this benefit.
- *Economies of scale* exist because some own-account operations are too small to be run economically in their own right. If they are linked together with other small operations, then the larger system that results is likely to be more economical. A single large depot may be necessary instead of three or four depots for all of the different companies. This will provide savings in overheads, better utilization of equipment, etc.
- For individual client companies, there is a likely *cost lag* or *cushion effect* as increased costs are delayed before the third-party company can pass them on to the client. This is particularly apparent in times of high inflation.
- It may be the case that the *change-over costs* of moving from own-account distribution to third-party distribution are such that it does not make good economic sense. Problem areas are the sunk costs of existing own depots, fixed low rents, and vehicles and equipment.

Organizational factors include the following:

- One of the prime reasons quoted for the move to the use of a third-party distribution company is the opportunity for users to *concentrate on their core business*, be this manufacturing or retail. There are both organizational and cost benefits to be gained from this.
- It is claimed that the use of third-party distribution leads to a *loss of control over the delivery operation*. Any lack of control can be reduced, however, by buying the right service at the outset, and by carefully monitoring the performance of the distribution company in terms of the service it is actually providing.
- There may also be a *loss of control over the company's logistical variables* if a third party is used. This means that the company is no longer in a position to define the number, type or size of depots, or vehicle types and sizes etc. Once again, if this is important, the company must choose the third-party structure that suits it the best.
- Third-party distribution companies may *lack the experience* of client companies' products and markets, although the growth in specialist distribution companies has helped to change this point of view. In contrast, it is felt that the use of a third-party company can provide the user company with access to leading-edge technology, a wider management experience and knowledge beyond that of their own industry and that this may enhance the opportunities to improve their operation.
- It is thought that *service levels are poorer* among third-party distributors than own-account operators. For dedicated operations, there should be no significant difference. For multi-user operations this should not necessarily be true, because many third-party distributors make frequent and regular deliveries to high-street outlets. In addition, in remote rural areas, the use of a third party can greatly improve service levels because deliveries are more frequent.
- The *balance of power is shifted* away from the user in favour of the contractor, as the contractor owns the systems and the distribution resources.
- There is a *loss of distribution and logistics expertise* in the user company. This will make it more difficult for the user company to revert back to an own account operation should it so wish. Also, distribution and logistics expertise, if maintained within the client organization, will help to enable a better monitoring and assessment of the true performance of the contractor.
- There can be a problem trying to *co-ordinate* third-party *delivery service with* a client company's *sales service*. For example, the salesperson may call and an order be placed, but the delivery of that order may not be completed for some time afterwards due to the fixed delivery cycle. This potential problem can often be overcome by better co-ordination of order and delivery schedules.

- The use of a third party can often mean the *loss of direct influence at the point of delivery* because the driver is delivering a number of different companies' products. This can be an issue as the driver is very often the only direct physical link between the supplier and the customer. For multi-user operations this can be limited if a salesperson is also used as a contact point. For dedicated operations this should not be an issue because the driver is only delivering for a single client company.
- A third party cannot guarantee *brand integrity*. The value of advertising on a vehicle may be thought to be important. Using a third party means that the company does not have its own livery and brand name on a vehicle. For dedicated contract distribution the livery can be and is used.
- There may be a problem with *the confidentiality of information* when using a third-party distribution service. This may arise because products can be mixed with those of competitors.
- There may be an issue with *cultural incompatibility* between contractor and client. It is now recognized that company cultures can vary quite dramatically from one to another. It is important that there is no clash of culture in a contractor/ client relationship because this may lead to problems in the way the operation is run.

Physical factors include the following:

- The use of a third-party distribution operation should offer *greater flexibility* to the user company as it seeks to develop its products and markets.
- For some companies, the move to a third-party operator provides a major opportunity to solve any *industrial relations problems* that might otherwise be difficult or costly to eradicate. Legislation, such as the Transfer of Undertakings (Protection of Employment) Regulations in the UK, has however diminished the potential impact of this aspect.
- The *drop characteristics* of some products may be incompatible in some third-party operations. This may relate to the frequency of deliveries required (eg a large number of small drops for high-value items) or the nature of the product itself. It is likely that some form of specialist distribution system can provide an appropriate alternative.
- *Vehicle characteristics* and requirements can differ between products and product ranges. Vehicle size, body quality, equipment and unit load specifications may all be relevant dependent on weight/volume ratios and any 'special' product features. Once again, the use of a specialist third-party company could be appropriate.

- *Basic delivery systems* may be incompatible. This would apply, for example, to the use of pre-selected orders against van sales, and also the need for a 'mate' to help unload some bulky or heavy products. It is important to ensure that products are not being distributed via incompatible delivery systems, as this can be both costly and inefficient.
- Some *products may be incompatible*, a particular problem being the danger of contamination. Many third-party companies get around the problem by the use of special sections in vehicles.

Many of the debatable issues identified in the previous section refer more specifically to multi-user operations rather than dedicated operations, because the client requiring a dedicated operation is able to define and buy a specially designed service from the supplier. Clearly, as well as the main decision whether or not to take the third-party route there is also a crucial decision for a company to make as to whether to use a dedicated or a multi-user operation. The decision, as so often in distribution and logistics, is a question of trade-off between cost and service. What then are these key trade-offs? They are summarized in Table 4.3.

Table 4.3 The key trade-offs between dedicated and multi-user distribution services

	Dedicated	**Multi-user**
Advantages	<ul><li>Organization and resources are focused exclusively on the customer</li><li>Specialism and loyalty of staff</li><li>Specialism of depots, handling equipment and delivery vehicles</li><li>Confidentiality of customers' product specifications / promotional activity</li></ul>	<ul><li>Scale economies gained by sharing resources between a number of clients</li><li>Consolidation of loads enable higher delivery frequency</li><li>Ability to find clients with different business seasonality to maximize utilization of assets</li></ul>
Disadvantages	<ul><li>Total costs of the operation are borne by the customer</li><li>Seasonal underutilization of resources</li></ul>	<ul><li>Conflicting demands of each customer can compromise service</li><li>Staff do not gain specialist customer knowledge</li><li>Equipment is not specialized and may not exactly meet individual customer requirements</li></ul>

The choice between own-account and third-party distribution needs to be carefully quantified and analysed. This should be undertaken with care, using a structured approach. Such an approach is outlined and discussed in Chapter 31 of this book.

KEY ISSUES IN THIRD-PARTY DISTRIBUTION AND LOGISTICS

Surveys are undertaken on a regular basis to try to identify what the critical factors are in a user's choice of a third-party distribution company. The results of such a survey, conducted in the UK, are shown in Figure 4.5.

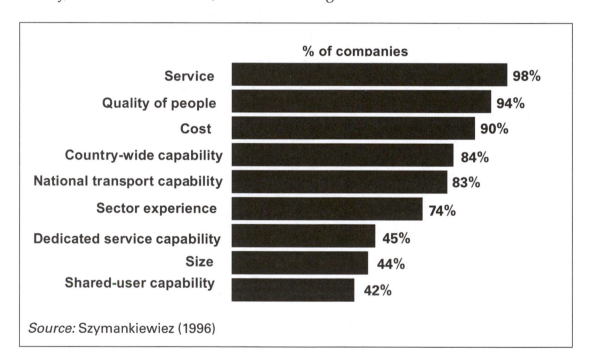

Source: Szymankiewiez (1996)

Figure 4.5 Critical factors in the choice of which third-party distribution company to use

Service comes out as the most important factor. Cost, although extremely critical, comes third, with the quality of people used the second most important. This reflects the continued concern for many users that it is the quality, commitment and ability of the personnel involved in any distribution operation that is paramount to its success.

Other relevant factors from the most recent survey are that users are only 'generally satisfied' with contractors' performance (68 per cent) – there is, in the minds of users, ample opportunity for improvement. Also, users feel that contractors are mainly reactive rather than proactive in their relationships with users (only 37 per cent are proactive). Users are looking for a more positive approach from contractors to identify and pursue ways and means of improving service and cutting costs. One major issue is that users think contractors have a very limited influence over wider supply chain developments (only 16 per cent have a major influence), and it is here that many users feel there is a real opportunity to identify improvements.

One of the reasons put forward for this lack of proactive development is that the mainstream offering of third-party contractors is little more than a commodity, with no obvious means of differentiating between different companies and with very low return on investment for the industry. Some related issues are:

- Significant time is still required to manage third-party providers.
- The nature of contracts is such that third-party providers will concentrate on asset utilization to reduce their own costs rather than in developing a customer-focused approach to logistics.
- Third-party providers can only offer a limited range of wider supply chain skills.
- Third-party providers cannot contribute to opportunities to optimize operations over the wider supply chain.
- By their very nature, contractors are more likely to be concerned with one-off cost savings rather than continuous improvement, which is what users are most concerned with.

Contractors claim, however, that they are rarely given the opportunity to develop new ideas that allow for a broader supply chain perspective. Users tend to adhere to the traditional concept of contract-driven relationships that give very limited scope for the contractor to identify innovative solutions and put forward supply-chain-wide solutions. These arguments are paving the way for what is known as fourth-party logistics. This is where an external organization is able to provide a user with an overall supply-chain-wide solution by incorporating the resources and expertise of any number of third parties to best effect. The fourth-party provider will be involved in both the design and management of a client's logistics system and will act as a co-ordinator for many different types of service, which may include distribution, information systems, financial services, etc. It will be a challenge for third-party providers of distribution services to become amongst the leaders that can offer such a service. This is further explored in Chapter 34.

Another important development is the move to establish pan-European and global third-party companies. Currently, even the largest of the third-party providers can only offer a partial service across regional boundaries, having to subcontract or establish co-operative arrangements with other contractors. As manufacturers and retailers have moved towards global businesses, then they have an expectation that there should be global logistics companies to support them. Thus, it is thought that these integrated global contractors should evolve in the next few years.

For a number of user/third-party relationships there has been a move towards building closer partnerships. One of the aims is to create a more positive and co-operative alliance between the user and the contractor and to eliminate the combative culture that has evolved in some relationships. Historically, many relationships have been very much contract-driven, with both user and third party at times squabbling over the small print of a contract to the detriment of the overall operation and to the business relationship itself. The ideal is for a constructive alliance where both parties work together to identify ways of improving service and reducing costs.

One means of creating more constructive partnerships has been the use of incentivized contracts. Here, the contract is drawn up with clearly defined opportunities for the service provider to identify and introduce methods of service improvement or cost reduction. The key is that the service provider is rewarded for identifying these improvements. In more traditional contracts, it is not in the interest of the service provider to introduce cost savings because these have the effect of reducing the income the contractor receives.

Another development has been a move to a much more rigorous selection of contractors. There is now a clearly laid-out process for contractor selection, which most large companies adhere to. This process is considered in detail in Chapter 31.

SUMMARY

This chapter has been concerned with channel choice and selection, the main aspects covering:

- the physical and the trading channel;
- alternative channels of physical distribution;
- channel characteristics;
- an approach to channel selection;
- third-party versus own-account distribution;
- different types of third-party distribution operation;

- major players;
- types of service offered by third-party companies;
- key drivers for third-party distribution; and
- key issues.

Channel choice and selection, and particularly the increased use and sophistication of third-party distribution services, are all very important aspects of modern-day logistics. This is an exciting area of change within the industry and there is ample scope and opportunity for growth and development in the future.

5

Key issues and challenges for logistics

INTRODUCTION

In recent years there have been very significant developments in the structure, organization and operation of logistics, notably in the interpretation of logistics within the broader supply chain. Major changes have included the increase in customer service expectations, the concept of compressing time within the supply chain, the globalization of industry – both in terms of global brands and global markets – and the integration of organizational structures. These particular developments are discussed elsewhere in this book. There are, in addition, a number of other influencing pressures that may provide an impact on a company's logistics system. These may be external to logistics, such as deregulation, or may indeed derive from changes within logistics, such as improved handling or information technology.

It is possible to view these different influences at various points along the supply chain. This chapter outlines these factors under the consideration of:

- the external environment;
- supply;
- distribution;

- retailing;
- the consumer.

THE EXTERNAL ENVIRONMENT

One key influence that has become increasingly important in recent years has been the development of a number of different economic unions (the EU, ASEAN, NAFTA, etc). In some instances the formation of these unions may be felt to hold an important political element, but experience has shown that there will also be significant economic changes – most of these, hopefully, beneficial ones.

It is clear that one of the major consequences is deregulation within these internal markets, and this has a particular impact on companies' logistics strategies. Within the European Union there have been significant advances in, amongst others:

- transport deregulation;
- the harmonization of legislation across different countries;
- the reduction of tariff barriers;
- the elimination of cross-border customs requirements;
- tax harmonization.

Within logistics, this has led many companies to reassess their entire logistics strategy away from a national approach to embrace a new cross-border/non-national structure. There are many examples of companies that have significantly reduced depot numbers and associated inventory and storage costs whilst maintaining or improving customer service.

Another important development that has had a particular impact in Europe is the rise in importance of 'green' or environmental issues. This has occurred through an increasing public awareness of environmental issues, but also as a result of the activity of pressure groups. The consequences for logistics are important. They include:

- the banning of road freight movements at weekends (Germany, Switzerland);
- the attempted promotion of rail over road transport;
- the recycling of packaging – sometimes referred to as reverse logistics;
- the 'greening' of products;
- the outsourcing of reverse logistics flows;
- the design of products to facilitate repair/refurbishment, recycling and the elimination of packaging.

For most cities throughout the world one very visible external impact is that of *road congestion*. The fact of severe traffic congestion may well have a very negative effect on some of the new concepts in logistics – in particular the idea of JIT and quick-response systems. Allied to this problem is that most forecasts predict a significant increase in vehicle numbers at a time when, in most countries, there are very limited road-building programmes. Many Western countries try to reduce congestion through a combination of road tolls, lorry bans, access restrictions, time restrictions and usage tax – all of which have an impact on logistics costs and performance. There is no generally accepted solution. Companies try to alleviate the problem through strategies such as out-of-hours deliveries, stockless depots and depot relocation closer to delivery points.

The extreme changes and developments in logistics thinking and logistics and information technology has also led to another issue – the impact that this has on the *availability of suitable management and labour*.

The need for a strategic view of logistics and the need for an appropriate under-standing of the integrated nature of logistics are both important for today's supply-chain-oriented networks. Many managers do not have the relevant experience or knowledge that provides this view. Add to this the rapid changes in technology, and it is understandable why there is such a shortage of suitable logistics manage-ment. This problem is also reflected in the quality of labour available to work in the many different logistics and distribution functions.

SUPPLY

There have been many important developments in supply or inbound logistics. These have resulted from both technological and organizational changes. Within the context of raw material sourcing and production these include:

- *New manufacturing technology* (CIM, etc), which can accommodate more complex production requirements and more product variations.
- *New supplier relationships* with the emphasis on single sourcing and lean supply, thus enabling suppliers and buyers to work more closely.
- *Focused factories* with a concentration on fewer sources but necessitating longer transport journeys.
- *Transnational sourcing*, emphasizing the move away from local or national sourc-ing to a more global strategy.
- *Postponement*, where the final configuration of a product is delayed to enable reduced stock-holding of finished goods in the supply chain.

● *Co-makership:* the development of partnerships between supplier and buyer to help take costs out of the supply chain through quality and information improvements. This represents a positive move away from the more traditional adversarial relationship that has been common between buyers and suppliers.
● *Co-location:* the joint physical location of supplier operations on or next to customer production sites.

Associated with many of these developments has been the impact of changes in product range. Typical examples include the shortening of product life cycles, the wider product range expected and provided, and the increase in demand for time-sensitive products – especially fresh and prepared foods. These may all pose added logistics problems with respect to the impact on stock levels and in particular the speed of delivery required.

DISTRIBUTION

In many ways, there have been fewer changes in the distribution elements of the supply chain than in most of the other elements. In an operational context the major developments have been technology-based:

● 'new' vehicle systems – demountable bodies, etc;
● stockless depots operating cross-docking arrangements;
● paperless information systems, particularly in depots;
● interactive routeing and scheduling for road transport operations.

An important and still expanding area is that of *third-party distribution*, or the outsourcing of distribution operations. This has been a significant feature of logistics in the UK for many years, and now many continental European countries have begun to follow the same track. The major advantage is that outsourcing allows a company to specialize in its own core business, be it manufacturing or retailing, without spreading its resources to cover distribution as well (see Chapter 4).

There are still major opportunities in many markets. Most third-party contractors will now claim to have one or a number of specializations (food, hanging garments, etc), and many strive to provide an increased portfolio of 'value added' activities, which allows them to obtain additional business (relabelling, assembly, etc). There is currently a move to establish partnership arrangements, but the main questions are still whether to outsource at all and what to outsource.

Finally, within the aegis of distribution, one distinctive feature of recent years has been a concentration on improving asset utilization. This has been demonstrated in many ways: in grocery distribution with the building of composite depots and the use of compartmentalized vehicles; the backloading of delivery vehicles; and the development of shared-user contract distribution.

RETAILING

In Europe as a whole there have been several trends in the retail sector that have had and will continue to have an impact on logistics and supply chain development. The importance of the grocery multiples cannot be overestimated as many logistics-related changes have emanated from this sector. In general, there has been a growth in multiple stores and a decline in independents. Overall the number of retail outlets is in decline, but the average size of outlets has increased considerably. A fairly universal development has been the growth of large out-of-town 'one-stop' super-stores and hypermarkets.

These changes have all had an influence on logistics strategies and operations. Perhaps the most far-reaching effect however has been from the combination of inventory reduction policies. These include:

- the maximization of retail selling space – at the expense of retail stockrooms;
- the reduction in depot stock-holding due to cost-saving policies;
- the reduction in the number of stock-holding depots;
- JIT philosophies and concepts;
- vendor-managed inventory policies.

An important retailing policy has been the move to maximize selling space in stores, often at the expense of shop stockrooms. Developments in information technology have also been at the forefront, particularly the use of electronic point of sale systems, which provide a much more accurate and timely indication of stock replenishment requirements at shop level. Linked to this has been the introduction in the USA of vendor-managed inventory policies whereby the supplier rather than the retailer is responsible for shop stock replenishment. Finally, many retail operations have also adopted policies to streamline the activities within the retail environment through the movement of activities back into the depot (labelling, unpacking, etc).

The consequences are that stocks and buffers in retail stores have been reduced or eliminated in favour of the continuous flow of products into the stores. This necessitates more responsive delivery systems, more accurate information and more timely information. Thus logistics operations must perform with greater efficiency but with fewer safeguards.

THE CONSUMER

Linked directly with retailing operations is the gradual move into non-store shopping or *home shopping*. This phenomenon has been relatively common in the USA and Europe through the use of direct selling and mail order catalogues. It now seems likely to 'break through' and make significant inroads into more conventional retail shopping. The means for such a change are now in place through the development of cable TV, home computers, automatic banking and, of course, the Internet. Clearly any significant change will have a fundamental impact on logistics. The very nature of the final delivery operation will alter dramatically, and this will influence the whole of the supply chain. Typical implications will include:

- shops become showrooms where stock replenishment is no longer an issue;
- a major increase in direct home deliveries;
- new distribution systems may evolve (small drops into residential areas, community depots, etc);
- existing delivery systems may have a new life (post, milk delivery);
- customer ordering systems will be linked directly to manufacturers' reordering systems;
- a high rate of returns – dependent on the sector, this can vary between 30 and 50 per cent.

This major change to non-store or home shopping has always been 'just around the corner'. With significant advances in the spread of home computers and free use of the Internet, it is now reasonable to say that the time has arrived for these changes to happen. In some sectors (eg white goods, brown goods), home delivery is already common practice. There are already third-party contractors who specialize in home delivery. The rapid growth in online selling companies, such as Amazon, means that home shopping has now arrived, with all the implications for logistics that e-fulfilment will bring.

The importance of *customer service* has been previously discussed (see Chapter 3). It should be re-emphasized that this increased importance has had and will have a major impact on logistics, such that the logistics function becomes perhaps the key element in customer service strategy. Relevant developments include:

- the development of 'customer-facing' organizations and operations;
- a move towards service policies based on market segmentation;
- JIT and quick-response systems requiring markedly more frequent and reliable delivery;
- 'brand image' becoming less strong – the dominant differentiator being availability.

SUMMARY

This chapter has identified some of the key impacts and influences on logistics and supply chain development. It is possible to see major changes occurring throughout all of the different links within the supply chain, as well as broader external changes.

These various developments are only symptomatic of more fundamental changes. In particular the relationships between manufacturer, supplier, distributor and retailer may need rethinking. The concept of logistics and supply chain management is now moving towards the need for logistics and supply chain partnership. The overall trend, reinforced by information technology, is towards greater integration throughout the whole supply chain.

Part 2

Planning for logistics

6

Planning framework for logistics

INTRODUCTION

The need for a positive approach to planning was discussed in Chapter 2, together with the concept of a logistics planning hierarchy. In this chapter a more detailed planning framework for logistics is described and some key strategic considerations are introduced. A generalized approach to corporate strategic planning is outlined and this is linked to a specific logistics design strategy. The main elements of this design strategy are described. Finally, some of the fundamental physical influences on logistics design are detailed, in particular product characteristics, product life cycle, packaging and unit loads.

PRESSURES FOR CHANGE

Historically, many organizations have adopted a piecemeal and incomplete approach to their strategic planning. This is particularly true in the context of logistics where, often, individual functions within the logistics or supply chain have been sub-optimized to the detriment of the logistics chain as a whole. One of the reasons for this incomplete approach is the pressure for change exerted on companies from a wide variety of sources. Figure 6.1 provides an illustration of some of these pressures. They include:

- a significant improvement in communications systems and information technology, including such developments as enterprise resource planning systems (ERP), electronic point of sale systems (EPOS), electronic data interchange (EDI) and of course the Internet;
- regulatory changes of which the Single European Market (SEM) is one example amongst many economic unions, but also including various environmental and green issues;
- increasing customer service requirements, especially where the levels of service that logistics can provide are often seen as the competitive edge between companies and their products;
- a shortening of product life cycles, particularly for high-technology and fashion products;
- the need for improved financial performance at a time when companies and economies are under severe pressure;
- the development of new players with new roles in channels of distribution – this includes the growth of third-party service providers and their move to offer global and pan-European operations and to develop supply partnerships;
- the never-ending pressures to reduce inventories and their associated costs – through depot rationalization and the adoption of JIT concepts;
- the need to adopt a wider supply chain perspective when planning and re-designing logistics operations.

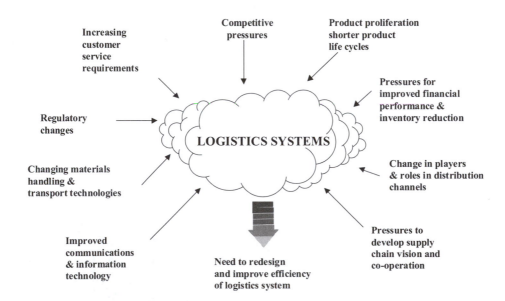

Figure 6.1 Pressures influencing logistics systems

The danger for any organization is to over-react to this need for change. Thus a measured response is required that enables distribution and logistics systems and structures to be developed as a whole in the context of company strategic plans. In this way, the likelihood of the sub-optimization of some logistics activities can be avoided. To this can be added the need to link the quantitative modelling of logistics requirements as a second stage of strategic business planning. This chapter thus focuses on the development and use of a framework and approach that takes into account broad organizational and business issues as well as more detailed logistics issues.

STRATEGIC PLANNING OVERVIEW

A generalized approach to corporate strategic planning is depicted in Figure 6.2. This is in many ways a classic strategic planning approach. There is nothing fundamentally new in this type of overview. One important point is that it does clearly identify the logistics function as a part of the strategic planning process. This may not always be the case in some corporate planning processes.

The initial phase of a strategic study should incorporate a review of the external environment within which a company operates. This includes such factors as the economic climate, current regulations and potential regulatory changes, and any relevant technological developments. Also of importance for most companies would be some sort of evaluation of major competitors – particularly, in this context, any information regarding service and logistics strategies. One recognized approach to reviewing and evaluating the impact of the external environment is to undertake what is known as PEST analysis. A very broad view of external factors is taken and an assessment is made of the effects of these and how they might influence the strategy of the company. Typical factors to be assessed using PEST analysis are shown in Table 6.1.

The analysis of relevant internal factors is also important. A typical approach is to undertake a form of SWOT analysis (strengths, weaknesses, opportunities and threats). This type of approach provides the opportunity for a company to review its position within the market-place with respect to its products, the demand for its products, the service it offers its customers and the position of its competitors. This type of analysis can and should also be undertaken with respect to identifying a company's key logistical variables.

Approaches such as these enable a company to identify what its overall corporate strategy should be. One of the key questions that must be answered is to define what business the company is in. Many companies can be classified as 'retailers' or 'manufacturers', but often a further definition is important because it will have

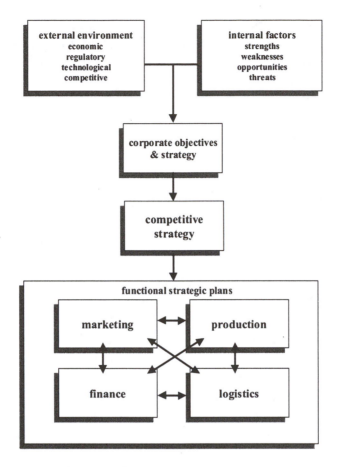

Figure 6.2 Corporate strategic planning overview

an influence on how the overall business is organized and structured. Beer provides a useful example. Typically, the brewing of beer has been seen as the key feature of the industry, and the brewing industry has a strong tradition that endorses this. Thus, the brewing of beer is the main activity. However, there are many different elements that need to be considered when determining how best to get the beer to the people. There are different parts of the supply chain that can be influential and can necessitate the development of a very different type of business environment. These might be:

● *Brewing the beer*: this is the traditional role concerned with production and packaging. Beer production is often seen as a magician's art. Varieties of beer are produced and they can be packaged in a number of different ways – barrels, kegs, cans, bottles, etc.

Table 6.1 PEST analysis: external influences

● **Political/legal** Monopolies legislation Environmental protection laws Taxation policy Foreign trade regulations Employment law Government stability	● **Economic** Business cycles, Interest rates Money supply, Inflation Unemployment Disposable income Energy availability & cost
● **Socio-cultural** Population demographics Income distribution Social mobility, Lifestyle changes Attitude to work & leisure Consumerism, Levels of education	● **Technological** Government spending on research Government & industry focus on technological effort New discoveries/developments Speed of technology transfer Rates of obsolescence

- *Environments in which to drink beer*: traditionally these have been pubs, clubs and bars. For the brewing industry a key question is whether or not to own these outlets (and thus have an assured sales outlet), or whether to concentrate solely on the production of the beer. A linked logistics issue is how best to get the beer to the outlets.
- *Environments in which to eat food and drink beer*: these are often known as leisure or lifestyle experiences. Typical are restaurants or 'theme' restaurants where the family might go to eat, drink and play. A major issue for these establishments is the supply and preparation of food as well as drink. For a brewer, this significantly changes the basic business objectives – there are other aspects to consider apart from brewing. Again, there are some obvious implications for logistics.
- *Drinking beer at home*: another important development is the increase in the home consumption of beer and the fact that this is primarily bought from supermarkets, specialist shops, wholesalers or corner shops. The brewer is unlikely to have the option to own these outlets (although, of course, beer is bought from pubs and bars for home consumption) but there are very different business, marketing, packaging and logistics implications in competing in this environment.

These represent an overview of some of the alternative business choices a brewer might have. Before attempting to design a competitive strategy and identify possible functional strategies, a company must be clear about which business it is in and what it wants to achieve within this business – a strategy based on set objectives.

In addition to a company's corporate or business strategy, the other element that is crucial is the competitive strategy the company plans to adopt. Competitive strategy has a major influence on the development of logistics strategy and in the way the physical structure of the operation may be configured. There are a number of important factors, but the key ones are the extent of globalization, the type of competitive positioning adopted and the degree to which the supply chain is an integrated one. These factors were discussed in Chapter 2, but the major logistics implications of globalization can be summarized as:

● extended supply lead times;
● extended and unreliable transit times;
● multiple break bulk and consolidation options;
● multiple freight mode and cost options;
● production postponement with local added value.

A company should adopt a competitive strategy by competing as a service or cost leader, or where possible as both of these. A service leader is a company that is trying to gain an advantage over its competitors by providing a number of key service elements to differentiate it and give it a service advantage. A cost leader is a company that is trying to utilize its resources by offering the product at the lowest possible cost, thus gaining a productivity advantage. Either of these extremes, or a combination of both, will necessitate a very different logistics structure.

The move towards integration within different supply chains has been relatively slow; indeed, most companies have fairly limited integration within their own organizations. Full external integration is quite unusual, but many companies have moved to functional integration with some achieving an element of full internal integration. The extent of integration will have a big impact on the logistics structure of a company. A company with limited integration will hold stocks in many parts of its operation. A highly integrated company will hold very limited stocks, with the emphasis on the steady flow of product throughout the physical system.

LOGISTICS DESIGN STRATEGY

On completion of this initial phase of the business planning process it should be possible to identify corporate strategy and objectives, and to determine a specific competitive strategy. The next task is to prepare appropriate functional strategic plans. The remainder of this chapter will concentrate on the functional strategy for logistics.

There are several important issues concerning the development of a suitable logistics strategy. The first is the need to link the logistics or distribution plan directly with the corporate plan. This is best achieved by ensuring that logistics is an integral part of the corporate plan and that factors related to these functions are used as inputs in the overall planning process.

The second point concerns the extent or coverage of the logistics strategic plan. This will clearly vary from one company to another. It may well just be a 'distribution' functional plan. It is most likely that it will be necessary to incorporate elements from other functions (marketing, production, etc) to represent the fully integrated nature of logistics or the supply chain.

The third, and in many ways most important, issue is whether or not a company has a structured logistics plan at all. Many still don't, so a first and major step may be to ensure that such a plan is developed, based of course on the company's business and competitive strategic plans. To achieve this, a logistics-planning framework is outlined in Figure 6.3.

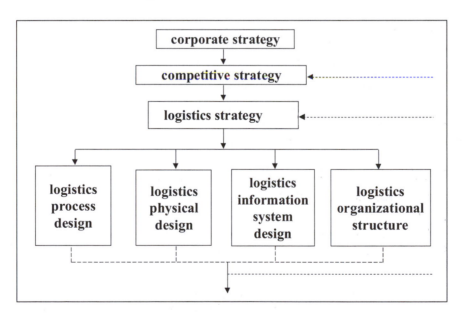

Figure 6.3   Framework for logistics design

As can be seen from the diagram, there are four key design elements that need to be considered. Traditionally, logistics planning and design have evolved around the question of depot numbers and location, but it is now recognized that as well as these physical logistics elements, there are other factors that also need to be considered. These are the design of logistics processes, logistics information systems and logistics organizational structure.

Logistics *process design* is concerned with ensuring that business methods are aligned and organized so that they operate across the traditional company functions and become supply-chain-oriented. Thus they are streamlined and are not affected or delayed because they are working across functional boundaries. A typical logistics process is order fulfilment, designed to ensure that customers' order requirements are satisfied with the minimum of disruption and the maximum of accuracy. The process should be designed as a seamless operation from the receipt of the order to the delivery of the goods and not as a series of different operations that occur each time a different internal function is involved – sales department, credit control, stock control, warehouse, transport. Other logistics processes that might be considered are information management, new product introduction, returns or spare part provision. Processes might need to be differentiated for variations in customer type, customer service requirements, product group, etc. Logistics process design is considered in more detail in Chapter 7.

Logistics *physical design* refers to the more traditional elements of logistics strategy. These include aspects related to the physical flow of the product through a company's operation, such as the manufacturing location from which a product should be sourced, the inventory that should be held, the number and location of depots, the use of stockless depots and final product delivery. One key to the determination of an appropriate physical design is the use of trade-offs between logistics components and between the different company functions. Typical trade-offs were described at the beginning of Chapter 2. A detailed approach to physical design is provided in Chapter 8.

Logistics *information system design* should include all of those information-related factors that are vital to support the processes and the physical structure of the operation. As well as these, however, it is important to recognize that there are also enterprise-wide information systems (enterprise resource planning or ERP systems), such as SAP, Baan, Peoplesoft, Oracle or JDE, which may have a direct influence on logistics process and physical design. Typical information systems that may support logistics process and physical design might be electronic point of sale (EPOS), electronic data interchange (EDI) between companies, warehouse management systems, vehicle routeing and scheduling and many more. These are outlined in Chapter 30.

The final design element is that of the logistics *organizational structure*. It is the experience of many companies that an inadequate organizational structure can lead to substantial problems. These include issues such as sub-optimization whereby functions tend to concentrate on their own operation in isolation from the rest of the company, or even worse examples where different functions and their managers compete against one another and develop antagonistic attitudes often styled as a 'blame culture'. These types of attitude work against the company but are also detrimental to customers and customer service. Organizational issues are further discussed in Chapter 9.

Each one of these different factors needs to be planned in association with the others. It is inappropriate to concentrate on any one without understanding and taking into account the influence of the others. Although Figure 6.3 indicates that process design should be the first factor to be considered, this is not necessarily the case. For different companies it may be any one of the other factors that plays the most dominant role. For example, a company that has introduced an enterprise-wide information system may find that this has a primary influence on how logistics strategy is formulated. Equally so, a company may feel that it is necessary to put a workable logistics organizational structure in place before it attempts to redesign its logistics processes and physical operations.

The different tools and techniques for undertaking logistics design are described in the next few chapters. Before considering these it is worth while considering some associated factors that may also have an influence on how a logistics operation is designed.

PRODUCT CHARACTERISTICS

One of the major factors to be considered when planning for logistics is, perhaps not surprisingly, the product itself. The product is, in fact, perceived to be an amalgam of its physical nature, its price, its package and the way in which it is supplied (ie the service). The implications regarding customer service were considered in Chapter 3. In the remainder of this chapter, the importance of the physical nature of the product and its package are discussed with respect to the planning of logistics operations.

For the logistics planner, the physical characteristics of the product and package are seen to be of great significance. This is because, in distribution and logistics, we are directly concerned with physical flow – movement and storage. The physical characteristics of a product, any specific packaging requirements and the type of unit load are all-important factors in the trade-off with other elements of distribution when trying to seek least-cost systems at given service levels. In the consideration of the product and its package, the potential for trade-off should continually be borne in mind.

There are a variety of product characteristics that have a direct, and often important, impact on the development and operation of a distribution system. This impact can affect both the structure of the system and the cost of the system. The major characteristics are:

- volume;
- weight;
- value;
- perishability;
- fragility;
- hazard/danger; and
- substitutability.

It is possible to classify these into four main categories:

1. volume to weight ratio;
2. value to weight ratio;
3. substitutability; and
4. special characteristics.

Volume to weight ratio

Volume and weight characteristics are commonly associated and their influence on logistics costs can be significant. A low ratio of volume to weight in a product (such as sheet steel, books, etc) generally means an efficient utilization of the main components of distribution. Thus, a low-volume/high-weight product will fully utilize the weight-constrained capacity of a road transport vehicle. Similarly, a low-volume/high-weight product will best utilize the handling cost component of storage (most other storage costs are not significantly affected by low volume/weight ratios).

The converse, a high volume to weight ratio, tends to be very inefficient for distribution. Typical products include paper tissues, crisps, disposable nappies, etc. The products have a very high space utilization, and are costly for both transportation and storage. In Europe, for example, there is a noticeable increase in the use of draw-bar trailer outfits in an attempt to increase vehicle capacity and so decrease the transportation costs of high-volume products.

Thus overall distribution costs tend to be greater for high-volume as against high-weight products. This effect is shown in Figure 6.4. It can be seen that the total costs of movement and storage tend to increase as the volume to weight ratio increases.

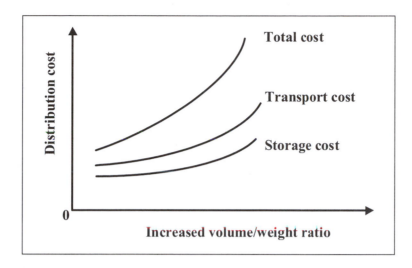

Figure 6.4   Effect of product volume to weight ratio on logistics costs

Value to weight ratio

Product value is also important to the planning of a logistics strategy. This is because high-value products are more able to absorb the associated distribution costs. It is often essential for low-value products to have an inexpensive distribution system because the effect on the total cost of the product might then make it non-viable in terms of its price in the market-place.

Once again, it is useful to assess the value effect in terms of a weight ratio, the value to weight ratio. Low value to weight ratio products (eg ore, sand, etc) incur relatively high transport unit costs compared with high value to weight products (eg photographic equipment, computer equipment, etc). Storage and inventory-holding unit costs of low value to weight ratio products tend to be low in comparison with high-value products because the capital tied up in inventory is lower.

Figure 6.5 shows that there is a trade-off effect as value to weight ratios increase.

Substitutability

The degree to which a product can be substituted by another will also affect the choice of distribution system. When customers readily substitute a product with a different brand or type of goods, then it is important that the distribution system is designed to avoid stock-outs or to react to replenish stocks in a timely fashion. Typical examples are many food products, where the customer is likely to choose an alternative brand if the need is immediate and the first-choice name is not available.

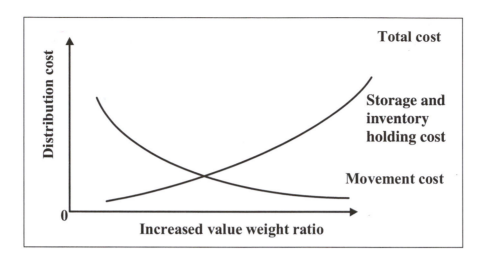

Figure 6.5 Effect of product value to weight ratio on logistics costs

In a distribution system, this can be catered for either through high stock levels or through a high-performance transport mode. Both options are high cost. High stock levels will decrease the likelihood of a stock-out, but will raise average stock levels and, thus, costs. The provision of a faster and more dependable transport function will reduce acquisition time and length of stock-out, but this increase in service will be at a higher transport cost.

Special characteristics

The various special characteristics of products (perishability, fragility, hazard/danger, contamination potential, extreme value) represent a degree of risk associated with distributing the product. The need to minimize this risk (sometimes a legal obligation) means that a special distribution system design must be used. As with any form of specialization, there will be a cost incurred. Examples of this effect include the following items:

● Hazardous goods may require special packaging, a limited unit load size, special labelling and isolation from other products. Regulations for the movement of hazardous goods differ between the different modes of transport.
● Fragile products require special packaging to take account of handling and transport shocks. Specialist distribution service providers now exist for some types of fragile goods.

- Perishable goods in many instances require special conditions and equipment for their distribution (eg refrigerated storage and transport facilities for frozen and chilled food).
- Time-constrained products – almost all foods are time-constrained now that 'best before' dates are so common – have implications for distribution information and control systems (eg first in, first out). Some products have fixed time or seasonal deadlines. Daily newspapers have a very limited life span, which allows for no delivery delays; fashion goods often have a fixed season; agro-chemicals such as fertilizers and insecticides have fixed time periods for usage; there are the classic seasonal examples of Easter eggs and Christmas crackers, which are time-constrained. There are significant implications for the choice of distribution system for many products such as these.
- Very high value products – cigarettes, videos, etc – are attractive products that require especially secure means of distribution.

There are many and varied product characteristics that can impose important requirements and constraints on all manner of logistics operations. They also affect the interrelationships between the different logistics functions, providing quite complex alternatives that need to be carefully assessed according to the implications on service and on cost.

THE PRODUCT LIFE CYCLE

One marketing concept that concerns the product and is also very relevant to distribution is that of the product life cycle (PLC). The principle behind the PLC is that of the staged development of a product. This starts with the introduction of the product into the market and follows (for successful products) with the steady growth of the product as it becomes established. The life cycle continues with the accelerated growth of the product as competitors introduce similar products, which stimulates total demand, and ends as the product life runs into decline. The PLC concept is illustrated in Figure 6.6.

It is important that the performance of a logistics operation is able to reflect the life cycle of a product. This can be differentiated as follows:

- *Introductory stage*: need for a high response to demand with a logistics structure that gives stock availability and quick replenishment, and can react to sudden demand increases. Initial retail stock-holdings are likely to be low so there is a need for speedy information and physical logistics systems probably from a centralized stock-holding base using a fast mode of transport.

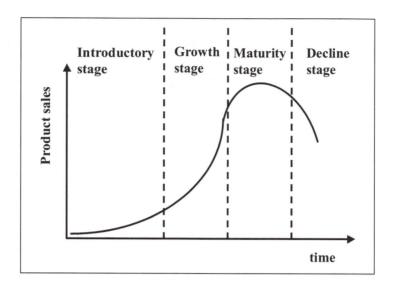

Figure 6.6 Standard product life cycle curve showing growth, maturity and decline

- *Growth stage*: here, sales are more predictable. The requirements for distribution are now for a better-balanced, more cost-effective system. The trade-off between service and cost can be realized.
- *Maturity stage*: where the introduction of competitive products and substitutes will increase price and service competition. An effective logistics operation becomes vital in order to maintain market share, especially for key customers.
- *Decline stage*: the product is becoming obsolete. Here, the logistics system needs to support the existing business but at minimum risk and cost.

There is a clear requirement to take into account the PLC concept when planning for logistics. A different emphasis needs to be placed on certain aspects of the logistics system according to the stage of a product's life. For operations where there are many products at varying stages of their PLC, this will not be crucial. In some instances, however, there will be a need to plan for a logistics operation that is suitably dynamic and flexible.

PACKAGING

In discussing the product, it is important to be aware of other relevant physical characteristics that can influence any decisions regarding the choice of logistics operation. In terms of the physical nature of a product, it is not generally presented to the logistics function in its primary form, but in the form of a package or unit load. These two elements are thus relevant to any discussion concerned with the relationship of the product and logistics.

The packaging of a product is broadly determined for product promotion and product protection, the latter being the function that is particularly pertinent to logistics. There are also some other factors that need to be considered when designing packaging for logistics purposes. In addition to product protection, packages should be easy to handle, convenient to store, readily identifiable, secure and of a shape that makes best use of space – usually cubic rather than cylindrical.

Once again, there are trade-offs that exist between these factors. These trade-offs will concern the product and the logistics operation itself. It is important to appreciate that, for those involved in logistics, the package is the product that is stored and moved and so, where possible, should be given the characteristics that help rather than hinder the logistics process.

Packaging is very much a part of the total logistics function and the design and use of packaging has implications for other functions such as production, marketing and quality control, as well as for overall logistics costs and performance.

UNIT LOADS

The idea of a unit load for logistics was developed from the realization of the high costs involved in the storage and movement of products – particularly in the inefficient manual handling of many small packages. The result of this has been the unit load concept, where the use of a unit load enables goods and packages to be grouped together and then handled and moved more effectively using mechanical equipment. Two familiar examples are the wooden pallet and the large shipping container, both of which, in their different ways, have revolutionized physical distribution and logistics. From the product point of view it is possible to introduce unit load systems to alter the characteristics of a product and thus make more effective logistics possible. One classic example has been the development of the roll-cage pallet that is in common use in the grocery industry. Although the cages are expensive units, the trade-off, in terms of time saving and security, is such that overall distribution costs decrease significantly.

Much of distribution and logistics is structured around the concept of load unitization, and the choice of unit load – type and size – is fundamental to the effectiveness and economics of a logistics operation. Choosing the most appropriate type and size of unit load minimizes the frequency of material movement, enables standard storage and handling equipment to be used with optimum equipment utilization, minimizes vehicle load/unload times, and improves product protection, security and stocktaking.

SUMMARY

This chapter has described the key elements of a logistics design strategy and has introduced a specific planning framework for logistics. The importance of under-standing and taking account of a company's corporate and competitive strategies has been emphasized. The detailed application of these different steps in logistics design is described in the next few chapters.

The chapter began with an outline of some of the main pressures exerted on companies such that they need to consider the replanning of their overall strategies. These covered a number of different internal and external aspects. A strategic planning overview was defined to incorporate a review of:

- the external environment to the company;
- internal factors;
- the development of a corporate strategy;
- the development of a competitive strategy;
- the development of functional strategic plans.

A framework for a logistics design strategy was proposed. This incorporated the four key aspects of logistics design:

1. process design;
2. physical design;
3. information system design; and
4. organizational structure.

Some of the major factors that need to be considered when planning for logistics were also considered. These included the product type, the product life cycle, packaging and unit loads.

7

Logistics processes

INTRODUCTION

As discussed in Chapter 6, one of the key elements of planning for logistics is concerned with the design of appropriate logistics processes. These processes are the methods used to ensure that the business operates effectively so that all the major objectives are achieved. The aim is for a streamlined operation that works across the various functional boundaries existing within any company. Thus, processes need to be supply-chain-oriented. One of the main problems with logistics processes is that they are very often tied in with a number of different functional elements of the business and so it is difficult for them to operate efficiently. The results of this are usually seen to be either additional costs within the logistics system or lower levels of customer service. In many operations both of these effects occur.

This chapter will consider the importance of logistics processes and the need to move away from functional and towards cross-functional process development. The main reasons for adopting more streamlined processes are discussed. Some of the key logistics processes are described, and the 'process triangle' is introduced as a means of categorizing the different processes. A broad approach to process design is outlined and the main steps in this approach are discussed. Finally, some key tools and techniques are described. These can be used for logistics process redesign.

THE IMPORTANCE OF LOGISTICS PROCESSES

The reason that the concept of logistics processes has been highlighted in recent years is a development of the move away from the functional view of logistics. Although functional excellence is important – if you are running a fleet of vehicles, it is still important to ensure that it operates cost-effectively and fulfils all the necessary requirements – the idea of trade-offs within logistics is now an accepted aspect of sound logistics planning. Some parts of an operation may sacrifice their efficiency to the greater good of the operation as a whole. Following on from this, there is the perspective of the supply chain where logistics is viewed not just across internal company functions, but also across the broader expanse of different companies. The chief beneficiary of this has been the final customer. The aim of any supply chain is to ensure that cross-company and cross-supply-chain activities are directed at achieving customer satisfaction for the end user. Thus, processes need to be developed to make this happen. They need to be able to span across internal functions and across company boundaries to provide the type and level of customer service required.

Unhappily this is not the case within many companies. Processes have generally been derived that act as a means for each separate function within an organization to undertake its particular role but they are not streamlined to act across all company functions as a united whole. Thus an effective process should be designed as a seamless operation rather than as a series of different elements. The order fulfilment process provides a good example of a typical logistics process. The aim of order fulfilment should be to ensure that a customer's order is received, checked, selected and delivered according to the customer's requirements, with no disruption and with complete accuracy. The process within many companies does not always work like this! As well as the possibility of error or delay within functions there is also the same possibility between the different functions. Typical functional errors might be:

- incorrect transcription of the original order requirements;
- incorrect notification of availability;
- incorrect selection or picking of the order;
- damage to the goods;
- late delivery;
- delivery to an incorrect address;
- invoicing to the incorrect address.

In addition, there might also be errors and delays associated across the functional boundaries. Examples might include:

- Order taking may be delayed because another function has to check stock availability.
- Stock may appear to be available but is actually pre-allocated to another customer.
- Order details may be incorrectly transcribed when moved from one information system to another.
- Credit control may delay the progress of the order – but the customer may not be informed.
- Different goods may be picked because the original requirement is out of stock so the 'next best' is selected. The customer may not be informed of this.
- Goods may not be delivered as part orders due to some product unavailability, when partial delivery may be better than no delivery.
- Goods may be physically delivered via an incorrect channel – to the customer's cost (next-day rather than the normal three-day service).

It is usually quite easy to identify problems that occur within individual functions and then put into place control measures to overcome these problems. It can be much more difficult to identify problems that occur between functions. Firstly, there is usually an unclear line of demarcation between functions, which makes it no easy matter to determine that there is a problem, let alone what the problem is. Secondly, it is very difficult to determine what is the cause of the problem – not least because of the associated 'blame' culture that often exists between functions, so that they will traditionally blame the other regardless of the true issues.

To avoid problems such as these, some companies now seek to redesign their key logistics processes. There are three essential elements. Properly designed processes should be customer-facing, that is, they should aim specifically to satisfy customer demands and expectations. They should also be cross-functional or indeed where possible they should be supply-chain-oriented in that they cross not just company functions but they also cross the boundary between companies. For most companies, the aim of achieving cross-functional processes is a big and sufficient challenge. Finally they should be time-based in that they need to reflect the importance of time as a key element in the logistics offering.

KEY LOGISTICS PROCESSES

What then are the key logistics processes? These will, as expected, vary between different companies, different sectors and different industries. Typical examples are:

- *Order fulfilment* – probably the most common that is quoted. Order fulfilment is concerned with the ability to turn a customer's specified requirements into an actual delivered order. Thus it embraces many of the traditional functions usually recognized as being a part of the logistics operation. Order fulfilment will involve the information elements of receiving and documenting an order through to the physical means of selecting and delivering the goods. For some 'make-to-order' manufacturing operations this will also have an impact on the production process itself. Some companies maintain the divide between the order-taking component (which is information-based) and the order-delivery component (which is both information-based and physical). This is a reasonable first step in process redesign, but ultimately there should ideally be a seamless process for the operation as a whole.
- *New product introduction.* This is an area where many companies find they have problems. There are many logistics issues related to the introduction of new products into the market-place. Very often existing, standard logistics structures and processes are insufficient to enable a satisfactory launch of a new product. One of the main problems is the inability to respond sufficiently quickly. Standard processes are designed to deal with known products. The consequence of introducing new products using existing processes is usually one of two possibilities. The first is that the product takes off very quickly and very well and there is insufficient ability in the supply chain to ratchet up supply to the required levels. The alternative is that demand is lower than initially expected and so there is an oversupply of stock, which eventually leads to products being sold off at discount rates or to obsolescence.
- *New product development.* In this example the idea is to design the product so that it can reach the market as quickly as possible from the initial design plan through to availability. The aim is to link the development of the product with the logistical requirements so that all secondary developments (of which there are normally very many) can be identified and re-engineered in the shortest possible time. The automotive industry has led the way in setting up processes to cut significantly the time that is required to bring a product to market from initial design.
- *Product returns.* There is a growing requirement in many businesses to provide an effective process for the return of products. This may be for returns that come back through the existing distribution network or through a new one that is specifically set up. It may also be for product returns that will be reworked or repackaged to go into stock, product returns for subsequent disposal or for packaging returns that may be reused or scrapped. In the light of developments in environmental legislation this is a very important area for process design or redesign.

- *The provision of spares.* For many companies the supply of a product or series of products is inextricably linked to the subsequent provision of spare parts to support the continuous use of the initial products. For many logistics operations, neither the physical structure nor the associated processes are really capable of providing a suitable support mechanism for spare parts as well as for original equipment. This then is another example of the need for the development of processes specifically designed to undertake a particular task.
- *Information management.* Advances in information technology have enabled a vast amount of detailed data and information to be available and manipulated very easily. This has led some companies to recognize the need to devise suitable processes to ensure that data is collected, collated and used in a positive and organized way. For logistics this means detailed information can be made available for individual customers, concerning not just their product preferences but also any customer service requirements that are distribution-specific (delivery time preference, order size preference, invoicing requirements, etc). This enables a much more positive, proactive approach to be adopted when considering particular customer relationships.

There are other associated processes that could also be relevant, such as:

- supplier integration;
- quality;
- strategic management;
- maintenance;
- human resource management;
- environmental management.

A number of different concepts have been proposed to try to help differentiate the type and importance of the various processes that might be relevant to any given company as it tries to position itself with its customers. Perhaps the most useful of these is known as the process triangle. This is shown in Figure 7.1. The process triangle seeks to identify three different bases for process requirement, and then to use these to accentuate those that need to be highlighted for particular development. These are as follows:

1. *Basic processes*: those processes that are not really recognized as essential to a business but are nevertheless a prerequisite.
2. *Benchmark processes*: those processes that are seen to be important to the customer and must be of at least an acceptable standard to even begin to compete satis-factorily in a given market.

3. *Competitive processes*: those processes that are of direct significance to the competitive area. Good practice and excellence in these processes will provide a competitive edge and ensure that the company is active and successful through its logistics operations.

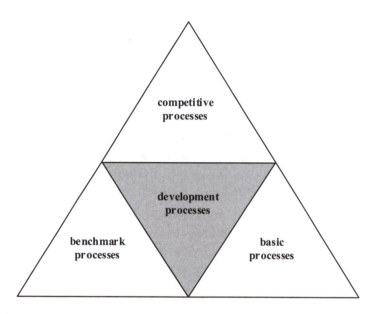

Figure 7.1 The process triangle

An assessment of what is required in these three areas and then the identification of what is missing – the 'gap' – will enable the development processes to be identified. These are the processes on which further work is necessary to ensure that the company will achieve or maintain a suitable competitive position.

It would be difficult for any company to develop a suitable process to cover all possible contingencies. Thus it is useful to understand some of the main methods of differentiating between the various factors that are fundamental to most logistics operations. Processes can then be developed to suit different requirements. Typical differentiating factors will include:

- *market segmentation*: by sector – engineering, automotive, chemicals, etc;
- *customer types*: may vary between, for example, industrial and consumer, or international, national and local;
- *product groups*: broken down according to a variety of categories, dependent on the industry – household, industrial, consumer, or hardware, software, spares, etc;

- *customer service requirements*: same day, next day, normal, special, etc;
- *order type*: made to order, off the shelf, postponement (partial production);
- *channel type*: direct, via depot, via wholesaler.

APPROACH

A broad approach to process design is outlined in Figure 7.2.

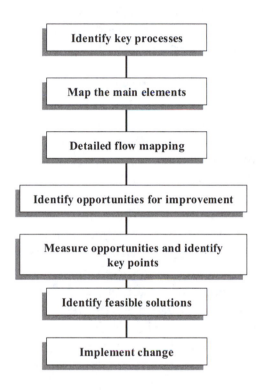

Figure 7.2 Approach to process design or redesign

The first step is to identify the key processes for design or redesign. This can be undertaken in a variety of different ways, but it is important to include representatives of all the main functions from within the company. Typically, some type of brainstorming exercise will provide the initial ideas linked closely with a customer service study similar to that described in Chapter 3. As usual, it is imperative to get a clear view of customer service requirements and these can only be truly identified through close contact with the customer. Any opportunity to benchmark against key competitors will also be advantageous.

The next stage is to map out the main elements of each process to be redesigned. The objective is to identify the key steps in each process and clarify which departments and people are involved. Key outcomes are to provide an understanding of what the process is all about, what it is trying to achieve, what some of the main problems are and perhaps an indication of some of the potential improvements that might be introduced.

Allied to this initial mapping approach is the next stage, which is to undertake a much more detailed flow mapping exercise. Here, the work flow is identified in detail as it progresses through each relevant department. Each crucial part of the process is identified together with the specified amount of time taken to complete each of these parts. Any problems are identified and noted. As already indicated, the order fulfilment process is likely to be one of the key processes that needs to be mapped. The complicated nature of this process in most companies indicates that the mapping exercise itself is likely to take a lot of time and effort. In general, the specific opportunities that should be identified are those with a high potential for positive change, and those that are either very high in cost or very high in terms of the time taken to complete that respective part of the process, or of course all of these. Additionally, it may be possible to identify some parts of the process that are entirely superfluous. This is not uncommon with many processes that have been allowed to develop over time without any specific replanning.

Once the detailed flow mapping has been completed and opportunities for improvement have been identified, it is useful to set up a specific team to undertake the remaining stages of the process redevelopment. This team should be one that has the full backing of senior management and should also be representative of the main departments to be affected by the redesign. The team should be in a position to complete any additional or more detailed mapping or measurement, as necessary. It should identify and measure the effects of any feasible solutions and then get overall agreement for any changes it feels should be put into practice.

The final stage, once agreement for change has been reached, is to implement any change. This may be undertaken on a pilot basis at first to test the effectiveness of the redesigned process. Subsequently, measures should be put in place to monitor the process continually into the future.

TOOLS AND TECHNIQUES

There are a number of different tools and techniques that can be used to help with logistics process redesign. These range from ones that provide assistance with the initial categorization of key process objectives to those that offer a detailed assessment of the processes themselves and thus can be used to identify opportunities for improvement. Some of the main alternatives are:

● *Pareto analysis.* Sometimes known as the 80/20 rule, this is a crucial method used in logistics for identifying the major elements of any business or operation. By identifying these main elements it is possible to ensure that, for analytical purposes, any assessment is based specifically on the key aspects and is not taken up with the peripheral detail. A typical Pareto curve is shown in Figure 7.3. In this example, which is common to most companies, 20 per cent of the product lines or SKUs (stock keeping units) are responsible for 80 per cent of the sales in value of the company's products. This type of relationship holds true for many relationships in logistics and distribution – the most important customers, the most important suppliers, etc. Thus it is possible to identify a limited number of key elements that are representative of the main business and to concentrate any major analysis on this important 20 per cent. Another useful result of Pareto analysis is to identify the items (customers, products or whatever) that make up the final 50 per cent of the 'tail' of the curve. These are often uneconomic to the company and should be considered for rationalization or elimination.

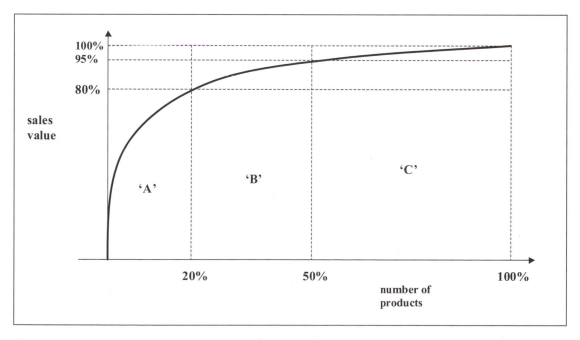

Figure 7.3 A typical Pareto curve showing that 20 per cent of products represent 80 per cent of sales value

In Figure 7.3, 'A' class products represent 20 per cent of the range of products, but account for 80 per cent of sales, 'B' class products represent 30 per cent of the range of products, but account for 15 per cent of sales and 'C' class products represent 50 per cent of the range of products, but account for just 5 per cent of sales.

- *Market or customer segmentation.* One of the main objectives of the design of suitable logistics processes is to ensure that they are 'customer-facing' and to align them in such a way that all customers' needs are met. Clearly, not all customers are the same and therefore not all customer requirements are the same. It is important to be able to identify different types of customers and different types of market and to adopt the appropriate service requirements to take account of these differences. Through the use of suitable customer service studies (as described in Chapter 3) it should be possible to categorize companies according to different types of service requirement. Suitable processes can then be based around the different categories of customer or segments of the market.
- *Customer service studies.* As already described in Chapter 3, a customer service study should be used as the basis for identifying key service requirements on which to design suitable logistics processes.
- *Relationship mapping.* This is used at an early stage of logistics process design to identify the main departments within a company (or across the broader supply chain if this is possible) that are specifically involved in a particular process. An example is given in Figure 7.4. As well as identifying these key departments, so that they can be brought into the design process, this will help to pinpoint the major relationships and will highlight the complexity within any particular process, thus indicating its need for redesign.
- *Process charts.* These can be represented in a variety of different guises, whether by straightforward flow charts or by a matrix, as shown in Figure 7.5. The flow chart approach can be based on traditional flow charting techniques. This is useful because standard shapes are used to represent different types of activity (storage, movement, action etc), and the importance of flows can be highlighted in terms of the number of movements along a flow. The matrix chart provides a more systematic way of representation and can be beneficial where time is to be represented.
- *Value/time analysis.* This type of analysis can be used to identify where in a process value is actually added to the product. The aim is to highlight those parts of the operation that in fact provide a cost but add no value. Traditionally, for most manufactured products, value is added when a process changes the nature of the product (such as production, which alters the physical attributes,

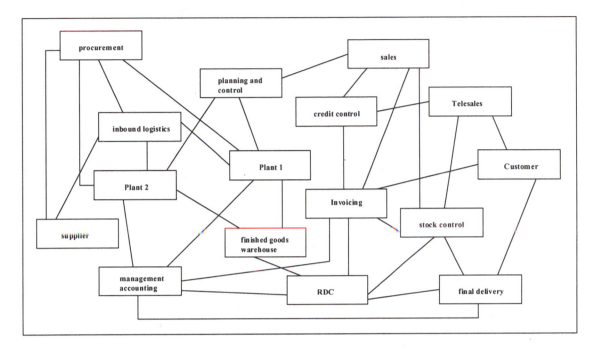

Figure 7.4   Relationship mapping: used to identify key departments and inter-relationships

or transport, which alters the physical location). Value is not added, but waste occurs through the passing of time, when the product is stored (as work-in-progress or as finished goods stock in a depot). Figure 7.6 provides an example of a value/time analysis. This is not an easy type of analysis to undertake, especially for the early downstream activities when it becomes difficult to isolate the true time and costs attributable to partially manufactured products.

SUMMARY

In this chapter the importance of logistics processes has been reviewed. The need to move away from functional and towards cross-functional process development has been highlighted. The main reasons for adopting more streamlined processes were discussed. Some of the key logistics processes were described, the main examples being:

● order fulfilment;
● new product introduction;

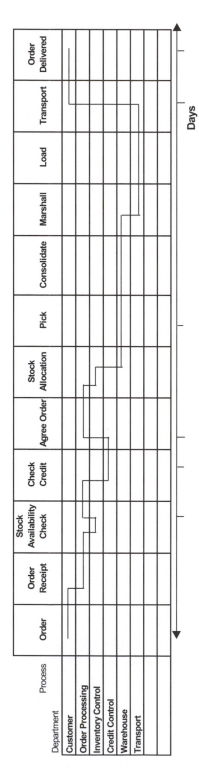

Figure 7.5 A matrix process chart

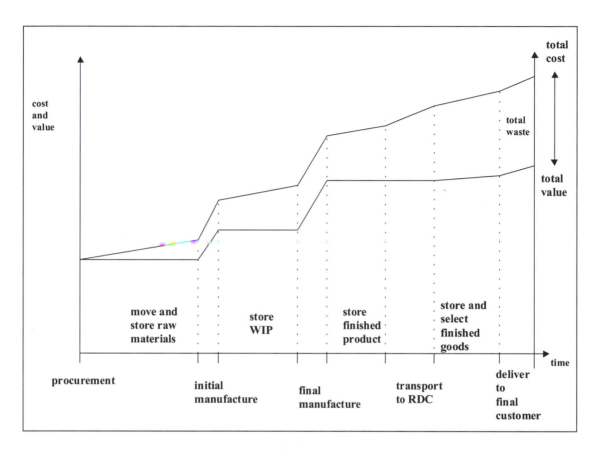

Figure 7.6 Value/time analysis

- new product development;
- product returns;
- the provision of spares;
- information management.

The process triangle was used as a means of categorizing the different processes.

A broad approach to process design was outlined and the main steps in this approach were described. Finally, some of the key tools and techniques for logistics process redesign were described.

8

Planning physical distribution

INTRODUCTION

In this chapter a particular approach to the planning of physical distribution strategy is developed and described. The main content follows on from, and links very closely with, the planning framework that was proposed in Chapter 6. As well as considering the key flows and cost relationships, various aspects associated with depot and facilities location are reviewed. There are both theoretical concepts and practical considerations to be taken into account. Some of the major points for discussion are:

- the role of depots and warehouses;
- distribution cost factors and relationships;
- a methodology for planning a physical distribution structure;
- an overview of different modelling techniques;
- qualitative assessment; and
- depot site considerations.

The question of the number, size and location of facilities in a company's distribution system is a complex one. There are many different elements that go to make up the distribution mix, and it is necessary to take into account all of these when considering the question of physical distribution structure or facilities location. Prior to the depot location decision a lot of work must be undertaken. This is necessary to help to understand the key requirements of the company and to collect and collate sufficient data that represents a numerical picture of the distribution structure so that appropriate analysis can be carried out to test potential options for improvement.

Before trying to determine the most appropriate number and location of depots, it is also necessary to ensure that there is an efficient flow of products from source to final destination. This assessment of the different patterns of product flows is known as sourcing analysis.

The complexity of sourcing and location decisions has led to the development of some quite sophisticated mathematical models that attempt to find the optimum flows and the optimum number of depots to serve a system. The detailed mathematical principles used as the basis for these models will not be covered, but consideration will be given to the relationships involved, and the approaches that can be undertaken when making location decisions.

It is worth while to begin the discussion by concentrating on the most practical aspects of importance to an individual company. The main point to appreciate is that the vast majority of location studies are undertaken when the company already has a number of depots and associated delivery areas. Thus, location studies are rarely based upon the premise that the 'best' results can be applied at the end of the day. Generally, it is necessary for a compromise to be reached between what is 'best' and what is currently in existence. The very high cost of depots and vehicle fleets is the main reason for this, as well as the high cost and great disruption involved in making any changes to existing systems.

Despite this, it is very important for companies to know how their distribution networks might be improved. Although some networks are planned from the beginning of a company's operation, this is a rare occurrence. The majority of systems are unplanned; they just evolve very much as the company evolves. This may be a steady growth (or decline), or may be in short steps or large leaps as mergers and take-overs occur. Perhaps the most common reason why distribution networks are out of balance is that of inertia, because of the great amount of work and effort required to make changes.

It needs a forward-looking management or a particularly significant change for a company to undertake a large-scale study of this nature. The recent realization of the importance of distribution to most companies, and the need to cut costs and improve efficiency have provided sufficient impetus for a number of companies to review their logistics and distribution structure with a particular emphasis on the use and location of depots and warehouses.

THE ROLE OF DEPOTS AND WAREHOUSES

There are a number of reasons why depots and warehouses are required. These vary in importance depending on the nature of a company's business. In general, the main reasons are:

- to keep down production costs by allowing long production runs, thus minimizing the time spent for machine set-up;
- to help link demand requirements with production capabilities, to smooth the flow and assist in operational efficiency;
- to enable large seasonal demands to be catered for more economically;
- to provide a good customer service;
- to allow cost trade-offs with the transport system (bulk delivery, etc); and
- to facilitate order assembly.

These reasons emphasize the importance of the facilities location decision, and also give an indication of the complex nature of that decision. It is possible to summarize the main reason for developing a physical distribution network as 'the need to provide an effective service to the customer, whilst minimizing the cost of that service'. Service and cost factors are thus of paramount importance when determining facilities number, size and location.

For the best possible customer service, a depot would have to be provided right next to the customer, and it would have to hold adequate stocks of all the goods the customer might require. This would obviously be a very expensive solution.

At the other extreme, the cheapest solution would be to have just one depot (or central warehouse) and to send out a large lorry to each customer whenever his or her orders were sufficient to fill the vehicle so that an economic full load could be delivered. This would be a cheap alternative for the supplier, but as deliveries might then only be made to a customer once or maybe twice a year, the supplier might soon find himself losing the customer's business.

There is obviously a suitable compromise somewhere between these extremes. This will usually consist of the provision of a number of depots on a regional or area basis, the use of large trunk vehicles to service these, with smaller delivery vehicles to run the orders to customers. For certain operations, of course, even these simple relationships will vary because of the need for very high levels of customer service or the very high value of products.

In addition, it should be noted that there are a number of different types of depot, each of which might be considered in the planning of a suitable physical distribution structure. These might include:

- finished goods depots/warehouses – these hold the stock from factories;
- distribution centres, which might be central, regional (RDC), national (NDC) or local depots – all of these will hold stock to a greater or lesser extent;
- transhipment depots or stockless, transit or cross-docking depots – by and large, these do not hold stock, but act as intermediate points in the distribution operation for the transfer of goods and picked orders to customers;
- seasonal stock-holding depots;
- overflow depots.

Distribution network and depot location strategies are aimed at establishing the most appropriate blend of storage and transport at a given customer service level. The interrelationship of the different distribution elements, and their associated costs, thus provide the basis for decision making.

COST RELATIONSHIPS

To plan an efficient logistics structure it is necessary to be aware of the interaction between the different distribution costs, specifically as to how they vary with respect to the different depot alternatives (number, size, type and location), and what the overall logistics cost will be. This is best done by comparative analysis of the major alternative configurations. Before this can be achieved, the detailed make-up of the individual distribution cost elements must be understood.

Many companies have cost information based on their conventional accounting systems, but almost always these costs are too general to allow for any detailed breakdown into the integral parts that reflect the company's distribution structure.

Without this information, and the understanding that goes with it, it is impossible to measure the effectiveness or otherwise of the existing operation. It is also impossible to gain the necessary insight into the distribution operation to allow for successful planning and management. The component parts of a distribution system necessarily interact with one another to form the system as a whole. Within this system, it is possible to trade off one element with another, and so gain an overall improvement in the cost-effectiveness of the total system. An appreciation of the make-up and relationship of these key costs is thus a vital link to successful distribution planning and operations.

The major cost relationships are outlined in this section, starting with storage and warehousing costs. The major cost breakdown is outlined below, with the percentage values indicating the approximate relative importance of the different factors based on conventional warehouses:

	%
Building costs (rent, rates, depreciation)	24
Building services (heating, lighting, etc)	16
Equipment (rental, leasing, maintenance)	13
Labour (direct)	38
Management and supervision	9

The relationship of these costs will, of course, vary under different circumstances – industry, product type, volume throughput, regional location, age of building, handling system, etc. In general, the direct labour cost is likely to be the greatest element, with the building cost likely to fluctuate from very high (new building, prime location) to very low (old building, peppercorn rent, low rates).

With respect to the cost relationship with other parts of the distribution system, the importance of storage and warehousing costs will be dependent on such factors as the size of the depot and the number of depots within the distribution network as a whole.

The effect of depot size is illustrated by the economies of scale experienced if larger depots are operated. It has been established that the cost of operation of a depot and the amount of stock required to support a depot tend to be higher (per unit) for a small depot than for a large depot. This is because larger depots can often achieve better space and equipment utilization and can benefit from spreading overhead costs over the higher throughput. With stock-holding, the larger a depot, the less buffer and safety stock is required. It should be noted that, eventually, diseconomies of scale could occur, because very large depots can be adversely affected by such conditions as excessive internal travel distances, problems of management, etc.

The effect of a different number of warehouses or depots in a given distribution network can be seen by developing the economies of scale argument. If a distribution network is changed from one depot to two depots, then the overall depot/ storage costs will increase. The change is likely to be from a single large depot to two medium-sized depots. This will not, therefore, double the costs because the change is not to two large depots. It will certainly increase costs, however, because there will be a need for more stock coverage, more storage space, more management, etc. In simple terms, this can be described by a graph, illustrated in Figure 8.1.

Thus, as the number of depots in a distribution network increases, then the total storage (depot) cost will also increase.

One point that should be appreciated is that some care must be taken over any generalization of this nature. In practice, it will be found that each individual depot may differ in its cost structure from the other depots in a system for a variety of

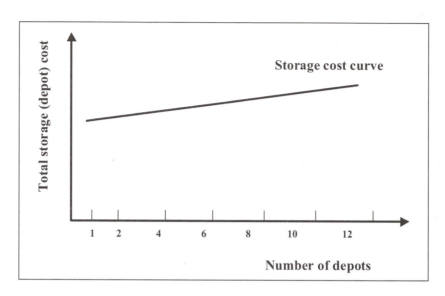

Figure 8.1 Relationship between number of depots (ie storage capacity) and total storage cost

practical reasons. These may include, for example, high (or low) rent and rates according to the locality of the depot (eg very high in cities) or high (or low) labour costs.

The two most important categories of transport costs are trunking and final delivery. These are affected differently according to the number of depots in a distribution network.

Delivery transport is concerned with the delivering of orders from the depot to the customer. This can be carried out by a company using its own fleet of vehicles or by a third-party carrier. Whichever alternative is used, the cost of delivery is essentially dependent on the mileage that has to be travelled. Delivery mileage can be divided into two types: 1) 'drop' mileage, which is the mileage travelled once a drop or delivery zone has been reached; and 2) 'stem' mileage, which is the mileage to and from a delivery zone. While the 'drop' mileage remains the same whatever the distance from the supplying depot, the 'stem' mileage varies according to the number of depots in the system. The greater the number of depots, the less the stem mileage. This can be described by a graph, as shown in Figure 8.2.

The *trunking* or primary transport element is the supply of products in bulk (ie in full pallet loads) to the depots from the central finished goods warehouse or production point. Once again, the number of depots affects the overall cost of this type of transport. In this instance, the effect is not a particularly large one, but it does result in an increase in primary transport costs as the number of depots increases. The effect is greatest where there is a smaller number of depots, as the graph of Figure 8.3 indicates.

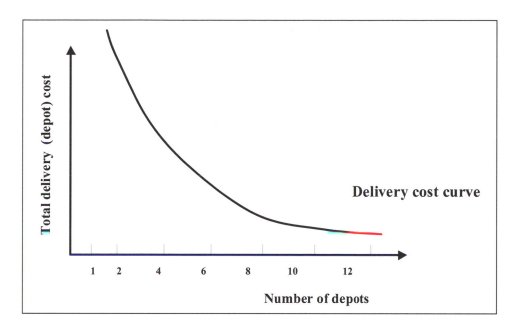

Figure 8.2 Relationship between the number of depots and total delivery costs

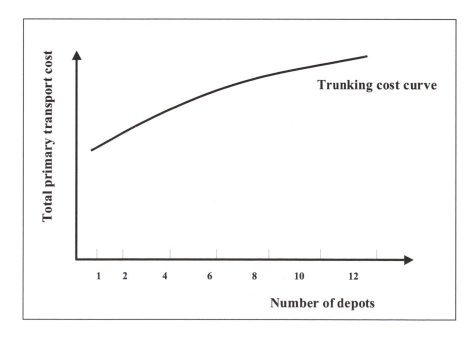

Figure 8.3 Trunking costs (total primary transport costs) in relation to the number of depots

If the cost for both delivery and trunking are taken as a *combined transport cost* then the total transport costs can be related to the different number of depots in a distribution network. The overall effect of combining the two transport costs is that total transport costs will reduce, the greater the number of depots in the system. The effect can be seen in the graph of Figure 8.4.

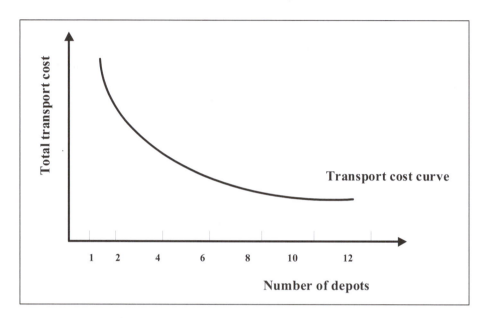

Figure 8.4   Total transport costs (delivery and trunking) in relation to the number of depots

Another important cost that needs to be included is the cost of holding inventory. The main elements of inventory holding are considered in detail in Chapter 12. The key costs can be broken down into four main areas:

1. *Capital cost* – the cost of the physical stock. This is the financing charge, which is the current cost of capital to a company or the opportunity cost of tying up capital that might otherwise be producing a return if invested elsewhere.
2. *Service cost* – that is, stock management and insurance.
3. *Storage costs* – which were considered earlier with warehousing costs.
4. *Risk costs* – which occur through pilferage, deterioration of stock, damage and stock obsolescence.

These costs, when taken together and measured against the number of depots in a system, can be represented as shown in Figure 8.5.

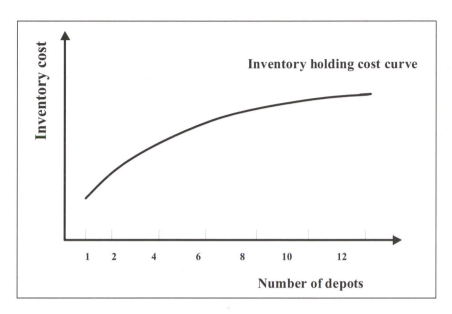

Figure 8.5 Inventory holding costs in relation to the number of depots

The final cost element for consideration is that of information system costs. These costs may represent a variety of information or communication requirements ranging from order processing to load assembly lists. In recent years, there has been a significant move from manual systems towards the use of computerized information systems to provide these requirements. These costs are less easy to represent graphically because of the fast rate of change of information systems and because costs can vary considerably dependent on the level of technology introduced. These costs can be broadly represented as shown in the graph of Figure 8.6.

By its very nature logistics operates in a dynamic and ever-changing environment. This makes the planning of a logistics structure a difficult process. By the same token, it is not an easy matter to appreciate how any changes to one of the major elements within such a structure will affect the system as a whole. One way of overcoming this problem is to adopt a 'total' view of the system, to try to understand and measure the system as a whole as well as in relation to the constituent parts of the system.

Total logistics cost analysis allows this approach to be developed on a practical basis. The various costs of the different elements within the system can be built together. This provides a fair representation, not just of the total logistics cost, but also of the ways in which any change to the system will affect both the total system and the elements within the system.

The total cost approach can be represented in a graphical format by building up a picture from the graphs used to illustrate the cost elements in the earlier section

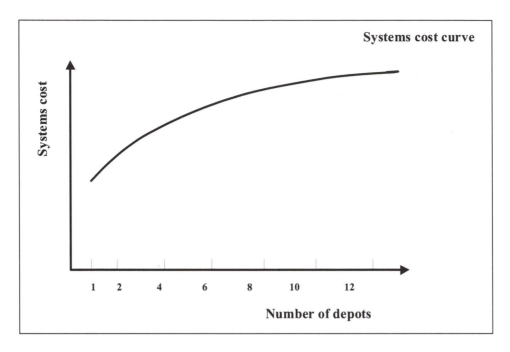

Figure 8.6 Information system costs in relation to the number of depots

of this chapter. This is illustrated in Figure 8.7 and demonstrates how the individual distribution and logistics cost elements can be built up to give the total logistics cost. It shows, for example, the effect of a different number of depots and the related costs on the total distribution cost.

For facilities location planning, for example, the overall cost effect of using a different number of depots can be explained by such a graph. The top line on the graph shows the overall distribution cost in relation to the different number of depots in the network. It is obtained by adding together the individual cost curves of the key distribution elements that correspond to each number of depots. For just a single depot, for example, there is a large local delivery cost to add to the much smaller costs of trunking, inventory, storage and system costs.

It can be seen from the graph that the least expensive overall distribution cost occurs at around the seven-to-nine depot number (in this example). The minimum point on the overall distribution curve represents this lowest cost solution. The results, in practice, will depend on a number of factors – product type, geographic area of demand, service level required, etc.

These relationships are the key to the planning of physical distribution strategy and structures. As will be discussed later in this chapter, models have been devel-

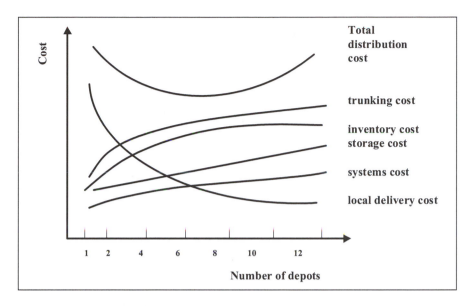

Figure 8.7   Overall distribution cost in relation to the number of depots, showing the constituent cost elements that make up the total

oped that allow this type of detailed quantitative analysis to be carried out so that least-cost solutions can be identified and implemented.

Trade-off analysis

An understanding of this total cost approach to logistics is important in order to appreciate the concept of trade-off analysis in logistics planning. It has been shown that any change in one of the major elements within a logistics system is likely to have a significant effect on the costs of both the total system and the other elements. By the same token, it is often possible to create total cost savings by making savings in one element that creates additional costs in another but produces an overall cost benefit. This can be seen in Figure 8.8.

In this example, a depot rationalization policy has been adopted whereby the number of depots in a logistics system has been reduced. Although this has led to an increase in local delivery costs, savings in some of the other main elements of distribution have produced overall cost benefits.

The cost and service trade-offs within any logistics structure will, of course, vary from one company to another depending on the role the company plays within the supply chain as a whole. In the main, however, the following major costs and their associated trade-offs may need to be considered and assessed:

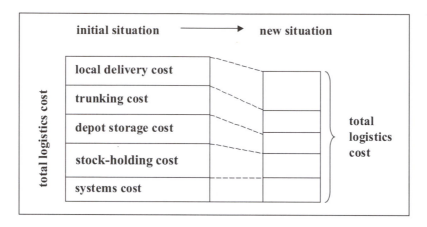

Figure 8.8   Trade-off analysis

- *Production costs.* These will vary according to the type of production process or system used and the type of product manufactured. Make to stock or make to order will also be relevant. Factories may be 'focused' on one or two specific types of product or may make a large range of different products. Different distribution structures may be required to support different types of product. The effect on primary transport costs will be very relevant.
- *Packaging costs.* These are mainly concerned with the trade-off between the type of packaging and the handling and transport costs. The type of load unitization will also be important.
- *Information systems costs.* These cover a wide area from order receipt to management information systems. The type of depot network will affect many of these costs.
- *Lost sales costs.* These might occur because of inadequate customer service, and are very relevant in the context of proximity of the depot to the customer, together with the reliability and speed of service.
- *Inventory costs.* These include the cost of capital tied up in inventory as well as the cost of obsolescence, etc. They have a fundamental relationship with the depot network in terms of the number of stock-holding points and the hierarchy of stock-holding according to depot type.
- *Transport costs.* The number and location of depots within the distribution structure, and the associated throughputs significantly affect transport costs. Both trunking and final delivery costs are affected by depot numbers and location.
- *Warehousing costs.* These costs vary according to the type of storage and handling systems used, together with the volume and throughput at the depot. The size and type of depot will thus be important, as will the location.

A PLANNED APPROACH OR METHODOLOGY

An approach to logistics and distribution strategy planning is outlined in Figure 8.9. This approach describes the practical steps that need to be taken to derive a physical distribution strategy from a corporate business plan, as described in Chapter 6. This type of approach requires the collection, collation and analysis of a great deal of data. It is thus quantitative, although a degree of qualitative assessment may also be necessary.

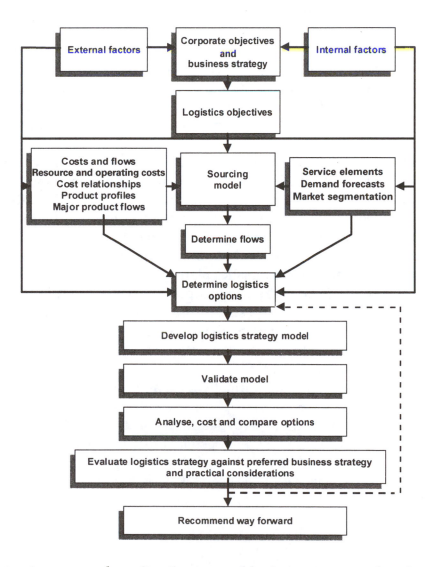

Figure 8.9   An approach to distribution and logistics strategy planning

Some initial points to note are:

- Various inputs to the corporate planning process will also be important inputs into the logistics planning process. These will include both external and internal factors.
- It is important to take great care in defining exactly the overall problem. It is likely to be concerned with the use and location of depots within a distribution network, but it is often vital to have clear limits and boundaries. These might include, for example, whether all production facilities must be retained or whether there are existing depots that need to be included.
- What period into the future is to be assessed?
- All relevant cost relationships need to be identified and understood.
- The relevant product flows for different patterns of demand and supply need to be established. Important aspects will include the type of products, the origin of these products (factories, etc) the destination of products (shops, hospitals, factories, etc) and the amount and type of product going through the system (throughputs, etc).
- The identification of all relevant data and information requires consideration. There are always problems in finding and obtaining the data and information required. It may be necessary to make compromises over the data that is available. Data collection is often the largest part of a study. It is helpful to collect data in the way that you will finally want to use it.
- A sourcing or 'flow' model is likely to be an important link in the process of moving from a corporate to a logistics plan.
- Both cost and service elements are vital inputs to the logistics planning process.
- Essential to the development of a suitable logistics plan is the need to carry out some fairly detailed quantitative analysis. In Figure 8.9, this is represented by the sourcing model and the logistics strategy model.
- Additional planning tools and models may also be used as an add-on to this planning process, but they are normally used as a second stage. They include, for example, inventory models (to determine levels and location) and vehicle routeing and scheduling models (to determine fleet size and vehicle mix, etc).
- Once a suitable logistics strategy has been identified it is essential to undertake the dual process of evaluating this strategy against the preferred business strategy and ensuring that due account has been taken of any practical considerations.

External factors

Any number of external factors may be relevant in a logistics-based study, and these will of course vary according to the industry, the company, the market-place, etc. Some of the factors that may be relevant will include:

- transport mode availability;
- infrastructure changes (eg the Channel Tunnel);
- regulatory changes (implications of SEM);
- information technology (EDI, EPOS, etc);
- technology changes (new vehicle design, unit load technology, etc);
- environmental impacts;
- industry trends.

Examples of these factors were described in Chapter 6.

Internal factors

The importance of the many internal factors will certainly vary from industry to industry. It is generally possible to categorize these in two ways: firstly, qualitative or descriptive factors that relate directly to the operation under review; and secondly, quantitative facts and figures. Both qualitative and quantitative information are used to help 'describe' the business in an operational context. These factors will be developed in much greater detail to represent the inputs into the modelling process for costs, product flows and customer service requirements.

Logistics objectives

An assessment of corporate objectives and business strategy together with the most relevant external and internal factors should allow for clear logistics objectives to be determined. As discussed in Chapter 6, these should be linked to the specific competitive strategy the company plans to adopt.

Costs and product flows and customer service

This is the data that will be used as the basis for the logistics modelling and analysis that will underpin the entire strategy planning process. Typical examples of descriptive data include:

- product groups;
- own and bought-in sourcing locations;
- number and type of sites and facilities;
- major transport modes;
- handling systems used;
- unit load types;
- own versus third-party operations;
- main customer groups;
- customer service levels;
- logistics information systems.

Examples of quantitative data are:

- major product flows;
- transport modal split for the major flows;
- demand by region, by major product group, by customer type, etc;
- market segmentation;
- customer service goals and achievements;
- carrier analysis;
- inventory holding profile;
- product profile;
- customer profile.

For the logistics strategy model itself, the key variables and key data requirements will generally be as follows:

Variables

- location and capacity of each plant, distribution depot or transhipment depot;
- cost functions for storage, trunking and local delivery;
- demand locations and amounts.

Data

- customer location and demand;
- depot location and throughput;
- trunking costs (fixed and variable);
- local delivery costs (fixed and variable);
- speeds, work period and other costs;
- hazards location and penalty.

Quantitative data may not always be readily available, so descriptive information or alternative data may have to suffice. For example, it may be recognized that customers can be broadly profiled in terms of, say, national accounts, key accounts, dealers, distributors and specialist users. It may not be possible to make precise quantitative comparisons in terms of tonnage distributed per annum to each grouping, but some type of value analysis may be available.

The quantitative data derived is crucial to the analytical process carried out and thus to the final conclusions and recommendations made. Although collection is extremely time-consuming, it is important that it is correct and that it does adequately reflect the real flows and costs within the business.

Further discussion on customer service and the means of determining customer service requirements is given in Chapter 3.

Modelling complete logistics structures

Many modelling techniques used in logistics concentrate on the detailed representation of specific parts of the logistics operation, eg production optimization, depot location and vehicle routeing. These methods, however, have the potential risk of optimizing only part of a logistics operation when greater economies or benefits could come from changes to other parts of the operation or from a complete restructuring of the operation.

The problem with such multi-faceted optimization is that suitable techniques do not exist to consider simultaneously all the possible alternatives. The combinatorial problem of considering all products, made at all sites, shipped via all modes, to all customers, via all depots is simply prohibitive. If the techniques did exist, solutions would require uneconomic run times on large computers.

A similar situation exists in the specialist area of production planning known as MRPII, where the technique of rough-cut capacity planning was introduced. Instead of trying to produce initial plans at a most detailed level, a rough-cut plan considers the overall requirement for key resources.

The consideration here can be described as trying to establish the 'economic footprint'. The economies of scale of production, the customer service requirement and the logistics cost are all considered to give an optimum factory size and radius of operation, hence the economic footprint. A brewery with canning lines has large economies of scale and a product with sufficient shelf life to give a medium to large economic footprint. A bakery has much lower economies of scale and a product with a short product life and thus has a smaller footprint.

A means of 'rough-cut modelling' for the whole of a logistics operation is to use sourcing models. Costs of raw materials, production rates and capacities, together with approximate logistic costs across a geographical area, are used to calculate the trade-off between the major elements.

Sourcing models

With multiple products from multiple sources it is only too easy to assume that the lowest-cost solution is to source each market from the closest available source with available capacity. In some situations this is true, but if plants have significant change-over (set-up) times and if different products can be produced at different rates in different plants, then a very counter-intuitive sourcing pattern can result.

> Example 1
> In a period of high demand, 'everything that is made can be sold'. In this instance, it is often better to run plants for specialist products and not incur change-over times but concentrate on maximizing production. Additional transportation costs may arise but gross margin will be greater and therefore will more than compensate for this.

> Example 2
> Product A can be made more efficiently than product B on Plant 1; on Plant 2 product B can be made more efficiently than product A. In this situation, extra transportation costs can be incurred to achieve the production efficiency.

Thus the first step in rationalizing a logistics system is to investigate optimal sourcing patterns. One definitive pattern may not be sufficient as sourcing could change according to market conditions, product price, raw material costs and transport costs.

Linear programming is a mathematical technique that finds the minimum cost or maximum revenue solution to a product sourcing problem. All available sources are described with capacities, change-over penalties and raw material costs. Approximate logistics costs from sources to markets are defined as linear cost functions. Under any given demand scenario the technique is able to identify the optimum solution for the sourcing of products. Most spreadsheet packages have an optimization feature that allows this type of analysis to be undertaken. A typical sourcing model equation operates under the following constraints:

- the availability of each plant for production and change-over;
- that customer demand should be met;
- the least-cost solution is required.

The objective of a typical sourcing model equation is to minimize the following, given the run rate of each product at each plant:

- raw material cost;
- material handling cost;
- production variable cost;
- logistics cost from plant to customer.

Generating alternatives and options

For any strategic review it is important to enable any innovative alternatives to be considered within the planning process because the length of planning time horizon is likely to be one that takes the logistics evaluation outside the scope of the existing operation. This can, not surprisingly, be difficult in many organizations as there is likely to be a very limited familiarity with new concepts and new technologies that might become appropriate as the requirements of a dynamic logistics system develops.

This problem can be overcome through the introduction of external specialist consultants and the use of techniques such as lateral thinking and brainstorming sessions.

With approaches such as these, it is usually possible to develop a long list of options (some of which may, initially, appear to be less than ideal) and then by fairly simple analysis determine which of them, or which combination, may be feasible in the context of the planning horizon. A short list of alternatives can then be drawn up for quantitative evaluation in the modelling process.

Logistics modelling

The output from such a sourcing study is to identify the major product flows from source points to final customer. The next stage is to take these flows and to develop the most cost-effective logistics solution in terms of the most appropriate number, type and location of depots, transport mode, etc. Thus, the overall trade-offs of the supply chain have been considered and assessed and a preliminary sourcing allocation has been made. The detailed logistics of modes, rates and depot structure can now be considered.

Cost trade-off analysis can be used as the basis for the planning and reassessing of logistics and distribution systems. Clearly, this approach is a time-consuming and often daunting task, not least because of the difficulty in obtaining the appropriate data and information from within a company's accounting system, but also because of the somewhat complicated models that have to be used.

Mathematical programming uses a number of well-known mathematical techniques (such as linear programming) that are particularly applicable to solving the depot location type of problem. Basically they use a logical step-by-step procedure to reach the optimal or 'best' solution. The main drawbacks with these techniques are that linear relationships are not always adequate (if linear programming is used) and some solutions can be 'local' optimums, that is, they are not the best from the overall point of view.

Heuristics is a Greek-based word, used to describe the method of solution that is derived on a 'rule-of-thumb' principle. Heuristic methods are determined by using experience and common sense to reject unlikely solutions from the outset. In this way, problems can be reduced to a more manageable size in terms of the number of alternatives that need to be tested. This type of approach is often very valid for depot location problems, because there are always a number of locations that are totally inappropriate.

Simulation is a widely used operational research technique, which is capable of representing complex problems and cost relationships. It is not an optimizing technique, so does not produce the 'best' answers, but is used to evaluate any alternatives tested. The inability to produce optimal solutions has previously been seen as a drawback, but in fact a carefully derived simulation model, used with the practical expertise of a distribution specialist, is likely to result in realistic and acceptable solutions that can be readily implemented. Simulation models allow for various 'what if' questions to be asked to test alternative strategies.

The common approach to determining depot location solutions is to use a logistics strategy simulation model. A variety of software has been developed. The common technique is to simulate the cost of operation for a particular configuration. A variety of heuristic techniques such as hill climbing or centre of gravity is used to suggest depot locations. As indicated, these methods are essentially 'what if' simulation systems, which will always give best results in the hands of an experienced user. Recent innovations have included the use of high-resolution colour graphics to give a detailed representation of the geography and logistics involved.

The two essential stages of logistics simulation are model validation and option testing. The validation exercise involves taking a known situation, reproducing flows and customer service to test whether the costs are predicted with reasonable accuracy. It is essential to ensure that the model or method of analysis is truly representative of the system being investigated. There is a consequent requirement during the modelling process to check and test the appropriateness of the model and the results produced. When agreement has been achieved or variances have been understood, then a variety of alternative options can be tested. Often the simulation of a future scenario will involve the synthesis of new databases of customer location and demand.

An additional stage in the modelling process when sourcing models have been used is to rerun the allocation with the logistics costs as modified in the logistics simulation. This should not lead to major changes if the original cost estimates are realistic and robust solutions are obtained.

MATCHING LOGISTICS STRATEGY TO BUSINESS STRATEGY

Having modelled the logistics options, and selected one or more that perform well when measured against service and cost, then the impact of these on the total business strategy must be assessed. Three main areas where this will impact are:

1. *Capital costs.* If increased factory storage, new depots, new equipment or new vehicles are required, then capital or leasing arrangements will be needed. In certain situations capital constraints can exclude otherwise attractive options. In other cases an increase in working capital (eg stock-holding) may exclude an option.
2. *Operating costs.* The minimum operating cost is frequently the main criterion for selection between options. In some situations increased operating costs can be accepted in the light of future flexibility.
3. *Customer service.* Although options should have been developed against customer service targets, the selected short list must be examined for the customer service level achieved. The balance of the mix might have changed in an effort to reduce costs. Stock held close to the customer might need to be increased to improve service reliability.

Qualitative assessment

One additional means of matching logistics strategy to business strategy is to undertake some associated qualitative analysis. There are several reasons for doing this but the key ones are to back up the quantitative analysis and to use in place of quantitative analysis where it is impossible to derive good quantitative measures. A series of key assessment criteria can be developed and used to help in the comparison of the different strategic options identified. These can then be weighted according to their importance in the decision-making process, and scored according to how each particular option is thought to perform. As well as the more obvious cost indicators, there are other criteria that may also be important. Typical assessment criteria might include:

- capital cost;
- depot cost;
- inventory cost;
- transport cost;
- overall cost;
- customer service – reliability;
- customer service – response/speed;
- market presence (eg stock-holding);
- flexibility (for subsequent change);
- ease of control;
- product quality;
- change from present;
- company image;
- risk;
- management of change.

DEPOT SITE CONSIDERATIONS

After a suitable series of depot locations has been determined, there are various factors that should be taken into account when deciding on a particular site in a preferred general area:

- size and configuration of site;
- site access;
- local authority plans;
- site details;
- financial considerations;
- legislation and local regulations;
- building factors;
- availability of skilled labour;
- availability of suitable sites;
- proximity to transport infrastructure;
- government grants.

These can have an influence on the overall effectiveness and operation of a depot, and on the scope of any projected future expansion.

The size and configuration of the site have to be sufficient to accommodate the proposed depot building and any ancillary or other building facilities (eg vehicle workshops, vehicle wash, separate office, canteen or amenity blocks, waste disposal facilities, security office, etc).

The amount of space required for vehicle movement on site, for vehicle parking, manoeuvre and access to the depot building, is often underestimated. This can lead to congestion and time being wasted on vehicle movement, as well as potential inconvenience to customers' and suppliers' vehicles. Estimates of space required, of course, necessitate knowledge of the number and type of vehicles using the site. In this context, consideration has also to be given to parking for employees' private cars, and it is usual for local authorities, when giving planning permission, to insist on the provision of a minimum number of employee car parking spaces. Vehicular access will be required to site buildings for fire-fighting vehicles.

Without initially having the benefit of detailed layout plans, some assessment should be made about the general shape and configuration of the site, and its consequent ability to enable a sensible layout of the depot building and other ancillary structures and site roads. Finally, consideration should be given to the extent to which the site should also be able to accommodate future anticipated expansion.

An estimate will be needed of the number, type and size of vehicles using the proposed site, including some measure of future expansion, in order to check that suitable access can be provided on to the site. This should clearly take account of the traffic characteristics for different operations, in terms of vehicle size and numbers coming on to the site, and also in terms of access for employees, whether on foot, by car or by public transport. In this context, the external roadway system and access need to be considered as well as the likely internal site roadways. Any future plans for development of the road network in the vicinity of the site that could possibly affect the ease of site access should be explored. Generally, goods will arrive and leave by road transport so that local links to the motorway network or other major roads are of significance.

Any development of a depot will require planning permission, but checks should also be made about local development plans for the area, for adjacent land and the general environment. This is to ensure that there is nothing that would adversely affect depot operation in terms of future plans for expansion. This might relate to physical growth, the extension of working times or shifts, site access, the availability of suitable labour and the overall operating environment, especially as it might affect potential customers.

Certain site details relating to the features of a potential site should be considered. These can influence any proposed depot building, and also influence such aspects as construction costs, site security and depot operation. In general the site should be suitable in terms of soil conditions (load-bearing), slope and drainage. Such factors may exert a significant influence on construction costs in terms of piling, excavation, backfilling and similar civil engineering factors. The necessary services should be available, or planned, and accessible – power, water, sewage, telephone links.

The adjacent properties to the proposed site can also influence such considerations as site security (eg if open space is adjacent) or the feasibility of working outside 'normal' day hours (eg if housing is adjacent).

Financial considerations are also important. The cost of site acquisition, rental or other ownership costs should be established, as should the probable levels of commitment for rates, insurance and any other services or site-related charges. On the other side of the cost equation, there may be investment or other grants that apply, which could influence the overall cost picture.

When occupying a site and either putting up new buildings or taking over existing buildings or facilities, there will be legislation and local regulations and planning requirements to be considered and met.

When considering the site, some typical constraints are a requirement for a minimum number of employee car parking spaces, an upper limit on the height of any building to be put up on the site and limits to the type of building to be constructed.

It is not unusual for a warehouse or depot operation to be set up in an existing building not specifically designed for the operation it is to accommodate. This applies typically on industrial and trading estates where the buildings have been put up by a developer. In this sort of situation a number of building factors that can influence depot operation need to be considered:

- type and size of building
  - clear space between stanchions or other obstructions
  - clear working height
  - total working area
  - configurations of the working space – length and width;
- building access for incoming and outgoing goods including the number and size of access doors, raised or level vehicle loading docks;
- quality and strength of floor for fork-lift truck operation, racking and point loadings;
- availability of required services;
- security factors
  - car park outside the security fence
  - facility to segregate drivers and warehouse operations;
- other available facilities

- offices
- cold/chill store
- fork truck maintenance bay
- fork truck battery-charging area
- canteen and amenities.

SUMMARY

The approach to logistics strategy planning outlined here must of course flex to suit particular industries and business situations. The important theme is the use of a formalized framework that takes into account business issues as well as more detailed logistics issues and combines the conceptual and quantitative evaluation techniques that are available. The basic methodology can be followed in any organization.

The various roles of depots and warehouses were discussed, and once again the influence of the different elements within the distribution system was noted.

The basic cost relationships within distribution have been described. These relationships have been brought together to produce a total distribution cost. It has been shown that trade-off analysis can be used to help optimize the cost-effectiveness of distribution systems, even where this may mean that individual cost elements are increased.

A formal planned approach for developing physical distribution strategy was described. The major discussion points have been the need to determine appropriate product flows and the planning of depot and facilities location. A number of different aspects have been covered, and it has been emphasized that the problem is a complex one, involving a great deal of data manipulation and the need for quite sophisticated modelling techniques.

In the final section, a number of factors were put forward for consideration when a preferred general area of location has been identified. These factors are all influential in ensuring the effective operation of a depot.

Based on articles written and work undertaken by Alan Rushton and Richard Saw, Cranfield School of Management.

9

Logistics management and organization

INTRODUCTION

This chapter is concerned with the way in which logistics and distribution are organized within the company. The importance of the integration of the logistics function into the business as a whole has been emphasized at various times throughout this book. In addition to the need for integration in a business sense is the need for the organizational structure to reflect a similar form of integration. Thus, the organizational structure and the human resource or 'people' aspects are considered in this chapter.

There are several factors covered, the first being a brief summary of those aspects, discussed in Chapter 2, related to the relationship of logistics and distribution with other corporate functions. Allied to this, a number of different organizational structures are discussed. These include traditional structures as well as those that provide more emphasis on logistics and those that allow for a process-oriented, cross-functional integrated approach to the organization.

The role of the logistics and distribution manager is considered – both with respect to his or her position within the company and also with respect to key functional responsibilities. The results of some work undertaken to identify 'what makes a world-class logistics professional' is reviewed. This provides some common denominators and identifies some key ingredients for the success of a number of senior European logisticians. Finally, a more 'grass roots' view of logistics is taken with a discussion on the payment schemes used within the distribution and logistics environment.

RELATIONSHIPS WITH OTHER CORPORATE FUNCTIONS

In the first two chapters, logistics and the supply chain were considered in the context of business and the economy as a whole. In particular, the interfaces with other corporate functions were discussed, the major ones being with production, marketing and finance. There are many occasions when the importance of these corporate relationships has been emphasized, not least because of the move to a cross-functional, process-oriented view of the supply chain. This importance is particularly valid where the planning of corporate strategy is concerned. The need to adopt such a view was discussed in Chapter 6.

There are two key points that bear re-emphasis at this stage. First is the fact that logistics is, for many companies, such an integral part of the corporate being. Because of this, the second major point becomes apparent – the need for logistics planning and strategy to be recognized and used as a vital ingredient in the corporate plan.

The first point – that logistics is such an important element within a company's total business structure – can be illustrated using the interrelationships of logistics with other functions:

With production	Production scheduling
	Production control
	Plant warehouse design
	Raw material stocks
	etc
With marketing	Customer service
	Packaging
	Depot location
	Inventory levels
	Order processing
	etc

With finance

> Stock-holding
> Stock control
> Equipment financing
> Distribution cost control
> etc

The need to include the planning of logistics and distribution into the overall corporate plan is thus self-evident. The business planning process was previously shown in Figure 6.2. Even within this strategic framework it can be seen that distribution and logistics factors should provide a vital input. Within the strategic planning process, such elements as market analysis and policy determination cannot be derived without an understanding of customer service requirements and channel choice alternatives. With any policy assessment exercise and in any subsequent determination of competitive strategy, knowledge of key logistics elements is essential. Any factors related to the procurement, storage and movement of goods must, of necessity, be relevant to the determination of a company's business plan.

The reason that companies fail to take sufficient account of the logistics input to corporate planning is probably due to the dynamic nature of the logistics environment and operation. Logistics is seen to be very much about doing and providing. As such, it can be viewed and treated as a short-term factor, with little direct relevance to long-term planning.

Logistics is a function with both long- and short-term horizons. Its very dynamism tends to mould the one into the other, making it difficult at the operational level to distinguish between the two. In addition, the consequence of inappropriate planning is often seen as a short-term operational problem. In effect, the size and extent of financial and physical investment makes it imperative that the differentiation between the long and the short term is made and that, where necessary, the relevant elements of distribution and logistics are included in the overall business plan.

LOGISTICS ORGANIZATIONAL STRUCTURES

Associated with the failure to include relevant logistics factors within the corporate business plan is the need to recognize that the logistics function may also require a specific organizational structure. For many years, logistics was barely recognized as a discrete function within the organizational structure of many companies. Although recently the importance of distribution and logistics has become much more apparent to a broad range of companies, a number have failed to adapt their basic organizational structures to reflect this changing view.

Such companies have traditionally allocated the various physical distribution functions among several associated company functions. This failure to represent distribution and logistics positively within the organizational structure is thus often a result of historical arrangement rather than a specific desire to ignore the requirement for a positive logistics management structure. Clearly, some positive organizational structure is essential if the logistics function is to be planned and operated effectively.

A typical structure, showing logistics and physical distribution functions based on traditional lines is illustrated in Figure 9.1. The problem with this type of organizational structure is that lines of communication are unclear. Thus, it is often impossible to optimize the efficiency of the different logistics sub-functions, let alone create an overall logistics system that is both effective and efficient.

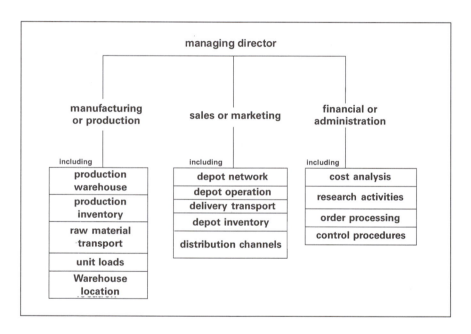

Figure 9.1   Traditional organizational structure showing key logistics functions

Several of the more forward-looking logistics-oriented companies have seen the need for some formal organizational change to represent the recognition now being given to the distribution and logistics activity. This new functional approach emphasizes the need for logistics to be planned, operated and controlled as one overall activity. The precise structure will obviously differ from one company to another. A typical structure might be as illustrated in Figure 9.2. This type of structure allows logistics to be managed as a function in its own right although the need for close liaison with other company functions remains vital.

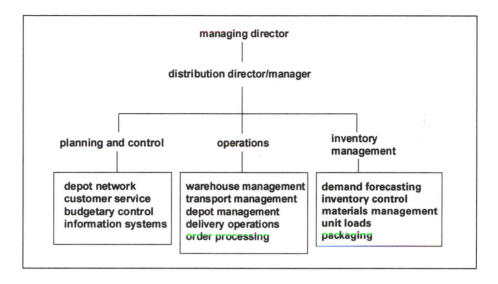

Figure 9.2 Functional structure showing logistics activities linked together

ORGANIZATIONAL INTEGRATION

One important feature that has evolved with the refocusing towards supply chain integration is the need to rethink the way in which logistics operations are organized. This has led to a change in thinking in organizational terms away from functional structures and towards process-oriented structures. This is in many ways a reflection of the key changes that have been outlined in previous chapters:

- the emphasis on the customer, and the need to ensure that internal processes support the requirement to achieve customer satisfaction;
- the concentration on time compression throughout the whole supply chain, and the need to identify and manage suitable trade-offs;
- the move to globalization and the requirement to plan and manage the logistics network as a complete system.

Traditional organizational structures do not really lend themselves to this new way of thinking. They are essentially functional and inwardly focused, with several directors of functional activities reporting to a chief executive officer (see Figure 9.3). There is a tendency for these functional boundaries to create barriers to integration – with the power barons at the head of each function fighting to protect their own power base, rather than serving the overall company objectives.

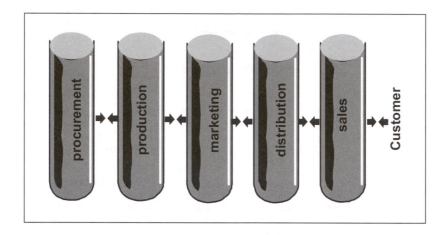

Figure 9.3 Traditional silo-based functional organizational structure

Thus there has been a move away from these silo-based functional structures towards more process-oriented organizations. These are based on key business processes, such as those described in Chapter 7. They attempt to reflect the need to support, in particular, the customer-focused approach that many companies are trying to achieve. These new structures try to increase the visibility of market demand and enable an integrated supply chain response. An example of such an approach is shown in Figure 9.4.

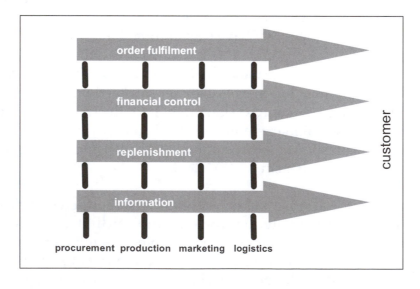

Figure 9.4 A customer-facing, process-driven organizational structure

This type of structure is known as mission management and is based on the concept of the management of systems or flows. This is undoubtedly relevant to logistics and distribution, which are concerned with material flow and the associated information flow often from raw material through various processes, storage and movement to the final customer.

Clearly the potential problems lie in the inability to manage and co-ordinate across functional boundaries. However, where good management practices have been followed, and in the appropriate operational context, organizational structures such as these have been made to work very effectively. They are particularly relevant for customer-service-oriented businesses. Some of the larger chemical companies, for example, adopt this type of management structure to provide co-ordination and control throughout the supply process of particular products.

Mission management is cross-functional, and as such can pose problems in a traditionally functional organization. For many companies this type of mission management structure has not been an easy alternative, with traditional managers loath to make such a dramatic change to an approach that they have been familiar with for many years. Because of this, a further development, matrix management, has evolved. Here, the product or flow is planned and managed by a 'flow' or logistics manager, whilst the traditional functions provide the necessary inputs as they are required.

For some companies a mixed or matrix approach seems to have been the most successful. This accepts that there is a need, at the *planning* level, to reorganize on a process basis, which crosses traditional boundaries, but recognizes that it is important to retain specialists at an *operational* level to ensure the efficient running of operational functions such as transport and warehousing. The different emphasis in these two approaches is demonstrated by comparing Figures 9.5 and 9.6.

As well as changes to process-oriented management structures, there have been broader supply chain initiatives, in particular the need to rethink buyer–supplier relationships. A major aim is to move away from the traditional combative arrangements towards the building of stronger and more positive partnerships that reflect the need for companies, within a supply chain, to work together to achieve commercial success. This involves the development of a structure where the link is not merely with the traditional sales/buyer, but also includes co-ordination and co-operation with other relevant groups across company boundaries. This might include research and development, marketing, distribution and any other functions that, with a suitable link, can benefit from such a partnership approach. Figure 9.7 demonstrates the change in approach from a traditional single point to a co-ordinated multiple approach.

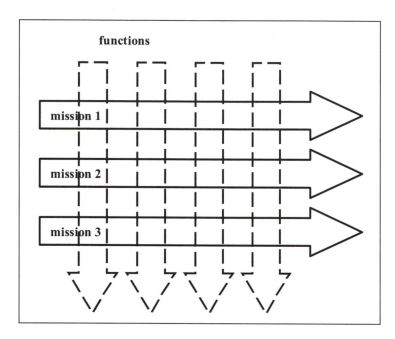

Figure 9.5 Mission management, which acts directly across traditional functional boundaries

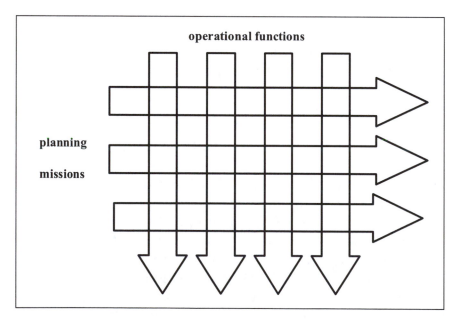

Figure 9.6 Matrix management, which emphasizes both planning and operational elements

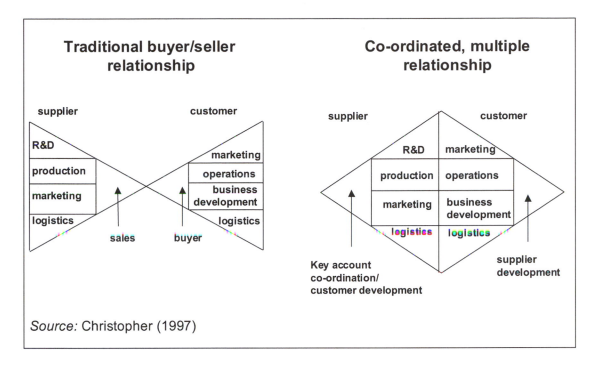

Figure 9.7 Buyer/seller relationships: a single versus a multiple linked approach

THE ROLE OF THE LOGISTICS OR DISTRIBUTION MANAGER

The role of the logistics or distribution manager can vary considerably from one company to another, dependent on the internal organizational structure, the channel type (own account, third party, etc), the industry or product, and the customer profile. Factors such as these will certainly affect the extent of the operational role and to a lesser extent the nature of the planning role.

In an earlier section of this chapter, the need for companies to include the planning of logistics and distribution in the overall corporate strategy was emphasized. It is useful here to consider the part that the logistics or distribution manager can play in the planning process. M A McGinnis and B J Lalonde have discussed this question. They take three main themes: the contribution that the logistics/distribution manager can make to corporate strategic planning; the advantages of this contribution; and the preparation that the manager can make to increase the effectiveness of his or her input.

The main points are as follows:

1. *Contribution to corporate strategic planning*
   - an understanding of the functional interfaces
   - an understanding of distribution's activities
   - familiarity with the external environment as it relates to distribution
   - insights regarding competitor distribution strategies
   - familiarity with customer distribution needs
   - familiarity with channels of distribution
   - distribution data;
2. *Advantages of contributing to corporate plan*
   - understanding of impact of corporate strategy on distribution activities
   - increased physical distribution responsiveness
   - increased sensitivity to the distribution environment
   - identifying distribution opportunities
   - improving communications;
3. *Preparation for strategic planning*
   - know the company
   - develop a broader perspective of distribution
   - know the distribution environment
   - develop rapport/liaison with others
   - know customer needs
   - improve communication skills.

Logistics-related planning activities are thus a vital input in the overall business strategy. The more specific activities were outlined in the early chapters of this book. They involve a medium- to long-term planning horizon and will include aspects such as the number of facilities, their size and location, transport networks, fleet size and mix of vehicles, stock levels, information systems, etc.

As already indicated, the operational role for managers can vary significantly according to the size and nature of the business, the product, the channel type and the customer profile, among other factors. Also, there are a number of different job titles and job functions that exist. These range from the distribution or logistics manager, who might have overall responsibility for an entire distribution network including central depots, regional depots, trunking and delivery vehicles, stock location and control, computer systems etc, to a shift manager or supervisor who might, for example, be concerned with the detailed performance and control of an order picking operation on a night shift.

Traditionally, the three main operational areas of responsibility are related to:

1. *transport* – trunking, delivery operations, vehicle routeing and scheduling, vehicle procurement, etc;
2. *warehousing* – goods inward, bulk storage, order picking, marshalling, materials handling equipment, etc; and
3. *information* – stock location, stock control, order processing, budgeting, monitoring and control, etc.

For many logistics managers these areas may be expanded to cover other aspects such as procurement, inbound logistics, inventory levels, forecasting, telesales, production planning, returns, packaging, etc.

In addition to these broad functional areas, there is a staff role concerning the management of human resources, union negotiation, health and safety and the linkage to other corporate interfaces such as production, supply, marketing, sales and finance.

Over and above all of these aspects of the operational role, and probably common to all types of distribution organizations, is the responsibility for, and the need to control, the balance between the service to the customer and the cost of providing this service.

From the point of view of supply chain planning, the key roles for a logistics manager with a broad remit might be summarized as:

● to lead the design, creation, configuration and parameter setting of the entire supply chain;
● to create the framework and the dialogue that determine the performance targets along the whole chain;
● to drive the systems and monitor and report the entire logistics operational performance against agreed targets;
● to review how problems can be solved and performance improved.

A WORLD-CLASS LOGISTICIAN – THE LOGISTICS DIRECTOR

Recently a study was undertaken by Cranfield to determine 'what makes a world-class logistics professional' and to identify some of the common denominators and key ingredients for the success of such a person.

Forty-eight leading European logistics practitioners were questioned. The majority of the respondents were working in manufacturing, although several were in retailing. Of the survey's respondents, 39 per cent were employed as logistics directors or logistics managers and 17 per cent were chief executive officers or managing directors. Very few had supply chain manager or supply chain director in their title. A further finding was that 64 per cent of respondents had global responsibility for logistics, and another 27 per cent had European responsibility. This represented a good selection of very senior directors who had overall responsibility for their company's logistics and supply chain operations.

The study found that over 80 per cent of respondents had degrees from a university or technical school. A large number of these degrees were in engineering, followed by business and management studies, and economics. Logistics, not surprisingly, was a long way down the list, mainly because logistics degrees were not available when many of the respondents undertook secondary education. A limited number of respondents had additional second degrees, possibly a reflection on the age of those surveyed. The study found a strong spread of language skills. All could speak English and most could speak at least one other European language.

Some key factors were:

- *Current experience.* Compared with an earlier survey, this latest survey showed that logisticians now have more field experience. The survey also highlighted, perhaps surprisingly, the respondents' lack of experience and expertise in information technology. Arguably, with their seniority, this experience may not be necessary because there will be staff who have the appropriate capabilities.
- *Responsibility.* Most of the people in the survey were responsible for outbound and inbound transport, and warehousing. Some were also responsible for processing customer orders. A few were involved in forecasting, and raw material and inventory management. Thus, the traditional area of distribution was still the most strongly represented.
- *Incentives.* The main driver of logisticians was their ability to develop long-term solutions for the business. Teamwork was also high on the list, followed by the opportunity to manage change, and developing people. Remuneration came quite low at sixth place. Fire-fighting operational problems were also low on the list.
- *Personal success factors.* The most important personal success factor was the development of an overall vision of the business and the industry. This was followed by the ability to communicate, manage change, and team leadership.
- *Next move.* When asked about their likely next career move, some respondents said it would be to a general management position. Some had no idea what

they would do next; others felt that retirement was the next step. In the previous survey, participants were more certain of where they were going, and retirement was not on the agenda for most of the respondents.

● *Important logistics issues.* Customer service enhancement was the most important logistics issue quoted by the respondents. This was followed by the need to pursue supply chain relationships and to develop information technology. More fashionable areas, such as benchmarking, outsourcing, and efficient consumer response, were low on the list of important issues.

● *Reason for job.* A quarter of respondents had taken on their job in order to implement strategy, 20 per cent to develop a strategy and 19 per cent to manage existing operations more effectively. When asked how they spend their time now, the overall results were similar: 25 per cent were implementing a strategy and 20 per cent were developing a strategy. Despite this apparent similarity, jobs had changed significantly for many individuals, as requirements moved naturally from strategy development to implementation to operational management.

● *Job change.* Only 9 per cent of respondents were doing the job they were first employed to do. Half said their job had changed by 50 per cent or more, while 41 per cent said their job had changed by 25 per cent. This is perhaps a natural reflection that logistics and supply chain management is a dynamic environment where change is the norm, especially in the higher echelons of an organization.

PAYMENT SCHEMES

One relatively neglected area in the literature on logistics and distribution concerns the payment mechanisms and incentive schemes that are used within the industry. Having looked at the broad roles and responsibilities of the logistics manager and director, it is interesting to gain a better understanding of the grass roots position related to the type of payment systems that are commonly used.

There are a number of different types of payment mechanism. These can be broadly divided into the three main systems of daywork, piecework and payment by results. These three systems are illustrated in Figure 9.8. Daywork is a method of payment based entirely on the hours attended at work; piecework is payment entirely related to the amount of work undertaken; and payment by results is a mixture of these, providing a basic wage plus a bonus based on work undertaken.

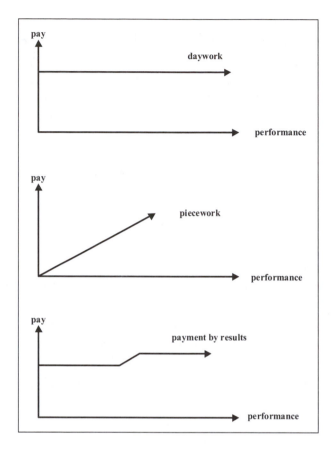

Figure 9.8 The main types of payment mechanism, showing the relationship between performance and pay

The main payment systems can be summarized as follows:

- *daywork* (also known as graded hours, fixed day, etc) – based entirely on the hours worked;
- *measured daywork* – basic attendance wage plus bonus for achieving a given level of work performance;
- *stepped measured daywork* (stabilized incentive scheme, premium payment plan) – introduces 'steps' in the measured daywork scheme, so providing additional incentive;
- *merit-rated bonus scheme* (incentive bonus scheme) – a bonus scheme on top of a basic wage, but not productivity related;
- *piecework* – payment related entirely to the amount of work completed;

- *payment by results* – in its purest form this is piecework, but usually it is a results-based payment on top of a basic wage;
- *commission* – a piecework or payment-by-results scheme, but based on effort and achievement (eg sales, cost savings); a common type of management bonus scheme;
- *group or plant-wide schemes* – collective bonus schemes based on collective performance, which can be related to costs versus sales, increased output or improved efficiency;
- *fringe benefits* – various non-performance-related add-ons covering such items as holiday pay, Christmas bonus, subsidized canteen, clothing allowance, etc; eventually, these types of benefit become taken for granted;
- *profit sharing scheme* – related to the company profit, and aimed at fostering employee interest in the company;
- *share schemes* – usually limited to managers and directors, though there are some notable company-wide share schemes;
- *team working* – rewards for small groups, usually used for management teams;
- *annualized hours* – systems that are formally organized for working time on the basis of a number of hours per year rather than hours per week; they have become recognized as useful schemes where there is a distinct seasonal or peak nature to the work and thus are matched to the needs of the business to meet customer requirements and are popular in warehouse operations.

For motivational financial schemes it is important to distinguish between schemes that provide an incentive, reward or bonus, because they can have a varying impact on workforces. The main differences are:

- *Incentives.* These stimulate better performance in the future because they are payments for the achievement of previously set and agreed targets. Incentives tend to have the most direct impact on employee behaviour and motivation because the conditions of payment are known in advance.
- *Rewards.* These recognize good performance in the past. They are likely to have a less direct impact on behaviour and motivation due to the level of uncertainty of the amount of the pay-out.
- *Bonuses.* These are rewards linked to performance but paid out in a lump sum.

Clearly, the applicability of these methods of payment varies considerably from one type of distribution company to another, and from one type of distribution job to another. Productivity-related incentive schemes are only valid in operations that will benefit from schemes of this nature, ie where increased worker effort will mean an increase in output. For many distribution operations the need for accurate, timely order picking may far outweigh the number of picks made per picker per hour. Additionally, it is likely to be both dangerous and illegal to propose a driver incentive scheme that gives additional payment for the speed with which the work is completed.

It is worth emphasizing two particular aspects related to payment schemes, and to show how these vary according to the type of scheme operated. The first is the relationship between different schemes and financial incentives. This is illustrated in Figure 9.9. In contrast, Figure 9.10 shows the extent of supervision required for the different schemes. One is the direct converse of the other, indicating the high levels of supervision required for payment schemes that offer strong financial incentives.

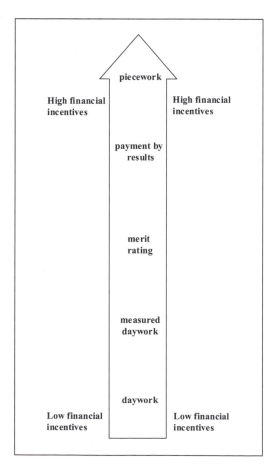

Figure 9.9 Hierarchy of payment schemes in relation to financial incentives

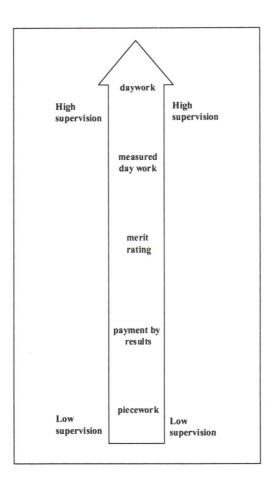

Figure 9.10 The extent of supervision required for different payment schemes

The relevance of these different schemes for distribution is best summarized according to the main breakdown of distribution personnel – drivers and warehouse staff.

Drivers are most likely to be paid on hours worked or hours guaranteed – some form of daywork. There may also be a special rate for the job, based on work experience or driving qualifications. In terms of incentive, a form of 'job and finish' might be operated, giving extra leisure rather than extra cash as the incentive. Financial bonuses might be offered as a form of payment by results based on such things as miles run, cases delivered, etc. Once again it must be emphasized that any bonus payments are prohibited if they endanger road safety.

Warehouse staff are also likely to receive remuneration based on hours worked or guaranteed. In the more controlled environment of a warehouse, daywork is likely to be measured. Additionally, there are likely to be different rates according to different job functions (fork-lift truck drivers, pickers, etc). Merit-rated bonuses based perhaps on attendance might be offered, and certainly productivity-related bonuses are likely to be very common, based on cases picked, pallets moved, etc. Measured performance schemes are operated based on work-study standards for specific tasks. In addition, as already indicated, many companies are now introducing annualized hours because it can lead to a much more efficient use of the labour force.

SUMMARY

This chapter has considered various aspects of the organization of logistics and distribution in the company. The first section concentrated on the relationship with other corporate functions and concluded that there is a need to include the planning of logistics and distribution within the overall corporate/business plan, and that this should be reflected in the upper echelons of the organizational structure of a company.

The next section discussed the basic organizational structures that are used in logistics. These included:

- traditional structure;
- functional structure;
- mission management; and
- matrix management.

The need to reflect the development of process-driven operations by adopting cross-functional organizational structures was emphasized.

The role of the logistics and distribution manager was assessed with regard to his or her input into the planning process and with respect to operational role. In addition, a picture of a 'world-class' logistician was derived from the results of a recent survey of top logistics directors.

Finally, the different types of distribution payment and incentive schemes were outlined. The applicability and relevance of these various schemes to distribution and logistics were discussed – especially regarding drivers and warehouse staff. The implications on staff of financial incentives and the degree of supervision required for the range of schemes were noted.

10

Distribution: tactical and operational techniques

INTRODUCTION

This chapter is designed to include a selection of simple but very practical techniques that may be applied to certain common situations very quickly and easily. The selection of techniques for inclusion has been arbitrary. However, techniques have been broadly selected from three areas:

1. the management of people;
2. the management of assets;
3. the management of money.

For example, a typical day-to-day problem is the selection and use of temporary staff and assets. This is addressed here through the use of checklists to aid the decision-making process. Obtaining the best utilization of vehicles is central to running a slick transport operation, therefore a few hints have been included here that may prove useful. How much should a given operation cost? This is a question that often plagues managers. Zero-based budgets can help answer this important question, therefore a simple approach is described below.

One or two other handy hints are included that may prove useful in certain situations. It is important to sound a note of caution at this point. This chapter does not contain an exhaustive list of techniques. It is simply a selection of very practical techniques that have proved useful in the past and are worth including on that basis alone.

THE SELECTION OF TEMPORARY STAFF AND ASSETS

Most distribution operations today can ill afford to waste money on human or physical assets that are not fully utilized. The days of the spare vehicle or driver are a distant memory. However, the realities of business are that operational requirements regularly swing between peaks and troughs, often on a daily basis. This inevitably means that vehicles, drivers or hired transport will be required at some stage to deal with the peaks. Indeed if an operation never has any requirements for temporary assets, then that is usually a sign that the operation has too many assets in the first place. The objective must be to utilize the operation's core assets to the maximum and to use hired assets for the peaks. Other situations also lead to short-term hiring such as staff taking their holidays or suffering from bouts of illness as well as vehicles breaking down just at the wrong time. Planning to deal with these temporary situations in advance will avoid problems when they occur.

Temporary drivers attract a great deal of criticism for various reasons but very often many of the situations they are held accountable for are not of their making. Too often harassed managers telephone a temporary staff agency late in the day and request a driver without having invested the time in the necessary preparatory work. Many simply look for the cheapest price and then complain when things go wrong. The following is a checklist that will help avoid disappointment:

1. Set aside time to investigate the temporary staff agencies in your area. Don't just select the cheapest. Many reputable agencies will be members of the Federation of Recruitment and Employment Services (FRES).
2. Check with other companies in the area about who the best agencies are and why.
3. Key points to be established with any potential agency are:
    –   How are drivers selected?
    –   How often are driving licences checked?
    –   Are the drivers examined to establish their level of understanding of relevant legislation?
    –   Are drivers' employment histories and references checked?
    –   Are drivers' full-time employees of the agency?

- Does the agency have all the relevant insurances such as employer's and public liability cover? What insurance do they have to cover damage caused by their drivers' negligence? If you have an excess on your motor insurance policy this last point could be significant.
- What training does the agency provide for its employees?
- Does the agency have 24-hour telephone cover?
- How will the agency inform you about the hours of work the driver has completed before undertaking your work? When was the last weekly or daily rest period? How many driving hours have already been used?

Any agencies that cannot give satisfactory answers to any of the above questions should be avoided.

4. Having selected an agency, try to establish a good working relationship with them. Invite them to your premises so that they can gain a better understanding about the specific needs of your business. If the agency is of the right calibre they should suggest this themselves.

5. Ensure that rates of payment are agreed for a given period. This will ensure that rates are negotiated at leisure and not under pressure.

6. Tell the agency exactly what you expect from any driver they send. If they are to be up to a standard that you have set, then ensure that any who do not meet those standards are rejected. Sometimes this is difficult to achieve if the alternative is letting a customer down, but in this case agree penalty clauses in advance. This allows them to be invoked retrospectively if such a situation arises. A financial penalty is usually very effective. A percentage reduction in the fee for that driver could be effective, especially if it has been agreed in advance.

7. Supply the agency with all relevant health and safety information in advance to allow them time to brief their drivers. Include any specific rules about your premises such as smoking policies or protective clothing.

8. If your delivery drivers have regular delivery points try to compile a library of direction sheets to hand out to temporary drivers. This could save a lot of time and trouble.

9. If security is important then insist that temporary drivers are provided with identity cards that display the driver's photo on them. Obtain the name of the driver being assigned to your work and ensure that your staff are made aware of whom to expect.

10. In large operations some agency staff will become almost permanent fixtures due to their continued presence covering for holidays and sickness. Make an effort to include the agency in any information bulletins that are circulated to drivers. This will be especially important in the case of health and safety information or BS5750 quality management information.

The above list has concentrated on temporary drivers but may be easily adapted to cover other temporary staff. With warehouse staff, fork-lift training certificates will be important.

Hiring vehicles and trailers to cover short-term needs is always easier if the hire company has advance warning of your requirements. Unfortunately, many short-term requirements are needed to deal with the unforeseen such as breakdowns. However if peaks in business needs, such as Christmas or harvest times, occur regularly every year then it is worth establishing what extra vehicles are needed in advance and communicating this to your chosen hire company in good time.

Another way of dealing with short-term peaks is to use the services of a third-party haulier. Spot hire rates are likely to be higher than rates negotiated on the basis of a long-term relationship. When establishing such a relationship check the following:

- What are the conditions of carriage?
- Ask to see a copy of their operator's licence.
- What levels of goods-in-transit insurance do they have?
- Take a look at the hauliers' vehicles. Do they look well presented and maintained?
- Do their drivers wear uniforms and are they generally well presented?

The cheapest is not always the best. Poorly maintained vehicles may break down while engaged on your work. Remember that these hauliers will be representing your company to your customers. If you establish a good working relationship with reputable hauliers, they are more likely not only to be in business for the long term but also to put themselves out to ensure that you receive a good service.

VEHICLE UTILIZATION

The effective use of vehicles is vital to the cost-effective running of any transport operation. Therefore this section covers a method for calculating vehicle utilization and performance. A detailed description of vehicle costing is to be found in Chapter 25. Idle vehicles will attract the fixed costs associated with their ownership whether they are working or not. These fixed costs will normally include:

- depreciation;
- insurance;
- licences (vehicle excise duty and operator's licence (only vehicles over 3.5 tonnes gross plated weight)).

Let us say that this vehicle is a 17-tonne distribution vehicle with a cost new of £45,000, and your accounting policy is to depreciate the vehicle over five years on a straight-line basis. The cost of insurance is £2,000 per annum and the vehicle excise duty is £1,320. Operator's licence is £34 per annum. A daily 'charge' (assuming 260 working days in the year) for fixed costs could be calculated as follows:

Depreciation	= £45,000/5 years	= £9,000 per annum
	£9,000/260 days	= £34.62 per day
Insurance	= £2,000/260 days	= £7.69 per day
Licences	= £1,320 + £34	= £1,354 per annum
	£1,354/260 days	= £5.21 per day

Daily fixed cost 'charge' = £34.62 + £7.69 + £5.21 = £47.52 per day

NB Whilst the costs used are reasonably representative at the time of writing they will change regularly.

The above calculations can be easily adapted to account for more shifts or more working days, but the purpose here is to illustrate that there is a cost attached to not using the vehicles.

Given the importance of using the vehicles, one of the useful performance measures for utilization relates to daily or shift use in a given period. Let us say that our vehicle is used on a two-shift basis, six days a week. This will mean that there are 12 shifts in every week that the vehicle is available for use.

It is worth mentioning at this point that a week is a useful period of measurement given that transport requirements can change so rapidly that constant vigilance is important. Another important point is that, where possible, regular vehicle maintenance should be carried out when the vehicle is not needed for work. In this case that will mean on Sunday. Of course this is not always ideal but it must be a goal towards which you strive. If it is not achieved, cost will be incurred twice, because either the work your vehicle should be doing is being covered by subcontracting its work or the work is lost completely. In the above case a calculation will have to be done as to whether the cost of maintenance being carried out on a Sunday is greater than the cost of having the vehicle unavailable for duty during the working week.

The performance measure for daily utilization may be calculated as follows:

shifts available = 12 shifts (ie 6 days with 2 shifts)
shifts used = 10 shifts
daily utilization = 83.33% (10 / 12 × 100 = 83.33)

Naturally the above calculation would normally include all the fleet vehicles.

VEHICLE CAPACITY

It is not only the daily use of vehicles that is important. Equally important is the use of the capacity of the vehicles. Different types of product carried have different needs but most situations are constrained by either volume or weight.

If the products are very heavy then strenuous efforts need to be made to reduce the unladen weight of the vehicle carrying the goods on the one hand, and on the other emphasis must be placed on loading as much weight on the vehicle as is permissible within the legal weight limits. Assuming that the vehicle fleet has been thoughtfully specified to reduce unnecessary unladen vehicle weight then the performance measurement that will be most useful is the achieved payload weight. This may be calculated thus:

gross vehicle weight   = 41 tonnes
unladen weight   = 14 tonnes
available payload   = 27 tonnes

number of journeys × 27 tonnes = total available payload weight for a given period

By adding together all the actual payload weights and dividing them by the total available payload weight for that number of journeys and multiplying the result by 100, a percentage payload utilization figure is achieved, for example:

number of journeys   = 3
available payload   = 27 tonnes
total available payload weight   = 81 tonnes

actual payloads achieved – journey 1   = 25.6 tonnes
                          journey 2   = 26.1 tonnes
                          journey 3   = 26.3 tonnes
              total actual payloads = 78 tonnes

therefore 78 tonnes / 81 tonnes × 100 = 96.3% payload utilization

Where goods are constrained by volume due to their size then weight may not be quite such a useful way of measuring vehicle utilization. In many cases operators may opt to use a straightforward visual measurement made by the loaders at the time of loading expressed as a percentage. Despite the obvious difficulties with this visual approach some measure of capacity utilization should always be attempted.

FLEET UTILIZATION

Another useful way of evaluating the utilization of vehicle capacity is to add together the overall carrying capacity of a group of vehicles and trailers. The best results are obtained when vehicles engaged on the same type of work are grouped together. Once the total carrying capacity has been calculated this may be plotted on a graph as a straight line.

The next stage is to record actual tonnage carried by this group of vehicles on a daily or shift basis. These details are then also plotted on the graph. If there is a significant over- or underuse of capacity on a regular basis then consideration should be given to acquiring or disposing of vehicles.

Example
A vehicle fleet of 10 41-tonne gross vehicle weight tractors and 18 tri-axle trailers are all engaged on primary distribution runs for a major customer. Each tractor/ trailer combination can carry 27 tonnes payload. Therefore at the start of each period there is available 486 tonnes of payload space, ie 18 trailers × 27 tonnes = 486 tonnes available payload. Obviously a tractor can only tow one trailer at a time. Therefore with 10 tractors only 270 tonnes could be used at any given time. This may be too simplistic an analysis because some trailers may be pre-loaded to allow tractors to work with a minimum of downtime. On the other hand there may well be too many trailers for this operation. This type of analysis should help highlight the true picture.

Figure 10.1 shows a real-life example of this approach in action. The total available payload tonnage is 97.6 tonnes and the fleet is seven rigid vehicles engaged in local distribution work from a depot in Northampton.

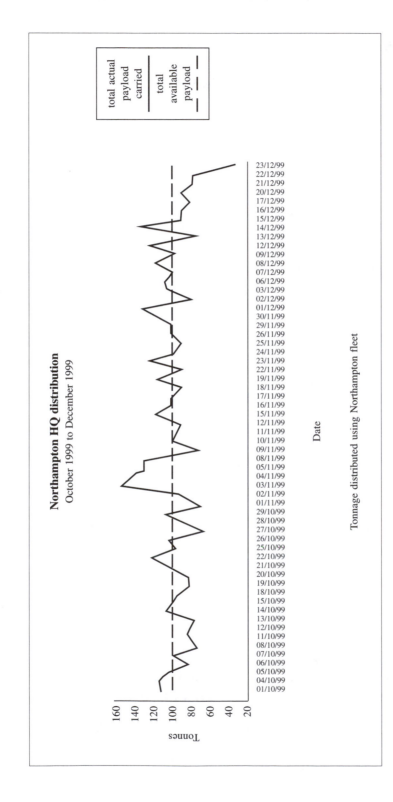

Figure 10.1 Record of tonnage carried

VEHICLE MONITORING

Many modern vehicles are equipped with computerized telemetry equipment that is able to measure in detail all aspects of the vehicle's daily duty cycle such as time used delivering goods, time the vehicle is left with the engine idling or the time that the vehicle's engine is being driven at excessively high revolutions. This information can be very useful but it must always be remembered that a skilled person will have to spend time analysing the mass of information. On the other hand there is considerable anecdotal evidence to show that drivers will positively modify their driving behaviour if they believe they are being closely monitored.

ZERO-BASED BUDGETS

In most companies part of the annual cycle is the time in the year when the next year's operating budgets are prepared. Very often this is nothing more than an exercise by which last year's budgets are increased incrementally, usually by the rate of inflation. For most operations this approach will produce a workable budget, but where questions about cost-effectiveness have been asked then another approach may be required. One such approach is known as zero budgeting.

This form of analysis requires a return to first principles. It is almost as though the operation has never existed and is being planned for the first time, hence the name 'zero' or back to the starting-point. Each element of the operating budget must be analysed line by line. For example, the cost of fuel will be calculated by examining the fuel consumption of the different types of vehicle in the fleet according to the manufacturers' technical figures, which will be divided into the annual mileages for this type of vehicle and finally multiplied by the cost of fuel, for example:

> 38-tonne gvw 4×2 tractor should achieve say 8.5 miles per gallon
> There are six similar vehicles in this fleet
> Their combined annual mileage is 480,000 miles
> The current cost of fuel is say £2.50 per gallon
> 480,000 miles / 8.5 mpg = 56,470 gallons × £2.50 = £141,176 pa

This process will have to be repeated for all the different types of vehicle in the fleet to achieve the final budgetary figure. Unless the operation is already in excellent shape then the chances are that the figure arrived at will be less than the current cost of fuel used. This is because part of the process entails using the best possible achievable figures such as the manufacturers' fuel consumption figures or the best bunkered price for fuel.

The object of the exercise is firstly to have managers take a fresh look at their operations. Secondly, because the best possible figures are used to formulate the budget, it highlights areas for improvement. Perhaps the drivers are not achieving the best fuel consumption achievable and require training? Maybe more can be done to achieve a better price for the fuel used?

The exercise will cause managers to ask many uncomfortable questions about their area of responsibility. Some will find this so uncomfortable that they will simply attempt to replicate the current system by using their current fuel consumption figures and fuel purchase prices. This should be avoided as the best results accrue from an honest line-by-line re-evaluation of the operating budget. If diligently undertaken the resultant budget will be accompanied by a number of action points that will serve to improve overall operational cost-effectiveness.

SUMMARY

This chapter has described in some detail practical techniques that can easily be applied to any distribution operation. Guidance on how to obtain the best from temporary staff and hired assets was given. The best utilization of commercial vehicles is central to running a cost-effective transport operation. Easily calculated performance measures were illustrated, which covered capacity as well as the daily use of vehicles. Finally, a zero-based approach to budgeting was discussed, with illustrations included, which showed how an agenda for improvements in cost-effectiveness might be achieved.

11

Manufacturing and materials management

INTRODUCTION

As noted earlier, materials management is an important and integral part of logistics management. This chapter aims to give the reader an overview of some of the most common forms of manufacturing planning and control techniques. It is not intended to examine these systems in great depth but rather to explain the basic principles of the various approaches and explain some of the terminology.

The following approaches will be covered:

- just-in-time;
- manufacturing resource planning (MRPII) incorporating material requirements planning (MRP);
- flexible fulfilment or, as it has come to be known, postponement.

Before we look at these planning and control systems in detail it is worth explaining a few terms that are often used when production scheduling systems are discussed.

Push and pull systems

A 'push' system of manufacturing is one where goods are produced against the expectation of demand. In other words goods are not produced specifically to order but are produced against a forecast demand. Demand forecasting has to be carried out where raw material suppliers' lead times for delivery have to be considered. If there is a one-month lead time for a given raw material then it will be necessary to forecast what the level of demand for the finished product will be in one month's time. These forecasts are usually based on historical sales information. The difficulty arises when either there is a higher level of demand than expected and sales are lost, or there is a lower level of demand and finished product stocks grow too large. Lost revenue from missed sales opportunities is the result on the one hand, and higher inventory carrying costs or product obsolescence costs are the result on the other. MRPII (incorporating MRP) is a 'push' system.

A 'pull' system of manufacturing is one where goods are only produced against known customer orders. This is because only actual orders from customers are being produced on the production line. None of the goods are being made to keep as finished product stocks that may be sold at a later date. It is said that this type of firm customer order is 'pulling' all the materials through the process from the material suppliers and culminating in the delivery to the final customer. Just-in-time is a 'pull' system.

Dependent and independent demand

Dependent demand is created due to the demand for the constituent parts of the finished product. In other words, because it is planned to make a given finished product, this decision triggers the demand for all the constituent parts of that product. In this situation there is no uncertainty and activities may be planned accordingly. Therefore when the production scheduling activity is taking place the quantity and required delivery dates of the constituent parts are known to the schedulers.

Independent demand is quite the opposite. In this situation the schedulers do not have a clear view of customer demand and are therefore forced to forecast demand in the best way they can. The demand for spare parts for products sold in the past is a good example of this type of demand. This is a very difficult situation, which is full of uncertainty. The schedulers must try and ensure goods and services are available just when the customers require them. In this sort of situation almost by definition there will always be a state of imbalance between supplies of the goods and services and the demand for those same goods and services.

Just-in-time

'JIT aims to meet demand instantaneously, with perfect quality and no waste' (Bicheno, 1991). Strictly speaking this is not so much a clearly defined system of materials management but more a set of management philosophies that work together to create the desired effect.

This approach was first developed in Japan by Toyota, the automobile manufacturer, in the 1970s. In its early days it was known as the 'Toyota manufacturing system' or 'Toyoterism'. The label 'just-in-time' was applied later.

One of the central ideas of this system is the elimination of waste ('muda' in Japanese) from the manufacturing process. In this context 'waste' does not refer simply to reworking or scrapping substandard products. Waste within the just-in-time environment means waste in all its manifestations. It seeks to reduce what are known as 'the seven wastes':

1. overproduction;
2. waiting;
3. transporting;
4. inappropriate processing;
5. unnecessary inventory;
6. unnecessary motions;
7. defects.

Elimination of wasted time

Because only customers' orders are being produced and the speed of the production process is known, it is possible to synchronize deliveries of raw materials to the end of the production line (or to the precise point on the production line in some cases) with little time to spare before use. The whole purpose of this exercise is to reduce the working capital used in the overall manufacturing system. In turn this produces a better return on capital employed. The other benefits are that there is little or no requirement for factory space to be used for storage and a reduced requirement for labour to manage the stock. This is the origin of the name 'just-in-time'.

Movement through the manufacturing process

If materials move through the system in a straight line it is reasonable to suppose that the minimum distance has been covered. In many manufacturing systems this is not always possible. In fact it has been identified in some manufacturing processes that components and sub-assemblies are moved around the factory in a very erratic pattern before they all come together in the finished product. Attempting to minimize the overall distance that materials have to travel through the system helps avoid wasted travelling time and effort.

Kanban

The word Kanban (the signal) refers to a system of cards (other methods such as marked squares on the floor or balls are used in some cases), which are used to organize the progress of materials through the manufacturing process. It may be easier to understand the system if squares marked on the floor of the factory are imagined. The squares contain work-in-progress required by the next step in the manufacturing process. The squares become empty as the materials are used. The next batch of materials may only move into a square when the square is empty. This approach is replicated as materials move progressively from one step to the next. Thus no build-up of goods occurs and materials move through the system in an orderly fashion.

The problem is that goods will have to move through the system at the speed of the slowest element in the chain. However, large online work-in-progress stocks will be eliminated. This too contributes to the reduction of working capital being used by the system.

Right first time

Quality problems in the form of scrapped or reworked products are waste of the first order. The Japanese developed several strategies to counter this problem. In one case they built their factory with no area to store scrap on the principle that having an area for scrap encouraged its production. Quality circles were created, where workers were allocated time specifically given over to discussing quality issues and their elimination, the target being zero defects. The philosophy of Kai zen, or continuous improvement, was engendered as a working culture in these organizations with support at the very top. Systems of quality management such as total quality management (TQM) and ISO 9000 seek to achieve the same ends.

The causes of scrapped or reworked production may not originate in the factory itself and may be caused by substandard raw materials being supplied to the process. Increasingly suppliers' performance is critically appraised and measured in defective parts per million, or in some other way. Working in a positive environment with suppliers to eliminate problems quickly is the preferred approach. Involving suppliers in new product development helps eliminate potential problems before they are translated into the production process.

Finished product stocks

These stocks only contain goods produced to a specific customer order. This too contributes to a reduction in working capital.

Because of the needs of brevity it has only been possible to skim the surface of the JIT philosophy. Subjects such as the reduction of set-up and change-over times, team working and empowerment, total productive maintenance, levelled production schedules and many more are arguably no less important.

MANUFACTURING RESOURCE PLANNING (MRPII)

Although MRP pre-dates MRPII, it is easier to see MRP in the context of MRPII rather than the other way round.

As the name implies, manufacturing resource planning deals with more than simply production scheduling. Whilst the basic material requirements planning system is incorporated into MRPII the wider system brings other activities into the picture. The objective is to harmonize and control more of the activities within the production plant. Areas outside an MRP system but included in MRPII system usually are:

- maintenance management;
- cost accounting;
- stock management;
- sales orders;
- procurement;
- personnel levels.

MRPII requires considerable computing power to operate because of the inclusion of virtually all the activities within a production plant. Implementation of such a sophisticated computer-based system is an enormous task and should not be undertaken lightly.

MATERIAL REQUIREMENTS PLANNING (MRP)

This principle of production scheduling is based on the premise that if one knows what product needs to be produced then one should also know how many constituent parts are required in order to make the product. A useful analogy is the preparation of a meal. Let us say that the meal in question is a traditional cooked breakfast. Depending on taste you may choose two rashers of bacon, a fried egg, some mushrooms, tomatoes and toast. Whilst describing the contents of the breakfast we have also prepared a list of the constituent parts. If we needed more than one single breakfast then we would simply multiply the quantities of ingredients by the number of breakfasts required. We now have our 'bill of requirements'. This would allow us to go shopping for the ingredients and also allow us to purchase accurately only the ingredients required to avoid wastage through having too many ingredients or disappointment through not having enough ingredients to meet the demand. The success of this system relies on us knowing how many breakfasts are required and how many diners actually turn up for the meal. In other words success relies on matching the forecast with actual demand.

If we were building a complex piece of machinery rather than our meal then we could apply the same principles. The numbers of different machines could be broken down into the numbers of sub-assemblies required, which in turn could be further broken down into components. Orders could be placed with suppliers for the required quantities and delivery times agreed. These orders would be made in the light of any existing stock of parts already available for use. This sounds very simple but in practice is an enormously complicated process that usually requires the assistance of a computer package. In fact the whole system was developed as a computer system for scheduling production. This is due to the number of transactions required in a short space of time for the schedule to be of any use.

The situation is further complicated when orders are cancelled at short notice or increased without warning. The adjustments will need to be made quickly to avoid failing to meet customer requirements or conversely being left with an excessive amount of component stock.

THE MRP SYSTEM

The following is a simple explanation of the basic structure of an MRP system.

The master production schedule

This is a list of all the products or services to be supplied within a specific period of time. This period of time must be sufficiently long to allow for the ordering and delivery of required sub-assemblies and parts, as well as allowing sufficient time for manufacturing the product in question. This schedule may be made up of forecast demand and actual known demand, ie customers' orders. This master schedule lists all the required outputs from the system. It will also list when the goods and services are required through the use of a 'due date'. Therefore the contents of the schedule will dictate the contents of the bill of requirements.

The bill of requirements

This is also referred to as the bill of materials (BOM). As explained earlier, this will list all the sub-assemblies, components and parts required in total to produce all the goods listed in the master schedule. It will also show the different levels at which these constituent parts are put together in order to produce the finished goods.

For example, the finished product may contain two sub-assemblies that together complete the product (see Figure 11.1). The finished product is said to be at level 0. These assemblies will be numbered sub-assembly 1 and sub-assembly 2. Together these sub-assemblies are said to be at level 1. Both sub-assemblies are made up of one component and one further sub-assembly each. This level is described as level 2. Due to the fact that the two major sub-assemblies at level 1 themselves contain one further sub-assembly each at level 2 then a further level is created at level 3. At level 3 it can be seen that one of the sub-assemblies at level 2 contains two components and the other contains four components.

This process (sometimes referred to as netting) is continued until all the constituent parts are broken down and listed at different levels. It can be quickly seen that if the bill of requirements for each product is viewed from the opposite direction to the finished product, ie the highest-level number first, then one is looking at a sequence for assembly. The components are put together to form sub-assemblies, which in turn are put together to form the finished product.

This bill of requirements, having detailed all the required parts and sub-assemblies, will allow the MRP program to create the required orders to be placed with suppliers. One important thing to remember is that it also lists in detail the order and timing when these parts are required.

Noting the level of detail in the bill of requirements for just one product described above, it may be easier to understand the level of complexity involved in scheduling many different products that may contain many more components. It will also underline the complexity involved in changing the master schedule due to cancellations or additional orders. For anything more than a very basic schedule a customized computer program will be required to deal with the large number of transactions required to effect the most straightforward of changes to the schedule.

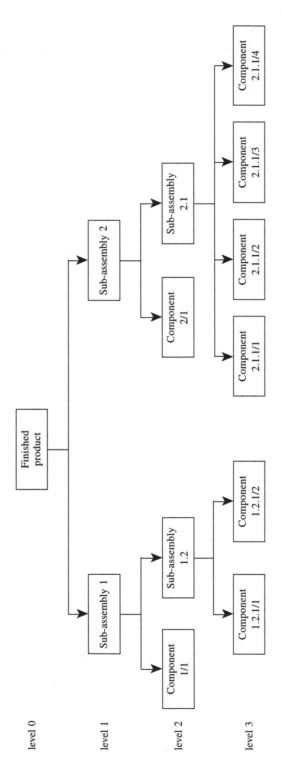

level 0

level 1

level 2

level 3

Figure 11.1   A bill of requirements for one product

Opening stock

The master schedule and the bill of requirements together form the framework of what is required and when it is required but two other factors must be fed into the computer program at the same time. The first of these will be the current level of unallocated stocks of parts, components and sub-assemblies available for immediate use. There will be in total larger stocks on hand but these will already have been allocated to production via the system and are therefore unavailable. This information will, of course, modify any orders for raw materials placed on suppliers.

Opening capacity

The final fundamental factor required by the MRP program is the current level of available unallocated production capacity for not only the finished product but any components or sub-assemblies that are manufactured in house.

All of the above information – the master schedule, the bill of requirements, the opening stock and the opening capacity – will be fed into the MRP computer program. The program will then produce as required the following:

- a list of purchase requirements, which will list what needs to be purchased and when;
- a manufacturing schedule, which will list what will be made and when it will be made;
- the closing stock of parts, components and sub-assemblies after the master schedule has been completed;
- the closing capacity available after the master schedule has been completed;
- a list of anticipated shortfalls in production – these may be due to shortages of parts or capacity.

The whole MRP process is iterative and therefore must be repeated periodically. This may be done on what is known as a 'regenerative' basis or a 'net change' basis.

The 'regenerative' basis involves assuming that no previous MRP calculation has taken place. Therefore known or forecast demand is used to create a new bill of requirements, with available parts of stock and available production capacity being allocated disregarding any previous calculations. For the purposes of this approach all parts and capacity are assumed to be unallocated, as existing orders and work in progress will be covered by the new master schedule. This approach tends to be used where demand and therefore output are fairly consistent. This method also has the advantage of not perpetuating any previous computation errors as each new calculation starts from fresh current data.

The 'net change' approach concentrates on changing only those parts of the program that have changed rather than recalculating the whole program. Thus if changes are made to the master schedule then only those parts of the program that are affected will be changed. This method tends to be used more in situations where demand is more volatile and so changes are more frequently needed.

FLEXIBLE FULFILMENT (POSTPONEMENT)

Flexible fulfilment is a method of manufacturing that attempts to delay the final definition of a product to the last possible stage in the supply chain – hence the popular description of 'postponement' for this system.

The advantages gained from this method can be dramatic, especially where companies trade on a world-wide scale. Consider the problems raised by the different voltages available around the world for the use of portable electrical goods. If the manufacturer supplies goods around the globe, then stocks of finished products might have to be kept for each different type of power supply, very likely in or close to the particular market in question. This will increase inventory carrying and, especially in the electronics business, the possibility of product obsolescence. However, if it were possible to have a number of different power supply packs that all fitted the same product then it would be necessary to have only one 'global' product, which could be quickly adapted by changing the power module alone to suit the market concerned. This would mean that there would no longer be country- or market-specific products and products could be transported and sold anywhere in the world at short notice.

This method has considerable implications for product design in that products need to be designed so that any variations dictated by markets can be adapted by changing modules only. Different keyboards for laptop computers are required to allow for the different alphabets to be found around the world. Manufacturing a laptop with a keyboard that is not easily substituted for another creates large inventories of language- or alphabet-specific stocks in those countries. Postponement means that the bulk of the laptop is produced and shipped around the world, but the final definition of the product only takes place when the alphabet-specific keyboard is attached.

Other examples of postponement can be seen when promotions of a product such as 'Buy product A and get product B free' occur. The attachment of product A to B creates a third product C. This product can be produced by wrapping the two products A and B together in some form of outer. This operation can be undertaken in the distribution centre prior to final delivery, which will avoid the necessity of forecasting and shipping stocks from further up the supply chain. The product C could almost be made to order via the wrapping process. If the promotion goes well then only increased levels of product A and B need be shipped.

THE EFFECTS ON DISTRIBUTION ACTIVITIES

These developments in manufacturing planning and control systems have had a significant impact in the management of traditional distribution activities. In the case of flexible fulfilment, where final modifications to products are taking place in distribution centres, this has caused traditional distribution managers and companies to redefine their role and approach. Distribution companies have had to start offering these services as part of their portfolio of services. Distribution managers have had to create the working environment for these activities to take place as well as providing a suitable trained workforce to deal with the new requirements.

The effects on distribution systems of just-in-time (JIT) deliveries have led to more frequent deliveries of smaller quantities to stringent delivery timetables. This has had effects on vehicle fleets and scheduling as well as developments in linked information systems between manufacturer, supplier and transport provider. Without these developments JIT would be virtually impossible.

Distribution requirements planning (DRP) systems were developed as a logical extension of MRP systems. The principles have simply been extended into a forward distribution planning system.

SUMMARY

This chapter has provided an overview of materials management in the production area as a part of supply chain management. Explanations of the following were included:

- push and pull systems;
- dependent and independent demand;
- the philosophy of just-in-time, including a description of the 'seven wastes', Kanban, and a 'right first time' approach to quality management;
- manufacturing resource planning (MRPII) and material requirements planning (MRP);
- flexible fulfilment, which has come to be known as postponement.

Finally, the effects of these manufacturing planning and control systems on distribution activities were briefly discussed.

Part 3

Procurement and inventory decisions

12

Basic inventory planning and management

INTRODUCTION

One of the most important aspects of logistics concerns questions related to inventory. The amount of inventory that should be held and its location within a company's logistics structure is vital in order to meet customer service requirements and expectations. But there is, potentially, a large cost associated with holding inventory. It is vital to get right this balance of service versus cost. This chapter sets out to explore the basic concepts behind the inventory holding decision.

In the first part of the chapter the main reasons for holding stocks are considered. The many different types of inventory are then described. These include raw material stocks through the supply chain to finished goods stocks. The implications of inventory holding policy on other logistics functions are highlighted, with particular emphasis on the need to provide the balance between cost and service that was indicated above. The need to avoid the sub-optimization of logistics resources is also discussed.

The two main inventory replenishment systems are described. These are the periodic review and the fixed point reorder systems. Also outlined are the impacts that end-user demand changes have on requirements further up the supply chain. The means of identifying reorder quantities using the EOQ method is described and it will be noted that it is important to take other factors into account when determining order quantities in this way.

Two methods of demand forecasting are discussed, moving average and exponential smoothing. It will also be shown that demand can be broken down into trend, seasonal and random factors.

THE NEED TO HOLD STOCKS

There are a number of reasons why a company might choose or need to hold stocks of different products. In planning any distribution system it is essential to be aware of these reasons, and to be sure that the consequences are adequate but not excessively high stock levels. The main reasons for holding stock can be summarized as follows:

- *To keep down productions costs.* Often it is costly to set up machines, so production runs need to be as long as possible to achieve low unit costs. It is essential, however, to balance these costs with the costs of holding stock.
- *To accommodate variations in demand.* The demand for a product is never wholly regular so it will vary in the short term, by season, etc. To avoid stock-outs, therefore, some level of safety stock must be held.
- *To take account of variable supply (lead) times.* Additional safety stock is held to cover any delivery delays from suppliers.
- *Buying costs.* There is an administrative cost associated with raising an order, and to minimize this cost it is necessary to hold additional inventory. It is essential to balance these elements of administration and stock-holding, and for this the economic order quantity (EOQ) is used.
- *To take advantage of quantity discounts.* Some products are offered at a cheaper unit cost if they are bought in bulk.
- *To account for seasonal fluctuations.* These may be for demand reasons whereby products are popular at peak times only. To cater for this while maintaining an even level of production, stocks need to be built up through the rest of the year. Supply variations may also occur because goods are produced only at a certain time of the year. This often applies to primary food production where, for example, large stocks result at harvest time.
- *To allow for price fluctuations/speculation.* The price of primary products can fluctuate for a variety of reasons, so some companies buy in large quantities to cater for this.
- *To help the production and distribution operations run more smoothly.* Here, stock is held to 'decouple' the two different activities.

- *To provide customers with immediate service.* It is essential in some highly competitive markets for companies to provide goods as soon as they are required (ex-stock).
- *To minimize production delays caused by lack of spare parts.* This is important not just for regular maintenance, but especially for breakdowns of expensive plant and machinery. Thus spares are held to minimize plant shutdowns.
- *Work in progress.* This facilitates the production process by providing semi-finished stocks between different processes.

TYPES OF STOCK-HOLDING

The main stock types can be categorized as follows:

- *raw material, component and packaging stocks* – generally used to feed into a production or manufacturing process;
- *in-process stocks* – sometimes known as work in progress, these consist of part-finished stock that is built up between different manufacturing processes;
- *finished products* – stocks that are held at the end of the production line normally in a finished goods warehouse;
- *pipeline stocks* – probably the most common type of stock-holding, these are held in the distribution chain for eventual transfer to the final customer;
- *general stores* – containing a mixture of products used to support a given operation, for example a large manufacturing plant;
- *spare parts* – a special category because of the nature of the stock, which provides a crucial back-up to a manufacturer's machinery or plant where any breakdown might be critical, and also held by service and maintenance companies for supply to their customers to support service contracts.

Within the above categories, stock can again be broken down into other major classifications:

- *Working stock.* This is likely to be the major element of stock within a distribution depot's stock-holding, and it should reflect the actual demand for the product.
- *Cycle stock.* This refers to the major production stock within a production warehouse, and it reflects the batch sizes or production run lengths of the manufacturing process.
- *Safety stock.* This is the stock that is used to cover the unpredictable daily or weekly fluctuations in demand. It is sometimes known as 'buffer' stock, as it creates a buffer to take account of this unpredictability.

- *Speculative stock.* This can be raw materials that are 'bought forward' for financial or supply reasons, or finished stock that is pre-planned to prepare for expected future increases in demand.
- *Seasonal stock.* This is product that is stockpiled to allow for expected large increases in demand. Typically, this would include inventory built up prior to the Christmas demand peak.

THE IMPLICATIONS FOR OTHER LOGISTICS FUNCTIONS

There are many ways in which the need to hold stock affects other logistics functions and vice versa. It is essential for effective planning that the various costs associated with inventory are minimized in relation to other logistics costs. As already discussed in previous chapters, it requires a process of balance between these functions to avoid any sub-optimization and to create a cost-effective total solution. With this in mind, it is useful to review those areas where this balance may be needed.

The *number of depots* in a distribution system significantly affects the overall cost of that system. The reasons given for having a large number of depots are generally the perceived need to have a 'local presence' within a market and the need to provide a given level of service to customers. A distribution system that does have many depots will require high stock levels, specifically with respect to the amount of safety stock held. In addition, a large number of depots is likely to mean fairly small delivery areas, reflecting poor stock turn and higher unit costs in the warehouse.

Many companies have, in recent years, undertaken depot rationalization exercises whereby they have cut significantly the number of depots within their distribution network. This particularly applies to retail and to manufacturing companies. Although this leads to an increase in local transport costs because delivery distances are greater, there are large savings to be made in inventory reduction – specifically in safety stock reduction.

A simple rule of thumb exists for estimating these savings, known as the 'square root law'. Basically, the law states that the total safety stock-holding in a distribution system is proportional to the square root of the number of depot locations. The law thus gives a broad indication of prospective inventory savings from any depot reduction. For example, a depot reduction from, say, 10 to 5 can lead to inventory savings of 29 per cent as indicated in the following calculation:

$$\text{Inventory reduction} = 1 - \left(\frac{\sqrt{5}}{\sqrt{10}} \right)$$

$$= 1 - \left(\frac{2.24}{3.16} \right) \times 100$$

$$= 29\%$$

Another major factor to be considered is the effect that an excess of inventory can have on the size and operation of a depot. This might be for a number of reasons such as obsolete stock, dead stock, unnecessary storage of slow-moving lines, etc. This may mean that a depot is larger than necessary, that extra outside storage is required, or that the depot operation is hindered through a shortage of working space.

One means of tackling these problems is to be more aware of the range of products held. This can be achieved by using Pareto analysis (or ABC analysis). Pareto's law provides the '80/20 rule', which states that there is an 80/20 relationship for products in many conditions. For example, it is often found that approximately 20 per cent of storage lines represent 80 per cent of the throughput in a warehouse.

Using Pareto analysis, it is possible to categorize product lines on the basis of:

'A' lines = fast movers
'B' lines = medium movers
'C' lines = slow movers
'D' lines = obsolete/dead stock

Policy decisions can then be made, for example: 'A' lines should be held at all depots and have a 98 per cent availability; 'B' lines should be held at all depots but only at 90 per cent availability; 'C' lines should be held only at a limited number of depots and at 85 per cent availability; and 'D' lines should be scrapped.

Clearly this policy will differ according to product type, industry type, service level requirements, etc. The essential point is to be aware of the appropriate stock-holding costs and recover the costs accordingly.

There are several ways in which stock-holding policy and practice can affect a transport operation. One that has already been indicated concerns the number of depots in a distribution system. Whereas inventory savings can be made by reducing depot numbers, this will be associated with an increase in local delivery costs because mileage will increase as depot areas become larger. It is generally true, however, that any increase in transport cost will be more than offset by inventory and warehouse cost savings.

One other area where inventory policy can influence transport is in the provision of backloads for return journeys by trunking vehicles and sometimes by delivery vehicles. Empty return journeys are a recognized cost that transport managers are always keen to minimize. It may be possible to arrange for raw materials or bought-in goods to be collected by own vehicles rather than delivered by supplier's vehicles.

A company's stock-holding policy may also affect the distribution structure that the company adopts. There are three main patterns:

1. direct systems;
2. echelon systems; and
3. mixed or flexible systems.

Direct systems have a centralized inventory from which customers are supplied directly. These direct systems are of two main types – either supplying full vehicle loads, or specialist services such as mail order.

Echelon systems involve the flow of products through a series of locations from the point of origin to the final destination. The essential point is that inventory is stored at several points in the distribution chain. There may be several links or levels within these structures, perhaps from production warehouses through a central stock-holding point to regional and/or local depots. Typical examples include some of the manufacturers of FMCG products.

Mixed systems are the most common. They link together the direct and the echelon systems for different products, the key element being the demand characteristics of these products (order size, fast/slow moving, substitutability, etc).

INVENTORY COSTS

Inventory costs are one of the major logistics costs for a large number of manufacturing and retail companies and they can represent a significant element of the total cost of logistics. As has been discussed in several previous chapters, there are many major cost trade-offs that can be made with all the other key logistics components. It is important to be able to understand what the key cost relationships are within a company. To do this, an awareness of the major elements of inventory cost is essential.

There are four principal elements of inventory cost. They are:

1. *Capital cost*: the cost of the physical stock. This is the financing charge that is the current cost of capital to a company or the opportunity cost of tying up capital that might otherwise be producing a return if invested elsewhere. This is almost always the largest of the different elements of inventory cost.
2. *Service cost*: the cost of stock management and insurance.
3. *Storage cost*: the cost of space, handling and associated warehousing costs involved with the actual storage of the product.
4. *Risk cost*: this occurs as a consequence of pilferage, deterioration of stock, damage and stock obsolescence. With the reduction in product life cycles and the fast rate of development and introduction of new products this has become a very important aspect of inventory cost. It is one that is frequently under-estimated by companies. It is particularly relevant to high-tech industries, the fashion industry, and fresh food and drink.

Another important cost that needs to be understood is the reorder or the set-up cost for an individual product. The reorder cost refers to the cost of actually placing an order with a company for the product in question. This cost applies regardless of the size of the order. The set-up cost refers to the additional cost that may be incurred if the goods are produced specifically for the company. Here, the larger the order, the longer the production run and the lower the production unit cost of the items in question. Of course, orders for large amounts of a product will result in the need for it to be stored somewhere – at a cost! This is yet another classic logistics trade-off decision that needs to be made. The means of assessing appropriate order quantities are discussed in the next section but one of this chapter.

INVENTORY REPLENISHMENT SYSTEMS

The aim of an effective inventory replenishment system is to maintain a suitable balance between the cost of holding stock and the particular service requirement for customers. The need for this balance can be illustrated by considering the disadvantages of low stock levels (which should provide very low costs) and high stock levels (which should provide a very high service).

The disadvantages of low stock levels are that customers' orders cannot be immediately fulfilled, which may lead to the loss of both existing and future business, and that goods have to be ordered very frequently, which may lead to heavy ordering costs and heavy handling and delivery costs. High stock levels have a major disadvantage because capital is tied up that might be better invested elsewhere. Also, there is the risk of product deterioration (eg food and drink) and of products becoming outdated, superseded or obsolete if they are stored for long periods of time (eg computers, mobile phones and fashion goods). A final disadvantage, previously discussed, is the expense of providing additional storage space.

Inventory replenishment systems are designed to minimize the effects of these high/low stock level disadvantages by identifying the most appropriate amount of inventory that should be held for the different products stocked. There is a variety of systems, but the two major ones are the periodic review (or fixed interval) system and the fixed point (or continuous) reorder system.

The periodic review system works on the premise that the stock level of the product is examined at regular intervals and, depending on the quantity in stock, a replenishment order is placed. The size of the order is selected to bring the stock to a predetermined level. Thus, the order size will vary each time a new order is placed. The system is illustrated in Figure 12.1.

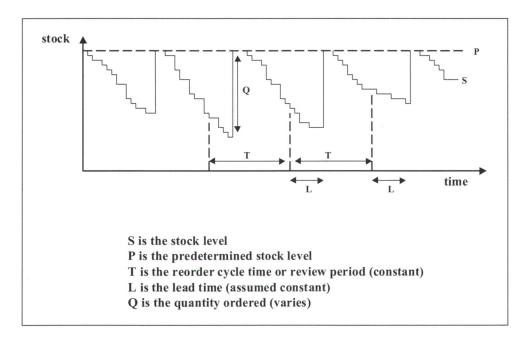

Figure 12.1 Periodic review

In Figure 12.1, the change in stock level can be seen by the pattern represented by the line S. T represents the reorder cycle time, which is the regular interval at which stock is reviewed – say at the beginning of every month. An order is placed at a quantity (Q), which will bring the inventory for this product back to the predetermined stock level (P). Note that the quantity ordered includes an allowance for the time it takes for the product to be delivered from the supplier (this is the lead time L). With this method, the quantity ordered is different each time an order is placed.

For the *fixed point reorder system*, a specific stock level is determined, at which point a replenishment order will be placed. The same quantity of the product is reordered when that stock level is reached. Thus, for this system it is the time when the order is placed that varies. This is illustrated in Figure 12.2.

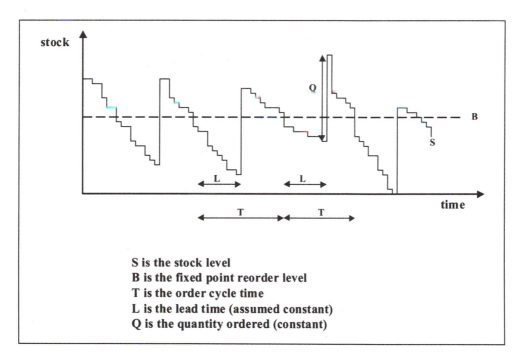

Figure 12.2   Fixed point reorder system

In Figure 12.2, the change in stock level can be seen by the pattern represented by the line S. When the stock level reaches the fixed point reorder level (B), a replenishment order is placed. This is for a fixed order quantity (Q). L represents the lead time for the order and the diagram shows that when the order arrives the stock level is increased by the set quantity that has been ordered. T represents the time period between orders, the length of which varies from one cycle to another for this system.

These systems, and variations of them, have been used for many years. Apart from the vagaries of lead time reliability they generally work quite well. They do have one significant drawback, however, which is that they can create unnecessarily high or low stock levels, especially when demand occurs in discrete chunks. This applies, in particular, to multi-echelon distribution systems where the demand at each level is aggregated at the next level up the supply chain. Thus, small changes in demand for finished products are amplified as they move back through the supply chain. This is because each part of the chain is acting independently of the others. The result is a surge in demand up the supply chain as each inventory location individually adjusts to the demand increases. This is known as the 'bull whip' or Forrester effect. It is illustrated in Figure 12.3.

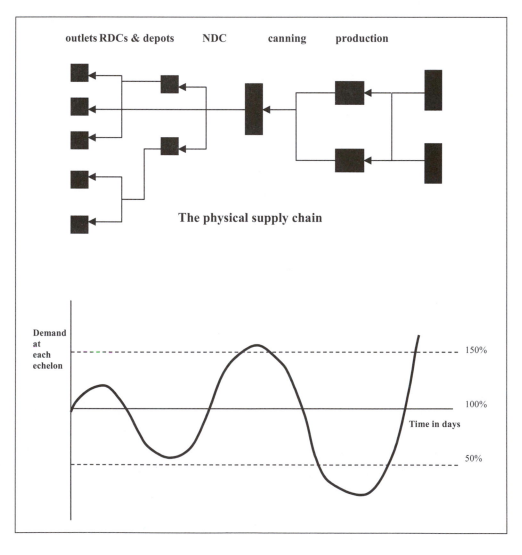

Figure 12.3   The 'bull whip' or Forrester effect

An example of this might occur where an unexpectedly hot day causes an increase in demand for cold soft drinks. This will lead to additional orders from a variety of outlets – supermarkets, pubs, corner shops, vending machines, etc. As these requirements move up the supply chain through the different channels of distribution, they will be converted into additional orders of various sizes and at different order frequencies. They might be for weekly mixed pallet loads from cash-and-carry outlets, twice-weekly full pallet loads from grocery RDCs and daily vehicle loads for manufacturers' NDCs. The consequence at the canning factory and point of production for the drink will be for a massive increase in product and a very confusing picture of what the true requirements are. This is echoed back into raw material and packaging supply.

Thus, it can be very difficult to forecast demand based only on the immediate next or lower level of demand. Accurate forecasts need to reflect the requirements at all levels, which is often very difficult because companies have traditionally been loath to share information with their suppliers. This is one of the reasons for the move towards more open information systems that provide a clearer vision of stock-holding and demand throughout the supply chain.

REORDER QUANTITIES

The two reorder systems described in the previous section require either fixed or variable quantities of different products to be ordered. The next question that needs to be addressed is how much product should be reordered. To answer this question is not easy, and there are many different views as to the best means of arriving at an answer. The traditional method of calculating the appropriate quantity is known as the *economic order quantity (EOQ) method*. This is shown in Figure 12.4.

The EOQ method is an attempt to estimate the best order quantity by balancing the conflicting costs of holding stock and of placing replenishment orders. The effect of order quantity on stock-holding costs is that the larger the order quantity for a given item, the longer will be the average time in the store and the greater will be the storage costs. On the other hand, the placing of a large number of small quantity orders produces a low average stock, but a much higher cost in terms of the number of orders that need to be placed and the associated administration and delivery costs. These two different effects are illustrated in the diagram of Figure 12.5.

The large order quantity gives a much higher average stock level (Q_1) than the small order quantity (Q_2). The small order quantity necessitates many more orders being placed than with the large order quantity.

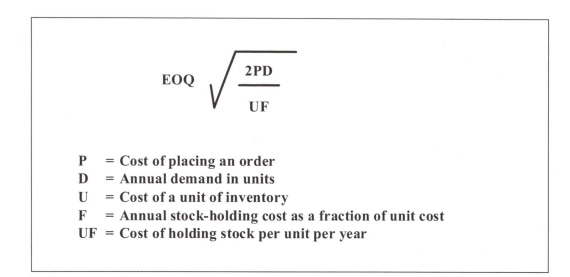

Figure 12.4 The economic order quantity formula

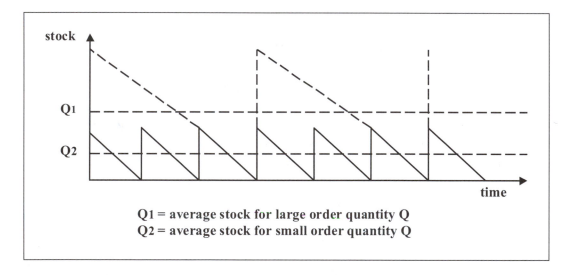

Figure 12.5 Reorder quantities

The best approach is, once again, one of balance, and it is this balance that the EOQ method aims to provide. Figure 12.6 helps to illustrate how this balance is achieved between the cost of holding an item and the cost of its reordering. There is a specific quantity (or range of quantities) that gives the lowest total cost (Q_0 in the diagram), and this is the economic order quantity for the product.

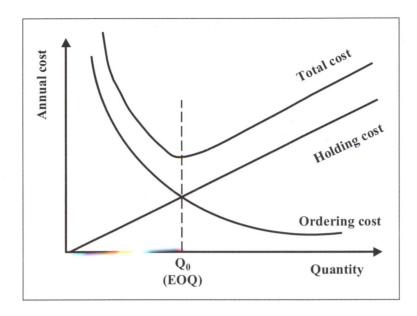

Figure 12.6 The economic order quantity (EOQ) principle

There are a number of additional factors that need to be considered before the final order quantity is confirmed.

These factors are of two types. The first type applies specifically to an individual company operation, or to a particular industry. The second type relates to factors of a more general nature, which tend to be relevant to most stock control or stock reorder systems. An important point to appreciate is that factors such as these may need to be considered as well as any suggested order quantity that derives from a stock control or stock reorder system. Some of these factors may be included within the stock reorder system itself, but this is often not the case.

The first series of special factors relates to specific companies or industries. The order quantity requirement for each product must be assessed and readjusted accordingly. The factors include the following:

- *New product lines.* These may be one-off items, or items that are expected to show a sharp increase in demand. There will be no historic data on which to base demand forecasts, so care must be taken to ensure that adequate stock levels are maintained.
- *Promotional lines.* National or local promotion (via TV, newspapers, special offers, etc) may suddenly create additional demand on a product, so stock levels must cater for this.

- *Test marketing*. This may apply to certain products, and may be for a given period of time, or be in a given area only.
- *Basic lines*. Some companies feel that a certain number of their basic stock lines should always be available to the customer as a matter of marketing policy. To provide this service, higher stock levels must be maintained.
- *Range reviews*. A company may adopt a policy to rationalize, or slim down, its range of products – particularly if new lines are being introduced. To do this it may be necessary to reduce the reorder quantities for some products.
- *Centralized buying*. Sometimes, where centralized buying occurs, it is necessary to hold excess stock, or run out of stock, because the buying department is negotiating large bulk discounts.

The more general factors that may need to be taken into account are:

- *Outstanding orders* – ie orders already placed but not delivered. It is important to include these in the analysis, otherwise overstocking may occur.
- *Minimum order quantities*. For some products there may be a minimum order quantity, below which it is uneconomic (or even impossible) to place an order.
- *Pallet quantities*. As with minimum order quantity, it is often more economic to order in unit load quantities – which are often a pallet or number of pallets. A good economic unit load order is often a full lorry load.
- *Seasonality*. Many products have a peak demand at certain times of the year. The most common peak occurs just prior to Christmas (toys, games, wines and spirits, etc). When estimating stock levels, and when forecasting trends in demand, it is essential to take these into account.

The EOQ method has been in use for many years, and used in association with other factors such as those previously indicated it is still valid for many companies. It does rely on a number of basic assumptions, however, some of which may not be so applicable with the new concepts and approaches to inventory that have been derived in recent years. These concepts are discussed in the next chapter.

DEMAND FORECASTING

There are many different forecasting methods available and it is important to select the most appropriate alternative for whatever demand is to be measured. Two of the most common methods of forecasting are described here. One of the most simple is the *moving average*, which takes an average of demand for a certain number of previous periods and uses this average as the forecast of demand for the next period.

Another, more complicated, alternative is known as *exponential smoothing*. This gives recent weeks far more weighting in the forecast. Forecasting methods such as exponential smoothing give a much faster response to any change in demand trends than do methods such as the moving average. Figure 12.7 illustrates this.

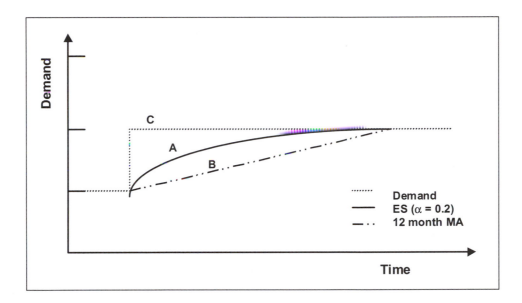

Figure 12.7 The moving average method (B) and the exponential smoothing method (A) of forecasting shown working in response to a step change in demand (C)

The dotted line (C) represents actual demand, the dash–dot line (B) represents a forecast using the moving average method and the single line (A) represents a forecast using exponential smoothing. It can be seen that the single line (exponential smoothing) responds more quickly to the demand change than does the dashed line (moving average).

There are a number of ways in which the demand for a product can vary. These different elements of demand are illustrated in Figure 12.8. It can be seen from the graphs that the overall demand pattern can be divided into the following patterns:

- A *trend line* over several months or years. In the diagram, the trend is upward until the end of year 4, and then downward.
- A *seasonal fluctuation*. This is roughly the same, year in, year out. In the diagram there is high demand in mid-year and low demand in the early part of the year.
- *Random fluctuations* that can occur at any time.

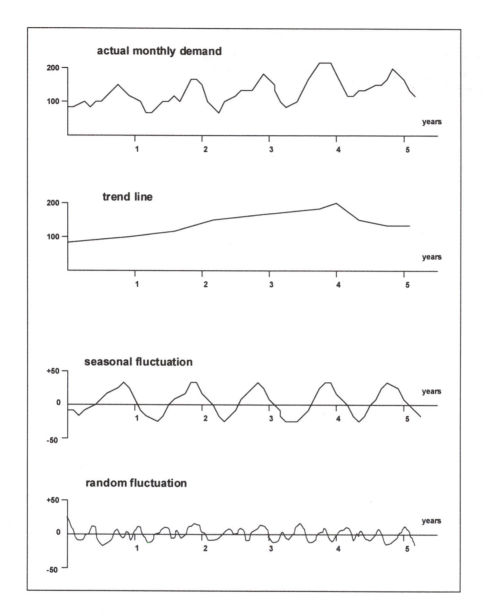

Figure 12.8   Elements of a demand pattern

Each of these elements should be taken into account by a good stock control system:

● the trend, by a good forecasting system;
● seasonality, by making seasonal allowances; and
● random, by providing sufficient buffer stock.

SUMMARY

This chapter has considered basic inventory planning and management, and a number of important factors have been outlined. In the first section, the reasons for holding stock were summarized. Following on from that, the main stock types were categorized as:

- raw materials, components and packaging;
- in-process stocks;
- finished products;
- pipeline stocks;
- general stores; and
- spare parts.

A further breakdown of stock includes five major classifications:

1. working stock;
2. cycle stock;
3. safety stock;
4. speculative stock; and
5. seasonal stock.

The implications of inventory holding policy on other logistics functions were highlighted, with particular emphasis on the need to provide a suitable balance between cost and service, and the need to avoid the sub-optimization of logistics resources.

The two main inventory replenishment systems were explained – periodic review and fixed point reorder. The Forrester effect was described, demonstrating the impact on requirements further up the supply chain as end-user demand changes. The question of reorder quantity was then discussed and the EOQ method was outlined. The need to take other factors into account when determining order quantity was emphasized.

Two methods of demand forecasting were outlined, the moving average and exponential smoothing. It was shown that demand could be broken down into trend, seasonal and random factors.

13

Inventory and the supply chain

INTRODUCTION

In the previous chapter, the basic inventory planning and management techniques were described. This next chapter provides a description of some of the very recent developments in inventory planning, particularly with respect to the way that inventory is viewed across the supply chain as a whole. In addition, the important relationship of inventory and time is discussed.

The chapter starts with a consideration of some of the problems associated with the traditional approaches to inventory planning. Inventory requirements are reviewed in relation to the different types of demand that can be found. The need for a company to hold inventory is explored with respect to the lead-time gap – the difference between the length of time it takes to complete an order and the amount of time a customer is prepared to wait for that order to be satisfied.

Different approaches to inventory reduction are considered and some of the main methods of measuring inventory and its relationship with time are reviewed. Finally, various new approaches to inventory planning for both manufacturing and retailing are described.

PROBLEMS WITH TRADITIONAL APPROACHES TO INVENTORY PLANNING

Inventory planning has traditionally been applied in particular at the finished goods end of the supply chain. It is now an activity that is seen to have relevance for stock held at all stages within the supply chain. Companies are beginning to understand that the cost of excess or unnecessary stock held anywhere in their supply chain, whether they have direct responsibility for it or not, is still going to have an impact on their bottom-line costs. Thus, raw material and component stock-holding levels are seen to be relevant and to provide an opportunity for cost improvement. Some retailers have begun to ask their suppliers to take responsibility for the planning and management of the stock of products they supply.

Because of this changing approach to inventory responsibility, the traditional methods of inventory planning are now becoming less applicable for many companies. This applies to the economic order quantity concept (EOQ) that was discussed in the previous chapter. Although still a useful and valid tool in many circumstances, some of the main assumptions on which it is based are less realistic for companies that have adopted a more streamlined approach to their logistics and supply chain activities. For example:

- Demand is not as predictable as it may once have been.
- Lead times are not constant – they can vary for the same product at different order times.
- Costs can be variable. Order costs relationships have changed with the introduction of automatic and EDI-related ordering procedures.
- Production capacity can be at a premium; it may not always be feasible to supply a given product as and when required.
- Individual products are closely linked to others and need to be supplied with them, so that 'complete order fulfilment' is achieved.

Thus the main assumptions that are the basis for the EOQ may not now hold true for many companies and their products. This can be linked to the introduction of continuous replenishment, which is now at the heart of many companies' supply policies. This means that orders are for much smaller quantities and are required much more frequently. The rules that once applied to inventory planning are undergoing a change. This is certainly true for many large companies, although the application of EOQ is still very relevant to many small and medium-sized enterprises.

DIFFERENT INVENTORY REQUIREMENTS

There are some important differences in the way inventory requirements are determined that are related to the type of demand for the products in question. The nature of this demand should have an influence on the approach adopted to manage the inventory. Some of these points were discussed in Chapter 11, but they are outlined again here.

One important way of differentiating between demand types is that of dependent or independent demand. The type of demand will have an influence on the nature of the inventory management technique chosen.

Independent demand occurs where the demand for one particular product is not related to the demand for any other product. Consumer demand for a desktop computer is, for example, independent. Indeed, most consumer products are independent of the demand for other finished goods. This is an important distinction, because products with an independent demand necessitate the use of forecasting to help determine expected demand levels and associated inventory requirements. The EOQ approach is commonly used for products with independent demand.

Dependent demand occurs where the demand for a particular product is directly related to another product. In the case of the desktop computer, for example, the demand for the power leads or the connecting cables would be directly dependent on the number of computers stocked as finished goods. Dependent demand can be classified in two ways. It may be vertical, eg the chip actually required in the production of the computer, or it may be horizontal, eg the instructional manual that is packed with the computer as a finished product. Typically, most raw materials, components and sub-assemblies have their demand dependent on the demand for the finished product. Because of this dependence, there is a far more limited requirement for the forecasting of the demand for these elements as the actual needs are directly related to the finished product requirements themselves. MRP and MRPII systems are used for these elements.

One feature that has become particularly relevant in recent years concerns the nature of the demand requirement. Is it a 'push' system or a 'pull' system? A *push system* is the more traditional approach where inventory replenishment is used to anticipate future demand requirements. A *pull system* is where the actual demand for a product is used to 'pull' the product through the system.

A push approach to inventory planning is usually based on a set plan that is predetermined according to certain rules of inventory reordering. This approach is a proactive one in the sense that it is planned on the basis of estimated, or forecast, demand for products from customers. The aim is to anticipate the extent and location of this demand and ensure that adequate stock is available in the right place at the right time. Typically, a push system is applicable for dependent demand and for cases where there are uncertainties in supply, source or production capacity limitations or the need to cater for seasonal demand. The EOQ method of inventory planning is based on the push approach. This was outlined in the previous chapter.

The pull approach is a reactive one where the emphasis is on responding directly to actual customer demand, which pulls the required product through the system. The idea of a pull system is that it can react very quickly to sudden changes in demand. The pull system is most useful where there is independent demand and where there is uncertainty of demand requirements or of order cycle time. The most common form of pull system is JIT, as the orders are placed only when working stock is at such a level that a replenishment order is triggered.

For many companies there is a need to adopt the concepts of both types of approach. Thus, hybrid systems are often used in practice.

THE LEAD-TIME GAP

One of the major reasons for the build-up of finished goods inventory is because of the long time that elapses between the moment when a product is ordered and the moment when the manufacture of that product starts. Ideally the customer would be prepared to wait the full amount of time that is required. If this were the case, there would be no need to hold any stock at all. This, of course, happens only rarely for special 'made-to-order' products. The vast majority of products are required either immediately, as for many consumer products at the point of sale in shops, or within a short time-scale, as for industrial products and also for consumer products when the retailer orders them in the first instance from the manufacturer.

The total time it takes to complete the manufacture and supply of a product is often known as the *logistics lead time*. Customers are generally prepared to wait for a limited period of time before an order is delivered. This is the *customer's order cycle time*. The difference between the logistics lead time and the customer's order cycle time is often known as the *lead-time gap*. The concept of the lead-time gap is illustrated in Figure 13.1. It is the existence of this lead-time gap that necessitates inventory being held. The extent of the lead-time gap, measured in length of time, determines how much inventory must be held. The greater the lead-time gap, the greater the amount of inventory that must be held to satisfy customer requirements. Thus, the more this gap can be reduced, the less inventory will be required. Recently there has been a move towards identifying different ways of reducing this gap. A number of these are described in the next section.

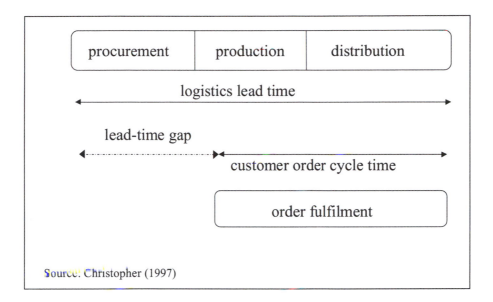

Figure 13.1 The lead-time gap

INVENTORY AND TIME

High levels of inventory are used by many companies to hide a number of problems that occur throughout the supply chain. Companies may have sound and acceptable reasons for holding stock – as outlined in the previous chapter – but some may also use high levels of inventory to protect themselves from those problems that they are unable or unwilling to solve by more direct means. The implications of this are illustrated in Figure 13.2. This shows that there is significant waste in many logistics systems made up of unnecessary inventory (the difference between A and B). This is used to cover up problems such as:

- unreliable suppliers;
- inaccurate forecasts;
- production problems;
- quality issues; and
- unpredictably high demand.

There is of course a very real cost associated with these high inventory levels. This is caused by the amount of capital tied up in the value of the inventory itself, and also of course in the other associated costs. These include the costs of the storage

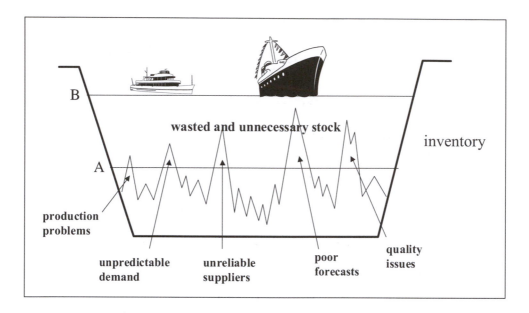

Figure 13.2 High inventory levels can hide other supply chain problems

facility and the cost of obsolescence when products become outdated and have to be sold at discount rates or even scrapped.

Finding a solution to these inventory-related problems can lead to a significant reduction in the requirement to hold stock. In Figure 13.2, their elimination would mean inventory coming down from level B to level A. How can inventories be lowered in this way? As well as confronting the particular problem areas directly, another approach is through what is known as *lead-time reduction*. This approach recognizes the importance of time within the inventory decision-making process. The aim of lead-time reduction is to reduce the amount of unnecessary time within the order-to-delivery process and thus reduce the need to hold so much inventory as cover for this time delay. This can be achieved in a number of different ways and some of these will be investigated in the remainder of this chapter. The main approaches are:

- *Manage the supply chain as one complete pipeline.* This will allow stock to be reduced at various stages in the total pipeline because it is clear that other stock exists to provide the necessary safety stock cover. The section on supply chain mapping will explain this further.
- *Use information better.* If there is a clearer picture throughout the supply chain of what the true *final* demand for a product is, then it will be much easier to

provide more accurate forecasts of the likely demand at other points in the supply chain.

- *Achieve better visibility of stock throughout the supply chain for all participants.* This will allow for clearer and more confident planning of stock requirements at the various stock-holding points in the chain and thus reduce the need to hold safety stocks.

- *Concentrate on key processes.* Make sure that the greatest planning and monitoring effort is spent on the most important processes in the supply chain. These may well be those that are providing the biggest bottlenecks or hold-ups in the system. It will often be necessary to undertake specific analysis to identify these bottlenecks using flow charts such as those described in Chapter 7.

- *Use just-in-time (JIT) techniques to speed up the flow of products through the supply chain.* These will reduce lead times and thus mean that less stock is required within the supply chain.

- *Use faster transport.* This is, of course, one of the classic trade-offs in logistics. Faster transport will almost certainly cost more, but there will be an associated reduction in the need to hold stock and savings will be made accordingly. Ideally this will provide an overall cost reduction in the supply of that product as a whole. It is also likely to result in a faster and more responsive service level.

- *Develop supply chain partnerships.* It is important to understand the need to identify lead-time reduction opportunities that lie outside a company's own boundaries. The most spectacular savings in stock reductions occur where companies in the same supply chain can work together, share information and build up a trust that allows them to reduce stocks with confidence.

ANALYSING TIME AND INVENTORY

To help understand the relationship of time and inventory it is useful to be aware of the concept of activities that add value to the supply chain and those that do not add value. An activity that adds value is one that provides a positive benefit to the product or service being offered. This can be assessed in terms of whether the customer is prepared to pay for this activity. An activity that does not add value is one that can be eliminated from the supply chain process and will not materially affect the finished product as far as the final customer is concerned. The analysis of supply chain activities in terms of the extent to which they add value to a product has thus become an important factor in the assessment of supply chain efficiency. The aim is to identify and eliminate those activities that add cost but do not add value. The holding of inventory within a supply chain is one such activity, and many companies are now trying to eliminate unnecessary inventory from their supply chains.

One method of highlighting unnecessary inventory is through the use of *supply chain mapping*. This technique enables a company to map the amount of inventory it is holding in terms of the length of time that the stock is held. An example of this technique is provided in Figure 13.3.

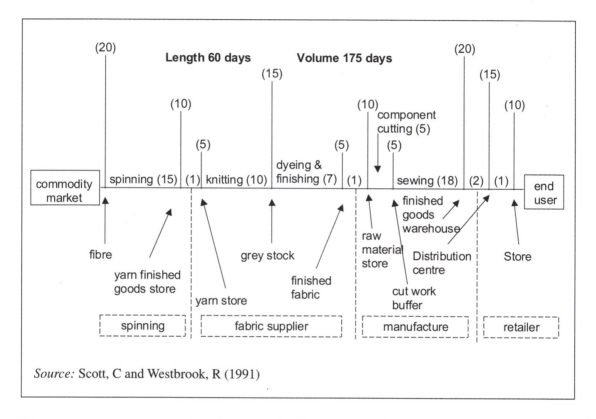

Figure 13.3 An example of a supply chain map showing inventory mapped against time

Figure 13.3 is an example from the US clothing industry. It shows:

- *Value-adding time*, which is represented along the horizontal axis. This shows the total of the manufacturing and transport time for the whole supply chain process from the initial fibre raw material to the supply to the end user. It is value adding because the product is changed either through a production process or through a movement process. It amounts to 60 days.

- *Non-value-adding time*, which is represented by the vertical lines that rise from the horizontal axis. These show the various occasions when the part-prepared or finished product is held as some form of inventory. This is adding no specific value to the product. This amounts to 115 days.
- The *total time* or pipeline time, which is the addition of the value-adding horizontal time and the non-value-adding vertical time. This therefore includes all the time that it takes through all the different manufacturing, storing and transport processes. This is a total time (or volume) of 175 days.

Note that in some instances transport is treated as non-value-adding (movement between production processes) and value-adding (movement to the final customer).

The example clearly indicates the opportunities for reducing time within the supply chain by reducing unnecessary inventory. Some inventory will be required, but as illustrated by this particular example there is a lot that is not. Very few companies undertake this type of analysis, and those that do are usually surprised by the results they get as large inventory levels are identified. It should also be noted that this type of analysis is particularly dramatic where a complete supply chain can be measured. Where a product moves from one company to another within a supply chain, then there is often evidence of large stock builds by both the supplier and buyer companies. This is due to a variety of factors, such as unreliable supply, a lack of confidence, uneven demand patterns and poor information on the real demand requirements for the finished product.

INVENTORY PLANNING FOR MANUFACTURING

Recent developments in inventory planning are aimed at solving some of the problems encountered by the use of the more traditional approaches to stock replenishment. They are based on the concept of *materials requirements planning* (MRP), which is a computerized system for forecasting materials requirements based on a company's master production schedule and bill of material for each product. Broadly, the system is used to calculate the time-phased requirements for components and materials with respect to production schedules, taking into account replenishment lead times, etc. This approach enables inventory levels to be significantly reduced, and service levels, in terms of shorter production lead times, to be improved.

MRP systems are now quite well established, as are other related techniques such as 'just-in-time' (JIT) or Kanban systems. The obvious advantages of these systems to manufacturing have led to the development of associated techniques for distribution – distribution requirements planning (DRP). *DRP systems* are designed to take forecast demand and reflect this through the distribution system on a time-phased requirements basis. DRP thus acts by pulling the product through the distribution system once demand has been identified. It is particularly useful for multi-echelon distribution structures to counter the problems of requirements occurring as large chunks of demand (the Forrester effect – described in Chapter 12).

The concept of *time compression* is an important approach in the planning of manufacturing inventory requirements or perhaps it should be termed as the planned reduction in manufacturing and WIP inventory. The opportunities for such reductions have been illustrated in the above discussion on analysing time and inventory. Typical approaches include:

- the need to take a complete supply chain perspective when planning;
- the need to undertake appropriate analysis;
- the identification of unnecessary inventory and unnecessary steps in key processes;
- work towards customer service requirements as well as cost minimization when planning for production;
- design products to be compatible with supply chain requirements;
- design production processes to be compatible with supply chain requirements.

These approaches have been discussed in Chapters 2 and 11.

INVENTORY PLANNING FOR RETAILING

In recent years power within most supply chains for consumer products has lain very firmly in the hands of retailers rather than manufacturers. This has applied to all but the strongest brand names. If anything, this power has continued to increase even further, although it will be interesting to see what impact the development of Internet and home shopping has in this direction. Many retailers have tended to outsource their distribution and logistics activities, but although this continues to be the case, retailers are now taking a much closer interest in the impact an effective logistics operation can have on their overall service offering and consequent company profitability. This applies to distribution and also particularly to inventory management policy and practice.

Inventory management at depot level for both retail NDCs (national distribution centres) and retail RDCs (regional distribution centres) poses similar problems to those experienced by manufacturers. At the retail store, however, inventory requirements can be quite different, depending on the product availability strategy and the merchandising policies that are used. New types of inventory management systems have been developed in recent years to cater specifically for these different requirements. The main planning techniques are:

- *Vendor-managed inventory (VMI).* This is where the manufacturer is given the responsibility for monitoring and controlling inventory levels at the retailer's depot and in some instances at the retail store level as well. Specific inventory targets are agreed and it is the responsibility of the manufacturer to ensure that suitable inventory is always available. Such arrangements depend on accurate and timely information, and suitable computerized systems have only become available in recent years. The main advantage for retailers lies in the reduction of operating costs and also the delay in payment for the products in question. For manufacturers, it is suggested that running a VMI system for a retailer provides the opportunity to develop a much closer, and hopefully more binding, relationship with the retailer as well as giving a much better visibility of real demand. This can make the planning of production much easier and can lead to significant reductions in inventory holding right through the supply chain.
- *Continuous replenishment (CRP).* The aim with CRP is to develop free-flowing order fulfilment and delivery systems, so that pipeline inventories can be substantially reduced. Such systems use up-to-the-minute point of sale information (via electronic point of sale – EPOS – systems) to identify real-time demand and to pull product through directly from the supplier, through the depot and on to the retail outlet. CRP systems are thus able to synchronize this flow of product by focusing on end-user requirements via the use of real-time demand, linked to flow-through distribution systems that allow for cross-docking, store-ready packaging and automated handling. Once again pipeline inventory is kept to a minimum or completely eliminated.
- *Quick response (QR).* A further development of the JIT approach is that of quick response (QR). Here the aim is to link the manufacturer more closely to the actual demand at the retail level. There are strong similarities with continuous replenishment systems, but with QR the emphasis is on time compression and the opportunity for the manufacturer to redesign production operations to allow for a 'little and often' approach to resupply. Short production change-overs and small batch sizes enable the manufacturer to respond to changes in demand in a very short time-scale. A classic example is the Benetton operation. This demonstrates most of the key characteristics of a QR system. It has allowed the company to offer an extremely responsive supply to its retail outlets to reflect the fast-changing nature of the fashion industry. Figure 13.4 provides more information.

Background

♦ **Integrated manufacturer and retailer**

♦ **Knitwear, casuals, accessories**

♦ **80 million garments a year**

♦ **<u>All</u> with a pre-placed order**

♦ **From 7,000 licensed Benetton stores**

♦ **In 110 countries**

Distribution

♦ **Distribution via automated central warehouse in Italy**

♦ **Automated and linked to factories**

♦ **Cartons bar-coded and electronically sorted**

♦ **15,000 cartons shipped per day**

♦ **50% air freight, 50% rail/sea/road**

Ordering

♦ **For each of two main fashion seasons:**

♦ **Store managers adjust product mix for local requirements**

♦ **Each store commits for 80% of orders seven months ahead, which are shipped on a 20-day order cycle to provide regular new 'collections'**

♦ **Remaining 20% by quick response in seven days**

♦ **Orders transmitted by EDI direct from shops to factory (via regional agents)**

Logistics efficiency

Provides:

♦ **Fastest order cycle times in the industry**

♦ **No excess work in progress**

♦ **No 'pipeline' inventory build-ups**

♦ **Little residual end-of-season stock for 'clearance'**

♦ **Extremely high customer service to stores**

♦ **Extremely responsive product provision**

Figure 13.4 The Benetton Group: initial quick response system

Efficient consumer response (ECR) is another concept that uses the most recent advances in information technology to allow a streamlined approach to the supply of products to retail stores. ECR was originally set up and run in the USA with the aim to improve service and reduce costs in the grocery industry by focusing on the efficiency of the supply chain as a whole, rather than on individual components in individual companies. The goal of ECR is therefore to develop a customer-driven system that works across the supply chain. One definition is: 'A seamless flow of information and products involving manufacturers and retailers working together in joint planning and demand forecasting. Both sides might take on functions traditionally handled by the other if they can do it better and at a lower cost. It will drive changes in business process, organization structure and information systems' (*Financial Times*, 1996). ECR combines a number of different concepts and strategies. The basic tenets of ECR are:

- a heavy use of EDI (electronic data interchange) for exchanging information with suppliers;
- an extremely efficient supply chain using cross-docking and direct store deliveries, thus keeping inventory holding to a minimum;
- the use of sales-based ordering, notably through continuous replenishment programmes (CRP);
- much greater co-operation with suppliers, using where appropriate co-managed inventory (CMI) or full vendor-managed inventory (VMI).

There are four key strategies in the use of ECR. These are the areas that companies believe should improve significantly:

1. replenishment – to get the right product into store at the right time, etc;
2. store assortment – ensuring the right mix of products in the store to maximize consumer satisfaction;
3. promotion – to link trade promotions with retail availability;
4. new product introduction – streamlining all processes to get new products to the consumer more quickly.

In general, the greatest benefits are to be found with the improvement in the first two of these – speedier replenishment and better store assortment. Overall, benefits can be found in both cost reduction and service improvement. The main benefits are:

- Automated systems reduce labour and administrative costs.
- Sharing information leads to more timely deliveries and falling inventory levels at the store.
- Cross-docking reduces inventory levels at the depot.
- Concentrating on fewer suppliers reduces transaction and administration costs.
- Offering the right products to the right customers increases volume sales and economies of scale.
- Customer needs are more fully addressed.
- The ability to tailor the products and services on offer in the store allows a company to take account of local preferences.
- Rapid replenishment can reduce out-of-stocks and this means that customers seeking a particular product or brand will not leave empty-handed.

A common approach for the implementation of ECR by a retailer is to focus on the consumer and then to develop a particular IT strategy and capability. This is likely to include the use of EDI, EPOS, computer ordering, computer routeing, etc. It is important to create a climate for change and to re-engineer existing business practices, as they are unlikely to be adequate for the successful implementation of ECR. The next requirement is to develop a responsive replenishment strategy jointly with key suppliers for key products. Finally, a workable flow-through distribution operation must be planned and implemented. A typical flow-through operation is likely to involve:

- *Pre-distribution identification.* Vendors pick, sort and pre-label final orders using bar codes.
- *Automated cross-docking.* This will require conveyors, diversion lines and bar-code readers.
- *A disciplined appointment scheduling procedure.* Inbound receipt scheduling will need to match available labour and minimize vehicle waiting.
- *New facility design.* This should ideally include shipping doors around the circumference of the building. The use of conveyors will eliminate put-away and picking.
- *Floor-ready merchandise.* Suppliers should provide tags and labelling to reduce DC and retail store work and handling.

In fact many cross-docking operations in an ECR environment can work well with much less automation than indicated above. Clearly, this becomes problematic for very large-scale operations. The major tenet for any quick response system is that the product should be continually moving.

SUMMARY

This chapter has considered the broader role of inventory within the supply chain as a whole. Some of the drawbacks of the traditional approaches to inventory planning have been discussed. The need to differentiate between demand types was highlighted, the major types being identified as:

- independent demand;
- dependent demand;
- push systems;
- pull systems.

The relationship between inventory and time was also reviewed. Two important elements were described: the lead-time gap and the opportunity for lead-time reduction. In addition, the technique of supply chain mapping was outlined, and it was shown how this could help in the analysis of inventory in the supply chain, and show how value-adding and non-value-adding time could be identified.

Recent developments in inventory planning for manufacturing were reviewed. These included:

- materials requirement planning;
- distribution requirements planning; and
- time compression.

Developments in inventory planning for retailing covered:

- vendor-managed inventory;
- continuous replenishment;
- quick response; and
- efficient consumer response.

The importance of new information systems to support these techniques was seen to be fundamental to their continued development and implementation.

14

Procurement

INTRODUCTION

Procurement is one of the key links in the supply chain and as such can have a significant influence on the overall success of the organization. Ensuring that there are sufficient supplies of raw materials at the right price, of the required quality, in the right place and at the right time is obviously crucial to any manufacturing plant. So important is this process that over the years many organizations have developed large departments to deal with the sheer weight of supplier transactions.

Recently, however, many companies have been reducing the number of suppliers they deal with in order to reduce the cost of these transactions.

In addition to supplier reduction programmes many companies have tried to move away from the traditional adversarial relationship with suppliers and towards a more partnership-based approach. This style of relationship recognizes that both parties need to make a profit to survive but that there may be areas where, through co-operation, real cost may be removed from the supply chain.

Of course, procurement is not just about raw materials. The following also need to be acquired:

- utilities – gas, water, electricity and telephones;
- fuel – diesel, petrol and heating fuel;
- capital assets – machinery, vehicles and buildings;

- corporate travel and hotels;
- stationery;
- consultancy;
- outsourced services – distribution contracts, IT services, etc;
- IT equipment – hardware, software and support.

Very large sums of money are involved in the above areas of purchasing with different emphasis placed on different elements depending on the business of the organization concerned. For a transport company, fuel may represent as much as 35 per cent of the total operating budget, but for a manufacturing plant the major cost may be in the plant running costs. These costs need to be carefully managed but the first step is to determine some purchasing objectives.

Managing suppliers is another crucial aspect of procurement. 'How many suppliers should we have?', 'How will we assess their performance?' and 'Should we make or buy this component?' are all key questions that need to be answered if a procurement strategy is to work to the benefit of the business.

Procurement is a very large subject area. The objective in this chapter is only to highlight the key areas.

SETTING THE PROCUREMENT OBJECTIVES

When setting procurement objectives consideration should be given to the following:

- ensuring the supply of raw materials and other supplies;
- the quality of supplies;
- the price;
- the origin of the supplies;
- the method of supply, eg JIT-style deliveries;
- the mode of transport used;
- a hierarchy of importance, eg key raw materials would have precedence over office stationery;
- whether to make yourself or buy from a supplier.

Ensuring the supply of raw materials

Clearly without an assured flow of raw materials into a manufacturing plant serious problems will ensue. These could take the form of plant stoppages, which will be enormously expensive. If expensive plant, machinery and labour are standing idle then costs may be incurred at an alarming rate. Not only will cost be incurred but customers may be let down as goods are not available for delivery at the appropriate time.

With this in mind procurement management can adopt several policies to ensure that supplies are always in the right place at the right time.

- The manufacturer could purchase the supplying company. This used to be common in vertically integrated organizations.
- Sufficient safety stocks may be held at the manufacturing plant to cover such eventualities. These stocks would attract inventory carrying costs but the alternative may justify this investment.
- A manufacturer may insist on the co-location of the supplier next to or close to the plant itself.
- Where commodities such as wheat or crude oil are concerned, then options to buy certain quantities may be negotiated in advance.

The quality of supplies

Ensuring that the goods and services purchased are of the right quality is important in that substandard supplies cause waste and a variety of problems:

- If the goods are unusable then their presence has created a shortage in the required quantity, which in JIT environments may be crucial.
- Substandard goods will need to be stored awaiting collection. This could be a problem if storage at the receipt stage is restricted.
- They will incur transaction costs, as paperwork and time will be involved in rectifying the error.
- They will undermine confidence in the supplier and the supply process.

Insisting on suppliers having quality management systems in place can help avoid these problems, as can extrinsic audits of suppliers' premises. These audits may be carried out by the company's quality auditors. Supplier assessment programmes will help highlight the main offenders.

The price

This is the area that most people associate with the purchasing process. The price will be dictated by certain factors:

- The negotiating skill of the purchasing team.
- The quality of the goods in question.

- Detailed knowledge of the product being purchased. For example, when multiple retailers purchase commodities such as flour they will have familiarized themselves with the costs of wheat and production before entering any negotiation.
- How much of the product is generally available for purchase. In other words if the product is scarce then prices tend to be higher as purchasers pay higher and higher prices for the goods. The opposite is true when the product is plentiful.
- The distance the goods have to travel from their point of origin to the delivery point. Associated with this is the mode of transport used. The cost of transporting the raw materials may represent a large part of the purchase price.
- If the goods are being purchased by a buying group, then prices should be lower. A buying group is a number of companies grouped together in order to pool their buying power.

The origin of the supplies

The origin of the raw materials may be critical. If the goods have to travel halfway around the globe then not only will the transport costs be high but the lead times to delivery may be unacceptably long. It is also the case that not all parts of the world enjoy political stability. If supplies are interrupted for unspecified periods of time by political strife then a company could be in dire trouble if it did not have an alternative source of raw materials. Important decisions must be made with these factors in mind.

The method of supply

Smaller, more frequent deliveries typify a JIT system of supply. Inventory carrying of raw materials may only be measured in hours and deliveries may even be made directly on to the production line itself. As more and more companies seek to reduce inventory carrying costs then these types of arrangement have become more common.

Some companies look to suppliers to provide vendor-managed inventory. In this system the supplier keeps and manages stocks of its product on the customer's premises. The customer only pays for the goods when they are used.

The process of receiving goods in a warehouse can be significantly speeded up if suppliers provide the goods in the right quantities, at the allotted time, correctly labelled and bar-coded where necessary. How the raw materials are to be supplied needs to be determined and then discussed in advance with suppliers because they may not be able to meet the necessary criteria. It will be no good insisting on bar-coded products if a supplier is unable to comply, and if a supplier can't comply, a buyer's receiving operation may be severely compromised.

The mode of transport used by suppliers

Many transport and delivery requirements need to be discussed prior to agreeing to deal with a supplier. In the past, company procurement managers have in some instances been guilty of making spot purchases of goods on the basis of price alone only to discover that the consequential cost of handling has been unreasonably high. Typical questions that need to be answered include:

- Will the goods be shipped by road, sea, rail or air?
- What sort of unitization is used?
- Will the goods be on pallets?
- What size are the pallets?
- Will the goods be stuffed inside containers and require considerable time and labour cost to unload?
- Should a railway siding be built to accommodate rail traffic?

The hierarchy of importance

> 'In our visits to firms, it never ceases to amaze us how most purchasing departments still treat a critical microchip in the firm's key product much the same as a paperclip purchase' (Jack Berry, Arthur D Little Inc).

This quotation says it all really. It is vital that appropriate amounts of time and effort are spent on the purchases that most matter to the organization. Therefore procurement management must ensure that purchasing is segmented accordingly. Products need to be classified according to their criticality to the business and the value of annual purchases. The four categories usually used are:

1. routine purchases;
2. commodities;
3. critical items;
4. strategic items.

Figure 14.1 demonstrates how purchases may be easily categorized by assessing how critical an item may be to the organization and by calculating the annual value of purchases. A strategic item is one that is both very critical to the business and has a high annual purchase value. At the other end of the scale, a routine purchase is one that has a low annual purchase value and is not critical to the business.

Once purchases have been categorized in this way the process by which they are to be purchased may be decided upon. Buying processes include:

- online catalogues;
- tendering;
- a system of approved supplies;
- strategic partnerships.

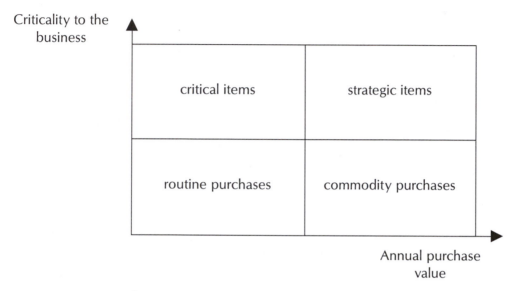

Figure 14.1 Purchase categorization

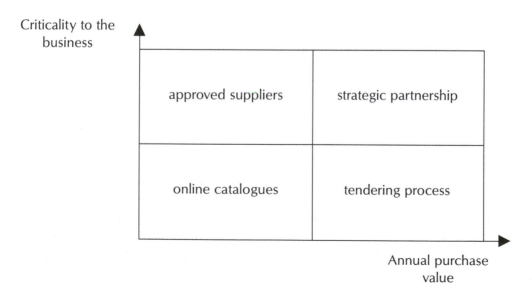

Figure 14.2 Appropriate buying processes

Figure14.2 shows how the appropriate buying process may be matched with the purchase categorization described in Figure 14.1.

Online catalogues available to employees will allow them to purchase routine items quickly and easily. This speeds up the process and limits the cost of these transactions (see the Texas Instruments example below).

The tendering process for high annual purchase value commodities will be appropriate where obtaining the best price is important.

A network of approved suppliers and a formal system for approving suppliers are most appropriate where items are critical to the business but have a low annual purchase value. Suppliers will have been able to satisfy the purchasing department that they are able to meet certain criteria satisfactorily on a consistent basis. The criteria used may include delivery reliability, quality of goods supplied and value for money.

Strategic partnership (see the section on partnerships later in this chapter) will be most appropriate where the purchase has high annual value and is critical to the business. In these cases, it is in the interest of both purchaser and vendor to develop a strong working relationship.

Make or buy?

The decision to make goods or provide a service as opposed to buying it in is one that is rarely straightforward. It is not always simply a question of cost. Other issues such as the company's reputation or production capacity may be included in the mix. The following is a list of some of the factors often considered:

- *Cost.* If the goods or services are to be provided in-house, then it is not simply the direct costs involved that need to be considered but the wider costs, such as the opportunity cost of the capital employed. In other words, could the capital tied up in this exercise produce a better return if invested in another activity? If the activity is to be provided by a supplier, then the costs associated with managing the supplier and the transaction costs (eg for processing invoices) should be included in the analysis.
- *Ensuring supply.* As mentioned above, if goods or services are not available when required then significant extra costs may be incurred. The reliability of the supplier and the quality of its offering is another crucial part of the decision-making process.
- *Production capacity.* Some parts of an operation may be provided by subcontractors because a company does not have sufficient capacity within its operation to do the job itself. This may be a very sensible approach to take in certain circumstances. A vehicle fleet, for example, should be kept working full time.

Therefore, it is better to have sufficient vehicles to achieve this end and subcontract any further work created by short-term increases in demand. Of course, the opposite is true in that if a production plant has spare capacity then it may be correct to use it rather than have it stand idle.

● *Competitive advantage.* There may be certain products, components or processes that the company wishes to keep secret and so it will not allow any other company to gain information about them. A revolutionary new product may fit this situation.

MANAGING THE SUPPLIERS

The following areas should be considered when managing suppliers:

● who the suppliers will be;
● how many suppliers there will be;
● how suppliers will be managed – adversarial or partnership approach.

Who the suppliers will be

Choosing your suppliers will involve all the elements already discussed but there are one or two further points that have to be considered. Of course this only applies in a situation where there is a choice. There are certain situations where no choice exists at all and one is forced to deal with a monopoly situation.

If a partnership approach is desired then suppliers need to be able to respond to this type of situation. They must also be companies that are sufficiently well established. Company accounts are public information and easily obtained. A check should be made to establish that a company is financially stable. It would be very unfortunate to spend time developing a partnership only to see a new partner going into liquidation.

Another consideration is whether or not a supplier wishes to become closely involved with a major customer. It will be necessary to share information and the supplier may also deal with competitors. This could place a supplier in a difficult position and it may decline the offer of closer ties. Another fear may be that the customer could become so close that it gets taken over.

How many suppliers there will be

This will obviously vary from industry to industry. The high costs associated with transactions are driving companies into supplier reduction programmes. The suppliers who remain will hopefully be the ones who perform best on supplier appraisals. They will also be the ones who have been prepared to share information and get involved in electronic data interchange (EDI) to reduce the cost of purchasing and who have the geographical coverage to match the client company. Increasingly global companies are seeking to do business with global suppliers.

A partnership or adversarial approach

In a traditional adversarial relationship between buyer and seller each party sees itself as being in competition with the other. The inevitable result of this kind of relationship is that one or other party inevitably 'wins' in any negotiation. This is often referred to as a 'win–lose' situation. Who and why one party is successful in this sort of relationship has much to do with the relative power that resides in one camp or the other. For example, a vendor with a rare product that is absolutely crucial to the process of the buyer would tend to be in a more powerful position. This would be especially true if the item on sale could not be substituted by another. The problem with this type of association is that, because both parties are secretive and defensive, inefficiencies in the supply chain are the result. These usually take the form of excess buffer stocks held by both parties, stock-outs and a lower level of customer service.

The idea of seeing a supplier as a partner makes a great deal of sense from a logistics point of view. The Toyota organization, like many other Japanese companies, has long seen its suppliers as co-makers of the product. The Japanese system of keiretsu epitomizes the approach. A network of suppliers is intimately bound to the client company in a complex web of interdependence. This type of association should be seen as a 'win–win' situation in which both parties gain more from the relationship than from the adversarial style.

It is worth introducing a word of caution at this point. Toyota reduced its supplier base to such an extent and was so reliant on JIT deliveries that when a fire occurred at the premises of one of its suppliers it was forced to stop its production lines in Japan for a week. At the time Toyota owned 22.6 per cent of the supplier, Aisin Seiki, a manufacturer of vital brake components. The fire occurred early in 1997 and brought Toyota to a standstill. This was not an isolated incident either because in 1995 after the Hanshin earthquake in western Japan car manufacturers were cut off from some of their suppliers by the disaster. By contrast Honda does not have such a closely knit keiretsu and has a policy of dual supply for all raw materials as a hedge against just such a situation.

These are extreme examples and should in no way inhibit companies from building closer ties for mutual benefit. As with all partnerships the partner has to be selected with care, as not all suppliers will either wish to engage in this sort of relationship or be suitable. Some prerequisites for a successful partnership will include:

- compatible cultures;
- high levels of trust already in place;
- compatible computer systems to aid the electronic sharing of information;
- the financial stability of both parties;
- a willing attitude to exploring the advantages of partnership.

In a partnership, members of equivalent departments in both organizations will meet regularly to discuss areas of mutual interest. For example, new product development people from both organizations will sit down together to see how products may be produced in such a way as to avoid causing problems for each other. In a similar way logistics personnel will associate more freely. Traditionally in the old adversarial way only buyer and seller would meet.

Through this closer liaison, information sharing occurs for mutual benefit. Real benefits have been achieved by linking together computer information systems. In this way, a retailer with an electronic point of sale (EPOS) system can provide the supplier with real-time data about the current level of demand for a given product. This kind of information can lead to real reductions of inventory carrying in the supply chain and a reduction in stock-outs. As the relationship matures then initiatives such as VMI may be introduced. Ordering and invoicing may be carried out via EDI, thus reducing transaction costs by the removal of expensive paper-based systems.

A practical example

Texas Instruments were able to save in excess of $30 million dollars by redesigning their procurement process. In some cases they were able to reduce the transaction costs associated with line items from $250 for a manually processed order to less than $5. These kinds of saving were achieved by using the following approach:

- Each division of the company had its own procurement system. This was changed so that the buying power of the whole company could be exploited.
- The supplier base of 34,000 was significantly reduced.
- Business processes were carefully examined and unnecessary steps or procedures eliminated. This saved both time and money.
- The newly streamlined processes then formed the basis of their computerized paperless procurement model.

- EDI links were established with suppliers internationally.
- Online catalogues of items were made accessible to employees. This system, known as Express Buy, allowed employees to select the everyday items they needed with speed and ease, the terms and conditions of these purchases having already been negotiated by the buying team.
- Savings were generated in labour costs and inventory carrying, buying power was consolidated on a global scale and the need to expedite critical parts orders was reduced.

These kinds of improvements and savings were not generated overnight. Texas Instruments started this process back in the 1980s but they had a clear idea about what they were seeking to achieve.

DELIVERED PRICE

Very often one area associated with the buying process that is overlooked is the cost of transporting the goods to the buyer's facilities. Often companies show a remarkable lack of interest in this area preferring to see it as somebody else's problem. Unfortunately, the delivered price may hide some extra cost that the buying company could avoid.

If raw materials are being sourced from a variety of locations whether it be on a national, European or global scale then there may be a possibility of removing some of the associated transport costs by employing a third party to co-ordinate this process. Large freight-forwarding companies may be able to pool one company's transport requirements with others so that a better price is obtained.

Another way of removing cost from the inbound side of a business is to use the vehicles delivering finished goods to collect from suppliers. This will allow a company to buy raw materials at ex-works prices and utilize its delivery fleet more effectively as well. It may be possible to have the same organization that handles final deliveries co-ordinating inbound raw material transport needs as well.

SUMMARY

This chapter has highlighted the crucial role played by procurement as part of the supply chain. The key areas covered were:

- the setting of procurement objectives with regard to ensuring supply, establishing a hierarchy of importance, quality, price, origin of goods, method of delivery and mode of transport used;
- how to manage suppliers with regard to the number of suppliers and who they will be, make or buy decisions, and whether to adopt an adversarial or partnership approach;
- a practical example of how Texas Instruments saved $30 million by redesigning their procurement process.
- delivered price and co-ordinating inbound and outbound transport needs in order to reduce overall supply chain costs.

Part 4

Warehousing and storage

15

Principles of warehousing

INTRODUCTION

The effective management of any enterprise requires that all its constituent activities operate effectively as individual units, and together as an integrated whole.

Within supply chains, warehousing is an important activity in the distribution of materials, from raw materials and work in progress through to finished goods. It is integral to the supply chain within which it operates and as such its roles and objectives should be determined by the objectives of the supply chain. It is not a 'stand-alone' activity and it must not be the weakest link in the supply chain.

Warehousing is costly in terms of people and of the facilities and equipment required, and its performance will impact directly on overall supply chain performance. Inadequate design or management of warehouse systems will jeopardize the achievement of required customer service levels and the maintenance of stock integrity, and result in unnecessarily high costs.

Some of the recent pressures on logistics – forever increasing customer service levels, inventory reduction, time compression and cost minimization – have inevitably changed the structure of supply chains and the position and working of warehouses within the supply chains.

Certainly the old concept of warehouses as places to store goods has been superseded. Warehouses, perhaps better referred to as distribution centres, exist primarily to facilitate the movement of goods to the end user. There are exceptions such as strategic stock-holding, but in general commercial applications, effective movement of goods to the customer is the key, even if some inventory has to be held to achieve this.

Warehouses come in all shapes and sizes, from facilities of a few hundred square metres handling modest throughputs, to – despite the previous comments – large capital-intensive installations with storage capacities in the 50,000-pallet-plus range, and very high – hundreds of pallets per hour – throughputs.

However, the concept of throughput rather than storage, and the pressure to reduce inventory with increased customer service have also seen the development of distribution centres that do not hold stock – the 'stockless depot' – such as transhipment depots and cross-docking operations, of which more later.

Another issue that has exercised minds in recent years has been the level of technology to utilize in warehousing operations. The range spans from conventional warehousing – racking and shelving with fork-lift or even manual operations – through to automated computer-controlled systems with conveyors and AGVs, and on to robotic applications. The reasons for the choice of a particular technology level are not always clear cut, and run the gamut of financial, marketing and other factors, from company image or flexibility for future change through to personal perception of the appropriateness of a particular technology to a particular business or company.

STRATEGIC ISSUES AFFECTING WAREHOUSING

Since warehouses, stores and distribution centres should operate as integral component elements within supply chains, key decisions when setting up such facilities must be determined by the overall logistics strategies for service and cost. The factors that should be considered include the following:

- *Market and product base stability.* Long-term market expectations for growth and for how the product range may develop will influence decisions on the size and location of a warehouse facility, including space for potential expansion. These considerations will also impact on the perceived need for future flexibility, which in turn can influence decisions on the type of warehouse and the level of technology.
- *Type of goods to be handled.* Goods handled can include raw materials, work in progress, spare parts, packaging materials and finished goods in a span of material types, sizes, weights, product lives and other characteristics. The units to be handled can range from individual small items through packages, drums,

sacks, palletized loads and on up to ISO containers. Special requirements for temperature and humidity may also have to be met, and all of these will impact on the type of warehouse and technology level.

- *Type of facility, size and location.* The type of operation, the design capacity and size of a warehouse and its location will all be influenced if not directly determined by its specific role and position in the supply chain, and the role, capacity and location of any other facilities in the chain. The customer base, amount of inventory, the need for inventory reduction, time compression in the supply chain and the overall service levels should all be considered when deciding on type, size and location. A further consideration here is whether the facility should be an own-account operation run by the company or outsourced and run by a third party.

- *Inventory and inventory location.* Within a supply chain there is the issue not only of what goods to hold and in what quantities, but also in what locations. Options can include distribution centres dedicated to specific markets or parts of the product range, distribution centres dedicated to serving specific geographic areas, or regional distribution centres that hold for example the fast-moving product lines, with the slower lines held only in a national distribution centre. The choice depends on such factors as customer base, product range and service levels required.

- *Level of technology.* The choice of the level of technology has already been noted, and the range can go from very basic installations with high manual input and minimum mechanization to automated and robotic installations. The decision can be influenced by company-wide strategic marketing or employment policies, as well as by more obvious financial considerations and the ability to achieve specified levels of throughput and provide the required levels of customer service. Other factors can include requirements for flexible operation to meet significant demand fluctuations such as seasonal variations, and the perceived future stability and growth of the market and product range. The level of technology adopted in any particular application should be chosen because it most nearly matches the given requirements and objectives. It is not true that automation or similar technologies are right in every case. It is true that good, probably computer-based, communication and information systems are vital in every application, irrespective of the technology level.

- *Choice of unit load.* The choice of unit load or loads – pallets, roll or cage pallets, tote bins – will be determined by the nature and characteristics of the goods passing along the supply chain, and this clearly encompasses an enormously wide range of goods, unit quantities, and pack types and sizes. This may appear as a very mundane factor more subject to operational than to strategic influences.

However, within the warehouse it can influence the choice of handling equipment and the choice and sizing of storage systems. In the wider context it will affect transport operations in terms of vehicle loading and unloading, and vehicle utilization.

COSTS

Since the early 1980s the Institute of Logistics and Transport has commissioned and published an annual survey of the distribution costs incurred by industry, analysed by the costs of inventory, transport, storage and handling of the inventory (warehousing), and systems. The movement trend of the figures has been somewhat variable, but the cost of warehousing, as a percentage of sales turnover, appears to be settling out at a figure of about 2 per cent or less – from an initial figure in the early to mid-80s of 2.5 to 3.5 per cent. As a percentage of the total costs of distribution the warehousing element ranges between about 30 and 40 per cent. By any measure, this represents a considerable expense to industry.

The operating costs of the individual components within warehousing clearly depend on such factors as the nature of the warehousing operation and the industry. The Freight Transport Association (FTA) annually publishes broad guidelines (*The Manager's Guide to Distribution Costs*) in which it emphasizes the great variability of such costs, but suggests the dominant costs are staff, accounting for about half the total, with building costs being a further quarter.

More detailed cost surveys for 'conventional' warehouse operations – reach trucks and pallet racking with case picking at ground level – have indicated average annual costs of:

- staff – up to 50%, of which half is accounted for by the order picking staff;
- building (rent or equivalent) – 25%;
- building services (maintenance, services, insurance, rates) – 15%;
- equipment – 10 to 15%.

From a cost point of view, the two key factors that emerge from these figures, on which designers and managers should put particular emphasis, are building space utilization and the design and management of order picking systems.

THE ROLE OF WAREHOUSES

Commercial warehouses and distribution centres have a prime objective, which is to facilitate the movement of goods from suppliers out to customers. In order to achieve this effectively they may have to hold stock, but that is not their *raison d'être*. Some stores on the other hand have a specific objective of stocking goods and material against particular contingencies, which it is hoped will never occur. Examples include some major spare parts such as steam turbine rotors for a power station, or emergency/disaster relief supplies. It must be said, though, that when such items are required, speed is of the essence.

The adoption of just-in-time and similar approaches to material supply, allied to computer-based information systems that provide up-to-the-minute information on stock availability and locations, have certainly challenged the need for holding stock and having warehouses at all. It is true that inventory levels have come down significantly over time. Nevertheless, even with closer integration of production and logistics planning, and accurate demand forecasting techniques, in many supply chains there will remain a level of mismatch and indeed conflict between supply optimization and demand. There will also remain the need to consolidate goods from different sources, for break bulk operations and for value-adding activities such as postponement.

Hence there are still valid reasons for holding stock, and for continuing to have warehouses and distribution depots in supply chains, including:

- to provide a buffer to smooth variations between supply and demand;
- to enable economies of long production runs in manufacturing;
- to provide a buffer between production runs in manufacturing;
- to enable procurement savings through large purchases;
- to cover for seasonal fluctuations and peaks, eg the Christmas build-up;
- to provide a wide range of different products, from different suppliers, in one location;
- to cover for planned or breakdown production shutdowns.

Other significant reasons for warehousing operations have included more operational objectives such as:

- order picking and assembly;
- packaging and repackaging;
- minor assembly operations to build specific product variants – postponement;
- kit marshalling for production and assembly.

Current developments in just-in-time, lean manufacture and similar approaches to inventory reduction and time compression will continue to depress inventories, and will also perhaps change the 'centre of gravity' of where inventory is held, pushing it further back up the supply chain. This however will not eliminate entirely the need for stock and the facilities in which to hold it.

The emphasis for warehousing has now shifted and become focused on:

- facilitating the flow of goods to the customer;
- meeting the requirements of customer service standards;
- incorporating value-added activities, such as postponement, as a means of reducing the numbers of product lines or stock keeping units (SKUs) in a system, and increasing the flexibility to meet customer requirements.

TYPES OF WAREHOUSE OR DISTRIBUTION CENTRE

Warehouses or distribution centres can operate at national or regional level, determined by the supply chain structure and strategic decisions on inventory levels and customer service, ie national distribution centres (NDCs) and regional distribution centres (RDCs). These can use conventional handling and storage systems, or can be designed to use automated or even robotic technology. At a local level there may be 'stockrooms' that serve a limited number of retail outlets within a close geographic area. They are stock-holding facilities.

However, a fundamental distinction to make is between stock-holding warehouses and stockless depots, and the latter have been receiving more attention in recent years as enabling fast stock movement and inventory reduction. There are two basic forms for a stockless depot: transhipment depots and cross-docking.

Transhipment depots tend to be located to serve specific areas of customer concentration. Orders for customers are picked at a stock-holding depot, typically an NDC, loaded to road trailers in reverse drop sequence and dispatched to the transhipment depot overnight, where the trailer is dropped. The overnight tractor returns to the NDC with the previous day's empty trailer. In the morning, a local tractor unit picks up the overnight trailer, delivers the customer orders and returns the empty trailer to the transhipment depot. The implications of this system are that all order picking, down to individual customer level, is carried out at the NDC, and there is no stock held at the transhipment depot, which need be only a small secure site without staff.

Cross-docking tends to operate out of an 'empty' building. Product ordered by product line (SKU) from suppliers in quantities sufficient to meet the next day's total customer orders is delivered to the site and unloaded, often along one (goods receipt) face of the building. It then goes directly to a (manual or mechanized) sorting system, which distributes the required quantities of each product to allocated order locations so that the orders build up, product by product, until the orders are complete. Completed orders are then loaded to outbound delivery vehicles parked along the dispatch face of the building. Dispatch vehicles leave to meet specified departure times to reach customer locations by given deadlines. The term 'pick by line' is often used to describe this sort of operation.

In a typical application, for fresh produce, products would start arriving from market gardeners at say 2 pm, build up to a peak at say 8 pm, and then slowly fall back as the evening progressed. Outbound vehicles might start to get away from say 7 pm onwards, to meet travel and delivery times to the customers' outlets. By say 3 am the building would be empty.

This concept can be very labour-intensive, with operators moving stock from the incoming vehicles to order collation and dispatch vehicle loading, using pallet trucks and manual handling of cases off pallets. On the other hand, there is no inventory, and goods movement is fast, giving short lead times.

Advanced systems can also be used in this situation, using conveyor sortation technology, enabled by techniques such as bar-coding to recognize individual items or cases. This is very capital-intensive.

WAREHOUSE OPERATIONS

As will be discussed later, there are various methods and equipment types that can be used for storing and handling material in warehousing operations, and for order picking and order assembly, and any specific application should be designed to meet the requirements of the supply chain within which it functions. Nevertheless, there is a basic flow of material that is common to most warehouse operations, although this may be modified in particular cases such as cross-docking operations. Figure 15.1 illustrates the basic warehouse functions and material flows.

Figure 15.1 shows the separation of reserve storage from order picking. The aim is to limit the distance that order picking staff would otherwise have to travel to access the full range of stock items, especially in warehouses holding high stock volumes. By limiting the amount of stock held in the picking area, travel distances for picking are reduced. Separation also helps to reduce the interference between order picking and bulk material movements. The risk however is that by concentrating all the picking activity into a small area, congestion will occur. Hence there is a trade-off between minimizing travel distance and avoiding congestion in the

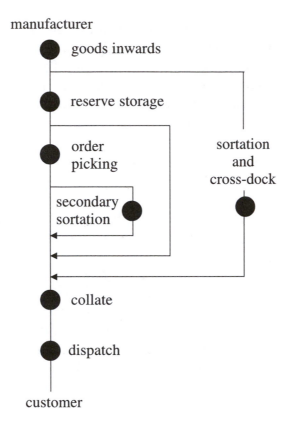

Figure 15.1 Warehouse functions and material flows

picking area. Clearly, however, if the total inventory for a stock item is small, it will not be appropriate to hold it in separate locations.

As will appear later, another significant compromise has to be faced in designing storage systems, between the most effective use of expensive building space and the ability to access stock quickly.

Warehouse functions are as follows:

- *Goods inwards.* This includes the physical unloading of incoming transport, checking, recording of receipts, and deciding where the received goods are to be put away in the warehouse. It can also include such activities as unpacking and repackaging, quality control checks and temporary quarantine storage for goods awaiting clearance by quality control.
- *Reserve storage.* Reserve or back-up storage, which is the largest space user in many warehouses, holds the bulk of warehouse stock in identifiable locations.

Goods are moved to reserve storage from goods inwards, and the locations communicated to the warehouse information system.

- *Replenishment.* This is the movement of goods in larger than order quantities, for example a whole pallet at a time, from reserve storage to order picking, to ensure that order picking locations do not become empty. Maintaining stock availability for order picking is important for achieving high levels of order fill.
- *Order picking.* Goods are selected from order picking stock in the required quantities and at the required time to meet customer orders. Picking often involves break bulk operations, when goods are received from suppliers in, say, whole pallet quantities, but are ordered by customers in less than pallet quantities. However, if a particular product is required in a sufficiently large quantity, for example a whole pallet load, it is picked directly from reserve storage. Order picking is important for achieving high levels of customer service; it traditionally also takes a high proportion of the total warehouse staff complement and is expensive. The good design and management of picking systems and operations are consequently vital to effective warehouse performance.
- *Secondary sortation.* For small sizes of order, it is sometimes appropriate to batch a number of orders together and treat them as 'one' order for picking purposes. In this case, the picked batch will have to be sorted down to individual orders, ie secondary sortation, before dispatch.
- *Sortation.* In some circumstances the use of information technology means that the ultimate destinations of a significant proportion of the goods coming into a warehouse are known. Recent developments have therefore used this facility to enable goods coming into a warehouse to be sorted into specific customer orders immediately on arrival, sometimes using high-speed sortation conveyors. The goods then go directly to order collation. This approach has been used for some years in cross-docking operations for grocery produce by major supermarkets.
- *Collate.* After picking, goods are brought together and consolidated as completed orders made ready for dispatch to customers. This can involve packing into dispatch outer cases and cartons, labelling operations, and stretch and shrink wrapping for load protection and stability.
- *Dispatch.* Picked and collated and packed goods are assembled for loading to outbound vehicles, and onward dispatch to the next 'node' in the supply chain – intermediate distribution centre, next transport leg such as air or ship, or direct to final customer.

The above list indicates the principal activities found in warehouse operations. In addition there can be a range of subsidiary activities such as packaging material stores, sub-assembly and packing areas, truck battery-charging area, equipment maintenance shop, offices and amenities, and in some cases services to support specific product environments such as chill or frozen goods stores.

OBJECTIVES AND PRINCIPLES OF GOOD WAREHOUSE DESIGN AND MANAGEMENT

There is an oft-quoted and almost universal definition, which used to be said to encapsulate the end point of good materials handling, and which in many ways sums up the objectives of all supply chain operations, including warehousing: *Getting the right goods in the right form, in the required quantities, to the right place, at the required time, in the required condition, safely and at the minimum overall system cost.* In some ways this statement is 'old hat', having been around for many years, but it is hard to fault as a statement of what distribution is trying to achieve.

Setting out a statement of good practice for the design and management of warehouse systems however is more open to discussion, and different authorities have expressed this in different ways. One early author produced a list of over 30 'principles'. A more succinct summary of the key principles, within an overall context of minimum overall system cost, and providing the required quality of customer service in terms of timeliness, accuracy and completeness of order fill, is set out in the following sections.

Choice of unit load

A unit load is an assembly of individual items or packages, usually of a like kind, to enable convenient composite movement, whether manual or mechanized. Examples include pallets in a range of materials although wood is still the most common, roll cage pallets, post pallets, cage pallets, tote containers whether plastic or steel, and ISO containers. The benefits of effective unitization include moving maximum quantities of goods per journey, so minimizing the number of movements, the ability to use standard handling and storage equipments, better use of storage space, stock protection and security, and facilitating the interface between warehousing and transport operations including vehicle loading and unloading.

Use of building space

As already indicated, warehouse space represents a very significant proportion of total warehouse costs, and space should be used effectively. Considerations for effective space utilization include:

- minimizing total stock-holding and eliminating obsolete stock;
- careful selection of appropriate storage and handling systems;
- effective use of building height, eg mezzanine floors where appropriate;
- minimizing aisle numbers and widths consistent with access and safety;
- use of random location systems for stock rather than fixed locations (see Chapter 16).

It is also important that there is clear access to stocked goods, and one of the important 'trade-offs' in warehouse design is to achieve good use of space whilst maintaining unrestricted stock access. Careful analysis of stock and throughput data will suggest where the emphasis should be put in any particular situation or for particular parts of the product range.

Utilization of resources

The design and management of warehouses should enable effective and efficient use of resources, including monitoring of equipment availability and utilization. In one warehouse example, inspection of the hour meters on the 12 fork-lift trucks showed an average use per truck of one hour per working day.

Minimum movement

Movement uses resources and, except for automated systems, involves operating staff time. Warehouse layout and the positioning of the various warehouse operations within the building clearly affect the amount of movement, as does the locating of stock within the storage systems. Ways to minimize movement include:

- locating 'popular' or fast-moving goods close to dispatch to minimize travel distances;
- separation of order picking and reserve stock to concentrate picking activity into the smallest feasible area whilst avoiding congestion;
- providing handling equipment to minimize manual effort and movement;
- computer planning of warehouse movement routes for minimum travel;
- movement planning to maximize people and handling equipment utilization and avoid travelling without payloads, eg dual cycling, in which both outward and return movements of an item of handling equipment are utilized for carrying goods.

Control and information systems

Any warehouse installation should have an effective, fast, accurate and flexible communication and information system. The functionality should include the ability to:

- log stock movements and maintain balances;
- control stock location;
- monitor productivity and the utilization and availability of resources such as handling and storage equipment;
- track the movement of goods through the system, and effective and ideally instantaneous communication between operators and the management system;
- sort order requirements into appropriate order picking tasks;
- plan optimum movement routes including order picking.

Product integrity

Warehousing and handling systems should be so designed and managed that product is maintained in a suitable state for the final customers. This implies having systems in place to minimize damage, loss or deterioration, and to satisfy stock rotation or product life requirements, and any legal constraints on storage environment such as temperature limits.

Working conditions and safety

Traditionally many warehouse tasks have been repetitive, monotonous, sometimes arduous, and often not in a particularly congenial environment. This is an area of increasing importance. Some recent significant innovations in fork-lift truck design, for example, have been specifically aimed at improving operator environment and minimizing risk of repetitive strain injury. Lighting levels, temperature and humidity, and hygiene also impact directly on operator environment and therefore on operator performance in the long term.

Safety has always been of prime importance in warehousing because of the amount of movement, lifting and manual handling involved. Even with the levels of mechanization and automation in some modern installations, safety remains of key importance. This is given further emphasis by the amount of legislation that has come from the Health and Safety Executive (UK), and the various European directives that have come from Brussels.

Safe working practice is a moral obligation and also makes economic sense by minimizing lost staff time, the costs that can be incurred in accident investigations, and the possible legal costs and claims that may be incurred. Accidents also result in material and equipment loss and damage, and loss of output.

Environmental issues

Environmental awareness has increased and is increasing, and is an aspect that more and more has to be taken into account in the design and management of warehouse systems. The obvious example is the packaging regulations and the additional responsibility and cost that have been imposed on suppliers.

COMMUNICATION AND INFORMATION

Warehousing is in essence a simple operation, although it can go spectacularly wrong. The usual reasons for performance failure relate to inadequate information and communication systems.

It is the authors' view that a good communication, monitoring and information system within the warehouse, and also communication out to the wider supply chain, are a *sine qua non* of effective warehouse management. Without such a system, and no matter how good the facilities and indeed the management and staff performance, overall performance will not achieve its full potential and may indeed fall far short of it.

PACKAGING AND UNIT LOADS

Before moving on to the detail of unit load handling and storage systems, it is appropriate to note the significance of packaging and unit loads to these operations.

Packaging

Definitions of packaging include 'the art, science, and technology of preparing goods for transport and sale' (BSI), and 'a means of ensuring the safe delivery of a product to the ultimate consumer in sound condition and at minimum overall cost'. Packaging is an integral part of the supply chain, and the design and use of packaging impact not only on storage and handling, but also on other functions such as production, marketing and the most appropriate type of unit load to be used.

Packaging fulfils different functions:

- to protect and preserve a product from physical, chemical and mechanical damage, deterioration or contamination;

- to contain the product;
- to facilitate ease of handling and ease of unitizing, and in some situations to act as a measure and dispenser;
- to communicate information, safety instructions and instructions for product use;
- to act as a marketing aid through appearance and presentation.

It needs to be compatible with the processes through which it will pass, such as filling, and with packaging machinery, and the design must also take account of potential reuse and of the disposal of the package after use.

It is possible to categorize packaging, and one example of this is:

- primary package in direct contact with the product, to protect, contain and seal, eg sachet, tube, sack or plastic envelope;
- secondary package, containing one or more primary packages, to provide physical protection;
- outer packaging or transport pack.

During handling and movement through the supply chain, packaging will be subject to potential damage and deterioration, including:

- mechanical shock, impact, vibration, compression or abrasion;
- environmental factors such as water (condensation, rain, sea water), pressure and temperature changes, light and other forms of radiation, odours and other contamination, and exposure to air;
- other potential causes of damage including infestation, vermin, fungi and bacteria;
- pilferage.

Unit loads

The unit load concept puts product in or on to appropriate standard modules for handling and storage, movement, loading and unloading. It enables the use of standard equipments irrespective of the products being handled, at the same time as achieving product protection and security, and economy in the use of space, and the amount of handling required for a given quantity of material.

Much of physical distribution is structured round the unit load concept, and the choice of unit load is fundamental to the effectiveness and economics of a supply chain. Examples of unit loads include:

- Small containers such as tote bins, made in galvanized steel or plastic, and used for small parts storage and handling.
- Wooden pallets made to standard sizes, although there are different standards, which can cause some problems with international movement. For example, the dominant pallet in Europe is the Europal (1,200 millimetres × 800 millimetres), and the dominant UK pallet is the ISO (1,200 millimetres × 1,000 millimetres). In addition to pallet size, other variables include the pallet construction: two-way or four-way fork entry, reversible or non-reversible (double-sided or single-sided), open- or close-boarded. The wooden pallet is probably the most commonly used type of unit load.
- Cage and box pallets, often of metal construction, fitted with corner posts and sides to contain the products, and usually stackable by means of bell ends fitted on the bottoms of the corner posts.
- Roll cage pallets, which consist of bases fitted with dolly wheels and cage sides. These are widely used in wholesale grocery distribution.
- Intermediate bulk containers (IBCs) represent the link between bulk handling and unit load handling, and are designed for payloads of one to two tonnes. They are used for solid particulate products such as building products (sand or gravel) and chemicals, and some are specifically designed for liquid products. There are rigid IBCs usually made of metal or plastic, collapsible IBCs made of canvas for ease of folding and return, and low-cost 'one-trip' IBCs made of fibreboard or similar. IBCs are used for in-plant storage or transport, and they cut out the need for conventionally sized sacks. They are usually designed for top filling and bottom emptying, and are handled by standard fork-lift trucks. They can often be block stacked.
- ISO (International Standards Organisation) freight containers are made in a range of standard external sizes that can fit and stack together for holding at container terminals and for loading on to land and sea transport. Standard handling, loading/unloading and stowing can therefore be used, which helps to reduce transport turn-round times and provide secure transit. Different designs of container, within the standard external dimensions, enable their use for general cargo, bulk solids, bulk liquids and refrigerated goods.

SUMMARY

This chapter highlighted and summarized some of the critical points of principle and key strategic issues that impact on the design and management of warehouse systems. These must be taken into account if warehouses are to function effectively within the wider context of the supply chain.

Warehouses and their handling systems are not stand-alone activities. Their roles and objectives should be determined by the overall supply chain within which they operate. They should integrate closely with the other components in the supply chain. They are expensive and should be well designed and effectively managed, and the way they operate will have an immediate impact on both customer service and costs.

The warehousing section of this book is concerned primarily with the handling and storage of unit loads. It is however considered that the basic principles that underpin the subject area are also valid in the context of other handling and storage operations such as the storing and handling of bulk solids.

The concluding section of this chapter outlined the significance of packaging and unit loads in the supply chain, and summarized their use and benefits.

16

Storage systems and equipment

INTRODUCTION

The storage function in the design of a warehouse is a major consideration if for no other reason than that it frequently occupies more space than any other activity in the warehouse, and hence accounts for a significant part of the building costs. Operationally storage systems impact on access to stock, product protection and integrity, the discipline of correct stock location and rotation, and the ease or otherwise of stock management.

The type of material passing through warehouses varies enormously, with different sizes, weights, shapes, levels of fragility and hazard characteristics. A major benefit of unit loads such as pallets is that they enable the use of standard storage systems and handling equipment, irrespective of what is handled. Nevertheless variations in throughput and order picking patterns make it appropriate to have different types of storage system, with different operational characteristics, so that systems can be selected that most closely match the needs of the wider system within which they are to operate.

Suggested clearances, vertical and horizontal, to allow safe access for goods into and out of storage equipment, and other guidance for the design and use of storage equipment can be found in a series of codes of practice published by the Storage Equipment Manufacturers Association (SEMA).

The key factors influencing the choice of a storage system are:

- the nature and characteristics of the goods and unit loads held;
- the effective utilization of building volume – horizontal and vertical;
- good access to stock;
- compatibility with information system requirements;
- maintenance of stock condition and integrity;
- personnel safety;
- overall system cost.

When comparing the costs of different storage systems, it is not only the storage equipment cost that should be taken into account. Other cost elements that could be affected by the choice of system include:

- space – land, building and building services;
- fire protection;
- handling equipment including maintenance;
- staff;
- information management systems.

One way of classifying storage systems could be:

- bulk storage for solids, such as silos, bunkers and stockpiles;
- loose item storage, eg casting and fabrications held loose on the floor;
- pallet storage systems;
- small item storage for individual items or small unit loads;
- non-standard unit loads such as long loads.

This chapter is concerned with unit load storage, and bulk storage systems will not be discussed.

STOCK LOCATION

The location of stock within a store is an important aspect of stock management and can be considered at different levels of detail. For example, the overall positioning of stock within particular areas of the warehouse can influence the total amount of movement required to get material into and out of stock. It can also affect the efficiency with which order picking operations can be carried out by affecting the distance order pickers have to travel to get to required stock.

At a lower level of detail, it is important to locate certain stock items for ease of operator lifting and handling. For example, heavy items should be near to ground level or to the level of the picking trolley platform to minimize operator lifting. Fast-moving product lines that have to be accessed frequently should be located at optimum operator arm movement levels, and not too high or too low (see Manual Handling Directive 90/269/EEC).

Fixed and random stock location

The effective storage capacity of a given installation is influenced by whether individual product lines are held in fixed and dedicated locations, or whether any product line can be located randomly in any available storage location.

If a fixed location system is used, any specific location can only be used for its designated product line, and never for any other product. Consequently the installation must be designed with enough capacity to hold the maximum stock of every product line.

With random location, when any empty location can be utilized for any product line as required, the size of installation can be reduced, since the probability of every product being in stock at maximum stock level at the same time is virtually nil. In this case, the required storage capacity can be calculated from the sum of the average stock levels for all product lines, inflated by a factor, say 10 per cent, to account for fluctuations about the average.

In any storage installation, the utilization of storage locations will always be less than 100 per cent since the movement of material creates empty locations that can never be refilled instantaneously. This effect must also be taken into account when calculating the number of storage locations required in a random location store.

Random location is often used for reserve storage, which tends to take up the largest area in a warehouse, and fixed location for order picking stock, which enables the use of concepts such as popularity storage – fast-moving product lines located to minimize picker movement.

As with other aspects of warehouse management, the ability to record quickly what stock is held in every location, and which locations are empty and therefore available for use, is vital for the effective management of the stock and the storage installation. Implicit in this is a requirement for an effective location identification system for stock locations.

PALLETIZED STORAGE

Block stacking

Block stacking does not use any storage equipment. Loaded pallets are placed directly on the floor and built up in stacks, one pallet on top of another to a maximum stable height (typically not more than six times the shortest plan dimension of the pallet, eg maximum stack height 6 metres for 1,200 × 1,000-millimetre pallets). Rows of stacked pallets are laid out side by side (see Figure 16.1). Typical clearances in a block stack would be 100 millimetres between each row of pallets and 50 millimetres between pallets in each row. When removing stock for use, free access is only to the pallets at the top and front of each row.

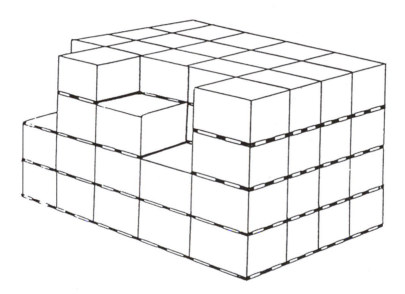

Figure 16.1 Block stacking

The pallet loads must be capable of carrying the superimposed pallets, and the top of each load should be flat enough to provide a stable base for the next pallet. If these conditions cannot be met, pallet converters or post pallets can be used, which carry the superimposed load directly to the next pallet below in the stack via corner posts or other means, and no weight is imposed on the 'payload'.

Any one row should only contain pallets of the same product, to avoid double handling, and should be emptied completely before being refilled in order to avoid trapping old stock at the backs of rows.

The front-to-back depth of any row should not exceed six pallets in from the truck access aisle, for safe fork-lift driving, which means blocks of 12 deep, back to back. In practice layouts may well incorporate rows of different depths to accommodate products with different stock levels.

Block stacking is suitable for that part of the product range where there are few product lines, each with high stock level, and where very strict first-in-first-out (FIFO) movement of stock is not required. The advantages are good use of area (although not necessarily of building height), flexibility to change the layout of the blocks and quick access to stock for rapid throughput.

Note that any working store will always have some unoccupied locations. For block stacking, where any row should be emptied before being refilled, typically some 30 per cent of the individual pallet locations can be empty at any one time. The effective utilization of the pallet positions is therefore 70 per cent. When designing for a random location block storage installation with capacity of P pallets, the number of pallet locations to be provided should be of the order of P/0.7. If a holding capacity for 1,000 pallets is required, then 1,000/0.7 = 1,430 (rounded) locations should be provided.

Drive-in and drive-through racking

Although this is a racked storage system, it is operationally similar to block storage. There should only be one product line in each row, and the effective utilization of the pallet positions is about 70 per cent. The racking structure supports the weight of the pallets so this system is suitable for high stock product lines, where strict FIFO movement is not required, but where the pallet loads are not strong enough or of regular enough shape to carry superimposed loads. Since pallets are supported by the structure, the height of the installation is not limited by pallet strength or stability.

This system consists of vertical support frames, tied at the top, with cantilever pallet support beams at different heights. Fork trucks enter the racking between the vertical supports to access the pallets sitting on the cantilever beams (see Figure 16.2). If access is all from one end the racking is called drive-in, and if pallets are fed in at one end and removed at the other the term drive-through is used.

Access for the fork trucks within the racking is tight because the cantilever supports have to be narrower than the width of the pallets, and pallets have to be moved in and out of the racking in a raised position. This tends to limit the speed of movement of pallets into and out of the racking, and driver strain can be a factor.

Since pallets are only supported along each side, pallet condition is important, and due to the narrow truck access the floor and the racking have to be built to tight tolerances to minimize the risk of the trucks colliding with the racking.

Figure 16.2   Drive-in racking (courtesy of Redirack Limited)

The suggested maximum height is 10 to 11 metres, with the front-to-back row depth of six pallets in from the fork truck access aisle, or 12 deep if back to back.

Push back racking

This type of racking is a comparatively recent development. Like drive-in racking it gives high-density storage and can be built to any height up to the maximum lift height of the lift trucks accessing it. Pallets can be stored up to about four deep in the racking, on either side of the access aisle.

Each level in each vertical row of the racking (let us call it a lane) is fitted with inclined rails along which trolleys can move, the incline sloping down to the front of the racking (see Figure 16.3). The trolleys 'nest' when empty. Incoming pallets

Figure 16.3 Push back racking (courtesy of Link 51 (Storage Products))

are lowered on to the trolleys and pushed up the incline and into the racking by fork-lift truck until the lane is full. As an outgoing pallet is withdrawn, the pallet behind moves down to replace it, until the lane is empty and can be refilled.

The basic operational difference between this system and block stacking or drive-in racking is the increased selectivity achieved. There should be no mix of product lines in any one lane, but there can be between the lanes in any row.

Adjustable pallet racking – APR

Adjustable pallet racking is probably the most widely used type of pallet racking, and offers free access to every pallet held. It can be built to match the lift height of any fork-lift truck.

It consists of upright end frames and pairs of horizontal beams on which the pallets are located, and beam heights are adjustable to suit the height of the pallet loads being stored (see Figure 16.4). In theory, to optimize the use of vertical space, beam heights can be altered if pallet load heights change. In practice, this does not often occur.

Figure 16.4   Adjustable pallet racking (courtesy of Redirack Limited)

Unit loads other than pallets can be stored using APR, and there is a range of accessories such as drum supports and channel supports for post pallets to facilitate this.

The conventional way of laying out APR is to have one row single deep at each end of the installation, with back-to-back rows in between. This gives every truck aisle access to two rows of racking, and minimizes the number of aisles required. Guidelines for the horizontal and vertical spacing of the racking components to enable safe access to the pallets are given in the SEMA codes of practice.

APR is a flexible, versatile storage system, which gives excellent stock access. It is simple in concept, easily laid out, and damaged parts are easily replaced. It can be suitable for fast-moving and slow-moving stock, and for product lines with high or low levels of palletized stock-holding. Typical utilizations for pallet positions in random location APR can lie in the range 90 to 95 per cent, depending partly on the effectiveness of the warehouse management system handling the location information.

However, APR does not make good use of building volume. In a typical installation using fork-reach trucks, each aisle (say 2.8 metres) is wider than the back-to-back pallets in the racking (2.1 metres, with ISO pallets positioned 1,000 millimetres deep into the racking). Hence, before allowing for any other space requirement such as transverse aisles, the building space utilization is well below 50 per cent, and this is important in the context of the building cost figures seen in the previous chapter.

High rack stacker trucks, equipped with rotating or sliding pallet handling mechanisms, do not need to turn in an aisle to access pallet locations, and in APR can typically operate in aisles of 1.8 metre or less. They can also lift higher than reach trucks, and these two effects increase the space utilization. However, there are cost penalties in providing the required floor strength and flatness for working in high but narrow aisles, and the trucks are significantly more expensive than reach trucks.

Double deep racking

If some loss of totally free access to stock can be accepted, although not nearly as severe as in block, drive-in or push back storage, space utilization can be improved using double deep racking. This supports pallets on pairs of beams as in APR, but improves space utilization by eliminating alternate access aisles, and using a 'double reach' fork-lift truck, which can access not just one but two pallets deep into the racking. The concept is illustrated in Figure 16.5.

The price of this space saving is the requirement for double deep reach trucks to access the stock, more costly than ordinary reach trucks, and some loss of selectivity since pallets are now stacked two deep into the racking, ie loss of absolute FIFO stock rotation. Pallet position utilization in double deep racking is likely to be of the order of 85 per cent. A practical requirement is that the bottom level of pallets in the racking has to be supported on a raised beam to allow the legs of a double reach truck to fit under the racking structure when accessing the pallet furthest in from the aisle. In single deep APR the bottom pallet can sit directly on the floor.

Figure 16.5 Double deep racking (courtesy of Redirack Limited)

Powered mobile racking

Powered mobile racking is effectively single deep APR, with the racking, except the end or outer rows, mounted on electrically powered base frames, which move on rails set into the floor as shown in Figure 16.6. Typically only one fork truck access aisle is provided, and the rack sections are moved to open up access as required to any specific pallet location. Floor loadings are high. Operationally it has similar characteristics to APR, but is slower in use, and the pallet position utilization is likely to be similar to APR at 90 to 95 per cent. Safety trips are fitted to each side of each mobile base frame to cut power in the event of any obstruction.

This type of system is expensive in equipment and floor costs, and it tends to be slow in operation. However it gives very dense storage, and is suitable for the typically large number of product lines forming the 'Pareto tail' of a product range,

Figure 16.6 Powered mobile racking (courtesy of Redirack Limited)

where individual product lines have low stock and low throughput. It also finds use in cold-store applications where space costs are especially high, and where temperature variations are reduced by cutting the air space in the storage area.

Pallet live storage

Live storage systems are made up of inclined gravity roll conveyors, laid out side by side and at a number of vertical levels (see Figure 16.7). Pallets are fed in at the higher end and removed as required at the lower. Such a system imposes FIFO. The only accessible pallets are at the outfeed end, so any one lane should only hold pallets of the same product line.

The incline of the conveyors is critical in these installations, and is perhaps best obtained by trial and error, by testing examples of the pallets that will be using the system. Braking devices and end stops are usually fitted to control the movement of pallets towards the discharge end.

Figure 16.7 Pallet live storage (courtesy of Link 51 (Storage Products))

Pallet live storage systems are suitable for very fast-moving product lines. They can provide effective order picking regimes, which automatically refill empty locations, and also provide physical separation between picking and replenishment operations.

Pallet live storage is expensive and pallet position utilization is not always high – say 70 per cent. Pallet type and condition are critical, and in some applications slave pallets may have to be used.

High bay and other automated storage installations

High bay warehouses, with racking accessed by computer-controlled stacker cranes, can be built with single deep or double deep racking. Stacker cranes typically require 1.5- to 1.6-metre aisles for standard pallet handling, and installations can be 40 to 45 metres high. They therefore tend to make good use of land area.

They are operationally similar to APR or double deep installations, with similar pallet position utilization figures, but they can be designed for very high rates of throughput, with 24-hour operation. These systems will be covered in more detail in Chapter 19.

Other automated storage and handling systems include block stacking accessed by computer controlled overhead cranes, and racked storage with pallets accessed by robot trolleys. These will also be discussed further in Chapter 19.

PALLETIZED STORAGE – COMPARISON OF SYSTEMS

One way to compare storage systems is the use of a matrix to 'rank' the importance of the different characteristics. This can be done by grading on a scale of say 5 (good) to 1 (poor), or purely qualitatively from excellent to poor. One author's (very subjective) example is shown as Table 16.1. Such a ranking will depend on the actual circumstances within which the storage system is to work.

SMALL ITEM STORAGE SYSTEMS

As with palletized storage systems, there is a range of different types of system for holding small items. In some cases these are operationally similar to their pallet holding 'big brothers'.

With small item storage it often happens that different systems are incorporated into one installation. For example, drawer units and cabinets may be built into a shelving installation. Consequently the concept of standard equipment sizes and modularity is important for small item storage systems.

Shelving – short and long span

Shelving is generally made from standard modular components that allow installations of different heights, vertical shelf spacing and shelf depths. The typical standard span width is 1 metre, but long span shelving is also available that facilitates holding longer items of stock. Subdividers can be used to provide more but smaller locations where this is appropriate for the stock being held.

Shelving can be accessed in various ways – from ground-floor level, from mezzanine levels or from fixed path or free path lifting equipment such as fork trucks and picking cranes. A variant on this concept is cantilever shelving, which is supported from the back and sides, and gives completely clear access from the front and hence flexibility for holding items of different lengths.

Table 16.1 Comparison of palletized storage systems

Factor	Block	Drive-in	APR	DD	VNA	Mobile	Live	Push Back	High Bay
Use of Floor Area	5	5	1	3	3	5	5	5	4
Use of Building Volume *	5 to 2	5	2	3	3	5 +	5	5	5
Ability to Go High	1	4	4	4	5	4	4	4	5 +
Speed of Throughput	4	3	5	4	5	1	5	3	5
Access to Stock	1	1	5	4	5	5	2	2	5
Suitability for Picking	2	1	5	4	4	1	5	1	1
Stock Rotation (FIFO)	1	1	5	4	5	5	5	3	5
Product Damage	1	3	4	4	4	4	4	4	5
Easy to Manage	3	3	5	4	5	5	5	3	5
Fire Protection	5	3	4	3	3	1	3	2	2
Rack Cost	5 +								
Other Costs†	no cost	3	4	3	3	1	1	1	3

* depends on building height
† depend on overall system

APR   adjustable pallet racking
DD   double deep racking
VNA   very narrow aisle racking – access by high rack stacker truck lifting to say 12/13 metres in say 1.8-metre aisle
FIFO   First-in-first-out stock rotation

Figure 16.8   Mobile small parts storage (courtesy of Link 51 (Storage Products))

Tote bins

Tote bins are made in a range of materials such as galvanized steel, polypropylene, wire mesh and fibreboard. They are made in modular sizes that are sub-multiples of standard dimensions, and this facilitates nesting and stacking, and the use of different sizes of tote within one installation.

A useful device for supporting tote bins, either in static storage locations or trolley-mounted for ease of movement, eg kit marshalling and movement from store to production assembly operations, is the louvre panel. It provides easy attachment and removal of totes, and also other attachments such as spigots for holding items such as gaskets, belts and other more awkward items.

Drawer units

Drawer units can be free-standing or incorporated into shelving modules or stores counters. Subdividers are used, which enable particularly good use of drawer space, and there is a range of other fittings suitable for such items as electronic components, machined items and other delicate components. Drawers give very good access to the stock and provide a clean and secure environment.

Dynamic systems – mobile and live storage

Just as for palletized stock, there are small item mobile storage systems with shelves mounted on moving platforms, which run along floor-mounted rails (see Figure 16.8). Unlike palletized systems, however, these are not usually powered, but are manually moved by turning a large wheel at the end of each section of shelving. This system finds wide application in banks and insurance companies for holding documents required only infrequently.

Small items and cartons can also be held in live storage systems, sometimes referred to as flow racking, with the goods located on inclined roller conveyors, fed in at the high end and taken out as required at the lower end (see Figure 16.9).

For both the above systems the operational characteristics are very similar to the versions for palletized storage.

Figure 16.9   Small parts live storage (courtesy of Link 51 (Storage Products))

Mechanized systems – carousels and miniloads

Carousels hold material on shelves, or in tote containers on shelves, supported and moved by chains, which are electric-motor-driven to bring specific product lines as required to an operator. The objective is to minimize operator movement when accessing stock, so carousels find application in small items order picking. Carousel units can give fast rates of accession to stock, and are inherently secure. There are two types of carousel, horizontal and vertical.

In the horizontal carousel (see Figure 16.10), stock is held in shelved cages or baskets suspended from a motor-driven overhead chain conveyor loop, and for each stock accession the chain is driven forwards or backwards to bring the required goods to the operator by the shortest route.

Figure 16.10   Horizontal carousel (courtesy of Dexion Limited)

In the vertical carousel (see Figure 16.11), stock is held on shelves suspended between two motor-driven vertical chain loops. The shelves are moved up or down, taking the shortest route, to bring stock items as required to the operator's static location. One advantage of the vertical carousel is that it can be built up to building roof height, so making good use of building space.

Figure 16.11 Vertical carousel (courtesy of Dexion Limited)

For carousel units, it is not generally practical to replenish stock at the same time as stock is being withdrawn, so a working pattern has to be established for these two aspects of the operation.

Another mechanized small item storage system is the miniload (see Figure 16.12). A (computer-controlled) crane operates in a central aisle to bring goods out of, or put goods into, the storage medium, shelving or tote containers set out on either side of a central crane aisle.

Figure 16.12   Miniload (courtesy of Morris Material Handling)

OTHER TYPES OF STORAGE

Material such as carpets, linoleum and engineering material such as bar, rod and tube are not suitable for the standard types of storage system discussed so far, and require special storage and handling.

Cantilever racking – supporting bars set at various levels and cantilevered out from back frames – is often used in engineering applications for long rigid items such as bar and tube stock. This type of storage is often accessed by four-directional reach trucks, side loaders or overhead cranes in order to minimize the aisle widths required for access. For items such as heavy sections of plate or sheet, vertical 'toast-rack' type storage is frequently used.

Other long loads that require some support along the length, such as rolls of carpet, can be stored in pigeon-hole racking, accessed by lift trucks fitted with long carpet booms, which are inserted into the centre of the roll to lift and position it.

SUMMARY

This chapter has set out the basic types of storage system for unit load storage, and the essential characteristics of the different systems. A key aspect for determining the most appropriate storage system for a particular application is to select one whose characteristics most closely match the overall requirements of the warehouse or store within which it is to work.

The basic factors for determining the most appropriate storage system for any application include:

- nature and characteristics of goods and unit loads held;
- effective use of space – building height, building area and access aisles;
- good access to stock for taking out and replenishing;
- stock layout for minimum movement;
- good information system and stock location system;
- integrity and security of stock;
- personnel safety;
- minimum overall system cost.

Storage systems that utilize building space most effectively often do not give particularly good access to the stock, and vice versa. A trade-off or compromise often has to be made between these two factors when deciding on the use of any storage system.

17

Handling systems

INTRODUCTION

It was Henry Ford who said that 'every time you pick up an article without changing its form, you add to its cost but not to its value' – an appropriate challenge when considering the handling and movement of material.

Handling in a warehouse or distribution centre will have a major impact on how effectively materials flow through the system, and on the cost, resource and time taken to get orders out to the customer. In addition, handling equipment can be capital-intensive, and the act of movement can be labour-intensive.

Various methods of handling goods are used in warehousing, from manual through to automated or robotic systems, and a broad categorization could be:

- manual handling;
- manually operated trucks and trolleys;
- powered trucks and tractors, operator-controlled and driven;
- powered trucks and trolleys, driverless, computer-controlled;
- crane systems;
- conveyors;
- robotics.

Whilst manual handling is recognized as a significant industrial activity, and one that accounts for a significant number of industrial injuries, the correct techniques for manual lifting and handling are not considered to be within the remit of this book.

Although this chapter will concentrate on powered trucks, cranes and conveyors, it must not be forgotten that there is a wide range of non-powered industrial trucks for pedestrian use. These include hand pallet trucks, order picking trolleys, stair climbing trolleys and a wide range of platform, shelf and cage trolleys. For some applications these will be the most appropriate methods for material movement.

Robotic applications will be discussed briefly in Chapter 19.

POWERED INDUSTRIAL TRUCKS AND ATTACHMENTS

Industrial lift trucks are used in warehousing for moving material over relatively short distances, for lifting into and out of storage, and for vehicle loading and unloading. Trucks facilitate load unitization, speed up movement, can handle large loads and consequently reduce the frequency of movements. Their lift ability enables the use of building height – the cost of building volume reduces as building height increases.

Powered industrial trucks have existed since the turn of the 20th century, but unit load handling trucks with lift capacity only came on the scene in the 1930s with the arrival of the counterbalanced truck. The disadvantage of this truck is its overall length and consequent requirement for a wide aisle if accessing stock in racking. Subsequent developments have resulted in trucks that operate in very narrow aisles, and lift to considerable heights.

The main types of powered truck used in warehousing and stockyard operations are:

- powered pallet trucks;
- counterbalanced fork-lift trucks;
- reach trucks including double reach and four-directional reach variants;
- stacker trucks;
- high rack stacker trucks – very narrow aisle;
- side loaders;
- order picking trucks;
- tugs and tractors;
- straddle carriers – container handling.

Truck power

Most trucks for use inside warehouse buildings have battery-powered electric motors, but counterbalanced trucks can also be engine-driven – liquefied petroleum gas (LPG), or diesel. Side loaders, frequently for outdoor use, are generally engine-driven.

Battery power is clean, quiet and compact, gives high initial acceleration and is suitable for intermittent work. If continuous shift working is required, spare batteries will be needed with one set in use while the other is being recharged. Traction batteries are heavy, and battery changing/charging facilities must be capable of handling accidental battery acid spillage, and dissipating the hydrogen and oxygen gases released during charging. A very low percentage of hydrogen in air forms an explosive mixture.

Gas- and diesel-powered trucks are robust and suitable for outdoor work. However, they are noisier than electric trucks, and the exhaust fume emissions make them less suitable for indoor work.

Most fork-lift trucks have rear wheel steering.

Fork-lift truck lifting capacity

The capacity of a fork-lift truck is usually quoted as a maximum load when the load centre of gravity is at a specified distance (load centre) from the heel of the forks (see Figure 17.1).

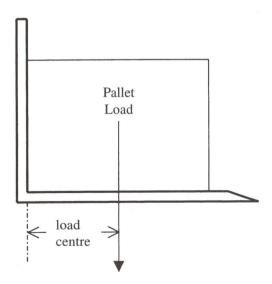

Pallet
Load

load
centre

Figure 17.1 Fork-lift truck load centre

If the load centre is longer than specified, the weight that can safely be carried must be reduced to avoid the risk of overturning. Manufacturers' technical literature usually indicates the magnitude of the consequent 'de-rating'. Further de-rating (reduction in permitted load weight) applies to some trucks if the design load is raised above defined height limits, because as loads are raised truck stability decreases.

There are three basic fork-lift truck mast configurations, ie single-stage, two-stage (duplex) and three-stage (triplex). The more stages the higher the mast can lift, and the lower the closed height of the mast.

With standard mast designs, when the forks begin to lift, the mast height immediately begins to extend. This can limit the use of the trucks for vehicle and ISO container loading and unloading. To overcome this there are 'free lift' mast designs that allow some raising of the forks without any increase in mast height. Fork truck masts also incorporate a tilt facility, forward tilt of about 5 degrees for picking up and setting down loads, and about 12 degrees backward tilt during travel and lifting or lowering.

Powered pallet trucks

Hand pallet trucks, with capacities up to a maximum of 2 tonnes, are probably the most commonly used trucks for the horizontal movement of pallets. It is not uncommon to see these trucks lifted on to the back of the vehicle for positioning pallets during loading and unloading. However, for frequent movements, and where there are inclines to be negotiated, battery-powered trucks are preferable in terms of operator effort and safety, and these can be pedestrian- or rider-controlled (see Figure 17.2).

Tugs and tractors

For long horizontal movements, the use of tugs and tractors may be more economic and appropriate than using fork-lift trucks. These trucks are often designed to carry loads and also to pull trailers. This can increase the number of units moved per journey compared to using pallet trucks or fork-lift trucks, and hence reduce the frequency of journeys.

Prime movers for this sort of use do not have to be driver-controlled, and there is a range of computer-controlled automated guided vehicles (AGVs) for horizontal movement, with the ability to interface with conveyor systems for picking up and setting down payloads. Some of these designs also have lifting facilities. This will be further discussed in Chapter 19.

Figure 17.2   Powered pallet truck (courtesy of Lansing Linde Limited)

Counterbalanced fork-lift trucks (CB trucks)

Counterbalanced fork-lift trucks carry the payload forward of the front wheels (see Figure 17.3), so there is always a turning moment tending to tip the truck forward. To balance this, a counterbalance weight is built into the rear of the machine – hence the name. Heavy components like engines and batteries are also positioned as far back as possible to help counter the overturning moment.

These machines are made with capacities ranging from 1,000 kilograms up to about 45,000 kilograms, the very large ones being typically for container handling applications. Smaller trucks, 1,000/1,500-kilogram capacity, sometimes have three wheels rather than four, which makes then more manoeuvrable, and some smaller models are also made for pedestrian control.

Since the load is always in front of the front wheels, CB trucks are long, necessitating a wide turning area, and trucks with a capacity of 2,000/3,000 kilograms will need a 90-degree turning aisle, eg for putting pallets into or out of racking, of some 4 metres. This compares with figures nearer to 2.8 to 3 metres for reach trucks,

Figure 17.3 Counterbalanced fork-lift truck (courtesy of Boss Group Limited)

and 1.7 to 1.8 metres for high rack stackers. Consequently, although CB trucks are very robust and fast, and are very good as 'yard trucks' and for vehicle loading and unloading, they are less appropriate inside the warehouse because of the space required for access aisles.

Battery-powered CB trucks are made in capacities up to about 5,000 kilograms with travel speeds up to about 20/25 kilometres per hour. Larger models tend to be LPG- or diesel-powered.

Figure 17.4 shows a container handling truck working in a dock environment.

The most recent development in CB truck design is a battery-powered machine with front-wheel steering, articulated so that the truck body 'bends' in the middle during turning (see Figure 17.5). The claims for this truck are a turning aisle width of as little as 1.7/1.8 metres, a lift height of up to 6/7 metres and a payload of up to 2,000 kilograms.

Figure 17.4   Dockside CB truck (courtesy of Lansing Linde Limited)

Reach trucks

Reach trucks (see Figure 17.6) are designed to be smaller and lighter than counter-balanced trucks and to operate in a smaller area. This is achieved by having a mast that can move forward or back in channels in the outrigger truck legs. When picking up or setting down a load, the truck is turned through 90 degrees to face the load location; the mast reaches forward, places or retrieves the load, and is retracted back into the area enclosed by the wheels. The truck travels with the mast in the retracted position. This virtually eliminates the need for a counterbalance weight, and reduces the truck length. Reach trucks are always battery-powered. They are widely used in conventional, ie non-automated, warehouses.

The typical range of capacities for reach trucks is 1,000 kilograms up to about 3,500 kilograms, with maximum fork-lift up to about 11 metres. Widths for 90-degree turning aisles, with trucks carrying standard pallets, would be in the range

Figure 17.5 Articulated CB truck (courtesy of Narrow Aisle Limited)

2.8 to 3 metres. Horizontal travel speeds would be up to about 12 kilometres per hour.

In the USA a more usual design has a static mast fixed back against the driver's compartment. The reach is achieved by the use of a pantograph (scissor) mechanism on the fork carriage, which reaches the forks forward and back.

Double reach trucks

A conventional reach truck can only reach one pallet deep into racking. For accessing double deep racking a double reach truck has to be used, which uses a pantograph mechanism to achieve the additional reach. Double reach can also be achieved on

Figure 17.6   Reach truck (courtesy of Lansing Linde Limited)

some lighter trucks by the use of telescopic forks. Double reach machines are also used for side-loading pallets on to road vehicles, working only from one side of the vehicle.

Four-directional (4D) reach trucks

On a conventional reach truck, the front wheels always face forward, and steering is from the rear wheels. The 4D truck has an additional option of being able to turn the front wheels through 90 degrees and lock them in this mode. This effectively converts the truck into a side loader and is especially useful in stores and warehouses where part of the stock range consists of long loads. For access to say cantilever storage, very wide aisles would be necessary if this option were not available.

Ergonomic developments

With reach trucks operating in narrow aisles and lifting to heights of 11 metres or so, there is considerable strain on drivers having to lean back and look up when accessing stock at high levels. The need for the operator to turn his or her head frequently according to whether the truck is being driven forwards or backwards imposes a further strain. This has resulted in repetitive strain injuries and associated conditions. Some of the recent developments in reach truck technology have been directed specifically to helping mitigate such problems. These have included positioning the driver's cab higher up the truck, rear tilting seats to reduce neck strain and improve visibility, seats that can turn in the direction of travel, and carefully designed seat and controls layout. For very narrow aisle trucks (see below), automatic height selection and rising cabs help to take the strain out of locating pallets and other work at high level.

Stacker trucks

These are fairly lightweight trucks with maximum capacities up to 2,000 kilograms. There are pedestrian, stand-on and ride-on versions. Superficially they look rather like small reach trucks, but the mast does not move. Pallets are put into or taken out of storage racking by the truck legs being driven into the space either under the bottom pallet (beam supported) or straddling round the bottom pallet (which requires wide clearances between pallets). When picking up pallets at floor level, the forks have to be lowered right down on to the outrigger legs, so perimeter-based pallets cannot be used, since they would be sprung apart as soon as the forks were raised. This problem is overcome if the lowest pallets are located on low beams with sufficient space underneath to accommodate the outrigger.

These trucks are usually limited to about a 6-metre lift, but they can operate in 90-degree turning aisles of only 2 metres or less.

High rack stacker trucks – very narrow aisle

These trucks (see figure 17.7), typically with lift capacities up to 2 tonnes and lifting to 12/13 metres, are equipped with mechanisms on the mast that can set down or pick up pallets from the racking without the truck having to turn in the aisle. Consequently they can operate in aisles of 1.8 metres or less.

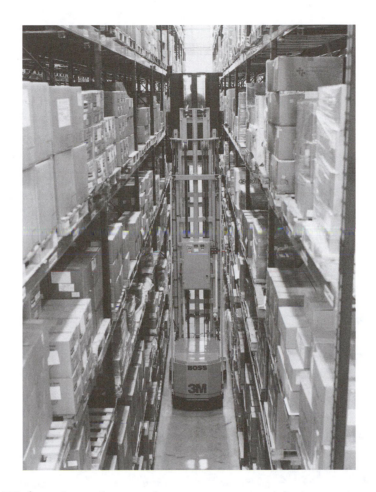

Figure 17.7 High rack stacker truck – very narrow aisle (courtesy of Boss Group Limited)

Some models have the operator at ground level, usually for pallet-in and pallet-out operations. Some form of automatic height selection is then necessary to assist the operator when locating or retrieving pallets at high level in narrow aisles. In other 'man-up' versions, the operator's cab rises with the forks, appropriate for high-level order picking operations.

The very narrow aisles and high lifts give good space utilization, but also necessitate very flat floors, which are expensive, to minimize the risk of collision between load and racking when manoeuvring loads. It is also necessary to have a guidance system to keep the trucks centrally positioned in the aisles. This is done either by fitting side wheels to the trucks which engage with guide rails fixed to the racking on both sides of each aisle, or by using 'wire-in-floor' technology whereby magnetic sensors in the truck follow an electric cable buried in the floor.

Side loaders

Side loaders (see Figure 17.8), frequently used for long loads and often for outdoor operations such as timber yards, have masts that reach at 90 degrees to the direction of truck travel. Typical load lengths can be 6 to 7 metres, handled in narrow aisles between stacks. To access a load positioned along one side of an aisle, the truck must enter the aisle with the reach mechanism on the opposite side of the aisle. These trucks are long and typically require cross-aisles of some 7 metres to move between aisles.

Figure 17.8 Side loader (courtesy of Boss Group Limited)

Stacker cranes

Stacker cranes, used mainly in automated high bay warehouses, run on floor-mounted rails with overhead guide rails. They can be single or twin mast design (for heavier loads) and installations can go to 45 metres or higher. They are always electrically powered, usually three phase 415 volts, supplied via suspended or reel feed cable. Aisle widths, which need to be only slightly wider than the unit load being handled, are typically about 1.5 metres. One of their strengths is their high operating speeds and hence unit load handling capacity.

This type of technology will be covered in more detail in Chapter 19.

Order picking trucks

There is a range of manual and powered trucks designed specifically for order picking operations. These range from trolleys, such as roll cage pallets, to ground-level pedestrian trucks such as long fork powered pallet trucks, up to multi-level trucks in which the operator is raised for high-level picking. These and other picking mechanisms and devices will be considered in more detail in Chapter 18.

Truck attachments

There is a wide range of truck attachments for handling loads that cannot be handled by forks, and for enabling additional degrees of movement when handling unit loads. It should be noted that all attachments have weight, and this must be taken into account when calculating the payload capacity of a truck where attachments are used.

Clamps

Clamp attachments consist of shaped or flat side arms, sometimes also fitted with non-slip surfaces, used for handling loads such as cartons and bales, drums, kegs and paper reels. They are powered by the truck hydraulic system, with the side arm pressure being adjustable to prevent crushing of the load.

Side shift

A side shift mechanism enables forks or other attachments to be shifted laterally by about ± 75 millimetres at right angles to the direction of truck travel, and is to facilitate the accurate positioning of loads, for example during loading pallets into ISO containers.

Rotating head

This device changes the orientation of a load. For example, reels of newsprint are usually stored with their axes vertical, but are required to be presented to printing machines horizontally.

Load push-pull

This device (see Figure 17.9) handles pallet-sized loads assembled on card or plastic skid sheets. A clamp fitted to a pantograph mechanism on the fork truck grips a lip on the skid sheet, enabling the load to be pulled on to a platen on the truck. Once there it can be lifted, moved and positioned effectively as though it were a pallet load. This enables 'palletless' handling, including loading vehicles for dispatch to customers. An implication of this is that the customer also must have the attachment to be able to unload.

Figure 17.9   Load push-pull (courtesy of Cascade (UK) Limited)

Non-powered attachments

All the above-mentioned attachments require power from the truck hydraulic system. There are also various attachments that do not require a power source. These include carpet booms, poles for reels and coils, and small crane booms.

Truck ergonomics

Although the cost of acquiring an industrial truck is significant, it is not the major element of total truck costs. One manufacturer has suggested that, taking total life cycle costs as 100 per cent, truck acquisition cost is only up to 25 per cent of the total cost, whereas driver costs can be up to 80 per cent, and energy and maintenance costs up to 15 per cent.

The basic message from this is that ergonomics and the driver's immediate working environment are crucial to good productivity,

CRANES

Cranes and hoists are for lifting and moving material on an intermittent basis. Except for mobile cranes they operate within an area circumscribed by the equipment configuration. Cranes therefore tend to be less flexible than, say, fork-lift trucks, but may be the most appropriate solution for regular lifting of heavy loads within a defined area. Cranes operating overhead can eliminate the need for aisles for material movement.

Equipment types include hand- and power-operated hoists, jib cranes, overhead travelling cranes, gantry cranes and crane attachments. Stacker cranes will be discussed in Chapter 19.

Hoists

Hoists are mechanisms for raising or lowering loads carried on a hook from a chain or wire rope, and they can be powered manually, electrically or by compressed air. They can be suspended from a fixed overhead point, from a slewing jib, from a trolley on an overhead runway system or from an overhead travelling crane. They are comparatively inexpensive items of equipment, and in general, for lower lift capacities, chain hoists are cheaper than wire rope hoists. However, for heavier and more extended lifts wire rope hoists are more appropriate. Typical applications include production and assembly shop operations, through to use for vehicle loading and unloading.

Slewing jib cranes

A slewing jib crane consists of a pivoted arm – the jib – either pillar-mounted or wall-mounted, with a hoist that can travel radially along the jib. The jib can be slewed about the pivot to position the payload within the arc defined by the radial jib. The load carried will determine whether the lift and travel mechanisms are manually operated, or powered lift, or powered lift and radial travel, or for heavy loads, powered lift, radial travel and slew. Power to the hoist is supplied by cable or air line suspended from the jib in such a way that it does not impede hoist operation.

Because of the high bending moments imposed at the pivot end of the jib, care needs to be taken when designing the floor or wall mountings. Most applications of jib cranes are in production and assembly operations.

Overhead travelling cranes

An overhead travelling crane consists of a bridge made up of one or more beams, the bridge being fitted with end carriages that travel along a pair of parallel high-level rails. A trolley, incorporating a hoist, travels on rails on the bridge structure. Consequently the payload can be moved:

- longitudinally by the bridge travel;
- cross-traverse by the bridge trolley travel;
- vertically by the hoist.

The length and span of the overhead supporting rails define the effective working area.

There are two basic designs of overhead travelling crane: 1) top-mounted, in which the bridge is carried on top of the end carriages; and 2) underslung, in which the bridge end is suspended from the end carriages.

Most overhead travelling cranes are electrically powered, and control can be from operator cab, by pendant and push-button control box or by radio.

There are obvious uses in the movement of heavy loads in manufacturing, but overhead cranes are also used in storage and handling for such materials as long loads and steel coil. Cranes can also be fitted with special attachments such as clamps for paper reel handling, and cradles for bar and tube.

Gantry cranes

Gantry cranes are also used for handling large and very heavy loads. The basic crane components are a bridge section carrying a transverse trolley and hoist mechanism, and supporting legs at each end of the bridge. The legs can run on ground rails or, for mobile gantry cranes, be supported on pneumatic wheels that allow free movement of the crane.

Gantry cranes tend to be slower in operation than overhead travelling cranes, being heavier but structurally less rigid. They do not require elevated running rails and are likely to be more appropriate for outdoor use where the construction of frames to carry the overhead rails would be very costly. In the handling of ISO containers on to and off cargo ships at container ports, gantry cranes are used that are designed to cantilever out to one side enabling the trolley and hoist to be positioned over the ships' access hatches.

Gantry cranes are made with capacities up to 1,500 tonnes, for example in shipbuilding, but smaller models, up to say 50 tonnes capacity, can be designed as mobile units, fitted with wheels rather than being rail-mounted. These give high mobility and are capable of operating over relatively uneven ground surfaces.

Crane attachments

In addition to the range of hook shapes and hooks with safety catches, there is a range of attachments designed to be safe, and to facilitate quick fitting and release for loads not easily lifted by hook. Examples include mechanical clamps and grippers, grabs, spreader beams, forks, magnetic and vacuum lifting heads, and the long-established techniques using slings of rope and wire.

Scissor lifts

Scissor lifts, used in manufacturing for positioning work at the required height, are also used for bringing loads to the correct height for vehicle loading, or for lifting and lowering forks trucks so they can be moved between working areas at different levels. They can also be used, generally mounted on a mobile platform, for personnel access for maintenance of high lighting and similar servicing activities.

The basic mechanism is a hydraulically actuated pantograph, which lifts or lowers a platform carrying the payload. Capacities range up to 200 tonnes, but more commonly in distribution activities the capacity will be up to say 10 tonnes. These devices tend to be slow in operation and are suitable for comparatively infrequent movements.

CONVEYORS FOR UNIT LOAD HANDLING

General characteristics

Conveyor systems are used for moving material between fixed points, for holding material as short-term buffer, for sortation and for process industry applications such as separation, grading and cooling. The latter, typically for bulk solids handling, are not within the scope of this book. This section concentrates on conveyors for unit loads, such as cases, cartons and pallets, and sortation is covered in Chapter 19.

The general characteristics of conveyor systems are:

- high throughput with few operators and low power requirement;
- suitable for fixed routes, and floor surfaces are not critical as they are for fork trucks;
- fast response and suitable for continuous or intermittent movements;
- can utilize very sophisticated movement control.

Conveyor systems now find very wide application in both conventional and automated warehousing. Recent years have also seen wide applications, associated with techniques such as bar-coding, for precise control of material movement, including very high throughput sortation systems for such things as parcels, and for routeing goods to prescribed destinations.

The less positive aspects of conveyor systems include:

- high capital cost;
- can obstruct working areas and access;
- inflexibility for future change;
- hence very careful system design required including safety features.

Gravity conveyor systems

Gravity systems require no power supply or associated motors and switchgear. Although simple in principle they do require careful layout and attention, especially to inclines, to achieve control of movement. Gravity systems include chutes, skate wheel conveyors and gravity roll conveyors.

Chutes

Chutes require very careful design to account for possible variations in friction coefficient between the loads and chute surface, especially if they are used to negotiate turns as in spiral chutes.

Skate wheel conveyors for lightweight cases and cartons

These consist of discs fitted to spindles mounted between side channels, and the discs carry the loads. These conveyors are often set into pantograph side structures, allowing them to be extended or shortened in use, and also enabling them to be 'bent' around corners. They are frequently used for vehicle loading and unloading.

Gravity roll conveyors

The gravity roll conveyor is probably the most common type of gravity conveyor, ranging from small-sized case conveyors up to pallet conveyors. The base of the load should be smooth and flat, and the rollers should be spaced so that there are at least three in contact with the load at any one time. As with any gravity conveyor, the incline is critical and these conveyors usually come with adjustable support legs to allow 'fine-tuning' during installation. It is also common to fit end stops or end ramps and, if appropriate, braking rollers part-way along each conveyor run.

Powered conveyor systems

Powered roller conveyors

Powered roller conveyors are used for similar loads to the non-powered versions, with widths up to about 1,500 millimetres, and the same requirements for smooth load bases and three-roller contact. Inclines are not recommended, and height changes are probably best achieved using flat belt conveying. For diverting loads on to branch conveyors, push mechanisms can be used, or skate wheel or chain sections that come up between the rollers and at right angles to them to move the loads off the rollers.

Flat belt conveyors

Flat belt conveyors are suitable for lightweight loads, and would not be suitable for the larger heavier loads such as pallets, which can be handled by roller conveyors.

A flat belt conveyor consists of a continuous belt running on supporting rollers between two end drums, one of which is electrically driven. Belting can be made from reinforced rubber or plastic, fabric, steel or steel mesh, and composites of these, and provides a continuous support surface for the loads being moved. These conveyors are quiet, can be taken through inclines, and have high throughput capacity. They are not suitable for accumulation unless special steel belting is used. To increase friction for use on inclines, ribbed or tread patterned belting can be used. Generally these conveyors are less expensive than powered roller conveyors.

Slat conveyors

In this type of conveyor, wood or steel cross slats are fitted between side chains, so providing a continuous rigid surface for the loads. They can be used for horizontal and inclined movement and, being robust, are used for heavy and awkward loads. They tend to be slow and noisy, and have a high power usage.

Chain conveyors

Chain conveyors carry loads on two or more parallel chains running in tracks parallel to the direction of motion. They are used for loads too heavy or otherwise unsuitable for roller conveyors, and also in short lengths as transfer units between sections of roller conveyor. They are generally slow. An extension of the concept bridges across the chains with regularly spaced flight bars. These run over a smooth bed along which they push the loads.

Tilt tray and tilt slat conveyors

Tilting conveyors are usually laid out in horizontal carousel configuration, with a series of tilting trays or slats fitted to a conveying chain, and capable of tipping loads off to left or right to branch conveyors or to off-take chutes. The slats can be tilted singly or in multiples according to sizes of load being handled.

Tilting conveyors are used for high-speed sortation operations such as parcel distribution, and for some cross-docking installations. The effectiveness and speed of these applications depends on information technology and coding systems such as bar codes. Each load is identified as it enters the system, which then instructs the conveyor to discharge the load to its designated destination.

Sorting rates typically quoted are between 6,000 and 10,000 units per hour per installation, but the rate is dependent on the size of installation, the number of in-feed points and the number of destination off-take chutes or conveyors.

Overhead conveyors

An overhead conveyor consists of a continuous chain running in overhead track, with loads on carriers suspended from the chain. These conveyors are roof- or building-supported and do not obstruct activities at floor level, but they can reduce the available working headroom. They are used for inclined as well as horizontal movement.

Applications include widespread use in manufacturing, moving materials between workstations, through paint booths, drying ovens or dip tanks. Warehouse applications include hanging garment movement and storage, and use in order picking operations. As with other types of conveyor, coding systems can be used to control movement and to enable loads to be directed to required locations.

Power and free conveyors

In this type of conveyor there are two tracks, one above the other, with the top track housing a continuously moving chain and the lower supporting load-carrying trolleys. Pushers on the chain act on the trolleys to move them along the bottom track. Spurs on the bottom track allow the carriers to be shunted into holding loops or diverted on to other conveyor lines, and these movements can be remotely or automatically controlled.

Accumulation

Accumulation is the ability of a system to form a queue in a conveyor line to act as a buffer if the rates of feed and off-take are not matched. Non-powered roller conveyors can achieve this effectively, but if the line is on an incline the pressure between one load and the next, known as 'line pressure', can be excessive. 'Pop-up' stops positioned one load back from the end stop can be used to take the pressure off the next load to be picked up.

Powered rollers can also be used for accumulation by incorporating rollers with friction clutches, which slip if the load is stopped, for example by an end stop. Other methods include powered chain conveyors fitted with rollers. When there is no resistance the rollers do not turn and the loads move forward with the chain. When the load is stopped, the chain continues to move forward but the rollers rotate backwards under the load.

SUMMARY

This chapter has reviewed the principal types of handling system encountered in warehousing and distribution centre operations, ie industrial trucks, cranes and conveyors. More technically advanced systems such as stacker cranes, sortation conveyors and AGV systems are considered in Chapter 19.

The factors to be considered when deciding on the appropriate type of handling system for a particular application include:

- types of load being handled including the unit load characteristics;
- quantity of material being handled;
- frequency of movement;
- distances to be travelled, horizontal and vertical;
- numbers and locations of pick-up and drop points;
- adjacent activities;
- nature of terrain;
- flexibility required.

The principles governing the design and use of handling systems include:

- control of position and movement;
- elimination of unnecessary movement and minimization of the necessary movement;
- selection of the most appropriate handling method to meet the system requirements;
- provision of adequate handling capacity;
- integration of handling with the storage and other adjacent operations;
- thorough and effective operator training;
- effective equipment maintenance for operational availability and safety;
- safe methods of handling and working practices.

18

Order picking and replenishment

INTRODUCTION

Order picking is the activity that brings together from the complete range of products held in a warehouse those products required to meet a customer order, in the quantity, quality and form in which they are required, accurately and to time. The effectiveness with which picking is carried out has an immediate impact on customer service factors such as completeness and accuracy of order fill, and completion of order in time to meet transport dispatch deadlines. It is perhaps the key activity in warehousing operations.

Picking can account for up to 50 per cent of the direct operating staff in a warehouse. Early studies suggested that, with manual picking methods and pickers moving between picking locations, 50 to 70 per cent of an order picker's time could be spent moving, with only a small proportion of the time being spent physically picking. For reasons of customer service, cost and effective use of staff, order picking systems merit attention to get them 'right'.

A typical picking operation could involve picking case quantities of products held on pallets in dedicated picking locations, and then checking, collating and packing the picked cases ready for dispatch.

There have been advances in handling technology, despite which there are still many picking operations using low levels of mechanization, and in many cases order picking remains manual and labour-intensive, repetitive, and prone to error.

Picking can also require unsociable working hours to meet service requirements and it is not uncommon for companies to offer next-day delivery for orders received up to say 6 pm.

Despite the above comments about technology levels, there have been significant developments in the techniques and technology of picking, and in particular the application of electronic data transfer and communication. These will be discussed in this chapter. It is pertinent to note that a number of very recent examples of 'automated' warehouses, with automated pallet handling and storage, nevertheless use 'manual' operator to goods picking at ground level, albeit using powered trucks and radio data communication. Such 'traditional' picking methods, allied to effective use of IT, often enable very high levels of productivity, as well as being flexible enough to accommodate future change.

PRINCIPLES OF ORDER PICKING

Underlying the effective design and management of order picking systems, there are basic principles that should be addressed:

- Picking methods and equipment should be appropriate for the application.
- Stock availability at the picking face must be maintained, with effective replenishment of picking locations to avoid stock-outs.
- Equipment should be laid out and stock positioned in the picking area for minimum movement but avoiding congestion.
- Picking stock should be concentrated into the smallest feasible area in order to minimize picker movement, whilst at the same time avoiding congestion. This often involves keeping reserve stock and order picking stock separate. This separation can be vertical, eg pick from racking at ground-floor level with reserve stock on the higher racking levels (see Figure 18.1), or horizontal, with reserve stock in one area and picking in another (see Figure 18.2).
- A prerequisite for effective picking is an information system. This can include sorting and batching orders, monitoring stock availability and triggering pick face replenishment, working out optimum picking routes, presenting information to the pick staff, and recording order throughput.
- Stock rotation and similar constraints must be met.
- Performance should be monitored for speed, accuracy and completeness of order.

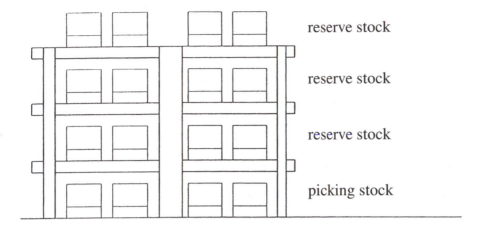

Figure 18.1 Vertical separation

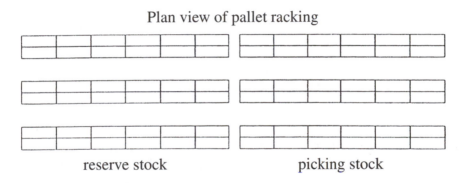

Figure 18.2 Horizontal separation

ORDER PICKING REGIMES

Different methods of order picking are discussed later in this chapter, but another classification must first be considered. In any one journey or circuit by a picker through a picking area, how many orders or how much of only one order should or can be picked? The answer clearly depends on the size of order, and also on the picking method, and size of unit load or container into which orders are being picked. A number of categories can be recognized.

Consignee picking

One picker in one circuit of the picking area collects the items required for one order. This is appropriate when one order will typically fill the capacity of the picking trolley or truck. An extension of this is when more than one order is picked per circuit, but each of the orders is accumulated into a separate container so that at the end of the picking circuit each order is discrete.

Batch or summary pick, and sort

For small orders it is not always economic to pick only one order per circuit. If it is not appropriate to pick multiple orders and to keep them separate during picking, a group of orders can be consolidated during order processing so that a picker assembles all the items required for that group of orders. At the conclusion of the picking circuit, the bulk-picked items are then sorted down to individual order level.

Zone picking

This approach is relevant where individual orders are beyond the capacity of one picker to collect in one picking circuit, and where for reasons of meeting dispatch times it is not feasible to pick sequentially until an order is complete. In this case, stock is laid out in zones, each zone holding a specified part of the product range and staffed by one picker. Each incoming order is subdivided by zones, and picking then takes place simultaneously in all zones until order completion.

Dynamic picking

There are various approaches to 'dynamic picking'. The concept essentially is to keep no separate picking stock but to have an open picking area. Incoming orders, for say four hours' worth of picking, are batched and bulk-picked from stock in whole pallet quantities, and transferred to the picking area. Picking of individual orders then occurs. Any residual items remaining on the pallets can be returned to stock before the next wave of picking, or if required in the next wave can be left in the picking area.

Combinations

In some situations it may be appropriate to make use of a combination of two or more of the above picking regimes within one picking system. A typical warehouse order will require just one or two slow-moving products, but a large quantity of fast-moving popular products. In this situation the picking area may be laid out with popular products near the dispatch area to minimize movement, with the less popular products, which require fewer picking visits, further away. If consignee picking is used because of order size, the slow-moving products could add significantly to the distance travelled by the pickers. In this situation, the possibility of consignee picking for the most popular products could be considered, with less popular slow-moving products for a group of orders batch-picked.

METHODS OF ORDER PICKING

There is a wide range of picking methods and equipment types. Deciding the most appropriate for a given situation will depend on such factors as the types of product, product sizes and weights, product range (how many SKUs), the picking frequency by SKU, order size range including the number of SKUs per order, number of items per order, and order frequency.

Discussion of methods of picking is presented under three categories – picker to goods, goods to picker, and automated and robotic systems.

Picker to goods

This category includes basic methods such as pickers pushing trolleys or roll cage pallets into which required items are placed as the picker moves along aisles between shelving or pallet racking. Generally pickers work from floor level, although in some cases warehouse ladders are used to access higher stock locations. In this case the slower or less popular product lines should be allocated to the less easily accessible positions. Depending on the type of goods handled and the order characteristics, such methods, despite their total reliance on pedestrian manual effort, can be very effective and achieve high rates of picking. The next stage of course is to use powered trucks carrying pallets or cage pallets (see Figure 18.3), with picking from floor level. Some powered trucks incorporate a step to enable pickers to reach not only ground-level stock, but also up to first-beam height in pallet racking.

For picking higher up from racking or shelving, the high-level picking truck incorporates a rising cab, which can lift the picker typically to four pallets high in pallet racking (see Figure 18.4). In addition, very narrow aisle high rack stacker trucks (see Chapter 17) fitted with rising cabs are also used for high-level picking. Picking rates for high-level picking are not as high as for lower-level picking.

Crane technology is also used for picking from narrow aisles, with pickers in crane-mounted rising cabs. Typical applications for this technology are in auto parts distribution centres holding large numbers of small-sized SKUs (see Figure 18.5).

Figure 18.3 Low-level powered picker (courtesy of Boss Group Limited)

A number of picking installations make use of conveyors. Basic systems have pedestrian pickers selecting required items from shelving and putting them on to conveyors to be taken away for subsequent packing and collation into customer orders. At the other end of the spectrum are systems such as 'pick cars'. A pick car operates up and down in a racking aisle, and is equipped with a rising cab linked by hinged joint to an inclined conveyor, which moves up and down with the cab. The other end of this conveyor is hinged and connected to a trolley running on rails in the aisle. Picked items are placed on this conveyor, which feeds them down to a horizontal conveyor running along the bottom of the aisle, and beneath the pick car. At the end of the aisle the picked items are removed and packed or palletized, and collated to make up customer orders.

Goods to picker

Various systems have evolved that are designed to reduce the very significant proportion of picker time spent in travelling in picker to goods systems. Generally goods to picker systems involve significant mechanization, and the established ones, carousels and miniloads, have already been outlined in Chapter 16. Being mechanized they can readily be linked in to computer control to present pickers with the

Figure 18.4 Multi-level picker (courtesy of Lansing Linde Limited)

required stock items in the appropriate sequence. These systems are generally suitable for small-item picking.

It is notable that many 'automated' warehouses with computer-controlled whole pallet movement and storage nevertheless incorporate manual order picking. This is understandable in view of the complexity of item recognition and positioning that picking can involve, and the cost. However, these systems automate the crane and conveyor movement of the required pallets of stock from the storage area to the static picking locations, thereby eliminating any picker travel. Part-used pallets are then conveyed back into stock, and completed orders are taken away for packing, wrapping and collation, also by conveyor.

Automated and robotic systems

The picking systems described so far, however much they mechanize or automate, all require an operator or picker, to physically pick the individual items required

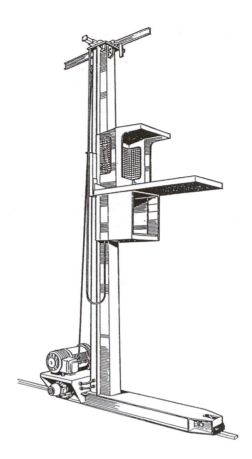

Figure 18.5 Pick crane

to make up an order. It is probably fair to say that, until quite recently, order picking technology had not been developed as much as storage and even movement systems technology. This is now changing, although some of the developments have a high price tag. There are now systems that not only move goods under computer control, but also carry out the picking by controlled mechanical means.

Dispensing

A dispenser consists of two lines of vertical magazines, one line on each side of a belt conveyor (see Figure 18.6).

The magazines are loaded with SKUs, which need to be in regularly shaped packages for ease of movement down the magazines, and fairly small, eg pharmaceutical packs, cosmetics and beauty products. As the conveyor moves between the two lines, the required order quantities of the required SKUs are dispensed

Figure 18.6   Dispenser (courtesy of KNAPP Logistik Automation, Austria)

under computer control, all items for one order being dispensed on to the same section of conveyor. When the accumulated items reach the end of the conveyor, all the items for the order are together and fall off the conveyor into a carton ready to be taken away for packing. An alternative is to have empty cartons already on the central conveyor belt, fed on at the upstream end. The picking operation is controlled and carried out by the machine, but there is often a heavy manual input required to keep the individual dispensers replenished as the stock is used up. These machines achieve very high item throughput rates.

Robotic applications

The use of robots for the routine stacking and de-stacking of cases on to and off pallets is well established. Robots can be programmed to stack to prescribed patterns, to build up layers on a pallet, and to use different patterns on adjacent rows to assist pallet load stability. Robots maintain quality and rate of throughput, and they do not get bored. In routine applications such as this, they offer significant benefits, especially for continuous 24 hours per day working, which if done manually would require three operatives.

The other established use of robots is for order picking, especially small-item picking in the pharmaceutical industry. A typical application has computer-guided trucks fitted with robot arms, carrying a number of containers. The trucks move through a shelving installation containing the pharmaceutical products, and items are picked and placed into the containers, each container being dedicated to a specific order. At the end of each picking circuit, the containers are automatically discharged into cases for dispatch. Very rapid response, say two hours from telephoned order to dispatch to pharmacy, is claimed.

There have also been recent applications in the brewing industry where larger unit loads, eg cases of canned product, have to be picked from pallets. In this case the number of SKUs is small. Typically, a computer-guided truck picks up an empty pallet from an in-feed conveyor, and then moves along a fixed route on either side of which are short conveyors holding pallets of product. As the truck moves along, it is followed by an overhead gantry robot, which picks the required cases of products, by suction head, and positions them on the pallet on the guided truck. When the order pallet has been stacked with the required cases, it is discharged on to an out-feed conveyor.

Sortation

Mechanized sortation systems use a continuous loop conveyor moving between off-take chutes or conveyors set around both sides of the main conveyor. Items for sorting, or for routeing to order accumulation points, are fed on to the continuous conveyor, and as they arrive opposite the appropriate off-take point are automatically diverted to join up with other items for the same destination. These systems are computer-controlled, and depend on some form of machine-readable coding system such as bar codes to identify individual items or groups of items as they move round the conveyor, so that they can be diverted down the correct off-take lines. These systems give very high rates of sort/pick, and are used in some cross-docking applications (see Chapter 15).

INFORMATION IN ORDER PICKING

Accuracy and completeness of order fill, together with timeliness, are key factors in picking performance, and a good information and communication system is a prerequisite for meeting these objectives. This includes appropriate presentation of the correct and sufficient information to the order picking staff, ideally with minimum clerical effort required from them, with the facility for them to communicate back to the managing system in the event of mislocated stock or shortage.

The information required by pickers is the picking locations they have to visit and the sequence of the visits, the SKUs to be picked and the quantities, and the destination or order reference for the picked goods. The traditional way for pickers to receive picking instructions was by paper picking lists, which itemized the SKUs to be picked and the quantities, and left space for the picker to record differences between required and actual quantities. There are now more sophisticated methods, mostly computer-driven.

Pick by label

A gummed label is printed for each item to be picked, and the labels for one order are produced on a backing sheet in the sequence in which they are to be picked. The picker attaches the relevant gummed label to each item as it is picked, and any labels remaining at the end of the pick circuit show what shortages have occurred.

Pick by lights

Every pick aisle has an indicator light, and every picking location is wired with an LED display panel, all controlled by computer. A picker starts by entering the aisle that shows an indicator light, and then goes to the first pick location in that aisle with an illuminated LED, which shows the quantity of items to be picked at that location. Having picked the items, the picker presses a cancel button and moves on to the next illuminated location. This process continues until order completion. This method is often supported by using a take-away conveyor for the picked items, and it is claimed to give high pick rates and very high levels of picking accuracy.

Radio data communication

This can provide online communication between designated warehouse workstations and warehouse management computer packages, and as such has application in order picking.

Bar codes

Bar codes are increasingly used in warehousing. One use is to identify uniquely every storage and picking location in a warehouse, and of course to identify products and product information such as batch identification. In picking operations this can be used to verify pick locations and the items being picked.

PICKING PRODUCTIVITY

Perhaps the most common measure of picking performance is the pick rate, expressed as the number of 'picks' per person per hour. Some companies mean by this the number of items per hour, and some measure the number of SKUs or order lines per hour. This can lead to confusion and it is important always to define the units.

Likewise, using such information to compare different operations can be misleading, since in very similar types of picking operation, and with the same units of measure, apparent performance levels can be surprisingly different. A survey of a number of warehouses in the same business sector, using the same technology and picking methods, produced figures for cases picked per person per hour varying between just over 300 to just under 100, with a mean value of about 170. Quite clearly there were other pertinent factors that influenced the figures. These include whether an incentive scheme was in operation, order characteristics such as the number of items per order line, the amount of 'back picking' due to stock-outs at the pick face, and whether pickers carry out other functions such as replenishment.

Pick rate should not be the sole measure of performance, and other key indicators to be monitored include accuracy of pick, completeness of order fill, timeliness to meet dispatch deadlines, returns and customer complaints, and stock damage during picking.

Other important issues that can impact on the effectiveness of order picking operations include:

- the way stock is laid out within the picking area;
- planning work to eliminate waiting time;
- balancing work loads across the various picking staff;
- ensuring timely replenishment of picking stock as it is used up;
- planning the interface between the picking and any subsequent packing operations;
- elimination of clerical work.

REPLENISHMENT FACTORS

Picking stock availability is necessary to maintain high levels of order fill. The potential consequences of low availability at the picking face are reduced service levels in terms of incomplete orders, or extra cost because of the need for pickers to revisit picking locations they have already visited and found to be out of stock.

Consequently any order picking system must be backed up by an effective replenishment system, which tops up picking stock when 'trigger' levels are reached or which initiates replenishment at regular time intervals based on known patterns of issues.

In addition, flow racking storage is often used in pick face design so that when one unit of stock is issued, or one unit load is emptied, the next one rolls forward and is immediately available for use.

Particularly for very fast-moving materials there is the potential for serious congestion at the picking face, and between the picking and replenishment operations. There are ways to alleviate this such as:

- incorporating multiple picking locations for fast-moving and popular product lines;
- laying out part of the racking or shelving so that every other aisle is for picking, and the alternate aisles are for replenishment – this physically separates picking and replenishment, although it usually involves using single deep racking or shelving, and is a compromise between utilization of space and rapid access to picking stock;
- carrying out the replenishment and picking operations at different times, either by using offset shifts, or in some cases by staggered breaks with stock replenished during the pickers' lunch break.

SUMMARY

Order picking is a key activity in warehousing, having an immediate impact on customer service and accounting for a major part of warehouse costs and operating staff numbers. Consequently picking systems should be designed and managed with particular care.

This chapter has reviewed the important principles for effective order picking, and presented an overview of the different equipment and picking methods available when designing a picking system. The importance of a good information and communication system was emphasized, and the need to support any picking system by effective picking stock replenishment.

19

Advanced systems

INTRODUCTION

This chapter will present an overview of some of the more sophisticated handling and storage systems to be found in warehousing applications. They include highly mechanized systems, automated systems with computers controlling the physical movement and storage of materials, and robotic applications. Such applications may be said to be at the technologically advanced end of the equipment and system spectrum in the context of warehousing, although some of the technology is well established and has been with us for many years.

'High-tech' installations are costly, involve 24-hour working, are somewhat inflexible and tend to require long payback periods. They should be based on some assurance of long-term demand for the products handled.

An example is the use of automated storage and retrieval systems (AS/RS) using computer-controlled driverless high lift stacker cranes in high bay warehouses, a concept that has been with us since the early 1960s. In this sort of application the computer is used to manage and control the physical movement of equipment, and hence of the materials being handled and stored. Many of the earlier stacker cranes were operator-controlled, but the facility for on-board operation is now more usually for maintenance purposes only.

The use of computers for warehouse management and for information handling and communication, ie the application of IT, is considered in Chapter 21.

During the last 10 to 15 years the pace of technological development and application has increased considerably. This has gone hand in hand with, and been encouraged by, the growth in information technology, and has been motivated by the increasingly tight requirements for accurate and timely customer service, and for inventory and cost reduction. However, there are still many warehousing applications that do not make use of advanced handling technology, and the authors' view is that high-tech solutions are not always the answer to every handling or storage problem. Systems should be designed that best meet the overall system requirements, and in some cases that will be a 'low-tech' solution. One example of this was the building of a new clothing warehouse that had to be able to meet peak seasonal sales of up to three times the volumes experienced at other times of year. In this case the flexibility of a labour-intensive solution, in which the company could 'throw people at the problem', was seen as a major requirement for meeting seasonality and peak sales volumes. An automated solution would have been underutilized for much of the time.

Systems to be discussed in this chapter include:

● AS/RS for pallets and other unit load storage;
● order picking systems – crane technology, dispensers, robotic picking;
● sortation systems;
● automated guided vehicles (AGVs);
● robotic applications.

It should be noted that some advanced systems, notably those for order picking (see Chapter 18), have already been discussed in previous chapters. This has been done to avoid an artificial split in the treatment of the subject.

AS/RS SYSTEMS FOR UNIT LOADS

The basic components of an AS/RS system are:

● storage medium, eg pallet racking, or shelving for small-item tote bins;
● storage and retrieval machines that operate in the storage medium;
● in-feed and out-feed systems, eg fork-lift trucks, conveyors, AGVs;
● controlling computer.

The controlling computer monitors the status of all the components of the system and, based on the warehouse stock and movement requirements, plans the work

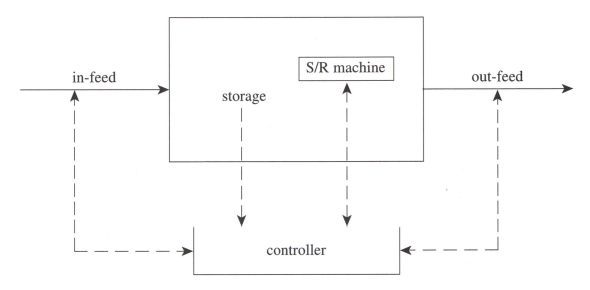

Figure 19.1 AS/RS principle

to be carried out within the system and instructs the equipment accordingly (see Figure 19.1).

A typical installation could consist of high bay pallet racking, with stacker cranes operating in the racking aisles to put pallets away to stock and to retrieve them as required. Note that there are single deep and double deep stacker cranes, enabling the use of single or double deep pallet racking on each side of each aisle. Installation heights of 45 metres or more can be achieved, and typical operating aisles for standard pallets can be about 1.5 metres. The computer would control the incoming and outgoing material flows, monitor the status of the pallet racking (what stock is located in each location and which locations are empty), and control the crane movements. Because of the generally tight clearances in such installations and to prevent possible jams in the racking, a strict profile check for incoming pallets is adopted to ensure that loads have not slipped on the pallets during transit, and that packaging material has not come loose. Pallets outside the dimensional specification are rejected, and have to be rectified before being accepted into the system.

A stacker crane (see Figure 19.2) consists of a vertical mast or pair of masts supporting a unit load handling mechanism, which can be raised or lowered. The crane travels on floor-mounted rails running the length of each aisle, and is guided by an overhead rail. The unit load mechanism can pick up and put away pallets from and to either side of the racking aisle. Cranes can be designed for accessing pallets in single deep and double deep racking.

Figure 19.2 Stacker crane (courtesy of Morris Material Handling)

The amount of storage racking required depends on the designed stock-holding capacity of the installation. The overall rack dimensions are then determined by the height of building (allowed by the local planning authority), and by the lift and travel characteristics of the cranes. This then determines the number of racking rows required and the number of crane aisles.

The number of cranes required is determined by the total amount of pallet movement that has to be carried out in a given period of time. If the number of cranes is significantly less than the number of aisles in the racking, a transfer facility can be incorporated into the design to enable the computer to move cranes between aisles as required. This usually consists of a transverse aisle at one end of the racking, equipped with one or more transfer cars on to which the cranes can be driven and moved between aisles. If the number of cranes required is close to the number of aisles in the racking, it is probably better to have one dedicated crane in each aisle.

There are various applications of this principle of automated storage. They include:

- small-item storage using 'mini' crane installations;
- long load storage of metal bar and tubing using cantilever racking – often in support of manufacturing operations;
- paper reel handling using overhead travelling cranes fitted with vacuum lifting heads, moving the reels into and out of vertical stack storage.

It should be noted that the term 'automated warehouse' is frequently used to describe installations that in reality are only partially automated. The handling of whole pallets into and out of racking may indeed be automated, but the order picking of cases from those pallets is in many applications still carried out manually. However, such applications will always be supported by a good information and communication system, using such techniques as bar-coding and/or radio data communication.

A frequently used term in automated warehousing is 'high bay warehouse'. Generally this refers to a crane-accessed AS/RS system, and there are cranes designed to lift in excess of 40 metres high. Other terms associated with this sort of installation include 'roof on rack' and 'clad rack'. These both refer to the specific building technique in which the walls and roof are supported by the racking steelwork, so avoiding the need for a separate enclosing building. This reduces the cost of building. There can also be tax implications according to whether the building is classified as a fixed asset or as 'plant'.

ORDER PICKING SYSTEMS

Order picking is a crucial operation within warehousing, being critical to order timeliness and order accuracy. Many order picking operations however are monotonous and labour-intensive, and require clerical effort from the pickers. They are often carried out during unsociable hours of work and in uncongenial environments, all of which militate against quality.

In recent years a number of 'advanced' systems have been developed for faster picking with high levels of accuracy, and minimum clerical and manual work input. Some of these are based on high levels of mechanization, and all rely totally on the use of IT. They include:

- operator-controlled cranes working in aisles between racking or shelving;
- carousel and miniload picking – the required goods are brought to the operator working in a static location;
- dispensing, with stock-holding magazines feeding automatically on to a conveyor belt;

- robotic applications in which guided trucks fitted with robot arms are used for small-item picking, eg pharmaceutical products;
- gantry robots used for larger-item picking, eg case picking of brewery products;
- pick by lights, using computer-controlled indicator lights on each picking stock location to guide picking operators along optimum picking routes, and to indicate the required quantities of items to be picked.

These have been discussed in Chapter 18.

Picking by lights has found numerous applications, especially for small and medium-sized items picking, including the picking of tape cassettes, videotapes, pharmaceutical products, and dairy products such as cheeses. The benefits include high rates of picking and hence productivity, little or no requirement for clerical input from the pickers, and very high levels of picking accuracy.

Robotic picking is expensive, but is fairly well established in the German pharmaceutical industry. Other robotic picking applications are beginning to appear, for example case picking of beer in the brewing industry.

SORTATION SYSTEMS

The concept of sortation is well established and has been used for applications such as parcels sorting for a long time. The traditional method of sortation was for items to be unloaded manually at a depot from local collection vehicles. They would then be trolleyed and dropped off in designated collation areas by geographic zone prior to loading on to vehicles for dispatch. This approach is also used in cross-docking operations (see Chapter 15), for example in handling fresh produce to collate loads for delivery to supermarkets. It is often viewed as a means of shortening the supply chain and reducing inventory.

The mechanized approach to sortation is the use of a conveyor, usually set out in a continuous loop, with a number of induction (input) feeds and rather more discharge chutes (see Figure 19.3). Items, appropriately coded, are unloaded from incoming vehicles by conveyor, and fed directly on to the sortation conveyor. As the items go round the conveyor they are identified by code reader and automatically diverted on to the appropriate discharge chutes by geographic zone or destination. As the consignments build up they are collated ready for loading on to dispatch vehicles. This technology is used in a number of major parcels distribution, and other, operations.

Other types of business, typically distribution depots supplying retail outlets, are examining sortation as a means of reducing inventory and shortening their

Figure 19.3   Sortation (courtesy of Vanderlande Industries Limited)

supply chains. The approach will only work if the supporting information system knows in advance the required quantities of which products are to be allocated to each destination. It also requires a tight discipline in the arrival and dispatch times of goods into and away from the distribution depot, and accuracy in the quantities of products coming into the system. In addition, sortation systems require considerable space and they are expensive. However, the potential benefits include reduced inventory, time compression and less handling – goods are not taken into stock and subsequently taken out again for picking.

AUTOMATED GUIDED VEHICLES (AGVS)

AGVs are electrically powered driverless trucks for picking up, moving and placing unit loads (see Figure 19.4). They are computer-controlled, although in some cases there can be manual over-ride. They are used in manufacturing operations to move work pieces between workstations and off the production line, and in warehousing operations for moving unit loads into, within and away from the warehouse system. They are usually designed to interface with other handling systems such as conveyors.

Figure 19.4 AGV (courtesy of Indumat Systems Limited)

A typical warehouse application would be the movement of palletized goods from goods receipt to the input conveyor of an AS/RS installation, and the subsequent movement of retrieved goods to order picking replenishment or to dispatch. In situations of high throughput and 24-hour operation, AGVs can give considerable productivity benefits, but as with any sophisticated handling system, careful planning and design are necessary.

AGVs can be controlled in a number of ways. 'Wire-in-floor' technology is well established. The truck follows an underfloor wire, which carries an alternating electrical current that induces a magnetic field around the wire. As the AGV moves, on-board sensors measure the field to detect any deviation of the truck from the prescribed path. In this event, correcting signals are sent to the steering motor to bring the truck back on course. (This technology is also used for very narrow aisle high rack stacker trucks.)

Optical guidance also uses (optical) sensors to follow a tape strip stuck to the operating floor, although such systems are susceptible to wear and dirt and have not found wide application.

The most recent method of control uses line-of-sight systems continuously to scan fixed datum points located throughout the working area. The scanned angles are transmitted by radio back to the controlling computer, which calculates speed and position of the truck and sends controlling and correcting instructions to the truck as appropriate.

ROBOTIC APPLICATIONS

Robotics enables the automatic movement and manipulation of items in predetermined ways. It has been used routinely in manufacturing applications for a number of years, including in welding, assembly and painting operations.

In warehousing, the stacking and de-stacking of cases on to and off pallets is a routine task that, given a high level of activity, lends itself to the use of simple robotics. Required stacking patterns and orientation of packages can be programmed into the system with, if appropriate, each layer stacked to different patterns to assist overall load stability. A typical application is the palletizing of cased products received from production during three-shift, 24-hour operation, which if carried out manually would require three shift operators carrying out monotonous repetitive work.

More recent and more sophisticated applications in order picking in the pharmaceutical and brewing industries have been outlined in the chapter on order picking, Chapter 18.

FACTORS INFLUENCING THE CHOICE OF TECHNOLOGY

Decisions on the type of technology to adopt in given situations can be influenced by a number of factors, both quantitative and qualitative, and also by the different perceptions and experience of the decision-makers. The image presented in the market-place has certainly influenced such decisions, where a company wishes to be seen at the leading edge in its use of technology.

Costs

Clearly capital and operating costs are critical factors, and it is generally true that the higher the level of mechanization and automation of an installation, the higher the capital cost.

A major justification for the high cost of highly mechanized or automated systems is the consequent reduction in operating costs (lower staffing levels), and this generally comes about if the installation is designed for very high levels of throughput, probably with shift operation. The physical size of an installation, determined by stock-holding capacity, is not of itself a justification for automation.

The basic costs when evaluating design options will include: 1) capital costs – land, building, equipment and systems; and 2) operating costs – staff, building services including insurance etc, maintenance and systems support. It will often happen that services costs will be lower with an automated installation, since the need for lighting, heating and ventilation is reduced because staff do not have to work in the main storage and handling areas.

Operational factors

Automated systems tend to be fast and accurate in operation, can handle short-term fluctuations in throughput levels within the design throughput capacity, and are eminently suitable for 24-hour operation. They provide a secure environment for stock, and if well designed they minimize damage to stock, although unit loads and pallets must be in good condition to avoid possible collapse during handling and storage. Most systems incorporate a stringent dimensional check on unit loads entering the installation, with a reject spur for restacking if necessary. Systems nowadays tend to be fairly reliable, and in general users report infrequent failures with typical downtimes of less than an hour.

A major operational factor is the low staff requirement for automated systems compared to more 'conventional' systems. However, an automated installation has to be designed for peak throughput rates, so it is appropriate to consider the proportion of the operating year that it will be working at or near full capacity, and how much of the time it will be underutilized. It is not desirable to have a major capital investment significantly underutilized. There are companies with high seasonal sales levels that have opted for low-tech warehouse solutions, which give greater flexibility to meet varying throughput levels by 'throwing people' at the problem.

Personnel factors

The skills required for highly mechanized and automated systems include some level of computer literacy, with a facility to work with and understand more complex equipment and systems, and this applies at all levels within the operation. The working environment can be more congenial than in more conventional operations, with the operators spending less time in the working, storage and handling areas. There is often however a need for shift working, although with the current trends in logistics and the need for rapid response and fast service, this also applies in many conventional operations.

Project considerations

It is probably still true that designing and building an automated system takes longer than a more conventional system, although as more experience is gained overall project times tend to reduce. A very approximate comparison would be that a conventional system requiring one year to design and build would take 18 months if automated. A significant part of the time requirement for an automated system is commissioning the control systems. Other key project considerations for some automated systems include obtaining planning permission from local authorities if a 'high bay' installation is proposed, and exploring the insurance and fire protection implications.

Other factors

There is a perception that automated systems are inflexible in the sense that they are designed for a specific set of operating parameters, and any significant change to the market or other requirements may not be easily accommodated. There is some truth in this, and certainly it can be difficult to dispose of or significantly modify such an asset if future changes make it inappropriate for the business. Hence long-term business forecasts are crucial in planning such an installation.

SUMMARY

This chapter has reviewed the principal developments towards higher levels of technology in warehouse applications, and highlighted the key factors in deciding the most appropriate level of technology for a given application. The adoption of 'high-tech' designs has varied considerably according to geography. Japan has led the way with AS/RS systems being built from the early 1960s. In Europe, Germany has been at the forefront of developments. There is now a much wider and increasing acceptance of the potential benefits of such systems and of their increasing reliability, and recent years have seen the numbers of such installations increase significantly.

Certainly the pressures towards higher customer service levels with fast and reliable response, and pressures on cost and inventory reduction, minimum staff levels and environmental factors, are all increasing the pressure towards high-tech designs.

A final word, however – good information and communication systems applied to conventional warehousing technology can enable high levels of performance, particularly in terms of speed and accuracy of customer service, minimum inventory levels and very effective use of staff and other warehouse resources and equipment. A high level of mechanization or automation is not the answer to every problem. The best design for any application is that which most effectively and closely meets the application objectives.

20

Warehouse design

INTRODUCTION

The design of a warehouse and handling system is not simply the production of a drawing showing the position and size of racking or other storage areas, and the aisle runs, handling areas, offices and truck charging points. It is that, but it is also the specification, *inter alia*, of the unit loads (eg pallets), equipment types and quantities, operating systems and methods including ancillary and service activities, information and communication systems, staff levels and organizational structure, and the capital and operating costs. It should also indicate the external layout and space requirements for vehicle access, manoeuvre and parking, and for car parking, site security and any other external activities.

A principle of good design is to define the overall system requirements, and by analysing the relevant data produce a design incorporating methods and equipment that most closely match those requirements. One implication of this is that it is not true to claim that one type or level of mechanization or automation is always the right solution to warehouse design. The old adage of 'horses for courses' applies, and the best design is that which most closely matches the initially specified system requirements and constraints. However, there is one overriding prerequisite: whatever design or level of technology is adopted for a given project, an effective, accurate and fast information system to drive and monitor the operation is a *sine qua non*.

DESIGN PROCEDURE

The design of a warehouse and handling system involves a number of stages, starting with the definition of system requirements and constraints, and finishing with an evaluated preferred design. Although set out sequentially below, the design process is iterative and involves checking back against the system requirements as the design is developed, and assessing the interactions that necessarily occur throughout the process. Any design process uses a range of skills and disciplines. As well as warehouse design expertise, it is appropriate to draw on the operational experience of managers and staff to incorporate their perspective and help produce a design that is technically, financially and operationally viable.

The design process includes the following steps:

- Define system requirements and design constraints.
- Define and obtain data.
- Analyse data.
- Establish what unit loads will be used.
- Postulate basic operations and methods.
- Consider possible equipment types for storage and handling.
- Calculate equipment quantities.
- Calculate staffing levels.
- Prepare possible building and site layouts.
- Evaluate the design against system requirements and constraints.
- Identify the preferred design.

Define system requirements and design constraints

The design requirements for a warehouse or distribution depot operation, taking account of future growth forecasts and other likely business developments, are likely to include:

- required capacities, both storage and throughput;
- service level to be achieved;
- specified facilities such as packaging, quality or other.

Relevant constraints can include:

- time, eg facility to be up and running by a specified date;
- financial, eg limit on capital expenditure or on cost per unit of throughput;

- technical, eg to be compatible with existing company technology, to enable flexible throughput to meet high seasonal variations, or technology level to present 'leading-edge' company image.

Any design must also comply with local authority and legal requirements, which amongst other aspects can cover building height constraints, limitations on working times, and safety legislation including, specifically, manual handling and fork truck codes of practice. Insurers also are likely to require measures relating particularly to fire prevention and control. The local fire officer will need to be satisfied about the measures for personnel safety and evacuation in the event of fire. Ideally, the local planning authority, local fire officer and insurer should be involved as early as possible in any design project.

The impact of environmental legislation and codes of practice is also likely to increase with time, affecting such issues as packaging, and package disposal and reuse.

Define and obtain data

The accuracy and completeness of the data on which any design is based will affect how well the final design meets the specified requirements. It is most unlikely that any design will be based on current levels of business, and it is important to establish anticipated growth and other changes to the business that the warehouse is to be designed to satisfy. However, there are often gaps in the available data, and on occasions assumptions have to be made based on informed opinion and experience, and they should be clearly highlighted and justified in the final design document. Depending on circumstances, it may be appropriate to draw up a data report, including any assumptions, for all interested parties to see and agree before the full design is carried out.

The data required for warehouse design includes:

- goods handled
  - handling and other relevant characteristics, size, weight, temperature or other constraints
  - packaging and unit load(s)
  - inventory levels by SKU – maxima, average, minima and seasonal variations
  - throughput levels by SKU – maxima, average, minima and seasonal variations
  - forecast growth trends;
- order characteristics – influence order picking system
  - service levels for time, and for completeness of order fill

  - – size distribution as SKUs per order and units per order
  - – order frequency
  - – package and unit load details
  - – special or priority order requirements;
- goods arrival and dispatch patterns
  - – vehicle sizes, types (end or side load), frequencies and times
  - – unit loads to be handled
  - – consignment sizes
  - – own vehicles or third party;
- warehouse operations
  - – basic operations to be carried out
  - – ancillary activities, eg packing and packaging store, returns, quality control, battery charging, offices;
- site and building (if existing) details
  - – location, size, gradients, access
  - – adjacent activities and scope for expansion, constraints or obstructions
  - – services available;
- any existing facilities or equipment that may be used
  - – size, condition, numbers.

Data is not always readily available and data collection almost invariably takes considerable time. Potential sources include computer records, existing operational records, market forecasts, customers, drawings for site and buildings, equipment records and equipment suppliers, and input from relevant management and staff.

Analyse data

The purpose of data analysis is to provide the foundation for the designer's proposals for appropriate operating methods and systems, equipment, layouts, staffing levels and costs.

Data may be analysed and presented in various ways, including graphs and charts, tables, drawings, statistical analyses, drawings and networks.

One very useful analytical tool is to present inventory levels, sales quantities and picking accessions in descending order of magnitude across the whole range of SKUs. This technique is known as Pareto analysis (named after an Italian economist), and is also sometimes referred to as the 80/20 rule or A B C analysis. The results of this analysis more often than not show that roughly 20 per cent of the stock range accounts for roughly 80 per cent of the total inventory, 80 per cent of the sales and 80 per cent of the picking effort. This enables the designer to identify

Table 20.1 A B C analysis

Product Group	Percentage of Product Range	Percentage of Total Stock	Suitable Storage Methods
A	20%	80%	block stack, drive-in, push back, live, double deep, very narrow aisle
B	30%	15%	VNA, APR
C	50%	5%	APR, mobile

the really important SKUs in the product range, and also to identify different characteristics for different sections of the product range and so devise solutions appropriate to the material being handled and stored. A simple example of this is shown in Table 20.1.

In practice, other factors such as throughput would also have to be superimposed on this analysis in determining the storage systems to be adopted for the different part of the product range.

Establish what unit loads will be used

Examples of unit loads include pallets, stillages, roll cage pallets, skid sheets, tote boxes and hanging garment rails.

Unit loads to be handled and stored in a warehouse, which may change as material moves through the warehouse, will influence the choice of equipment required and the ability to utilize space effectively, and should therefore be established early in the design process. Suppliers may impose the unit loads in which material arrives at a warehouse and customers may specify dispatch unit loads, but the warehouse designer should use whatever freedom of choice exists to ensure the most appropriate unit loads for the processes being carried out.

The benefits of using unit loads include equipment standardization, minimization of movement, material security, and facilitating and minimizing the time for loading and unloading vehicles. For example, roll cage pallets used for picking grocery products enable cases of different sizes to be accumulated and handled in a common unit. Standard handling equipment can be used for moving the roll cages, and if the cages are used for stores deliveries, there is no need to transfer picked goods into another unit load before vehicle loading.

The most common unit load is the wooden pallet, and there are various designs – single sided, double sided, two-way or four-way fork entry, and other variations. In the UK the most common size is the ISO pallet, 1,200 millimetres by 1,000 millimetres, although in Europe generally the most common is the Europal at 800 millimetres by 1,200 millimetres. The pallet dimensions determine how pallets can be loaded on to vehicles and such details as storage racking dimensions, so the point must be emphasized that the choice of unit load is critical. The disparity between the dominant UK pallet size and the European-sized pallet will ultimately have to be resolved.

Postulate basic operations and methods

The basic operations that will take place in a warehouse, and how they will be carried out, must be determined before it is possible to specify the equipment, space or staffing levels required for them. These will include vehicle unloading and goods receipt, storage, picking operations, order collation and packing, vehicle loading for dispatch and all associated handling.

The information and communication requirements for the operations must also be established, and this will build up into a specification for the warehouse management system to run the operations. This will include considerations of whether paper systems will be used, or 'paperless' systems, which can include radio data communication, picking by lights and the use of bar codes.

In addition to these fundamental considerations, however, there will be ancillary activities required to support the basic operations, which will require resources and space in their own right. These are sometimes tagged on to a design almost as an afterthought, but they really are an integral part of the total design and should be treated accordingly. They can include:

- packing operations and associated packaging material storage;
- pallet repair and empty store;
- returned goods area;
- waste disposal;
- warehouse cleaning and cleaning equipment;
- battery-charging area;
- maintenance workshop;
- services – heating, lighting, ventilation, fire prevention;
- stand-by generator, especially for chill stores;
- offices;
- amenities – changing and locker rooms, toilets, rest-room, restaurant, first aid;
- separate amenities for visiting drivers;
- security facilities including gatehouse;
- lorry parking and manoeuvre areas, car parking;

- vehicle wash;
- fuel supply for lorries.

Consider possible equipment types for storage and handling

The basic types of equipment used in warehouses have been outlined in Chapters 16 to 19. To be able to specify the appropriate equipment for a particular application clearly requires an awareness of what is available and an understanding of the basic operating characteristics of the different equipment types.

To illustrate this point, consider a requirement for pallet storage of 1,000 different product lines, SKUs, with only a small amount of stock associated with each SKU, say not more than two pallets, and fairly low throughput rates. Clearly block stacking, drive-in racking or even push back racking would not be appropriate since it is not practical to mix different SKUs in any one storage row, and the use of any of these methods would result in either very poor use of space or unacceptable levels of double handling. On the other hand, mobile racking or adjustable pallet racking could be considered. Mobile racking is expensive, but the good space utilization might reduce building costs. It provides random access to all pallets, and the inherently slow operation would not be a disadvantage with low throughput products. Adjustable pallet racking, however, would not give such good use of space, but is very much cheaper, and gives random access to all pallets. It is also inherently more flexible in the event of future changes to stock or throughput profiles. This sort of argument should be used, selecting equipment with characteristics that most closely match the system requirements, for all warehouse operations.

After the completion of warehouse design comes the procurement stage, identifying potential equipment suppliers, going out to tender, assessing suppliers on equipment performance, spares and service back-up, and the experience of other users, before finally deciding and placing orders.

Calculate equipment quantities

The amount of equipment required is calculated from the basic design data and equipment operational characteristics. Typically the stock-holding requirements will dictate how much storage capacity to incorporate into a design, and the type of storage will also influence the final numbers, eg block stack utilization typically 70 per cent, adjustable pallet racking 90 per cent (see Chapter 16).

Handling equipment requirements will be based on material movements in the warehouse, including seasonal variations and short-term peak loads, and operational data on equipment capacities, typically manufacturers' technical data plus operating experience. Shift working patterns will affect these calculations, and also determine whether spare batteries will be required for battery-powered trucks. The number of order picking trucks will depend not only on total warehouse throughput, but also on order sizes and frequencies.

Data on goods received, including delivery window and times required for vehicle unloading, will dictate receiving dock facilities such as access doors and dock levellers, and the handling equipment for vehicle unloading. Similar considerations apply to dispatch. The provision of raised docks or level docks will depend on the types of vehicle accessing the warehouse – end loading or side loading. Space requirements for order collation and assembly should take account of the working patterns of order arrival at dispatch, and the way in which vehicle schedules integrate with these internal work patterns.

Using stock and throughput figures, and equipment operating characteristics, the calculations of basic equipment requirements are generally straightforward when taken operation by operation. What is not easy to calculate however is the effect of all the mobile equipment and operating staff, working together, and interacting and interfacing, and sometimes getting in the way of one another, and causing queues and delays. This dynamic situation is nearer the real operational situation than is one based on merely calculating each operation in isolation. For this reason, computer-based dynamic simulation techniques are used, to validate the 'static' calculations and to take account of potential interference between activities when running simultaneously.

Calculate staffing levels

The requirements for operating staff are closely linked to the mobile equipment requirements, and in many cases will 'fall out' of the equipment calculations. Quite clearly, staffing levels have to be established as part of the design, and to enable a full costing of the warehouse to be made.

Prepare possible building and site layouts

The layout brings together all the components of the warehouse operation inside the building, and also the external site features.

Internal layout issues

The general principles for internal layout include:

- good access to stock;
- logical flow patterns with minimal cross-flows or backtracking of people or material, based on analysis of material and staff movements, generally in a rectilinear layout;
- minimizing the amount of movement required for people and for handling equipment;
- making the best use of building volume;
- safe systems of work including the provision where possible of separate movement aisles and access doors for people and for mobile equipment, elimination of dead areas in which operators could be trapped, eg no aisles with closed ends, and provision of fire escapes.

A fundamental decision is whether to adopt a 'through flow' or 'U' flow configuration. With 'through flow', goods enter at one end of the warehouse and leave from the opposite end, and all material flows across the full length of the building. This is appropriate when separate goods receipt and goods dispatch operations are required, perhaps for security or control reasons, or because goods inwards vehicles and dispatch vehicles are very different (platform height, nature of unit load), or when incoming goods arrive from an immediately adjacent production facility. A 'U' flow configuration has goods receipt and dispatch along the same face of the building, making better use of dock space and possibly of loading/unloading staff and handling equipment, and enabling popularity storage to minimize total goods movement.

Building costs have been discussed in Chapter 15, and a general rule is that the higher the building, the lower the capital cost per cubic metre of building space. Fork truck and pedestrian aisles take up a lot of building space, but aisle widths should be adequate to give reasonable and safe access to stock, and avoid congestion.

Other layout issues include:

- the use of raised or level docks for vehicle loading/unloading;
- the type of floor and floor flatness tolerances;
- the location of offices for good oversight of operations;
- provision of separate facilities for delivery and collection drivers;
- location of ancillary functions such as packaging store;
- battery-charging facilities.

Finally the likelihood of further expansion should be considered, with an internal layout that minimizes disruption if expansion has to be implemented.

External layout

The relevant factors that affect the site layout include:

- vehicle access to the site;
- security including barriers, gatehouses and separate access for cars and commercial vehicles;
- internal roads and directions of movement, one-way or two-way circuits;
- manoeuvre and waiting areas for vehicles waiting to being called forward for loading / unloading;
- car parking;
- access for fire appliances;
- locating new buildings with potential future expansion in mind.

Evaluate the design against system requirements and constraints

The original design objectives and constraints will have defined the commercial, financial and technical requirements to be met by the new warehouse, and these form the principal criteria for assessing the proposed design. The basic requirements for storage capacity, building size and layout, site layout and building position, and staffing levels can all be fairly readily validated. Capital cost (land, building, equipment, systems, etc) and operating costs (staff, equipment operating, maintenance, building insurance and rates, depreciation, etc) can also be obtained. As suggested earlier in the chapter, however, it is much more difficult to assess how effectively a warehouse will operate when all the components are working together and interacting with one another, and the use of dynamic simulation is a powerful final arbiter of the feasibility of a warehouse.

Identify the preferred design

As a design progresses, there will inevitably be a process of iteration, of checking back to the design requirements, and partial evaluation of ideas to assist the process of homing in on the final preferred design. The preferred design should then present the proposed operating processes and methods, services requirements, equipment specifications and requirements, staffing levels, capital and operating costs, and layout drawings.

SUMMARY

This chapter sets out a general procedure for the design of warehouse systems, starting from the definition of system requirements and any constraints on the design, and working through to an evaluated preferred design.

The key points of emphasis include:

- defining and agreeing terms of reference;
- obtaining accurate and relevant data (usually very time-consuming) and validating the data;
- checking the forecast stock and business levels on which the design is to be based;
- explaining and justifying any assumptions that have been used;
- involvement of all relevant management and staff as early as possible in the design process, and external bodies such as planning authority, local fire officer and insurance company.

The time and effort to achieve a good and soundly based design are well spent when compared to the cost of setting up a warehouse facility. Making changes to achieve a good design when a project is still 'on the drawing board' is comparatively easy and inexpensive. Rectifying design errors or misconceptions once a facility has been built is either impossible or very expensive (see Figure 20.1).

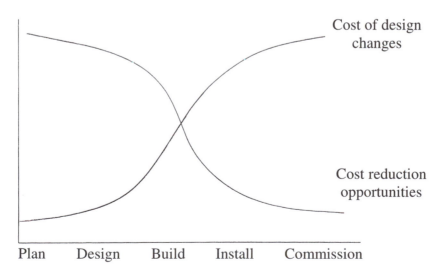

Figure 20.1 Design costs

Finally, the aim of a design should always be to get the right design and technology to meet the given requirements. Whatever level of technology is used, whether fairly basic or a very sophisticated automated or robotic system, an effective information and communication system, probably computer-based, should always be incorporated into the operational design.

21

Warehouse management and information

INTRODUCTION

A broad statement of the responsibilities of warehouse or distribution centre management would include effective planning and control, and the optimum use of resources to achieve the objectives of the operation.

More specifically, the objectives for an effective operation would include:

- meeting required customer service levels;
- cost-effective operation;
- effective and efficient use of resources;
- safe operation;
- maintaining stock integrity;
- meeting legal and local requirements for working environment and safety.

PERFORMANCE MONITORING

Performance monitoring is obviously essential to the effective management and control of any enterprise, and this certainly applies in warehousing. Although essentially a simple process, warehousing is often the last link before the customer, and it has to operate within tight service and cost standards. Failure to meet these can mean the difference between a successful and unsuccessful business. Effective monitoring necessitates an effective information system.

Clearly the performance indicators appropriate to a particular operation will be peculiar to that operation, but typical measures will include those detailed in the following sections.

Service levels

Measures can include:

- stock availability in the warehouse;
- order lead time;
- the percentage of orders completed on time;
- percentage completeness of order fill;
- accuracy of order fill;
- the number of outstanding back orders;
- damaged stock;
- returns and customer complaints.

Cost-effectiveness

This includes monitoring the costs of:

- staff, including overtime and other special payments;
- building and site;
- equipment and other resources;
- maintenance;
- pallets and pallet repair;
- packing materials and other consumables;
- services including any bought-in services.

It may be helpful to isolate the costs of specific operations such as order picking or packing, and monitor these as a proportion of total warehouse costs. It may also be useful to express some of these measures as ratios such as the cost per unit of throughput, the cost per pallet stored or the cost per item picked.

Resource utilization

This is concerned with how effectively the warehouse facilities are being used. It can include utilization of storage facilities – percentage fill – and also the utilization and availability of handling equipment, and how much availability is lost through maintenance and breakdown.

Safety and the effective use of staff

This includes performance and productivity monitoring such as pick and pack rates and order fulfilment rates. It is also concerned with the monitoring of overtime and absence, the provision of necessary skills and safety training, safe working practices and environment, safety audits and hazard monitoring. In this context risk assessment is a legal requirement – to examine the total operation and identify potential hazards, and to assess the likelihood of accidents and identify action to eliminate risk.

Stock integrity

This is concerned with the condition and security of stock, including minimizing loss, damage and deterioration. Relevant factors can include the control of stock rotation on the basis of first in, first out (FIFO), and the meeting of 'sell by' dates and shelf-life constraints.

An important control parameter is the measurement of stock turn, which indicates the rate at which goods move through the system in relation to the average stock level. For any stock line, stock turn is:

$$\frac{\text{annual throughput}}{\text{average stock level}}$$

For example, if a product sells 1,000 units per year, and the average stock level is 100 units, the stock turn will be 10, ie on average the stock is 'turned over' 10 times per year.

Meeting legal and local regulations and requirements

This particularly applies to working environment and safety. There is a wide spread of legislation that impacts on warehouse operations. It includes the Health and Safety at Work Act, Manual Handling Regulations, Self Propelled Industrial Trucks regulations, and even the Shops, Offices, and Railway Premises Act, covering the more mundane requirements for a working environment. It should also be remembered that there are codes of practice giving guidance on a wide range of warehouse operational issues, for example the Storage Equipment Manufacturers' Association (SEMA) codes of practice for racking, etc.

An increasing aspect of safety regulations is the requirement for formal risk assessments to be carried out within organizations to identify potential hazards and motivate preventative measures.

INFORMATION TECHNOLOGY

In recent years the dominant development in warehouse management and operation has been the use of computer technology and electronic data transfer, characterized by fast, accurate and comprehensive collection, analysis and use of data. It has enabled stepwise improvement in service levels, inventory reduction, use of people, utilization of resources (such as storage and handling equipment), reduction or elimination of paperwork and clerical effort, stock location and stock losses, and the facility for tracking goods through a supply chain.

Computer-based management packages are designed to handle information on goods receipt, stock balances, stock location, order picking replenishment, picking routes and pick sizes, order collation, and dispatch and vehicle loading. They are also used to monitor and work out overall performance measures to assist management control, and to log the output of individual operators as a basis for identifying training needs, and for calculating performance-related pay.

An increasingly important benefit of such systems is the ability to track individual goods and batches as they progress through a system, to provide quick and accurate information on progress and also to enable quality back-checks in the event of quality failures.

A representation of the sort of information and information links within a working warehouse are illustrated in Figure 21.1.

WAREHOUSE MANAGEMENT COMPUTER PACKAGE CHARACTERISTICS

The general characteristics of computer-based warehouse management packages include:

● accuracy by reducing the errors inherent in manual clerical recording, and by reducing or eliminating altogether the need for human data input or transfer;

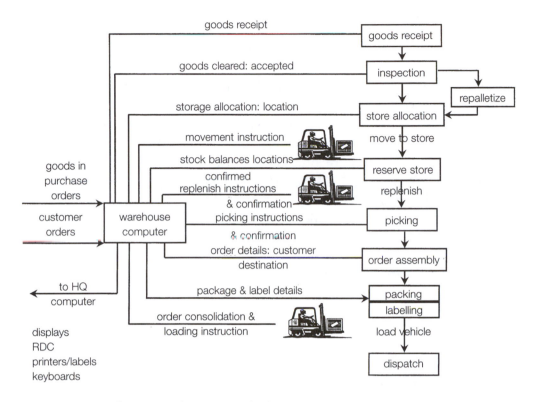

Figure 21.1 Warehouse information links

- speed of data collection, processing and communication, including immediacy of updating computer files and immediacy of information recall (particularly valuable in providing up-to-the-minute information on such aspects as stock levels and the status of customer orders);
- facility for work planning and allocation of staff and equipment;
- reduction or elimination of clerical effort;
- the ability to process and present information;
- the ability to track goods as they move through a system;
- the ability to work out and present performance-monitoring information, including the management of work-measured incentive schemes;
- information visibility.

Some of the specific benefits of such systems for warehouse operations include:

- improved customer service;
- accurate stock records;

- accurate stock location records;
- more effective use of staff, including identification of low productivity or poor picking accuracy;
- information to operators and the facility for them to interrogate the system in the event of problems;
- equipment utilization, eg better use of storage capacity by being able to use an emptied location more quickly (ie less time empty) or better use of handling equipment by minimizing the number of journeys when not carrying a payload (ie dual cycling);
- stock replenishment;
- verification of stock location and of picking quantities;
- stock rotation and maintenance of 'sell by' dates;
- fewer stock-outs;
- routine performance and status reports.

The information handling and analysis also provide data for optimizing stock zoning, location of picking stock, order picking batch sizes and picking routes.

DATA CAPTURE AND TRANSMISSION

An integral part of exploiting the benefits of computer management packages is the data capture and communication systems to which they are linked.

Data capture and transfer can be accomplished by a number of techniques. The most widely used in warehousing is bar-coding, which represents numbers and letters in printed bar form, and is machine-readable by appropriate scanning equipment. It is a fast and accurate technology, and fairly robust. There are various different bar-code types or 'symbologies', the most commonly encountered in warehousing being 'Code 39'. In warehousing bar-coding is used to identify goods and verify stock locations. It allows goods to be sorted and routed through a handling system, and enables them to be tracked as they move through the system. It simplifies stock checking, and a range of other data input and capture requirements. Bar-code labels are cheap although they can be damaged by scuffing, and the technology is established, reliable and fast.

Optical character recognition (OCR) technology uses labels that are both machine- and human-readable. It is appropriate in applications such as document handling and interrogation, and text scanning.

Voice data recognition is a system of data capture in which the sounds of an operator's voice are recognized and interpreted by the system. The system presents what it thinks it has heard on to a display screen for the operator to verify, and correct if necessary, before moving on to the next transaction.

Radio frequency uses small transmitter–receivers set into tags attached to the items to be identified or tracked. The tags can be interrogated and can communicate with a host computer. More complex tags can be re-programmed during use.

An interesting set of experimental data derived by the US Department of Defense gave the following results for error rates when capturing data.

Technique:	Error Rate (characters):
Written entry	25,000 in 3 million
Keyboard entry	10,000 in 3 million
OCR	100 in 3 million
Bar code (Code 39)	1 in 3 million
Transponders (radio frequency tags)	1 in 30 million

This data, although experimental, illustrates the levels of accuracy achievable using information technology. The use of an appropriate computer-based information and communication system is a *sine qua non* for effective warehouse management and the achievement of operational objectives. Without such a system, however high-tech or leading-edge the engineering technology, the operation will not function to the limit of its capability.

RADIO DATA COMMUNICATION

A technique of communication increasingly found in warehouse information applications is the use of radio data communication. This is usually linked in to the warehouse management computer system and provides radio communication between the computer and any required workstation, which can be static or mobile. It is now quite common to see fork-lift trucks fitted with remote radio data terminals (see Figure 21.2), and sometimes also with a label printer mounted with the terminal. The operator is online to the computer, takes instructions from the computer, confirms work carried out, and interrogates the computer for further information if required. This sort of technology facilitates major improvements in communication between the operator and the warehouse management computer, resulting in much greater speed of response within warehouse systems, and more efficient and productive utilization of people and equipment.

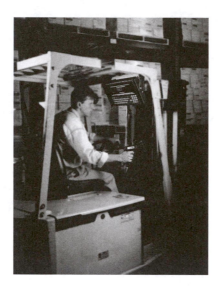

Figure 21.2   Radio data (courtesy of LXE Inc and Swisslog Software)

SUMMARY

Warehousing and associated storage and handling operations are not stand-alone activities, but integral and key elements in a supply chain. They use expensive resources – people, equipment, buildings, materials – and they play a vital role in the achievement of acceptable levels of customer service.

This chapter has discussed the fundamental responsibilities of management for warehouse and distribution centre operation, and the need for monitoring to identify potential performance failures and ensure efficient operation. The fundamental importance of information and communication in these processes has been emphasized, and the information technology utilized in these operations has been reviewed.

The pressures on management have been to reduce costs and inventory whilst maintaining or improving customer service, but in a context of increased legislation regulating such aspects as quality, safety and environmental constraints. Developments that have enabled management to meet these requirements include information technology and, where appropriate, the use of high levels of automation and robotics.

Nevertheless, achieving warehouse objectives and meeting management responsibilities still depend ultimately on the quality of management and staff running the operation. There has been significant development of management skills and awareness in recent years, as well as an upgrading of operational staff to exploit the potential benefits of technology and information systems.

Part 5

Freight transport

22

International logistics: modal choice

INTRODUCTION

The changing nature of logistics and the supply chain, particularly the move by many companies towards global operations, has had an obvious impact on the relative importance of the different modes of transport. In a global context, more products are moved far greater distances because companies have developed the concepts of focus factories, with a single global manufacturing point for certain products, and the concentration of production facilities in low-cost manufacturing locations. Long-distance modes of transport have thus become much more important to the development of efficient logistics operations that have a global perspective. So the need to understand the relative merits of, say, sea freight as against air freight is crucial. Nevertheless, for many localized final delivery operations it is still road freight transport that offers the only real alternative. All of these changes serve to emphasize the need to understand the particular advantages and disadvantages of the different freight transport modes.

In Europe, road freight transport continues to be the dominant mode of transport. A look at recent European statistics confirms this. The upward trend in the use of road transport has continued for many years but there is now an indication that this may have reached a plateau, although it seems unlikely that the importance of road freight transport will actually diminish in the near future. Rail freight has declined for many years, but is now holding its decline. Inland waterways are still important. The use of pipelines has continued for certain specialized movements. Figure 22.1, based on UK Department of Transport statistics for Europe as a whole, indicates the relative importance of the different modes for freight transportation.

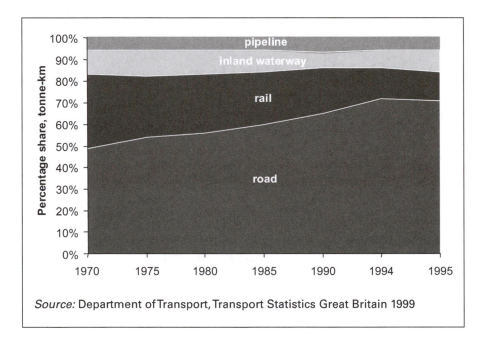

Figure 22.1 Share of freight transport in Europe

As previously discussed, for the movement of goods internationally the different modes continue to be important. The selection of the most appropriate transport mode is thus a fundamental decision for international distribution, the main criterion being the need to balance costs with customer service. There are very significant trade-offs to be made when examining the alternatives available between the different logistics factors and the different transport modes.

This chapter is concerned with the means of determining the choice of transport mode within the logistics environment. This covers the important operational factors that impose on the choice of mode, the characteristics of the different modes and an approach or method for selection.

OPERATIONAL FACTORS

Encompassing the many operational factors that may need to be considered are those that can be categorized as external to direct distribution-related factors. These are particularly relevant when contemplating the international context of modal choice because from country to country these factors can vary significantly. They include:

- basic infrastructure;
- trade barriers (customs duty, import quotas, etc);
- export controls and licences;
- law and taxation;
- financial institutions and services, and economic conditions (exchange rate stability, inflation, etc);
- communications systems;
- culture; and
- climate.

This list can be a long one, and the relevant inclusions will vary according to the country under consideration. A summary of some of the most relevant developments in international trade is given at the end of this chapter.

The particular customer characteristics may also have a significant effect on the choice of transport mode. Most of the characteristics will need to be considered for both national and international modal choice, that is, they are not specific to overseas distribution. The main characteristics to take into account are:

- service level / type of service location;
- delivery point constraints (access, equipment, etc);
- after-sales service needs;
- credit rating;
- terms of sale preference (CIF / FOB);
- order size preference;
- customer importance; and
- product knowledge.

From the modal choice standpoint, these characteristics can be classified into two broad areas: those related to customer service (speed, reliability, etc) and those related to physical attributes (order or drop size, location, delivery constraints, etc).

A more detailed discussion on the importance of customer service and logistics is given in Chapter 3.

The physical nature of the product is as important in determining modal choice as it is with all the other logistics functions. The main factors that need to be considered include:

- *Volume to weight ratio* – which concerns the relative amount of cubic capacity taken up by a given weight of product. For example, one tonne of paper tissues takes up far more space than one tonne of bricks. This is relevant when considering the different charging structures of the different transport modes – whether charged by weight or by cubic volume.
- *Value to weight ratio* – which takes into account the value of the product to be transported. The relative transport cost of a high-value, low-weight product is likely to be so insignificant to the overall value of the product that the choice of mode from a cost perspective is irrelevant (eg jewellery or computer chips).
- *Substitutability* (product alternatives, etc) – whereby if a product can be substituted by an alternative from another source, it may be worth while using a fast but expensive mode of transport to ensure the order is accepted by the customer. Where no substitute is possible, a slower and less expensive mode can be used.
- *Special characteristics* (hazard, fragility, perishability, time constraints, security). A hazardous product may be restricted in how it is allowed to be transported (eg some chemicals), and a time-constrained product may have to be moved on a fast and expensive mode of transport to ensure it does not miss its time deadline (eg newspapers and promotional products).

These characteristics are considered in more detail in Chapter 6.

The final series of important characteristics that need to be considered when determining modal choice concerns the other logistics components. These are the elements concerned with the classic logistics trade-offs described in Chapter 2. In any company's distribution structure there will be a number of factors that are interrelated. These may be fixed and unchangeable, and seen as sacrosanct by certain sections of the company. They may be subject to change – providing overall benefits can be identified from any change. These factors need to be known. There is no point in designing a system or choosing a mode that fails to allow for these other factors. It is important to be aware of the constraints that any fixed factors impose on any newly devised system, as the cost implications may well indicate that a trade-off would produce a better overall solution. The main characteristics may include:

- product locations;
- supply points;
- warehouse and storage facilities;
- own transport;
- marketing plans and policies;
- financial situation; and
- existing delivery system.

TRANSPORT MODE CHARACTERISTICS

The modal choice consideration so far has been concerned with the various operational factors that might need to be taken into account. The other main set of considerations involves the various attributes of the different modes themselves. It is not possible to describe here the detailed operations of the different modes, but it is important to indicate their major attributes specifically in relation to the factors described in the previous sections. This consideration is with respect to both cost and service and also with respect to the other distribution-related functions where trade-offs may need to be identified.

Sea freight

Of the main alternative types of sea freight, both the conventional load and the unit load are relevant. The unit load (container) is considered later. For conventional sea freight, the main points are:

- *Cost economies.* For some products, the most economic means of carriage remains that of conventional sea freight. This particularly applies to bulk goods and to large packaged consignments that are going long distances. Where speed of service is completely unimportant, then the cheapness of sea freight makes it very competitive.
- *Flexibility.* There are very many liners and tramp ships, and very many ports, both large and small. In addition to this, sailings are quite frequent, making sea transport very flexible in terms of the number of alternatives that are open.
- *Availability.* Liner services are widely advertised, extensively categorized and most types of cargo can be accommodated.
- *Speed.* Sea freight tends to be very slow for several reasons. These include the fact that the turnaround time in port is still quite slow, as is the actual voyage time.

- *Need for double-handling.* Conventional sea freight is disadvantaged by the inefficient handling methods still used. This is especially true when compared with the more competitive 'through transport' systems with which sea freight must compete. The problem is particularly apparent on some of the short sea routes.
- *Delay problems.* There are three major delay factors that can lead to bad and irregular services, as well as helping to slow up the transport time itself. These are over and above the journey time. They are pre-shipment delays, delays at the discharge port and unexpected delays due to bad weather, missed tides, etc.
- *Damage.* The need to double-handle cargo on conventional ships tends to make this mode more prone to damage for both products and packaging.

Road freight

As already indicated, road freight transport is the most important mode within Europe and the UK. In the context of international distribution, road freight transport is also important, particularly to and from the UK in terms of the use of roll-on, roll-off (RORO) ferry services and the Channel Tunnel route. The key characteristics are similar for sea or ferry crossings. This form of transport consists of the through transport of goods from factory or warehouse direct to customers' premises abroad.

Compared with the other forms of international freight transport, the major advantages and disadvantages of these services are as follows:

- They can provide a very quick service if ferry/tunnel schedules are carefully timed into the route plans.
- For complete unit loads with single origin and destination points, they can be very competitive from the cost viewpoint.
- There is a greatly reduced need to double-handle and tranship goods and packages, and for direct, full-load deliveries this is completely eliminated. This saves time and minimizes the likelihood of damage.
- For cross-Channel routes, there is a great flexibility for through movement as a unit load. This is because the system combines the large routeing choice provided by a road vehicle with the short ferry/tunnel crossings.
- Packaging cost can be kept to a minimum because loads are less susceptible to the extreme transit 'shocks' that other modes can cause.
- The system can provide regular, scheduled services due to frequent ferry/tunnel 'sailings', and due to the flexibility of road vehicle scheduling.

- The RORO/tunnel system loses many of its advantages when used for less than lorry-sized loads. These entail groupage and so involve double-handling (at both ends of the journey), additional packaging and time delay.

Rail freight

There have been recent developments in rail freight systems, including the development of containerized systems using ISO containers as the basic unit load, the regular scheduling of rail wagon services, and the introduction of the swap body concept of transferable road–rail units. The ISO container system has the particular attributes of all container systems, as discussed later. More conventional rail freight systems have the major benefit of being a relatively cheap form of transport. This is particularly true for bulky and heavy consignments that require movement over medium to long distances and where speed is not vital. The principal disadvantages of conventional rail freight are as follows:

- Shunting shocks can cause damage.
- There is a need to double-handle many loads because the first and last leg of a 'through' journey often needs to be by road transport.
- There is a limited number of railheads available – many companies with railway sidings on their premises have closed them down.
- In general, rail transport is a very slow means of carriage.
- Rail freight transport is also very unreliable. Batches of wagons may arrive at irregular intervals. This can cause further delays for international traffic if a complete shipment is on a single customs document.

Air freight

The use of air freight as an alternative transport mode has grown rapidly in recent years. Major developments in the areas of integrated unit loads, improved handling systems and additional cargo space, together with the proliferation of scheduled cargo flights, have increased the competitiveness and service capability of air freight.

The major attributes of air freight are as follows:

- Air freight compares very well with other transport modes over longer international movements. This is because it has very rapid transit times over these longer distances.
- It is a very fast mode of transport. There can be delays at airports, however, and this factor can often make a significant difference to overall journey times.
- One particular advantage is known as 'lead-time economy'. This is where the

ability to move goods very quickly over long distances means that it is unnecessary to hold stocks of these items in the countries in question (spare parts, etc). The short lead time required between the ordering and receiving of goods, and the resultant saving in inventory holding costs give this benefit its name of 'lead-time economy'.

● The air freighting of products allows for a great deal of market flexibility, because any number of countries and markets can be reached very quickly and easily. This is particularly advantageous for a company that wishes either to test a product in a given area or to launch a new product. The flexibility of air freight means that a company need not necessarily set up extensive stock-holding networks in these areas.

● The movement of goods by air freight can result in a marked reduction in packaging requirements. The air freight mode is not one that experiences severe physical conditions, and so its consignments are not prone to damage and breakages.

● Air freight transport is very advantageous for certain ranges of goods, compared to many of the alternative modes. This includes those commodities with high value to weight ratios (a lot of money is tied up, therefore an expensive freight on-cost is not significant), perishables (where speed is vital), fashion goods (which tend to both be expensive and have a short 'shelf life'), emergency supplies (speed again is vital), and finally spare parts (the lack of which may be holding up the operation of a multimillion-pound project).

● For the vast majority of products, air freight is a very expensive form of transport. This is by far its greatest disadvantage. In some instances, and for some products, cost is of very little consequence, and it is for these types of goods that air freight tends to be used. Although air freight is very quick from airport to airport, there is a tendency for this factor to become less of an advantage because a great deal of time can be lost due to airport congestion, and handling and paperwork delays.

● Air freight has suffered to a certain extent from having quite severe lapses in the security of the goods moved.

Container systems

Container systems can be viewed as a specialized mode of freight transport, although the container is now a fundamental feature of all the major national and international transport modes – road, rail, sea and air. Containerization makes possible the development of what is known as the 'intermodal' system of freight transport, enabling the uncomplicated movement of goods in bulk from one transport mode to another. (See Chapter 23 for more details.)

The main attributes of containers and container systems are as follows:

- They enable a number of small packages to be consolidated into large single unit loads.
- There is a reduction in the handling of goods, as they are distributed from their point of origin to point of destination.
- There is a reduction in individual packaging requirements, depending on the load within the container.
- There is a reduction in damage to products caused by other cargo.
- Insurance charges are lower due to the reduced damage potential.
- Handling costs at the docks and at other modal interfaces are reduced.
- There is a quicker turnaround for all the types of transport used. Port utilization also improves.
- The all-round delivery time is speedier, and so raises service levels.
- Documentation is much simpler – this applies to both company and customs documentation.
- The concept of 'through transit' becomes feasible, and allows for a truly integrated transport system to be developed.
- In the early days of containerization, the systems that were developed tended not to be well integrated across the different transport modes. This has considerably improved in recent years.
- There is a need for special facilities and handling equipment, and these are very costly. Thus, there is a limited number of transfer points available.
- The initial cost of the containers themselves is very high.
- The return of empty containers can often be an expensive problem. Trade is seldom evenly balanced so that return loads may not be available.
- Containers may leak, thereby causing damage due to rain or sea water.
- Loads may be affected by their position of stow, eg above or below deck.

METHOD OF SELECTION

A fairly straightforward approach can be adopted as a method of modal selection. This is based on the factors previously discussed and is as follows:

1. *Identify operational factors*
   - external
   - customer
   - product
   - other logistical.

2. *Identify transport mode characteristics*
   - sea
   - inland waterway
   - road
   - rail
   - air
   - container.
3. *Determine major consignment factors*
   - routeing responsibility
   - distance
   - cargo type
   - priority.
4. *Make trade-off*
   - service
   - costs.

Operational factors and transport mode characteristics are as described previously in this chapter. The major consignment or route factors are those that affect the decisions relating to the shipment in question. Often only a few of these will apply, but sometimes several need to be taken into account at one time. The main ones include those that are noted below with examples of some of the more important questions to consider:

1. *Routeing and through transit responsibility*
   - Is a direct route stipulated?
   - Who is concerned with the through transit?
2. *Distance*
   - What is the distance to be moved?
3. *Type of cargo*
   - If bulk or general cargo, will a certain specific route be best?
4. *Quantity*
   - Full load or part load?
5. *Unit size*
   - Small or large?
   - Will unitization help?
   - Is groupage an alternative?
6. *Priority*
   - How soon must the goods reach their destination?
   - Does 'Urgent!' really mean 'Urgent!'?

7. *Commodity value*
   - How important is the transport cost element?
   - If import/export, how is the commodity rated?
8. *Regular shipments*
   - How often will these shipments be made?

The final decision is the customary logistics trade-off between cost and service. This must be undertaken in relation to the relevant operational factors, transport mode characteristics and consignment factors outlined above. In theory, the volume of freight to be moved and the distance to be travelled dictate the choice of mode. This is summarized in Figure 22.2. In practice, other elements such as the speed of delivery required or the reliability of service may override these purely economic factors.

		short	medium	long	very long
Size of order/ load	**100T**	road	road/rail	rail/sea	sea
	20T	road	road	road/rail	rail/sea
	pallet	road	road	road/rail	air/sea
	parcel	post/road	post/road/air	post/road/air	post/air

Delivery distance

Source: Alan Rushton, Cranfield University (unpublished)

Figure 22.2   Modal choice matrix

ASPECTS OF INTERNATIONAL TRADE

This is a particularly exciting period for the development of logistics in a global context. The introduction of a number of international trade agreements and economic unions, such as the European Union, the North American Free Trade Association (NAFTA) and the Association of South-East Asian Nations (ASEAN) amongst others, has had a major impact on the globalization of trade. Many products are produced and distributed across regions and continents, and there has been a significant impact on transport opportunities. As these changes have taken place they have been a major influence on the structure of distribution and logistics systems throughout Europe and the rest of the world as trade barriers have broken down and new transport networks have been initiated.

In a European context, major barriers to trade have been or are being overcome. They include:

- physical barriers – removal of customs control, introduction of the single administrative document and removal of immigration and passport control;
- technical barriers – removal of all barriers to trade between member states, free movement of goods, capital, services and workers, harmonization of technical standards, common protection for intellectual and industrial property, and opening up of public procurement;
- fiscal barriers – approximation of indirect taxation (VAT and excise duties), and consequent removal of fiscal frontier checks;
- access to Central and Eastern European countries;
- introduction of the euro currency, which allows greater transparency of pricing.

Those provisions and changes that are particularly relevant to logistics can be summarized as:

- Goods and services can be bought anywhere in the community.
- Customs barriers have been virtually abolished.
- Documentation has been simplified and standardized.
- Operating (transport) permit restrictions have been removed.
- Testing standards are acceptable in all community states.
- There is free movement of capital.

Some significant opportunities have arisen for transport and distribution companies resulting from the development of economic unions. These have encouraged companies to increase the scope of their services across the wider geographic areas. They include the following:

- There is more competition between third-party companies because of the increased market.
- Transport and third-party distribution companies can give a more comprehensive European-wide service.
- There is easier and faster movement of goods across borders.

- Distribution and transport can be bought in any country – there is more cross-trading and cabotage (transport companies moving goods in other member states).
- Increased opportunities for joint ventures with other European and international operators enable European-wide and global integrated logistics and transport organizations.
- New depot locations and consequent transport flows can be determined to suit both sources and markets.

Identifying the most cost-effective opportunities in international transport and logistics requires a very sophisticated understanding of some of the key financial issues involved. There are many different elements that need to be taken into account when trying to identify the most cost-effective solution from a myriad of alternatives. The main factors include:

- *Types of payment.* These can include, in order of risk, an open account (where terms of payment are pre-arranged with the buyer), a draft (where title of the goods is retained until payment is received), a letter of credit (where the bank will authorize payment for an order once the precise conditions of the letter of credit have been met) and cash in advance (money paid up front – which few customers are happy to accept).
- *Taxes and duties.* These can have a big impact on the overall cost of a product. They may include import tariffs, value added tax or quota payments.
- *Transport costs.* These will include costs related to any of the different modes. Unless direct delivery is being undertaken using a single mode of transport, an allowance should be made for inland carriage from point of origin, plus international carriage, plus final delivery from the destination port.
- *Associated transport charges.* These can include port fees, bunker adjustment fees or fuel charges.
- *Other charges.* These can include insurance, break bulk, storage and handling.

It is important to be aware of the basic methods of undertaking business when concerned with international transport. There are a number of different ways in which goods can be purchased on an international basis, and it is essential that both the buyer and the seller are aware of which terms have been agreed. Different terms mean very different responsibilities for both the organization and the payment of the transport element of the order. These are known as Incoterms, and the main alternatives are outlined in Table 22.1.

Table 22.1 The main Incoterms

Ex-works	from the supplier's factory	The supplier makes the goods available at its premises at the agreed time, and the supplier arranges packaging and marking.
FCA	free carrier	A carrier, arranged by the buyer, collects the goods from the supplier after they have been cleared for export.
FAS	free alongside ship	The supplier pays for delivery of the goods to the ship at the port indicated by the buyer.
FOB	free on board	The seller pays for delivery on to the ship up to the point of export.
CFR	cost and freight	The seller pays for the freight to the destination port and is responsible for the export licence and the transport and packaging documentation.
CIF	cost, insurance and freight	This is the same as CFR, but the seller also arranges and pays the marine insurance.
CPT	carriage paid to	The seller pays the freight and costs to the destination point.
CIP	carriage/insurance paid to	This is the same as CPT, but the seller arranges and pays the cargo insurance.
DAF	delivered at frontier	The seller delivers the goods, cleared for export, at the frontier, but before the customs border.
DES	delivered ex-ship	The seller pays all the transport costs and delivers the goods to the buyer on board the ship at the destination port.
DEQ	delivered ex-quay duty paid	The seller pays all costs of transport and taxes to the port and clears the goods for import.
DDU	delivered duty unpaid	The seller is responsible for and pays all costs for delivery to the customer except duties, taxes and import costs.
DDP	delivered duty paid	The seller is responsible for and pays all costs for delivery to the customer.

Types of documentation are also very important. The requirements for these may vary according to the origin and destination of the shipment, and the mode of transport used. The most common documents are:

- the shipper's export declaration;
- bill of lading;
- consular documentation;
- single administration document (SAD);
- certificate of origin;
- packing note;
- insurance certificate;
- export clearance;
- customs requirements for import and export.

It is absolutely essential that all documentation is completed accurately and in good time, otherwise substantial delays can occur. In some instances, delays related to incorrect or inadequate documentation can lead to significant additional cost and, of course, loss of business. For this reason, and because of the particular complications concerning import and export documentation, many companies use the services of freight forwarders. Typical services that are offered include:

- preparation and checking of shipping documents;
- booking space with carriers;
- arranging the order collection from the point of origin to the shipping port;
- arranging the customs clearance and final delivery at the destination country;
- provision of advice in export regulations, documentation requirements, etc;
- detailed knowledge of carriers, ports, etc;
- knowledge of the different modes of international transport;
- knowledge of the different costs associated with different modes, destinations, etc.

SUMMARY

In this chapter the very broad area of transport modal choice has been described, initially by reviewing the relative importance of the different modes of transport. Emphasis has been given to the decision-making process involved in modal choice, covering the following aspects:

- operational factors relating to
  - the external environment
  - customer characteristics
  - the physical nature of the product
  - other logistics components;
- transport mode characteristics covering
  - sea freight
  - road freight
  - rail freight
  - air freight
  - intermodal systems;
- method of modal selection, indicating an approach that takes into account the main consignment or route factors;
- methods of undertaking business
  - Incoterms
  - documentation
  - the freight forwarder.

From the viewpoint of the different modes of transport it seems likely that the higher productivity and adaptability of road freight transport together with the increasing demands on service levels will put additional pressure on rail, and strengthen the already strong position of road transport. If concepts such as just-in-time continue to flourish with the requirement for regular, frequent deliveries, flexibility and reduced stock levels, then it will be less easy for rail and water transport to compete. Railway companies need to develop intermodal systems to offer flexibility and cost advantages comparable to road freight transport and container services. For long distance movement, rail should be able to compete with road. Air freight should continue to flourish in the niche area of fast delivery from global stock-holding centres. Computerized systems should enable improvements in reliability and transit times for all modes.

23

Intermodal transport

INTRODUCTION

What is meant by intermodal transport? The following is a useful definition from the European Conference of Transport Ministers: *the movement of goods in one and the same loading unit or vehicle, which uses successively several modes of transport without handling of the goods themselves in changing modes.*

Undoubtedly the introduction of unitized loads in the form of International Standards Organisation (ISO) containers and pallets revolutionized the movement of freight from the 1960s onwards. Pallets first appeared on the global transport stage courtesy of the United States military forces in the 1940s. The assembly of goods on to pallets allowed swift transfer of loads from warehouse to truck to train or ship or aircraft. The reduction in personnel required and transit times were remarkable. In 1958 Fred Olsen's reported loading 975 tons of unitized cargo in 10 hours with an 18- to 22-man long-shore gang (stevedores) instead of the usual 200 tons (Van Den Burg).

Rudimentary freight containers were certainly in use as early as 1911 when they were known as lift vans in the USA, but it was the 1960s that saw the birth of the ISO container for freight movement. Pioneering companies in container transport were Sea-Land Service Inc on the US Atlantic coast, Matsons on the US Pacific coast and Associated Steamships Ltd in Australia. A number of ISO recommendations helped the standardization of containers and therefore allowed for interchangeability between different modes of transport around the world:

- R-668 in January 1968 defined the terminology, dimensions and ratings.
- R-790 in July 1968 defined the identification markings.
- R-1161 in January 1970 made recommendations about corner fittings.
- R-1897 in October 1970 set out the minimum internal dimensions of general-purpose freight containers.

These standards allow the same container to be safely carried by truck, train, deep-sea cellular container ship and aircraft. This removes the requirement for multiple handling of the products, improves security, reduces loss and damage and above all speeds up the whole process of freight transportation. Containers of freight move around the globe with an ease that could only have been dreamt of at the start of the 20th century. This ability to move freight swiftly and safely aids the logistics process, as the elimination of wasted time is a key objective of logistics management. Containers also have another benefit in that they can be traced through the transport system and their progress monitored.

INTERMODAL EQUIPMENT

The following section is designed to provide an overview of the various types of equipment specifically used in intermodal transport. The list is not exhaustive but the most common equipment will be identified and described briefly.

Intermodal containers

ISO containers

ISO containers are so called because the International Standards Organisation have defined the important features of the container, such as dimensions, to allow for the widest possible use of this equipment around the world. Containers are usually rectilinear boxes constructed of steel. Open-topped versions, which are covered by a fabric curtain, are available for loads that may not fit into a standard container. Another common variation is the tanktainer, which is a steel frame that conforms to the ISO dimensions but has a tank container fixed inside the frame. This allows bulk loads of liquids or powders to be carried by intermodal carriers. Refrigerated versions are also available.

The most common sizes of container available are 20 feet, 30 feet, 40 feet and 45 feet in length. The height and width dimensions are the same for all lengths at 8 feet wide by 8 feet 6 inches high. As with most rules exceptions do exist, but these are the most commonly used dimensions.

Two acronyms used widely in intermodal circles are TEU and FEU. The initials stand for twenty feet equivalent unit and forty feet equivalent unit. They are often used as definitions of cellular container ship capacities. A ship may be described as being able to carry 6,000 TEU. The twenty feet equivalent unit refers to the 20-feet container. Therefore two 40-feet containers would equal four TEU or two FEU.

The swap body

These are a type of container used primarily on bimodal intermodal operations, which use the road and rail modes of transport. The swap body is a self-supporting body that has supporting legs that may be folded away when not required. Swap bodies conform to different international standards. There are three standard lengths of 7.15 metres, 7.45 metres and 7.82 metres. These lengths are used because the swap body will be carried by road transport for part of its journey and must conform to the strict requirements pertaining to vehicle dimensions inside the European Union.

The swap body is transferred from road vehicle to rail wagon by means of an overhead straddle crane, which has four arms that locate into slots permanently fixed to the bottom of the swap body.

A further version of the swap body is called the caisse mobile. These are 12 metres or 13.6 metres long, which conform to European Union dimensions for articulated semi-trailer lengths. Caisse mobiles do not usually have self-supporting legs but very often are able to be top-lifted in the same way as ISO containers. Unlike ISO containers, swap bodies cannot be stacked.

Road-Railer trailers

Road-Railer is the brand name for a method of effectively converting a road-going articulated semi-trailer into a rail-going rail wagon. This is achieved by placing a railway bogie under the rear of a specially designed road semi-trailer. This same bogie attaches itself to the kingpin of the following road trailer. This process is repeated until the train is complete. The road wheels of the semi-trailer are mechanically retracted to prevent them from interfering with the movement of the train. This system does not require specially adapted rail wagons and allows for a more rapid transfer of vehicles from road to rail. It does require that the road vehicles are specially designed for the purpose.

Unaccompanied trailers

Unaccompanied road semi-trailers may be used to send goods by roll-on roll-off sea ferry (RORO). This method does not require any adaptation of the road trailer and avoids the added cost of sending the tractive unit and driver with the trailer. This is important as tariffs on this sort of service usually relate to the length of the vehicle, and therefore unaccompanied trailers will be shorter and cheaper. The unaccompanied trailers are moved on and off the ferry by means of a motive unit (often called a tug) fitted with a hydraulic mechanism for attaching to the front of the trailer and lifting the semi-trailer without the need to raise the landing legs. This speeds up the operation at both ports.

Another effective use of unaccompanied trailers is called piggyback. This uses the same principle as the road–sea version but applies the principle in a road–rail context. In this situation, unaccompanied semi-trailers are carried on specially constructed rail wagons. Because articulated road semi-trailers tend to be higher at the front than at the rear a specially constructed well in the rail wagon allows the landing legs to sit at a lower level than the rear wheels. This has the effect of making the trailer sit on the rail wagon with the roof at an overall even height to the ground. The French have dubbed this method 'le kangarou' because of the well being likened to a kangaroo's pouch.

The problems caused by the landing legs and the road wheels are effectively overcome by a recent development known as the spine rail wagon (see Figure 23.1). In this system road trailers are loaded on the rail wagon with the road wheels and landing legs either side of a central spine on the rail wagon. This allows the semi-trailer to sit squarely on the rail wagon and reduces the overall height. The spine wagon is also able to carry ISO containers. In Figure 23.1, the third spine wagon from the left is carrying an ISO container, which demonstrates the versatility of the system.

These methods of unaccompanied transport have been in use for some time and are not always thought about when intermodal transport is discussed. However, they do fit the strict definition of intermodal transport above and use effectively the road, rail and sea modes.

Intermodal handling equipment

Transtainers

These are large devices mounted on rails, which are able to transfer containers from the sea-going vessel to trucks or rail wagons. A large boom spans the distance between the ship's cargo holds and the quayside. The transtainer is capable of moving along the quayside parallel to the ship's side to aid positioning.

Figure 23.1 Spine wagons being loaded by a reach stacker equipped with a grappler lift (courtesy of John G Russell (Transport) Ltd)

Gantry (or portal) crane

Sometimes referred to as a straddle carrier, this is a crane designed to lift containers and swap bodies (see Figure 23.2). It has four legs, one at each corner, with wheels at the bottom of each leg. It has the ability to straddle rail wagons and road vehicles. It is able to transfer containers and swap bodies quickly from road vehicles to rail wagons and vice versa. It is equipped with a spreader beam that has a twist-locking device at each corner, which locates in the corner casting of the container. The spreader beam is able to move in several directions to aid accurate location either of the spreader beam prior to picking up the container or when positioning the container on a road vehicle or rail wagon.

Grappler lift

This is a similar handling vehicle to the gantry crane except that it is fitted with four arms and is designed specifically to handle swap bodies. The arms locate in the special slots built into the bottom of every swap body. The vehicle straddles the vehicle, positions the four arms and then lifts the swap body.

Figure 23.2   Gantry crane loading ISO containers on to rail wagons double stacked

Reach stacker

This is a heavy-duty materials handling truck that is fitted with a lifting arm and a spreader beam. It is capable of lifting containers and swap bodies. It can be used to load and unload road and rail wagons (see Figure 23.3). It can also be used to stack containers one on top of the other and to reach over a row of stacked containers. Empty containers can be stacked up to eight high using specially equipped lift trucks.

INTERMODAL VEHICLES

Sea

The cellular container ship

These are custom-built sea-going vessels for the carriage of containers. The containers are loaded one on top of the other and guided into position by the means of vertical guides at each corner of the container. This aids the process of loading, as the guides position the container accurately enough to preclude the need for any further manoeuvring once the container is released by the overhead crane. It also eliminates the potential problems caused by the vessel listing or the crane not being accurately positioned.

Figure 23.3   Reach stacker loading an ISO container on to a road vehicle

Once in position the containers are secured together by means of a twist-locking device. The stacks of containers are also secured by means of deck lashings for added stability during the sea journey.

Containers may be stacked as much as four high above deck level. This ability is limited by the structure and stability of the vessel. Due to the cubic nature of the container load, which is at odds with ship design, some vessels carry other cargo in the spaces in the holds created by the squaring-off effect.

The service provided by these vessels is sometimes referred to as LOLO (lift-on lift-off). International freight carried in containers passing through UK ports has grown from 29 million tonnes in 1988 to 48 million tonnes in 1996 (see Table 23.1).

The roll-on roll-off ferry (RORO)

This type of sea vessel is designed to carry road vehicles. The vehicles are either driven on to the vessel by the driver or, as in the case of unaccompanied trailers, by port-based vehicles. This allows unaccompanied vehicles or trailers to be delivered to the port of departure and then collected from the port of arrival. International freight using the RORO system has grown significantly in recent years (see Table 23.1).

Other versions of the roll-on roll-off ferry are specifically designed to carry rail wagons. The decks of these vessels are equipped with railway lines to allow ease of loading rail wagons.

Table 23.1 Unitized international freight passing through UK ports (figures in million tonnes)

	RORO	Containers	Total Unitized
1988	35	29	65
1989	40	30	71
1990	40	32	72
1991	39	34	73
1992	42	36	77
1993	43	39	82
1994	47	42	89
1995	48	46	93
1996	48	48	96

Source: Department of the Environment, Transport and the Regions (1998)

River barges

On large inland waterways such as the Rhine/Danube in Europe and the Mississippi river in the USA there is considerable use made of the water as an artery of transportation. Roll-on roll-off facilities and container transport are used in this context and cannot be forgotten when considering long journeys using different modes of transport. This type of transport is useful for non-urgent freight as it is by definition slower than other modes.

Rail

It should be noted that a movement of freight that uses both road and rail to complete the journey is sometimes referred to as combined transport.

Rolling motorway

This is the rail version of the roll-on roll-off sea ferry. Vehicles are driven on to specially designed rail wagons by their drivers. In some cases the drivers stay with their vehicles and in others they are accommodated in a passenger car for the duration of the journey. This type of system is used in Switzerland to carry trucks that are heavier than the Swiss laws on vehicle weights allow between Germany and Italy where the weight limits are higher. Another use of this system is in the Channel Tunnel between the UK and France where it is known as Le Shuttle.

Piggyback and Road-Railer

These methods of carrying road trailers by rail were discussed above.

Double stacking

In some parts of the world, such as the USA and Australia, containers may be carried by rail double stacked, ie one container loaded on top of another. This method greatly improves utilization of equipment especially over the very long distances found in these countries (see Figure 23.2). This method is not practical in the European Union due to the restrictive loading gauges.

Multifret wagon

These are specially designed low platform rail wagons for use by intermodal trains using the Channel Tunnel.

Ferrywagon

This is a conventional rail wagon that is capable of being loaded on to a train ferry.

European rail containers

These containers are slightly wider than an ISO container, which is 2.4 metres wide. These containers are 2.5 metres wide and are used in the European rail system.

Road

Skeletal trailer

This is an articulated semi-trailer that is designed to carry ISO containers. It is fitted with twist-locks at various points on the trailer to allow the carriage of different sizes of container. It is called a skeletal trailer, as it does not have any loading platform as such. It is a framework designed to support containers alone. In effect the containers become the body of the vehicle when loaded on to the trailer.

Some skeletal trailers are equipped with hydraulic rams to facilitate the tipping of the container. Some granular and powder products may be carried in ISO containers. The product is loaded through the top of the container via a special hatch and the product is retained by means of a plastic liner inside the container. At the point of delivery the container is tipped up by the hydraulic ram and the product is allowed to flow out of another hatch set in the rear of the container. In some cases this process is assisted through the use of pneumatic conveyance.

Extendable trailers

These trailers are sometimes called 'slider' trailers because of their ability to be extended or shortened depending on the size of the container to be carried. In all other respects they resemble skeletal trailers.

44-tonne vehicles

Large goods vehicles that have six axles may operate at a gross vehicle weight of 44 tonnes in the UK provided they are being used for combined transport, ie transporting a 'piggyback' style trailer, an ISO container or a swap body (see Figure 23.4) from or to a railhead. The vehicle may be a three-axle rigid or articulated tractor towing a three-axle draw-bar or semi-trailer. These vehicles have to comply with special construction and use regulations, such as the need for road-friendly suspension on all non-steering drive axles. The drivers must carry documentation that details the railhead being used, and the time and date the load was collected from the railhead. Vehicles using the Channel Tunnel shuttle are specifically excluded from carrying 44 tonnes. In Northern Ireland only, a further use for the 44-tonne vehicle is allowed. Vehicles are allowed to carry intermodal containers to seaports as well as railheads.

INTERMODAL INFRASTRUCTURE

The European Union and UK government are committed to the promotion of intermodal transport. They see the removal of certain types of cargo from the EU's roads as an environmentally sound policy. The reduction of road congestion, improvements to urban environments and reduction of harmful gaseous emissions from road vehicles are the objectives. Consequently considerable investment is being made in intermodal infrastructure.

The Channel Tunnel

The fixed link between the UK and France has opened up new possibilities for the movement of freight by rail. Various distances are cited by railway economists for the point at which movements by rail become profitable. One thing is clear, that rail freight has a greater chance of being profitable if longer distances and full trainloads are involved. The Channel Tunnel has opened up the possibilities for much longer journeys into continental Europe.

Significant amounts of intermodal traffic pass through the fixed link every day and the quantities of traffic are growing. Table 23.2 details figures of freight tonnage carried through the Channel Tunnel and illustrates the growth pattern clearly.

Figure 23.4 44-tonne draw-bar road vehicle being loaded with a swap body (courtesy of Foden Trucks)

Table 23.2 International freight using the Channel Tunnel (figures in million tonnes)

	Shuttle	Through-train	Total
1994	0.8	0.4	1.2
1995	4.8	1.7	6.5
1996	6.9	2.3	9.2

Source: Department of the Environment, Transport and the Regions (1998)

International intermodal terminals and freight villages

These are road rail interchange points that have been strategically placed on the UK mainland and are directly connected to the European rail network via the Channel Tunnel. These terminals and freight villages usually have warehouse and distribution companies alongside the rail facilities. Break bulk and freight consolidation services are usually also available. Some of these facilities are classified as inland ports and so customs services are available.

The main international intermodal terminals in the UK are:

- Mossend, Glasgow;
- Trafford Park, Manchester;
- Seaforth Docks, Gartree (Liverpool);
- Hams Hall, West Midlands;
- Daventry International Rail Freight Terminal, Daventry;
- Doncaster International Railport, Doncaster;
- Wakefield;
- Willesden, London.

FREIGHT FACILITIES GRANTS

This is a grant paid by the UK government to help industry cover the capital cost of developing freight handling facilities that are used exclusively for rail freight. These may be completely new facilities or a reopening of old facilities. The applicants must demonstrate that without the facility the freight would be moved by road. The grant may cover handling equipment, sidings, rail wagons and locomotives.

TRACK ACCESS GRANTS

These grants are designed to help towards the costs payable to Railtrack for access to the UK's railway network. As Railtrack owns the railway network, anyone wishing to operate trains on the network pays a track access fee. These grants are designed to encourage industry to consider using the railways where practicable in preference to using the road network. They were introduced in the Railways Act 1993.

SUMMARY

This chapter has covered the area of transport known as intermodal transport. After briefly describing the history and development of unitization in the form of pallets and ISO containers, the equipment used in intermodal transport was described. ISO containers, swap bodies, Road-Railers and unaccompanied trailers were all briefly covered.

The equipment used to handle intermodal containers was explained and described. Included in this section were transtainers, gantry cranes, grappler lifts and reach stackers.

Each mode of transport has specially adapted vehicles designed to carry intermodal containers. The modes were looked at in turn, namely sea, inland waterway, rail and road. The workings of cellular container ships and roll-on roll-off systems were detailed. For rail, rolling motorways and other specialized methods were discussed. The use of 44-tonne road vehicles and skeletal trailers was included in the section covering road transport.

The intermodal infrastructure is obviously important for the development of intermodalism, and therefore a section was included that discussed the Channel Tunnel and international intermodal terminals.

Finally there were sections on the government grants available for supporting the movement of freight carrying away from the roads and on to the railways.

24

Road freight transport: vehicle selection

INTRODUCTION

As with most of the decisions that have to be taken in physical distribution, there are a number of aspects that need to be considered when trying to make the most appropriate choice of vehicle for a vehicle fleet. Vehicle selection decisions should not be made in isolation. It is essential that all the various aspects should be considered together before any final conclusions are drawn. There are three primary areas that need to be carefully assessed – efficiency, economy and legality.

Efficiency, in this context, means the most effective way to do the job, based on a number of important factors. These factors concern:

- the types of operation, ie the distance to be travelled, the types of terrain, etc;
- the type of load, ie physical features, weight, etc;
- the type of vehicle, ie chassis, body, etc.

The area of *economy* is concerned with the prices and costs of the different types of vehicle. There are a number of points that should be taken into account. These should be analysed and compared with the costs and performance of the various alternative vehicles. The main points concerning economy are:

- the fixed cost of a vehicle, ie the vehicle, the licences, etc;
- the variable cost of a vehicle, ie fuel, tyres, maintenance, etc;
- the residual value of a vehicle (some types of uncommon vehicle do not have good resale values);
- the whole life costs of the vehicle, ie a calculation of the above cost over a given life of the vehicle;
- the utilization factors, ie miles per gallon, cost per mile, etc;
- the ways of acquiring a vehicle, ie buy, hire, etc.

The third and final area for consideration in vehicle selection is that of *legality*. This emphasizes the need to ensure that vehicles are selected and operated within the existing transport legislation. Transport law is complicated and ever changing, so constant awareness is imperative. The major factors concern:

- operator's licences;
- construction and use regulations;
- weights and dimensions of vehicles;
- drivers' hours;
- drivers' records;
- health and safety features;
- environmental considerations.

In this and the following two chapters, these various aspects are considered in some detail. This chapter is concerned with those aspects of vehicle selection that relate to the physical effectiveness of the vehicle for the particular job in hand.

MAIN VEHICLE TYPES

There is a variety of vehicle types. It is important to be clear as to the precise definitions of each type because these definitions are used throughout the different areas of transport legislation. The main types are described in this section.

The motor vehicle is a mechanically propelled vehicle intended for use on roads. Mechanical propulsion covers all those methods that exclude the use of human or animal power. Thus, a vehicle driven by petroleum spirit (the internal combustion engine), by gas turbine, by electric battery or by steam generation is classified as a motor vehicle.

A goods vehicle is a motor vehicle or trailer that is constructed to carry freight. The term covers all such vehicles, but there are also distinct definitions that relate to the different weights of goods vehicles.

A trailer is a goods vehicle that is drawn by a motor vehicle. There are two main types of trailer: 1) a draw-bar trailer that has at least four wheels and actually supports its load of its own accord; and 2) a semi-trailer, which is the type of trailer that forms part of an articulated vehicle. This trailer does not support the load on its wheels, but only when it is standing with the use of legs or jacks at one end.

As previously indicated, an articulated vehicle is a combination of power unit and trailer (ie motor vehicle plus semi-trailer) (see Figure 24.1). Thus, the trailer carries the load and the power unit pulls the trailer.

Figure 24.1   Articulated vehicle made up of a tractor and semi-trailer (courtesy of Daf Trucks)

A rigid vehicle is a goods vehicle where the motor unit and the carrying unit are constructed as a single vehicle (see Figure 24.2).

A small goods vehicle is a goods vehicle where the permissible maximum weight does not exceed 3.5 tonnes. This weight includes the load and also any additional trailer that may be pulled. A medium goods vehicle is one where the permissible maximum weight, including any trailer, exceeds 3.5 tonnes but does not exceed 7.5 tonnes. A heavy goods vehicle is a goods vehicle where the permissible maximum weight, again including any trailer, exceeds 7.5 tonnes.

Figure 24.2   24-tonne rigid vehicle (courtesy of Daf Trucks)

The final definition, heavy goods vehicle (HGV), is still in common parlance. It used to refer to any goods vehicle that exceeds 7.5 tonnes gross vehicle weight. However, since 1 April 1991 the term has been replaced by large goods vehicle (LGV) for legal purposes when referring to driver licensing categories.

There are two main reasons why these definitions have been outlined so carefully. The first is to provide a clear definition of the main types of vehicle available. The second was mentioned earlier. It is to differentiate between vehicle types for the purpose of interpreting some of the legal requirements for transport. There are two major vehicle classifications used for transport legislation. First, a company must hold a special licence (an operator's licence) if it wants to use any vehicle that exceeds 3.5 tonnes gross weight. Thus, small goods vehicles are exempt from this requirement. Second, a driver who wants to drive a large goods vehicle must hold a special licence (an 'LGV' licence). This licence is required for the drivers of all vehicles exceeding 7.5 tonnes GVW. It should be noted that from 1 January 1997 new car drivers no longer have the entitlement to drive vehicles that exceed 3.5 tonnes but do not exceed 7.5 tonnes. Drivers of such vehicles require a C1 licence.

TYPES OF OPERATION

Goods vehicles are required to undertake a wide variety of jobs. For each of these different jobs, it is important that the most appropriate type of vehicle is chosen. Some jobs or operations may require a vehicle with a powerful engine, others may necessitate a good clutch and gearbox because of high usage. Consideration must therefore be given to the type of work in which the vehicle will be engaged for the larger part of its working life, and also to the conditions under which it must operate. The most important classifications are described below.

Vehicles that are required to travel long distances tend to be involved in trunking operations. A trunking operation is one where the vehicles are delivering full loads from one supply point (eg a factory) to one delivery point (eg a warehouse or distribution depot). Such long-distance journeys tend to include a large amount of motorway travel, and the vehicle is involved in continuous high running, carrying heavy loads. Clearly, for this type of work a very good 'workhorse' is needed. As already indicated, it is likely that the load carried will be a heavy one, so a powerful engine will be essential. Articulated combinations are favoured for these operations.

Increasingly for loads with a low weight but a high volume, draw-bar combinations are favoured, as they provide a higher cubic capacity for loading within the legal limits (see Figure 24.3). Articulated semi-trailers with two decks may also be used for loads that fall somewhere between the two extremes in terms of weight and volume (see Figure 24.4).

Vehicles involved in middle-distance runs (ie 100–200 miles per day) are probably delivery vehicles making one or two drops per day from a depot to large customers. Typical journeys might involve a mixture of motorway and A and B roads. The type of vehicle running on journeys such as these must, again, be a powerful one.

There are a number of different types of work that result in lorries travelling quite short distances in a day. The main example concerns local delivery work or what is often known as van deliveries. A vehicle involved in this type of work will probably be making a large number of deliveries in the day, and so may only be driving from 40 to 100 miles. Indeed, in some city centre areas the mileage may on occasion be even less. This type of operation tends to be concentrated in urban or city centres, although some of the delivery areas do involve rural settings.

Among the additional problems that this type of operation comes up against are the many constraints on vehicle size. Because of the problems of narrow streets, the banning of large lorries, and limitations on access at some delivery points, it is only possible to use vehicles up to a certain size. The size constraints, the relatively short distances and the 'stop and start' conditions of town and city traffic are the main factors that go towards vehicle choice for this type of operation.

Figure 24.3 A high cubic capacity draw-bar combination (courtesy of Daf Trucks)

Figure 24.4 An articulated vehicle featuring a double-deck trailer, in this case for carrying bread (courtesy of Daf Trucks)

As a consequence, the main vehicle type used is a rigid one with good gearbox and clutch mechanisms. Increasingly more operators are using urban artic combinations for this type of work because they offer a higher payload potential with the added bonus of being more manoeuvrable than certain rigid vehicles. They also reduce the likelihood of overloading the front axles in a diminishing load situation, ie where goods are progressively unloaded from the rear without the load being redistributed, which has the potential for overloading the front axle of a rigid vehicle.

Combination running concerns operations that constitute a mixture of features. A typical example is that of the urban delivery vehicle working out of a regional depot. Such an operation involves a vehicle making medium-distance runs to a given town or urban area, and then maybe six or seven drops or deliveries in that area.

There is a need to balance the requirements of distance running and local delivery, so a vehicle must have strong engine power, together with a chassis that does not violate any delivery size constraints. A small articulated vehicle, or 'urban artic', may be the most appropriate in this instance.

Multiple deliveries are made by vehicles where the distribution operations are concerned with the handling and delivery of many different types and sizes of commodities and packaging. They are sometimes known as *composite delivery operations*. Typical examples are haulage contractors or third-party operators that run their businesses by handling and moving other companies' produce. Thus, they may get a wide variety of loads, and may have to run short and long distances and make single or multi-deliveries. In this case, it is difficult to suggest any one type of vehicle that is the most appropriate. It is necessary to take account of all the different jobs undertaken, and then select a 'jack-of-all-trades' vehicle that can best cover them all, or provide for a mixed fleet of vehicles.

Site work is included as one of the main types of operation because there is a very high movement of sand, gravel, rubbish, etc to and from building sites and road works. Vehicles that undertake this type of work are only travelling short distances, but the conditions in which they work are amongst the worst of all the different types of operation. Many operators choose an eight-wheeled rigid vehicle for this type of work (see Figure 24.5).

International operations also present some particular problems that need to be taken into account. It is likely that all types of terrain may be encountered – flat, hilly and mountainous. Distances will clearly be very long. In addition, it is important to minimize the likelihood of breakdowns occurring in out-of-the-way places where it may be very expensive to complete repairs.

Figure 24.5 An eight-wheeled rigid tipper vehicle (courtesy of Daf Trucks)

Vehicles concerned in international operations thus need to be very powerful and very reliable. Such vehicles tend to represent the expensive end of the goods vehicle market. With the advent of the Single European Market and the opening up of Central and Eastern Europe to trade, it is likely that this category of operation will become significantly more important.

As we have seen when vehicles are being selected, many factors need to be taken into consideration before any choices are made. Prior to selecting a specific type of vehicle it is worth making a checklist of the requirements the operation demands. The following list is not exhaustive but does serve to illustrate the potential complexity involved:

- product characteristics
  - size
  - weight
  - unitization
  - susceptibility to damage
  - hazardous
  - frozen

- liquid
- powder
- hygiene requirements (food)
- live animals;
- method of loading or delivery
  - by fork-lift truck
  - by manual handling
  - by overhead gantry (height limitations)
  - by saddle carrier (containers)
  - from the side, rear, front, top or bottom;
- restrictions at the point of delivery or loading
  - narrow roads
  - low bridges
  - weight restrictions
  - night-time restrictions because of noise
  - lack of material handling equipment
  - low or limited building access;
- terrain to be covered
  - motorways
  - urban roads
  - low-quality rural roads or lanes
  - mountainous
  - flat geography
  - extremes of temperature: extreme heat or cold;
- fuel type
  - diesel
  - petrol
  - LPG
  - natural gas;
- vehicle configuration
  - articulated tractor and trailer
  - two-, three- or four-axle rigid vehicle
  - draw-bar combination
  - small goods vehicle;
- body types
  - curtain-sided
  - platform
  - skeletal suitable for carrying containers, demountable bodies or swap bodies
  - van bodies

- – tankers
- – tipping body
- – Road-Railers suitable for transfer to rail wagons
- – bulk carriers;
- legal requirements
  - – gross vehicle weight limits
  - – vehicle dimensions
  - – mandatory equipment
  - – vehicle licences
  - – insurances;
- vehicle economy
  - – fuel consumption
  - – tyre wear
  - – whole life costs
  - – residual values
  - – ease of maintenance;
- drivers' cab types
  - – sleeper
  - – day cab
  - – crew carrier;
- ancillary equipment required
  - – self-loading cranes
  - – blower units
  - – refrigeration units
  - – fork-lifts carried with the vehicle
  - – tail-lifts
  - – fire extinguishers;
- vehicle security
  - – locks
  - – alarms
  - – sealing devices
  - – tracking devices using GPS.

This list may appear to be lengthy but it is by no means exhaustive. These days, vehicle manufacturers are able to use computing power to aid the decision-making process. They can feed the details of vehicle dimensions, weights and terrain into computerized models, which then produce anticipated performance figures for the proposed vehicle. These might include the ability of the vehicle to turn in a given area, potential fuel economy for different-sized engines and driveline combinations and potential axle loading under different load situations.

LOAD TYPES AND CHARACTERISTICS

The particular load to be carried is another vital factor when choosing a vehicle. Once again, it is essential to consider the alternatives with the prime objective of selecting the best chassis and the best body suitable for the load. The principal load features are described below.

Light loads are those loads that consist of lightweight commodities that are extremely bulky. There are a large number of examples from the different industries. Some of these are:

- breakfast cereals;
- tissues;
- polystyrene products.

The important point is that light loads such as these are high space users of vehicles in relation to the weight of the goods being carried. This is known as having a 'high cube factor'. The consequence is that, although a vehicle may have a high cube (or space) utilization, it will have a very low weight utilization (ie it is not carrying as much weight as it could).

Where a light load is carried, the consequent low weight means that the motive unit of the vehicle does not have to be a particularly powerful one. It is important not to overspecify vehicle requirements, as the use of high-quality, powerful equipment is very expensive.

Two additional points concerning vehicle selection for light loads are firstly, that it is often possible to operate by using a large rigid vehicle together with a drawbar trailer (see Figure 24.3) and secondly that a double-decked semi-trailer could be used (see Figure 24.4). This increases the volume capability.

Very *heavy loads* pose problems for vehicle choice because of the gross vehicle weight restrictions on roads and also because of axle weight restrictions. Vehicles specifically designed to carry loads heavier than the maximum permissible gross weight are covered by the Special Types General Order (STGO) and fall into three categories, with a maximum of 150 tonnes permissible. Some loads are even likely to require special vehicle construction, although special low loader vehicles are available (see Figure 24.6).

Not all heavy loads are necessarily abnormal loads. For example, machinery that has a total weight within the legal limit can be carried on a standard trailer providing the weight is adequately spread over the axles.

The problem of *mixed loads* – where quite heavy products are mixed on the same vehicle as quite light ones – would not appear to indicate the likelihood of any constraining factors. The indication is that the mixture of light and heavy products

Figure 24.6   STGO Category 1 heavy haulage vehicle (courtesy of Daf Trucks)

would result in a balanced load where the total weight and the total cubic capacity are both about right for the vehicle, and this is indeed often true.

The problem that can occur, however, arises when a vehicle has to make a number of deliveries on a journey. What can happen is that the removal of parts of the load can change the spread of weight over the vehicle, and thus over the individual axle weights. These changes can mean that the vehicle suddenly has an illegally high weight on one of its axles – this is often referred to as 'the diminishing load scenario'.

This effect can occur on any delivery vehicle. When there is a mixed load of light and heavy goods, it can be much worse because of the variable spread of the load within the vehicle. Where this effect is likely to be a problem, it is important to select the most appropriate vehicle chassis and body from the outset, so that the problem can be overcome. A simple solution may be to equip the vehicle with a manual pump-up truck to assist the driver in quickly redistributing the load.

All *valuable loads* represent some sort of security risk. Vehicle selection must, therefore, take this into account. There may be a need for a special chassis or body construction. It should be appreciated that valuable loads are not just the more obvious ones such as money or jewellery. Many consumer products, when made up into a large vehicle consignment, represent a very high value. Examples include wine and spirits, electrical goods, clothing, etc. Thus, it is very often important to select vehicles that can be easily but securely locked during the course of daily delivery work. There are many anti-theft devices available on the market, including satellite tracking, intruder alarms and immobilizers. Drivers need to be trained to deal with various situations where criminal activities may be a problem (see Chapter 32).

Liquids and powders in bulk have to be carried by road tankers that are specially constructed (see Figure 24.7). They are subject to the construction and use regulations. They may also be subject to other specific regulations such as Pressure Systems Regulations or ADR. These regulations are related to the type of commodity that is to be carried. It is also important in vehicle selection to ensure that the correct input and output mechanisms are provided. For example, some products can be manoeuvred by gravity alone, while others require a variety of loading and discharging mechanisms for pumping products on to and off the vehicle. These mechanisms can create a lot of noise so consideration needs to be given to noise attenuation and ear defence for the drivers.

Figure 24.7   A four-wheeled rigid tanker (courtesy of Daf Trucks)

The bulk movement of *hazardous goods* by road is often carried out by road tanker, so the particular considerations for liquids and powders mentioned above apply automatically. In addition, the fact that hazardous substances are of a high risk means that care must be taken to select the correct material or lining for the tanker so as to avoid any potential chemical reaction. Another point to note is that special fitments may be necessary to prevent electrical flashes from the vehicle's engine from igniting inflammable goods.

MAIN TYPES OF VEHICLE BODY

The decision on the most suitable type of body to select for a vehicle should be based on both the operating and the load requirements. The various body types have particular advantages and disadvantages according to the work to be undertaken and the products to be carried. Nearly all of the different vehicle bodies considered below can be fitted either to a rigid vehicle or to an articulated trailer.

A box is an enclosed body that normally has a sliding door at the rear, often known as a box van (see Figure 24.8). As an alternative, some box vans may be fitted with side doors instead of or as well as doors at the rear. One common feature is the hydraulic tail-lift. This enables the load to be moved from the bed height to the ground automatically by lowering the tail-lift.

Figure 24.8 Articulated combination with 38-tonne tractor, enclosed box van body on the trailer and rear access (courtesy of Daf Trucks)

Box vans are by far the most common body type for urban delivery vehicles, especially for those delivering consumer products, food and packaged items. Their advantage lies in the protection to be gained from all types of weather, and also from the reduced risk of pilferage, because they are enclosed and so can be made secure. Increasingly, curtain-sided bodies are being used because of the ability to gain side access to the load if required. Large box vans are also now in very common use for trunking operations. The reasons are similar to those given for urban delivery vehicles. This additional popular usage has come about because of the great increase in the use of the wooden pallet as a unit load, and the fact that box vans with reinforced floors can be readily loaded by fork trucks.

The platform or flat bed is the traditional body type (see Figure 24.9). It consists merely of a wooden base above the skeletal trailer, with a possible range of heights of drop sides and rear. It is, of course, uncovered. It is still in common use for many raw materials and products that are unaffected by inclement weather. The majority of loads need to be roped and sheeted, a skilled but time-consuming occupation. It is for this reason that curtain-sided bodies are used more extensively than flat beds.

Figure 24.9 Platform or flat bed rigid vehicle with drop sides and rear – in this case fitted with its own crane to assist loading and unloading (courtesy of Daf Trucks)

The road tanker is another very common vehicle. The tank body can be used to carry a variety of liquids and powders. The different requirements for loading and discharging tankers, and the problems of hazardous goods in terms of selecting the correct material or lining, were indicated previously in this chapter.

The tilt body is quite a recent innovation. The tilt is a curtain-sided vehicle that broadly consists of a fabric cover over a framework secured to the platform of a lorry (see Figure 24.10). This fabric cover can be drawn together to cover the load completely and then fixed by lacing or strapping down the length of each side of the vehicle.

Figure 24.10   Articulated vehicle with tilt soft top on trailer, which provides all-round flexibility for loading and unloading (courtesy of Daf Trucks)

In appearance, a tilt body is very much like a box van, although the sides of the tilt van are, of course, made of flexible curtain fabric. The initial introduction of the tilt body was to eliminate the need for loads to be roped and sheeted, and thus to save considerably on loading and unloading times. If the tilt superstructure has to be stripped down to allow loading from above by crane, or even from the side, this can be very time-consuming as compared to the curtain-sided vehicle.

Figure 24.11 Curtain-sided trailer giving ease of access to the load (courtesy of Daf Trucks)

In addition, curtain-sided bodies are also used and have become very popular in recent years. They are different from tilt bodies in that they have a rigid roof, and one movable curtain each side of the body (see Figure 24.11). This is a very flexible and effective vehicle body that eliminates roping and sheeting and the problems associated with stripping out tilt bodies.

'Tipper' is the description that applies to vehicles that have the capacity to tip loads directly. These can be open-topped bulk carriers or tankers. They are normally worked hydraulically, and are used to discharge a variety of bulk materials, typical examples of which are grain, gravel, sand, cement and plastic pellets. They may be covered, depending on the particular characteristics of the product carried. The inherent dangers of tipping vehicles falling over are being overcome through the use of non-tipping tankers that use bottom discharge systems. These vehicles have the added advantage of being able to carry a higher payload.

As previously indicated, the low loader is used for the carriage of specifically large or heavy loads.

There are several other vehicle bodies used to carry certain types of product. These are basically self-explanatory, but in their construction they do reflect the

Figure 24.12 17-tonne rigid vehicle with maximum cube body for high-volume/low-density goods – in this case furniture (courtesy of Daf Trucks)

special needs and requirements of the products concerned (see Figures 24.12 and 24.13). Typical examples are those bodies used for livestock, furniture, hanging garments, transportation of cars and refrigerated products.

The final vehicle body to be considered is also a fairly recent alternative. This is the demountable box van or body, which is used in a similar way to a standard container. The demountable body can be carried directly on the platform or flat bed of the vehicle or can be mounted on the skeletal chassis. In direct contrast to the container, however, the body is removed by the use of jacks, which are positioned at each corner of the demountable body and then raised, allowing the vehicle to drive away.

There are a number of ways of removing the body. These may include screw-type jacks, power- or hand-operated hydraulic jacks, electrically operated portable jacks or power-operated lifting equipment fitted to the chassis of the vehicle. Demountable systems provide an increased flexibility to distribution operations by improving vehicle utilization and fleet economy.

The swap body is a body used by intermodal operators. It combines the features of a tilt body but it is detachable like an ISO container. These swap bodies conform

Figure 24.13   A car transporter (courtesy of Daf Trucks)

to standard sizes and may be used by both rail wagons and road vehicles. See Chapter 23 on intermodal transport.

THE WIDER IMPLICATIONS OF VEHICLE SELECTION

There are several additional points that should be considered when choosing a vehicle. Some of these are clearly associated with those factors and features that have already been discussed; some reflect quite clearly the wider implications of vehicle selection and others show how it is possible to use knowledge and experience to help in decision making. These associated factors can be summarized as follows.

Is there a proven model or make of vehicle that is known from experience will be good at the job in question? This knowledge may be obtained from looking at other depots and their fleets from within the same company, or it may be available from studying similar types of operation that are undertaken by other companies, or by reference to the trade press.

Similarly, it may be possible to assess the reliability of certain models and types of engine, etc by analysing the past history of similar vehicles. Thus various measures of performance can be produced and studied to give useful data on fuel economy, breakdowns, cost of maintenance, etc. Where information is not available from own company records, it is still possible to use a variety of published data, which is available from the commercial press and other sources. Some companies now use fleet management computer packages to provide this type of historical information.

In selecting a vehicle, it is important to be aware of the need to undertake maintenance and repairs. If a depot has its own maintenance facilities or garage available then this is not a great problem. The likely problems can and do arise for companies that do not have their own facilities, and discover that the nearest dealer or garage with appropriately trained mechanics for their make of lorry is situated at a great distance from the depot itself. With the new levels of vehicle technology it is becoming increasingly difficult for own maintenance facilities to justify the investment in the necessary equipment needed to maintain these types of vehicles. This will have wide implications for vehicle selection.

One area that is difficult to cater for, but must nevertheless be borne in mind, is that of likely future transport legislation that might affect the choice of vehicle. There are a number of factors that may be of importance, such as the construction and use regulations, drivers' hours, maximum vehicle weights, environmental issues, new levels of vehicle technology, etc.

Another point concerns drivers. It should be remembered that it is drivers who have to work with the vehicles every day of their working lives. They will understand many of the particular operational problems involved with the work that they have to do, and they will undoubtedly have an opinion on the 'best' type of vehicle from their point of view. It makes good sense to listen to this viewpoint. At least, it is important to consider the safety and comfort of drivers at work.

The final factor for which allowance must be made is, in many ways, one of the most important ones. It has been emphasized that there is a need to balance a variety of operational and economic aspects to ensure that the lorry is efficiently run. Another vital factor to take into account is that, as well as loading at the depot or warehouse and travelling legally on the roads, the vehicle also has to be able to get into the delivery points. Thus the accessibility at the delivery interface is a very important consideration. It is essential to be able to provide a vehicle that is capable of doing its job.

VEHICLE ACQUISITION

It has been shown that the process of vehicle selection is one that requires a good deal of thought and analysis to ensure that the most suitable one is used for the job that is to be undertaken. Having determined the vehicle requirements, the next task is to ascertain the most appropriate means of acquiring the vehicle. There are several options available – purchase, rent, lease or contract hire.

The traditional means of vehicle acquisition is that of outright purchase. This gives the operator unqualified use and possession, together with the choice of when and how to dispose of the vehicle. Discounts for cash may well be available, and there are tax allowances for capital purchases. The major problem is likely to be the lack of capital availability for purchases of this nature. Other ways of obtaining finance include bank overdrafts, bank loans, hire purchase and lease purchase. These have a clear cost associated with them and, although allowances can be set against tax, the recent reduction in capital allowances has made other methods of acquisition more attractive.

The leasing of vehicles is a popular alternative. Here, operators do not actually own the vehicles. With fixed-term leasing, operators make regular payments over an agreed period when they have full use of the vehicles. The payment covers all the usual financial costs, and may cover maintenance if required. Finance leasing means that operators cover the full cost of the vehicle over the leasing period, and so may be given the option of extending the period of use at a significantly lower lease cost. The main advantage of leasing is that the standing (fixed) cost of vehicles is known; the disadvantage is that operators must keep the vehicles for a prescribed period in which time, for example, operational requirements may alter. In addition, accounting practice (SSAP 21) means that vehicles acquired on finance leases have to be shown in the balance sheet, so the rate of return on capital employed is reduced.

Due to the changes in accounting practice previously mentioned, the contract hire of vehicles has become a much more attractive option. Contract hire arrangements can vary from the supply of the vehicle alone, through maintenance, insurance, drivers, etc to the provision of a complete distribution service. Thus, there has been a rapid growth in third-party distribution companies offering a variety of services. The financial advantages of contract hire include the release of capital and the easier, more predictable costing of operations.

Vehicles can also be acquired via rental agreements. The vehicle does not become the user's property, but can be operated as required. Agreements may include maintenance and driver. Costs are generally higher than for the other alternatives, but rental periods are often very short term, allowing the user greater flexibility, particularly providing the means to accommodate temporary peaks of demand. Costs are predictable and can be treated as variable for specific jobs.

SUMMARY

It can be seen from the various sections in this chapter that there are a multitude of factors that need to be considered when selecting road freight vehicles. The alternative options have been briefly discussed under the main headings, as follows:

- main vehicle types;
- types of operation;
- a vehicle selection checklist;
- load types and characteristics;
- main types of vehicle body;
- wider implications of vehicle selection;
- lease, hire or buy option.

A more detailed discussion on those aspects concerning vehicle costing and road transport legislation can be found in Chapters 25 and 26.

It is sensible not to treat the answers to the vehicle selection question as being hard and fast rules. They should be used as guidelines to be followed but not as strict rules. It must be remembered that companies, applications, operations and environments are all different in their own special ways, and all guidelines must be adapted to suit them accordingly.

25

Road freight transport: vehicle costing

INTRODUCTION

This chapter begins with a discussion of the reason why road vehicle costs need to be assessed separately from the costs found in most companies' financial accounts. The fundamental elements of road freight transport costing are reviewed, showing how these costs should be considered, and what can be gained from this type of information.

The need to know the details of vehicle and fleet performance is emphasized, as is the importance of gaining this information in good time. The two main uses of these types of costing systems are identified as the monitoring and control of operations and the formulation of budgets.

The major costs are categorized as standing costs, running costs and overhead costs, and examples show how these costs are calculated. The concept of whole life costing is explained. Some simple comparisons of different vehicle costs demonstrate the relative importance of the different types of transport cost, and show how this cost relationship can vary according to the size of vehicle.

REASONS FOR ROAD FREIGHT TRANSPORT VEHICLE COSTING

At the end of every company's financial year, the company has to produce a financial statement that shows how well or how badly it has performed during that year. This is known as a profit and loss statement. This statement is useful in a broad context because it can show whether or not the company has performed satisfactorily. It may also be possible from this information to ascertain a good picture of the overall performance of the company's transport operation for that year, but it does not provide a detailed account of exactly where any profit or loss is made within the operation itself. In short, it fails to give sufficient details of each vehicle and its operation to enable good control of the transport fleet.

There is another problem. The final profit and loss statement is produced after the financial year has ended. Because of this, it is too late for management to make any effective changes to the transport operation if the results show that its performance is not acceptable. The statement, therefore, fails to provide its information in sufficient time for any useful changes to be made.

In summary, there are two main reasons why a special form of cost reporting is beneficial to a manager running a transport operation. These are: 1) the need to know the details of the vehicle and fleet performance in order to control the operations; and 2) the need to know in sufficient time to make any necessary changes. It might be useful to consider an example of how such a system can be used for monitoring and control.

A weekly system of reports for every vehicle in a fleet will show, amongst other things, how many miles the vehicle has travelled and how much money has been paid out for fuel for this vehicle. For several weeks, the fuel costs for this vehicle may be very similar week on week. All of a sudden, the fuel cost increases considerably. Is this important? What can be done about it?

There are a number of reasons why this might have happened:

● The cost of fuel per gallon might have increased.
● The vehicle might have travelled more miles in this week, and so used more fuel.
● The vehicle might not be performing properly, so its fuel consumption per mile has increased.
● Figures have been incorrectly recorded.

It is important to know the real reason. In our example, we can perhaps see the following:

- The cost of fuel has not changed.
- The vehicle mileage has not altered – the vehicle has not run significantly more miles than usual.
- A check shows that figures have been recorded correctly.
- Measuring the amount of fuel used against the mileage travelled (which gives the vehicle miles per gallon) shows that the vehicle is travelling fewer miles per gallon than in previous weeks.

It can be concluded that the reason for the increase in the money paid out for fuel is not a rise in the cost of fuel nor an increase in miles travelled by the vehicle. It is because there is a fault in the vehicle – it is not operating cost-effectively. With this knowledge, the necessary steps can be put in motion to remedy the problem.

This example shows how useful an efficient costing system can be. In particular, it illustrates three important aspects of a good costing system:

1. to know, very quickly, that something is wrong;
2. to be able to identify where the problem lies;
3. to be able to take some form of remedial action and solve the problem.

THE MAIN TYPES OF COSTING SYSTEM

It has already been indicated that a good costing system can provide the means to make effective use of and keep adequate control over transport resources. Another important use for costing systems concerns the need to ensure that customers are being charged a sufficient price to cover the cost of the transport provided. This is clearly important for third-party contract operations. This type of costing system allows for costs to be budgeted in order to be able to determine an adequate rate at which to charge for the use of vehicles. For own-account fleets this will enable a company to determine an appropriate cost to add to the price of the product or order to ensure that all own transport costs are covered.

Two types or aspects of a costing system have been identified: 1) the recording of actual costs and performance in order to monitor and control the transport operation; and 2) the measuring of costs to identify the amount to allow to cover costs and to budget for a job. Both of these types of costing system require the same detailed collection of cost information. This information concerns the resources that are used in a transport operation. The types of transport resources that need to be considered are:

- men;
- machinery;
- materials;
- money; and
- minutes.

In order to be able to understand how costing systems can be used, it is helpful to be aware of common costing terminology in transport. These are:

- *Cost unit* – a unit of quantity in which costs may be derived or expressed. Examples include
  - cost per miles run
  - cost per tonne mile
  - cost per carton delivered.
- *Cost centre* – a piece of equipment, location or person against which costs are charged. Examples include
  - a lorry
  - a fleet of lorries
  - a driver
  - a depot.
- *Direct cost* – a cost that is directly attributable to a cost centre. For example, if a lorry is a cost centre, then direct costs would include
  - fuel
  - the road licence
  - insurance.
- *Indirect costs* – the general costs that result from running a business. They are also referred to as overhead costs, administrative costs or establishment costs. These costs have to be absorbed or covered in the rates charged to the customer. Thus, they need to be spread equally amongst the vehicles in the fleet. Examples include
  - office staff wages
  - telephone charges
  - advertising.
- *Fixed costs* – refer to the cost centre itself (ie the vehicle). These costs will not vary over a fairly long period of time (say, a year) and they are not affected by the activity of the vehicle, ie the mileage the vehicle runs over this period. They are very often, in transport, referred to as *standing costs*. Examples include
  - the cost of the vehicle
  - vehicle excise duty
  - vehicle insurance.

- *Variable cost* – the opposite of a fixed cost in that it varies with respect to the mileage the vehicle travels. Thus, it varies according to the amount of work the vehicle undertakes. It is sometimes known as the *running cost*. Examples include
  - fuel
  - oil.

It should be noted that some cost factors can be defined as direct costs, and then classified once again as either fixed or variable costs. In the examples above, fuel is both a direct cost (it is directly attributable to the lorry as its cost centre) and a variable cost (the amount used varies according to the mileage that the vehicle runs).

VEHICLE STANDING COSTS

In this section consideration is given to the different resources that are included as vehicle standing costs or fixed costs. Each of these resources must be paid for, regardless of the extent to which the vehicle is used. Thus, these resources are a cost that must be borne whether the vehicle is run for 5 or for 500 miles in any working week. Fixed costs, therefore, remain the same independent of the level of activity.

The vehicle is an expensive piece of equipment that in most companies is expected to last from about five to eight years. The working life of a lorry is dependent on the type of job that it has to do. A local delivery vehicle may carry relatively light loads and travel only 40,000 miles in a year. A long-distance trunking vehicle may be pulling heavy loads, and may be running for 80,000 miles a year or more.

Whatever the working life of the vehicle, it is necessary to take account of its cost over the period of its expected life. One reason for this is so that appropriate costs can be recovered for the service that the vehicle performs. Failure to do this might affect the ability to run a profitable operation.

The method of taking account of the cost of a vehicle is known as *depreciation*. This is a means of writing down the annual cost of a vehicle over its expected lifetime. There are a number of different methods used for calculating depreciation, and their use depends on the particular policy of each individual company. The two main types are: 1) the straight-line method; and 2) the reducing balance method.

The straight-line method of depreciation is the simplest method of assessing the annual cost of a vehicle. It requires three figures:

1. the initial cost of the vehicle (less tyres, which are treated as a running cost);
2. the anticipated resale or residual value of the vehicle (ie the amount for which the vehicle might be sold at the end of its life); and
3. the expected life of the vehicle in years.

The annual depreciation of the vehicle is then calculated by subtracting the resale value of the vehicle from its initial purchase price, and then dividing the result by the expected life of the vehicle.

Example

	£
Purchase price of vehicle	50,000
Less cost of tyres	6,000
	44,000
Less anticipated resale value	5,500
	£38,500

Expected vehicle life = 5 years

Annual depreciation

(£38,500 divided by 5 years)   £7,700

This is illustrated graphically in Figure 25.1.

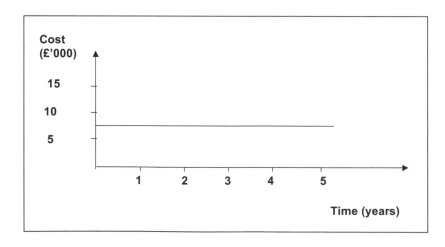

Figure 25.1   Depreciation – straight-line method

The reducing balance method is slightly more complicated, but probably more realistic. The method assumes that depreciation is greater in the early years of a vehicle's life, and becomes less severe in later years. This approach reflects the fact that assets lose a greater proportion of their value in their early years and also mirrors the fact that repairs associated with a vehicle's early life tend to be few and inexpensive, but tend to increase as the vehicle gets older.

The principle for the reducing balance method is to write down the vehicle to its expected resale value at the end of its life. This is calculated by reducing the value of the asset by an equal percentage each year. The same data requirements are needed as for the straight line method.

Example

£50,000 to be written down at 36 per cent per annum.

	£
Initial value:	50,000
Year 1 @ 36%	18,000
Written-down value	32,000
Year 2 @ 36%	11,520
Written-down value	20,480
Year 3 @ 36%	7,373
Written-down value	13,107
Year 4 @ 36%	4,718
Written-down value	8,389
Year 5 @ 36%	3,020
Resale value	£5,369

The relationship of the reducing balance method of depreciation with maintenance costs over time is shown in Figure 25.2.

There are three types of *tax and licences* that need to be costed against a vehicle. These are:

1. *vehicle excise duty*, which is based on the 'revenue weight' of the vehicle or tractive unit (eg the confirmed maximum weight, which for plated vehicles is the gross or train weight shown on the DoT plate);

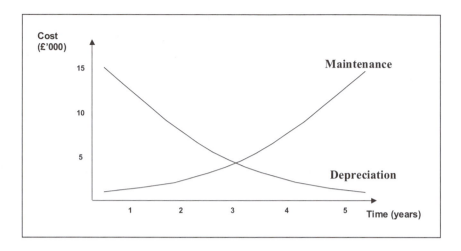

Figure 25.2   The reducing balance method of depreciation

2. *the operator's licence* – an indirect cost for the whole fleet, plus a cost per vehicle, and a legal requirement for a transport operator running a business;
3. *the driver's licence* required for individual drivers.

The excise licence is by far the most costly of the three.

The cost of *vehicle insurance* is also a fixed or standing cost. The actual amounts can vary for a number of reasons, such as:

● the area or region of operation;
● the number of vehicles in the fleet (ie discount);
● the type of loads carried;
● the value of the products carried;
● the accident history;
● the excess paid by the customer (eg the first £500 on each incident).

The sources for these costs are from company records or directly from an insurance broker.

Most companies treat *drivers' basic wages* as a fixed cost because they are payable regardless of whether or not a driver is actually 'on the road'. In addition to basic wages, allowances must be made for National Insurance contributions, holiday pay and pensions. Although basic wages are treated as a fixed cost, any additions, such as incentive bonuses and overtime, are classified as a running (or variable) cost, because they vary in relation to the amount of work that is done. Wages and other related costs can be found from payroll records.

An allowance for *interest on capital* is frequently omitted from cost calculations, being included, in the main, when assessing the overall performance of the company. It is an allowance that indicates one of two possibilities: 1) the cost of borrowing money (that is, the interest repayable on a loan); or 2) the cost of forgoing interest on a company's own capital (that is, the interest that is lost because the money cannot be invested elsewhere).

Because each individual vehicle is treated as a cost centre, the 'interest' can be included as a standing cost. This cost should be related to the current official interest rate or the rate at which the company can borrow money.

Vehicle standing costs are summarized in Figure 25.3.

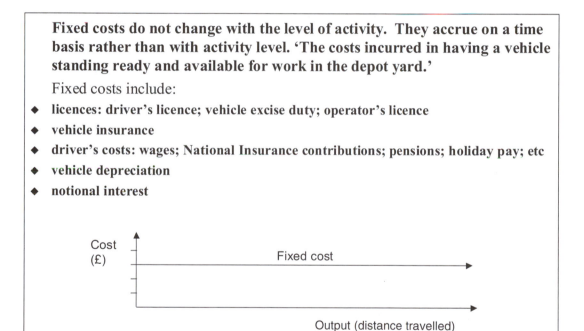

Fixed costs do not change with the level of activity. They accrue on a time basis rather than with activity level. 'The costs incurred in having a vehicle standing ready and available for work in the depot yard.'

Fixed costs include:

◆ **licences: driver's licence; vehicle excise duty; operator's licence**

◆ **vehicle insurance**

◆ **driver's costs: wages; National Insurance contributions; pensions; holiday pay; etc**

◆ **vehicle depreciation**

◆ **notional interest**

Figure 25.3 Vehicle standing (fixed) costs

VEHICLE RUNNING COSTS

This section concentrates on the second major category of transport costs – vehicle running or variable costs. A variable cost is said to vary in relation to the activity of the particular object with which it is concerned. The cost centre in this instance is the vehicle or lorry. The activity of the vehicle is the amount that it is used, which is the same as the mileage over which it is run. Thus we can see that the running cost is directly related to, and can be measured by, the mileage run by the vehicle.

Vehicle standing costs were defined as the fixed costs that had to be accounted for before a vehicle could be used 'on the road'. Vehicle running costs are the virtual opposite, being the costs that are incurred as a result of the vehicle being used. The major classifications of vehicle running costs are discussed below.

The cost of *fuel* is normally the largest of all the variable or running costs. There are two reasons why fuel is a particularly significant cost: 1) because of the high fuel consumption of commercial vehicles (ie low miles per gallon); and 2) because of the constant rise in energy costs due to periodic shortages and heavy taxation. Because the cost of fuel is such a significant portion of running costs, it is important that its usage is regularly monitored. Excess use of fuel can be the result of a number of factors, such as:

- fuel leaks;
- a worn engine;
- bad driving; and
- theft.

Running costs are related to an activity (ie the distance (in miles or kilometres) that a vehicle travels), so they are generally measured in pence per mile or pence per kilometre.

Example

Price of diesel = 70 pence per litre
Vehicle's average number of miles per litre = 4 mpl
Cost of fuel, in pence per mile:

$$\frac{70}{4} = 17.5 \text{ pence per mile}$$

The use of engine *oil and lubricants* is a very small variable cost. It is important to be able to measure usage, however, because high consumption may be a pointer to some mechanical problem. The costs of oil should also be measured in pence per mile (eg 0.5 pence per mile).

Tyres are classified as a running cost because tyre usage is directly linked to the distance the vehicle travels. Tyre usage is recorded as a variable cost in pence per mile as follows:

Example

Six-wheeled vehicle
Cost of tyres   £300 each
Estimated tyre life   40,000 miles each
Total cost of tyres
(6 x £300)   £1,800

Tyre cost per mile

$$\frac{£1,800 \times 100}{40,000 \text{ miles}} = 4.5 \text{ pence per mile}$$

Repairs and maintenance costs (including spare parts) tend to be the second highest of the variable costs, and are again related to mileage because vehicles are (or should be) regularly maintained after a given number of miles (eg every 6,000 miles). There are three principal factors that make up these costs. They are:

1. labour (fitters, mechanics, supervisors, etc);
2. spare parts; and
3. workshop or garage.

Records should be kept for each vehicle in respect of the work that is done. This is a legal requirement. Other information sources include mechanics' time sheets, suppliers' invoices, parts requisitions, etc. Costs are again in pence per mile. Many companies now outsource their repair and maintenance operations to third-party transport companies that specialize in vehicle maintenance.

As indicated in the section concerning standing costs, some of the costs associated with drivers are treated as variable or running costs. These are drivers' *overtime, bonus* and *subsistence* costs.

Vehicle running costs are summarized in Figure 25.4.

OVERHEAD COSTS

The two cost elements considered in the previous sections, vehicle standing costs and vehicle running costs, could both be classified as direct costs that relate directly to an individual vehicle. Vehicle overhead costs are indirect costs because they do not relate directly to an individual vehicle, but are costs that are borne by the whole fleet of vehicles. There are fleet overheads and business overheads.

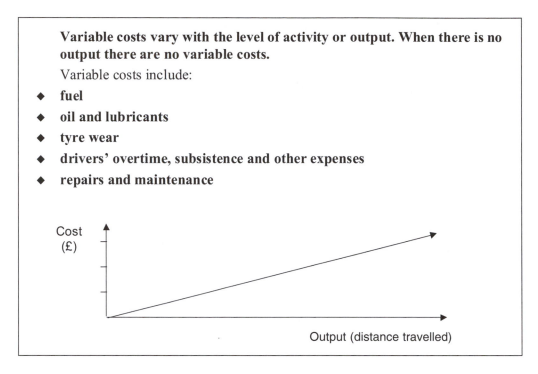

Variable costs vary with the level of activity or output. When there is no output there are no variable costs.

Variable costs include:

◆ **fuel**

◆ **oil and lubricants**

◆ **tyre wear**

◆ **drivers' overtime, subsistence and other expenses**

◆ **repairs and maintenance**

Figure 25.4   Vehicle running (variable) costs

Fleet overhead costs consist of the costs of all the 'back-up' or 'reserve' equipment and labour required to run an efficient fleet of vehicles. As such, they cannot be costed directly to a particular vehicle. The main resources are spare tractors and trailers, hired equipment and agency drivers. These are over and above what are called the 'on-the-road' requirements. The spare equipment is necessary to cover for the other vehicles as they are repaired or maintained, or if there is a breakdown. The agency drivers are necessary to cover for holidays and sickness during the year. These 'spares' are apportioned by taking the total cost over a period (eg a year) and then dividing by the number of vehicles in the fleet.

Business overheads can be subdivided into transport department and company administrative overheads. Transport department overheads consist of the charges and costs that are clearly concerned with the transport department but cannot be directly related to any one vehicle (eg salaries and wages for managers and vehicle schedulers, cars and expenses, telephone, fax, rent and rates, and training). Company administrative overheads are those costs that are central to the running of a business, and which have to be apportioned between all the different company departments. They include, for example, directors' fees, legal fees, bad debts and bank charges.

COSTING THE TOTAL TRANSPORT OPERATION

This section draws all the previous information together, so that it is possible to determine how to cost the total transport operation. The first step that must be taken is to estimate the likely vehicle utilization. This is essential so that vehicle costs can be divided according to the activity of the vehicle. The estimate should be based on the past history of vehicle usage and on any likely increase or decrease in this usage that might be foreseen.

There are two areas of utilization that need to be determined. These are for days worked in the year and mileage driven per year. Days worked can provide the basis for covering vehicle standing cost and distance travelled can be used for assessing vehicle running cost. Past history will indicate what the figures might be. Typical examples are:

Number of working days per year, eg
52 weeks × 5 days   = 260 days/year

Estimated annual mileage   = 80,000 miles

It is possible to determine the costs for the three main cost elements, as illustrated in the following example:

Standing cost
Annual standing cost   = £9,000

Therefore, $\dfrac{£9,000}{260 \text{ days}}$ = £34.62 per day

or $\dfrac{£9,000}{80,000 \text{ miles}}$ = 11.25 pence per mile

So the standing cost can be expressed on a daily basis or on an average mileage basis.

Running cost

	Pence per mile
Fuel	20.0
Oil and lubricants	0.5
Tyres	4.0
Repairs and maintenance	6.0
Total	30.5

Running costs should be calculated on a mileage basis.

Overhead cost

Apportioned vehicle overhead $\qquad$ = £1,200

Therefore, $\dfrac{£1,200}{260 \text{ days}}$ = £4.62 per day

or $\dfrac{£1,200}{80,000 \text{ miles}}$ = 1.5 pence per mile

As with the standing cost, the vehicle overhead cost can be expressed on a daily basis or an average mileage basis. With this breakdown of costs, it is possible to derive in detail the costs of different elements of the delivery operation that is being undertaken. If this is achieved, accurate and realistic charges can then be made to customers to ensure that transport costs are adequately covered.

If vehicles are allocated as a whole to a particular operation, it is easy to identify the appropriate standing, running and overhead costs, and to make the necessary charges or allowances.

Where vehicles are multi-user, and deliveries are made for a number of different customers, a further breakdown is required to reflect the extent of usage by the different customers. This is likely to be related to the number of cartons that are moved (or pallets, kilograms or cubic metres, depending on the measurement in use) and to the number of drops that are undertaken.

WHOLE LIFE COSTING

This approach to assessing the cost of owning and operating an asset has become accepted as a particularly good way of identifying the true cost of a vehicle. It is especially useful when trying to compare quotations from different companies. In this section, whole life costing is considered in the context of commercial vehicle acquisition and operation.

The idea is to include in the analysis all the cost elements that are involved in a vehicle's life, or at least that part of its life when it is owned by a particular organization. The major cost elements are:

the initial purchase price of the vehicle
plus
the total operating costs incurred by that vehicle during its life, ie maintenance, tyres and fuel
less
the achieved/guaranteed residual value of the vehicle

One obvious problem is that some of these figures will not be available until after the vehicle has been sold. This is true where companies purchase their vehicles outright and then manage them throughout their life until disposal. If these same companies change their vehicles every three years, whole life costing provides them with a valuable way of comparing not only how different makes of truck perform but also how different configurations of engine and drive-train perform. This can be invaluable when the time comes to make decisions about replacement vehicles. Armed with information such as fuel consumption and cost over a given mileage, cost of repair and maintenance and the value placed on this type of vehicle by the second-hand market, a transport manager can make discerning judgements about which trucks best suit the operation.

Before the adoption of whole life costing, decisions about truck purchase tended to concentrate solely on the initial purchase price of the vehicle. By looking at the costs incurred throughout the life of the vehicle it may emerge that it is better to pay a higher purchase price for the vehicle at the outset as the achieved economies in operating costs more than compensate for the initial extra outlay.

In recent years manufacturers have started offering whole life packages to commercial vehicle operators. This involves a purchase price, a cost for maintenance over a given mileage and a guaranteed residual value in the form of a buy-back price. Therefore it becomes possible for a potential purchaser to make a whole life comparison between manufacturers' offerings before the choice is made. Of course this will not include the performance on fuel consumption.

Information about achieved fuel performance may be obtained from the trade press, which often conducts vehicle road tests and publishes the results. Another good way of gaining a view about fuel economy is to ask the manufacturer for a demonstration vehicle that can be tested on the company's operations for a couple of weeks. This will provide useful practical information to aid decision making.

When making comparisons between different manufacturers' quotations a further sophistication may be introduced, which is to create a discounted cash flow (DCF) for each of the quotes. This is especially useful when pence-per-mile figures are quoted over different total mileages, purchase prices are different and residual values are also different. Unless systematically laid out in a DCF, it becomes very confusing to try to gain a true picture of which offering is the best. The discount factor is applied to each successive year's figures in order to represent the decline in the real value of money over time. By calculating a net present value (NPV) for each quotation, comparison becomes much easier. It is not absolutely essential that a discount factor is used because when the costs are laid out in this way a straight-forward addition will allow the quotes to be ranked in order of best value. The advantage of the NPV is that it provides a more accurate picture of the whole life cost of each quotation in today's money.

Table 25.1 demonstrates what a practical example will look like. The vehicles being purchased were 6×2 articulated tractive units, which were to be operated on a 24-hour basis at maximum gross vehicle weight. The life of the vehicles was to be four years at 120,000 miles per annum. The manufacturer offered maintenance either on the basis of a fixed price, which is described as inflation-proof, or on an annual review basis. In order to make allowance for this it has been assumed that an annual review would involve approximately a 3 per cent increase each year. It is worth noting that the guaranteed residual value is very generous because this manufacturer was attempting to increase its market share at the time. The resultant NPV appears to be better for the inflation-proof option but there is very little in it and the 3 per cent annual review figures are speculative. One very important aspect of this deal is that the guaranteed buy-back price is not only generous but it also insulates the operator from the vagaries of the second-hand truck market by trans-ferring the risk to the manufacturer.

When five or six of these DCF calculations are placed side by side for comparison, it is a powerful way of judging which is the best deal.

Whole life costings are widely used these days not only in the field of commercial vehicles but also in the field of company car fleet management because they are such a reliable indicator of the true cost of ownership.

Table 25.1 A practical example of whole life costing

	Purchase Price of Vehicle £	Inflationproof Maintenance £	Annual Review 3% £	10% Discount Factor £	Inflationproof Option Result £	Annual Review Option Result £
Year 0	£68,362.00	£0.00	£0.00	0	£68,362	£68,362
1		£3,515.04	£3,515.04	0.909	£3,195	£3,195
2		£3,515.04	£3,620.49	0.826	£2,903	£2,991
3		£3,515.04	£3,729.11	0.751	£2,640	£2,801
4		£3,515.04	£3,840.98	0.683	£2,401	£2,623
Less					£79,501	£79,972
Residual						
Value	£18,780.00			0.683	£12,827	£12,827
				NPV	£66,674	£67,145

VEHICLE COST COMPARISONS

It is important to be aware of the relative importance of the different elements of vehicle costs. This can be illustrated by the consideration of a typical road freight vehicle, in this instance a 38-tonne GVW articulated tractor and trailer. Figure 25.5 demonstrates that the driver costs, at about 29 per cent, and the fuel costs, at about 25 per cent, are by far the most significant costs for such a vehicle averaging about 70,000 miles per year.

It is also important to be aware that these comparative relationships may well change according to the type and size of vehicle. In a second example, a comparison is made between a large articulated vehicle and a smaller 7.5-tonne vehicle. Here, the relative importance of the driver of the vehicle, in cost terms, is much higher for the smaller vehicle, whilst the running costs are much lower. This is shown in Table 25.2.

SUMMARY

This chapter has considered the fundamental aspects of road freight transport costing – how these costs can be broken down, and what use can be made of this type of information. The major costs have been categorized as standing costs, running costs and overhead costs, and examples have shown how these costs are made up.

Standing costs	£pa	%
Vehicle Excise Duty	3,100	4.1
Insurance	1,696	2.2
Depreciation – tractor	7,217	9.5
– trailer	1,683	2.2
subtotal	*13,696*	*18.0*
Driver	22,257	29.3

Running costs	£pa	%
Fuel	19,265	25.3
Tyres	2,168	2.9
Maintenance – tractor	4,739	6.2
– trailer	2,839	3.7
subtotal	*29,011*	*38.1*

Overheads – transport	5,550	
– business	5,550	
	11,100	14.6

	£pa	pence per mile
Total	76,064	108.7

Figure 25.5 A comparison of vehicle costs, emphasizing the difference in importance of some of the main road freight vehicle costs

Table 25.2 Typical operating cost breakdown showing the relative cost difference for two different vehicle types

	Percentage breakdown	
	7.5-tonne	**38-tonne**
Depreciation	15%	10%
Driver	40%	25%
Running	20%	35%
– fuel, oil, tyres		
– repairs and maintenance		
Licence/Insurance)		
Overheads)	25%	30%

Emphasis has been placed on the need to know the details of vehicle and fleet performance and the importance of gaining this information in good time. The two main uses of these types of costing systems have been identified as the monitoring and control of operations and the formulation of budgets.

The concept of whole life costing was explained.

Some simple comparisons of different vehicle costs have demonstrated the relative importance of the different types of transport cost, and shown how this cost relationship can vary according to the size of the vehicle.

A more detailed discussion on the monitoring and control of logistics operations is given in Chapter 28. This identifies key indices for both costs (eg cost per mile) and performance (eg miles per drop or drops per journey) for road freight transport. It shows how they can be determined and used to help management ensure that the transport operation is run cost-effectively, and that any changes in both cost and performance can be readily identified.

The advent of a number of specific fleet management and costing computer programs and packages has enabled costing to be undertaken much more easily and with much greater accuracy. These packages are outlined in Chapter 27, which considers road freight transport information systems for planning and control.

26

Road freight transport: legislation

The legislation covering the road freight area is both vast in scope and complicated in nature. This chapter could not possibly deal with this subject in any great depth and it must in no way be viewed as a legal work of reference. The approach will be to highlight certain key areas that are common to all types of operation. It is highly recommended that matters of specific detail are clarified through reference to publications such as Croner's *Road Transport Operation* or the FTA's annual publication, *Road Transport Law*. It is also recommended that with regard to matters related to legal actions the opinion of professional legal advisers should be sought.

INTRODUCTION

The method by which the UK government chose to regulate road transport was fundamentally changed by the Transport Act in 1968. This act established the principle of managing the quality of road transport operations rather than controlling market access, as was the case prior to this piece of legislation. The act laid down certain key fundamentals that continue to form the basis of regulation to this day.

The UK's admission to the European Union in January 1973 introduced a further dimension to the legislation governing this area. Many EU directives and regulations are designed to harmonize the rules across the whole Union and much UK road transport legislation is derived from or directly based on EU legislation. Some specialist areas of operation such as the carriage of livestock and hazardous chemicals are covered by EU rules.

OPERATOR LICENSING

Road transport operators – both 'own account' and 'hire or reward' – who carry goods for commercial purposes on the public highway in the UK are required to hold an operator's licence. This licence may be one of the following:

- *Standard national.* This applies to the carriage of goods for hire or reward in the UK. Own-account operators may also apply for this type of licence, which will allow them to carry both their own goods and goods for hire or reward should they so choose.
- *Standard international.* This is the same as a standard national licence with the key difference being that it also authorizes the holder to travel abroad.
- *Restricted.* This licence is only available to own-account operators and covers these operations both in the UK and abroad. This licence has less stringent requirements than the two above.

The weight threshold for vehicles covered by operator licensing regulations is 3.5 tonnes maximum gross weight. However there are certain categories of vehicles that are exempted from these regulations. Examples include agricultural tractors, police vehicles and tower wagons. Once a vehicle is specified on a licence it will be issued with a windscreen disc. The disc will either be blue for standard, green for standard international or orange for a restricted licence. The disc will display both vehicle and operator details.

The criteria for obtaining an operator's licence cover the following areas:

- the operator's fitness to hold a licence;
- operating centres and their suitability;
- the organization and quality of vehicle maintenance arrangements;
- adherence to drivers' hours and tachograph regulations;
- compliance with vehicle loading restrictions;
- the financial resources of the undertaking;
- professional competence;
- good repute.

There are different criteria for financial standing depending on the type of licence being sought. The good repute and professional competence rules apply only to standard licences (national and international).

Operator licences are issued by traffic commissioners, and mainland Britain is divided into traffic areas. Currently different rules apply in Northern Ireland but this is under review and may change in the future. An operator may only hold one licence in each traffic area.

There are various bodies that have a statutory right to object to any application for a licence; they include the police, some trade unions and local authorities.

Once issued, a licence will run in perpetuity but will be formally reviewed every five years. There are rules governing changes to the licence such as a change in the number of vehicles, the operating centre or the professionally competent person.

Failure to adhere to the rules may result in the licence being revoked, suspended or curtailed. Traffic commissioners may decide to call operators before them to answer for their actions at a public inquiry.

DRIVER LICENSING

An EU-style driver licence, now in the form of a photocard, will be issued to any person over the age of 17 who has passed a driving test. This test comprises both a written and a practical test. This confers entitlement to drive motor vehicles up to a maximum authorized mass of no more than 3.5 tonnes and with no more than eight seats in addition to the driver's seat. This is a category B licence and essentially covers cars, light vans and small passenger-carrying vehicles.

Most existing ordinary licence holders will also have entitlement to drive medium-sized (not exceeding 7.5 tonnes maximum authorized mass – 'MAM') goods vehicles and, within certain limits, such vehicles towing trailers. These subcategories are known as C1 and C1+E.

Large goods vehicle (LGV) licences are divided into several further categories. It is important to note that any driver wishing to drive vehicles in these categories must first hold a category B licence and be 21 years old. Drivers have to pass the C category test before progressing to the C+E test. It is also possible to progress from B to C1 by passing a C1 test. Passing a C1 test allows the driver to drive vehicles of up to 12 tonnes MAM.

Large goods vehicle categories are as follows: category C – a rigid goods vehicle with a maximum authorized mass of more than 3.5 tonnes; and category C+E – an articulated goods vehicle or draw-bar vehicle combination. Essentially this category covers LGVs that tow trailers with a category C drawing vehicle.

Please note that the driver licensing rules are complex, with some differences in entitlement limited to the date when a licence was issued. Drivers' licences should always be visually inspected in order to verify their true entitlement, and regularly checked thereafter.

LGV licence entitlements will be valid after passing the appropriate test until the driver's 45th birthday or for five years, whichever is the longer. Thereafter renewal must be made every five years and be accompanied by a medical report. From the age of 65 the renewal process must be annual. The traffic commissioners retain some disciplinary powers relating to LGV entitlement.

DRIVERS' HOURS REGULATIONS

The European Union (EU) drivers' hours rules apply directly to drivers of most goods vehicles over 3.5 tonnes maximum gross weight undertaking journeys within the EU both domestically and internationally.

The rules apply to laden as well as unladen vehicles but not to purely 'private' driving. The weight of any trailer drawn must be taken into account. There is a long list of exemptions but these are often complex and should not necessarily be taken at face value.

Driving is deemed to be any period spent at the controls of a vehicle in motion or stationary with the engine running. Rest is deemed to be a period when drivers are free to do anything they choose other than work.

The basic rules are as follows:

- A tachograph must be used to record drivers' activities (see later).
- A week is defined as the period of time between 0000 hours on Monday and 2400 hours on Sunday.
- A day is any 24-hour period, beginning when the driver starts work after a rest period.
- A fortnight is any two successive fixed weeks.
- The daily driving limit is 9 hours. This may be extended to 10 hours twice a week.
- The weekly driving limit is not explicitly stated but is 56 hours in practice. The rules set a limit of 90 hours in a fortnight.
- Breaks from driving must total 45 minutes at or before the end of 4.5 hours accumulated or continuous driving unless a daily or weekly rest period is begun. This period can be split into breaks of at least 15 minutes. It is important to note that this rule has seen different interpretations over the last few years. If in doubt, professional advice should be sought.

- A daily rest period of 11 hours must be taken in every period of 24 hours commencing at the end of the last daily or weekly rest period. Three times a week this may be reduced to a minimum of 9 hours; however, any such reductions must be made up with equivalent compensating rest by the end of the following week. Separate reductions may be compensated for by one continuous period of rest of the appropriate length. These compensating periods of rest must be in addition to standard rest periods.
- Daily rest periods may be taken in a stationary vehicle equipped with a bunk.
- After a maximum of six daily driving periods a weekly rest of 45 hours must be taken. This may be reduced to a minimum of 36 hours if taken at home or at the vehicle's base. If the vehicle is away from base the weekly rest period may be further reduced to 24 hours. Any reductions must be fully compensated by the end of the third week following the week in which the reduction occurred. As with daily rest compensating periods, these must be additional to standard rest periods.

In some cases drivers exempt from the EU hours rules are covered by a limited set of rules known as the domestic hours rules.

In the future workers in the transport industry are likely to have their hours of work limited by the EU working time rules. They are currently exempt from the general EU directive. Apart from a 48-hour average weekly work limit, a limit on night work could also be imposed. Clearly these restrictions would have massive implications for any distribution operation and their proposed implementation has sparked off a vociferous debate within the EU.

TACHOGRAPHS

Goods vehicles over 3.5 tonnes gross vehicle weight must be fitted with a tachograph. Exemptions do exist but the majority of goods vehicles will require to have one fitted. These exemptions are identical to those regarding the EU hours rules. The tachograph must be used to record the driver's hours of driving, rest and other work.

Tachographs must also record distance travelled and vehicle speed. They must be properly maintained, calibrated and sealed at an approved tachograph centre. A two-yearly check is required and they must be recalibrated every six years.

Employers are bound to provide drivers with sufficient charts (see Figure 26.1), and ensure that the charts are returned within 21 days of use and retained for one year. For their part drivers must fill out the charts correctly, use a different chart

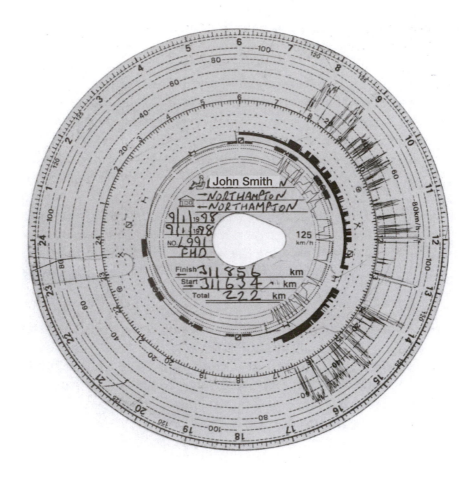

Figure 26.1 A tachograph chart

for each day worked and not tamper with the equipment. Employers must have an effective checking system to ensure that hours and tachograph rules are applied.

Tachographs provide a useful source of management information and can be used to achieve some of the following results:

- more economical driving habits, which will lead to improved fuel consumption and reduced maintenance costs;
- improved planning and routeing of vehicles, as real data on journey times and average speeds may be calculated;
- reduced vehicle accidents where drivers are aware that their driving performance and speed are being monitored;

- improved productivity from drivers;
- the prescribed method of ensuring compliance with the drivers' hours regulations.

As tachographs are the means by which both drivers and operators are prevented from working excessive hours, they have become the target for many forms of abuse. Some of the most common forms of abuse are listed below:

- winding the tachograph forward at the end of a duty period;
- removing the fuse;
- fitting a hidden switch to turn the tachograph on or off as required;
- putting a polo mint (lifesaver) in the middle of the disc to blur the reading;
- bending the stylus to give a false reading;
- placing chewing gum in a strategic place on the disc.

It has to be said that many of the more obvious forms of tachograph abuse have been superseded by the more sophisticated forms of fraud, which concentrate on tampering with the equipment's electronics. It goes without saying that all of these practices are illegal.

A new generation of digital tachograph based on a vehicle monitoring unit and a driver smart card will be introduced in the next few years.

VEHICLE DIMENSIONS

The length, width, turning circles and ground clearance are regulated for different classes of vehicles. There is no legal height limit for vehicles in the UK although the EU requires a 4.0-metre limit.

The standard maximum *width* for goods vehicles and trailers is 2.55 metres. This may be increased to 2.6 metres for vehicles constructed to carry goods at low temperatures but the walls of the vehicle must be at least 45 millimetres thick.

Turning circles for different classes of vehicle refer to the ability of the vehicle to turn within the confines of two concentric circles. For example, an articulated vehicle manufactured after 31 May 1998 must be able to turn within the confines of two circles with radii of 12.5 metres and 5.3 metres.

Maximum vehicle lengths are as follows:

Rigid vehicles	12 metres
Articulated vehicles	16.5 metres
Draw-bar vehicles	18.75 metres

Trailers and other vehicle combinations are also subject to length restrictions. These are the main dimensions:

Articulated semi-trailers
– from the kingpin to the rear of the trailer   12.00 metres*
– from the kingpin to any point on the front of the trailer 2.04 metres*

* These limits apply to trailers where the overall length of the vehicle and trailer is 16.5 metres.

Composite trailers   14.04 metres

For all goods vehicle trailers manufactured after 1 April 1984 a ground clearance of 160 millimetres is required if the trailer has an axle spacing of more than 6 metres but less than 11.5 metres. A clearance of 190 millimetres is required if the trailer axle spacing is 11.5 metres or more.

Vehicle weights

The gross vehicle weights of LGVs are clearly defined in the construction and use regulations. Maximum axle loadings and spacings are also of prime importance when specifying goods vehicles. The following list outlines the main maximum gross vehicle weights for vehicles operating in the UK. Please note that the maximum gross weights quoted below are the maximum possible, but they may be dependent on the fitment of road-friendly suspension (RFS), twin tyres, axle spacing and the type of work the vehicle is undertaking, eg 44 tonnes and road–rail.

- two-axled rigid – 18 tonnes;
- three-axled rigid – 26 tonnes (RFS);
- four-axled rigid – 32 tonnes (with RFS);
- four-axled articulated combination (two-axled tractor + two-axled trailer) – 36 tonnes (or 38 tonnes if the tractor unit does not exceed 18 tonnes and the semi-trailer does not exceed 20 tonnes, although the distance between the axles of the semi-trailer must be greater than 1.8 metres);
- five-axled articulated combinations (two-axled tractor + three-axled trailer and three-axled tractor + two-axled trailer) – 40 tonnes (44 tonnes under certain circumstances);
- six-axled articulated combinations (three-axled tractor + three-axled trailer) – 40 tonnes (or 41 tonnes if the drive axle does not exceed 10,500 kilograms, is

fitted with RFS and twin tyres, and the trailer has RFS; or 44 tonnes if on intermodal work – see Chapter 23);

- four-axled draw-bar combination – 36 tonnes;
- five- and six-axled draw-bar combinations – 40 tonnes (41 or 44 tonnes for six-axled draw-bars in certain circumstances).

The Government has indicated that it will allow a wider use of the 44 tonnes gross vehicle weight from February 2001 if vehicles comply with Euro II exhaust emission standards.

Construction and use regulations

These regulations are used to control the technical specifications of goods vehicles. They also control the maximum limits of use that the vehicles may be required to undertake. This area of the rules covers matters such as the extent to which a load may project over the sides of a vehicle and how this should be dealt with, eg with additional lights or markers.

The main areas covered by the regulations include:

- projecting and abnormal loads;
- marker board sizes and dimensions;
- braking systems;
- exhaust emissions;
- under-run equipment such as side and rear protection;
- horns;
- lighting;
- mirrors;
- noise emissions;
- speed limiters;
- spray suppression;
- suspension systems;
- steering;
- tyres.

This list is not exhaustive but it does illustrate the scope and depth of the regulation in this very technical area of road transport legislation.

SUMMARY

This chapter has set out the main areas covered by road transport legislation. It is an area that is very detailed and complex. Professional advice should always be sought where questions exist in the mind of the operator *prior* to engaging in any activity in order to avoid any future legal problems.

The main subjects covered were:

- the rules regarding operator licences and licensing;
- driver licensing;
- drivers' hours of work regulations;
- tachographs;
- vehicle dimensions;
- vehicle weights;
- construction and use regulations.

27

Road freight transport: planning and resourcing

INTRODUCTION

There are a number of reasons why road freight transport operations need to be carefully planned and resourced. These are discussed in the first section of this chapter. In addition, some of the main approaches for the management of vehicle fleets are reviewed.

The major content of this chapter is concerned with the basic methods of identifying fleet resource requirements. This can be achieved both manually and by computer analysis, and both of these approaches are considered. The main objectives of these types of analysis are discussed. In addition, the need to differentiate between strategic and tactical considerations is outlined.

The key data requirements are set out in some detail and then a particular approach to manual routeing and scheduling is used as an example. Finally, an identical analysis is undertaken using a computer package, and these results are reviewed.

NEED FOR PLANNING

There are some very general, as well as some very specific, reasons for carefully planning and managing road freight transport operations. As has been discussed in previous chapters, one of the real keys to creating an effective logistics operation is to get the right balance between customer service and costs.

This applies to an equal extent when considering the transport component of logistics. Some of the major elements include:

- *Assets.* Road freight transport fleets consist of some very high value assets, ranging from the tractors, trailers and rigid vehicles themselves to the drivers. It is important that these assets are made to 'sweat' through the development of efficient schedules that keep the vehicles and drivers on the road and active, and through the introduction of double- and treble-shifting of vehicles, which maximizes their use. Computer routeing and scheduling packages play a major role in achieving this high utilization, so a discussion of their characteristics will be a key part of this chapter. In addition, fleet management packages offer real opportunities to monitor very closely the costs and utilization of these assets. Both time and space (or load) utilization are important considerations.
- *Service.* Delivery transport acts as the main physical interface with the customer, so it is important that all customer service requirements are met. For transport this applies particularly to set delivery windows and timed deliveries. Once again, computer routeing and scheduling packages are key to achieving these goals.
- *Costs.* As well as the major assets discussed above, there are also costs associated with the operation of the vehicle, specifically the running costs such as fuel and tyres. Good scheduling can also help to keep these costs to a minimum.
- *Maintenance.* It is important to ensure that vehicles are maintained on a regular basis to reduce the occurrence of breakdowns, which can lead to both a loss of service and a higher operational cost.
- *Driver management.* This can be significantly improved by the use of appropriate tachograph analysis. As well as providing a better and more accurate picture of fleet efficiency, tachograph output can be used to monitor the detailed effectiveness of individual drivers.
- *Replacement.* A key decision for any transport manager is to be able to identify when vehicles need to be replaced and also which type of vehicle is the most effective for the particular type of operation that is being undertaken. A good fleet management system will be able to provide this information.

● *Security and tracking.* Some modern technology allows for the real-time tracking of vehicles. This enables up-to-the-minute information to be provided to schedulers and to customers, so can help to improve both operational effectiveness and service.

FLEET MANAGEMENT

Several different fleet management information systems have been developed that are aimed at assisting the transport manager to monitor, control and administer the transport operation. These are very broadly specialized database packages that are aimed specifically at fleet operations. The main functions covered are as follows:

● *Maintenance scheduling.* This includes the monitoring of the service life of vehicles in a fleet and the scheduling of routine and non-routine maintenance and repairs. Package features include
  – service history
  – maintenance schedule reports
  – workshop costs analysis.
● *Vehicle parts control.* This is the stock control function of spare parts requirements. Features may include
  – stock enquiry
  – maintenance of supplier information
  – stock location
  – stock reports
  – the generation of purchase orders.
● *Fleet administration.* Fleet administration packages are used to ensure that vehicles are legal and roadworthy. Package features may include
  – vehicle licence renewal
  – reports required by government regulations
  – insurance lapse reports, etc.
● *Fleet costing.* These packages provide detailed information relating to vehicle and fleet costs. They assist the manager by providing analyses and information concerning individual vehicle and overall fleet profitability. Features include
  – vehicle cost analysis
  – driver cost analysis
  – overall fleet costs.
● *Tachograph analysis.* Information from tachograph recordings can provide the input data for an analysis of driver/vehicle performance. A number of systems

are available that can read tachograph charts and produce itemized information on rest time, driving time and break time, as well as details of legal infringements. Typical package features are

- infringement reports
- driver and vehicle utilization reports
- fleet reports.

Tachograph analysis packages or modules are usually stand-alone, but can be integrated with other transport management modules.

TRANSPORT RESOURCE REQUIREMENTS

The basic method of assessing the road freight transport resources required for a given operation necessitates some very detailed and time-consuming analysis. This is the case whether the method adopted is a manual one or whether one of the many computer routeing and scheduling packages is used. Basically, it is necessary to identify specific delivery route requirements and then calculate from these how many vehicles and drivers are required to undertake the operation. Computerized systems for fleet planning and operations are used to help determine basic transport resource requirements but are also used to maximize the utilization and effectiveness of a given set of resources (eg an existing fleet of vehicles). In summary, there are two key areas for use: 1) determining fleet resource requirements; and 2) identifying effective vehicle schedules using an existing fleet.

These may have different implications according to the type of road transport operation that is being considered. The major use of these packages is for secondary delivery or local delivery. Here, vehicle routeing and scheduling is concerned with the efficient organization of road transport delivery to the final customer or retail outlet. Many large manufacturing, retailing and distribution companies have logistics structures with many depots spread across large geographic areas. Each depot will be responsible for supplying customers within a given region, that is, within the depot boundary.

This supply of products from a depot is often undertaken by a fleet of delivery vehicles that vary in size and capacity. Equally important, the particular demand for products from the depot may vary day by day and week by week. The two main problems are, therefore, to try to minimize the number of vehicles that are needed to achieve this, and to deliver this variable amount of goods and products as efficiently as possible. 'Efficiency' in this instance can be to maximize the amount of product moved on the vehicles and minimize vehicle mileage. It is principally about providing a balance between supplying an adequate service to customers on the one hand, and doing so at an acceptable cost on the other.

Other types of transport operation may also benefit from a similar approach to resource utilization, but the means of achieving this may require additional or different requirements. Two examples are trunking operations, which generally involve just one point of delivery for each vehicle, and stockless depot or demountable operations, which require a single stock-holding base plus additional stockless distribution points.

From the viewpoint of a depot manager or transport operator, objectives for local delivery can be stated quite simply as follows: *to plan journeys for vehicles operating from a single depot, delivering known loads to specific customers and returning to the depot after completing the journey.* Although this sounds relatively straightforward, there are a number of additional constraints that must be considered. Some examples are:

- the weight or volume capacity of the vehicles;
- the total time available in a day;
- loading and unloading times;
- different vehicle speeds;
- traffic congestion; and
- access restrictions.

A fairly general definition of the aim of vehicle routeing and scheduling has already been outlined. This can be summarized as the 'best' use of vehicles when providing a particular delivery service (known as the 'optimization' of vehicle usage). There are, however, a number of different ways in which this can be achieved, and any or all of these may be acceptable objectives for vehicle routeing and scheduling, depending on the particular transport operation concerned. Some examples of these different objectives are:

- to maximize the time that vehicles are used (ie make sure they are working for as long as possible);
- to maximize the capacity utilization of vehicles (ie ensure that all vehicles are as fully loaded as possible);
- to minimize mileage (ie complete the work by travelling as few miles as possible); and
- to minimize the number of vehicles used (ie keep the capital or fixed costs to a minimum).

VEHICLE ROUTEING AND SCHEDULING PROBLEMS

Vehicle routeing and scheduling problems are relatively complicated. There are several reasons for this: firstly, the different types of problem that can arise, each of which needs to be understood and approached in a different way; secondly, the many detailed aspects that need to be taken into account (some of these were listed in the previous section, and the detailed data requirements are reviewed later in this chapter); and finally, the various methods or algorithms that can be used to produce solutions.

The first point, concerning the different types of problem, is now described. These are linked very closely with some of the points made in the previous section of this chapter. They can, in fact, be categorized in four main ways:

1. strategic;
2. tactical or operational;
3. interactive; and
4. planning.

Strategic problems are concerned with the longer-term aspects of vehicle routeing and scheduling, in particular where there is a regular delivery of similar products and quantities to fixed or regular customers. Typical examples are most retail delivery operations (such as grocery multiples), bread delivery and beer delivery to 'tied' houses.

The main characteristic is that of a fairly regular demand being delivered to virtually the same locations. Thus, it is possible to derive vehicle schedules that can be fixed for a certain period of time (eg three to six months). Some changes will be necessary as shops open or close, or as new products come on to the market, but in general, the schedules can be maintained for a reasonable length of time. These schedules are drawn up on the basis of past or historical data. Strategic scheduling is now often undertaken by using modern computer techniques.

Tactical or operational problems are concerned with routes that have to be scheduled on a weekly or a daily basis. This type of scheduling is typically undertaken by parcels delivery companies, by companies supplying spare parts and by contract haulage companies that work for a number of different clients. The major factor of importance is that either the demand (quantity) of goods cannot be estimated (eg it is 'random' demand), or the location of delivery points can vary, or that both of these occur.

Thus, for tactical or operational scheduling it is impossible (or very difficult) to plan delivery schedules based on historical information. It is necessary to look at each series of orders on a daily (or weekly) basis, and plan vehicle routes and schedules according to this ever changing demand. This type of scheduling is often still undertaken manually by a load planner in a depot, but now computer applications are available that allow for 'live' scheduling. This is described below.

Many delivery operations are now planned on an *interactive* basis that allows the scheduler to use the computer to derive the most effective routes. Actual demand data is used rather than historical demand, and this 'real-time' data provides the basis on which routes are scheduled. Thus, much more accurate routes can be formulated. A rather obvious question might therefore be asked. Why aren't all sets of routes derived in this way? The answer is that the cost of setting up and using a routeing and scheduling package on a daily basis can be very expensive – both as to the cost of buying the package and also as to the time and cost of providing the demand data every day. Also, of course, when such packages are used for planning purposes, historical data is perfectly adequate.

Schedules produced in this way can result in very varied routes day by day. This is because the computer is able to reappraise demand requirements and come up with a completely original result each time it is used. One of the major benefits of an interactive approach is that the scheduler is in a position to make changes to routes as they are required. For example, should an urgent order be received after the initial routes have been planned using the computer, the scheduler can manually input the order into the package and assign it to an existing route. The computer will then check the route to see if the new order can be accepted. It may be rejected for a variety of reasons – insufficient capacity left on the vehicle, insufficient time available, etc. Thus the scheduler can use the package to ensure that the order is only placed on a vehicle that is in a position to complete the delivery both legally and within the allotted service constraints.

The final type of routeing and scheduling problem concerns the *planning* and measurement of the effect of change. This use of routeing and scheduling has really come into its own as a result of the development of computer-based techniques. Computer models may be used to test or simulate the effect of changing demand, new vehicle availability, legislative changes, etc. This is often known as 'what-if' planning. Some examples include:

- Third-party contractors typically use routeing and scheduling packages to help them respond to invitations to tender for business. The package will allow them to identify fleet and driver requirements and thus cost out the operation accordingly.
- A large manufacturer of soft drinks uses a routeing and scheduling package to help it to identify the implications of adopting different minimum order/drop

sizes for its various products to its many different customer types. Any reduction in minimum order size will bring an increase in revenue for the products, but will be associated with an increase in delivery costs, because many smaller orders have to be delivered. The routeing and scheduling package is used to test and identify these potential cost increases.

● Own-account operators use routeing and scheduling packages to help them identify the implications of changes in transport legislation. An increase in maximum vehicle weights is a case in point, as this will impact on the size of loads that can be carried, the buying policy for the fleet, etc.

The actual method used for routeing and scheduling varies according to the nature and difficulty of the problem, and whether a manual or computer-based approach is used. Each different method is known as an algorithm. The most common algorithm is known as the savings method. This can be explained by a relatively simple example, as indicated in Figure 27.1. Depot O services two delivery points, A and B. The distances between these two delivery points OA, OB and AB are a, b and c respectively. If each delivery point is served by a single vehicle from the depot, then the total distance is 2a + 2b. If only one vehicle is used in a single trip then the total distance covered is a + b + c. The savings achieved by linking together the two delivery points, A and B, are thus:

(2a + 2b) – (a + b + c), or a + b – c

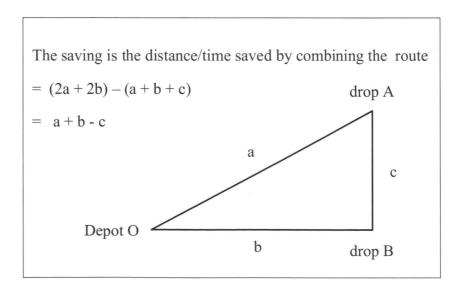

Figure 27.1 The savings method – a heuristic scheduling algorithm

In any problem with a significantly large number of delivery locations the advantage of using a computer is quite obvious. It would not be feasible to test all possible different routes manually.

The distance between every delivery location is recorded. A 'savings matrix' is then generated, recording the savings made by linking together each of these pairs of locations. Taking the link with the highest potential saving first, and then adding successive links, a route is put together, measured against the vehicle capacity and driver time constraints. Eventually all delivery points will be allocated to a vehicle route, and the schedule will be complete.

As indicated previously, other algorithms have been developed and are used in the many different computer packages available.

DATA FOR MANUAL AND COMPUTER ROUTEING AND SCHEDULING

It has already been noted that there are many different factors that need to be taken into account when planning the delivery operation of a road transport fleet. These factors require a great deal of data and information to be collected and collated. The advent of new computer techniques has enabled many more detailed aspects to be analysed, which more simple manual methods are unable to include.

As well as the basic demand data, routeing and scheduling require data that reflects the different characteristics of road transport delivery. The major areas for data are thus:

- demand data;
- distance factors;
- customer and service constraints;
- vehicle restrictions;
- driver constraints;
- route factors;
- product/unit load constraints.

The most important data requirement is for the *demand data*. Where possible this should be for weekly or annual demand by customer at the point of delivery. This can often be the most difficult data item to collect, will certainly be the most time-consuming, and will also require the most manipulation and clarification prior to use within the manual method or computer package. It may be necessary to undertake additional analyses (and collect additional data) to take account of peak demand periods because they are likely to require different schedules.

There are several ways in which demand data can be represented, which is fortunate because often the most appropriate choice of data is not available, so second or even third choice has to be sufficient. The key requirement is for the data that is collected to be representative of the *main measure* of vehicle capacity constraint. This might be weight-, volume- or unit-related. Examples include:

- weight (per product type delivered or as a total delivered tonnage figure – in kilograms or tonnes);
- cube or volume (in, say, cubic metres or cubic feet);
- carton/case/parcel (numbers to be delivered – common in retail distribution);
- unit load (eg numbers of pallets or roll cages – again common in retail distribution);
- value in revenue or sales (rarely appropriate because of the problem of interpreting value as a physical measure);
- product item (generally too detailed);
- product group.

Demand data can also be classified *by location* in a variety of ways. Clearly the level of detail and accuracy is very important in order to ensure good results from the scheduling process. Certain computer packages are more amenable to some classifications than others. The best alternative is usually the classification that is in general use within the company. Usually there is little (or no!) choice. The main alternatives are:

- postcodes or zip codes – the most common classification;
- Ordnance Survey codes, or any other type of map referencing system;
- 10-kilometre grid squares – useful simplification if there are many delivery points;
- gazetteer (main town or city) – rather imprecise, but easily recognizable;
- latitude and longitude – again, may not be sufficiently precise;
- population-based – can be a good approximation if there is no other data available;
- Plumbly management bricks (a marketing, sales-based system of identifying sales areas).

For routeing and scheduling analysis, there are various methods for estimating or measuring *distance travelled*. Distances include those from the depot to the many delivery locations and those between the different delivery locations. In the real world, these are of course the mileages travelled by the vehicles as they go about the distribution operation. The three main alternative methods of measurement are:

1. *True distance method* – where all the actual distances are physically measured on a road map. This is very time-consuming and could not be undertaken for large applications.
2. *Coordinate method* – where the depot and customer delivery points are located (on a map) by grid reference, and the straight-line distances are measured (sometimes called the 'crow fly' or 'aircraft' methods) and factored up to an approximate road distance. Typically, the factor that is used is 1.2 (this is sometimes called the 'wiggle' factor). This method uses 'barriers' to represent practical constraints such as rivers, railways, etc. A few computer applications adopt this technique.
3. *Digitized road network* – most computer scheduling systems now use a special digitized road network of the country concerned, which usually consists of the major roads and junctions of the national road network. These provide a very accurate representation of travel distances. They also make allowances for different road types (eg motorway, trunk, etc) and for land use (eg city centre, town centre, etc), which allows for variable speeds to be used when calculating the time taken to travel. The road networks of most major countries are now represented by digitized maps.

There are a number of *customer and service constraints* that may need to be taken into account during the scheduling process. These relate to the ease of delivery or the ability to make a delivery to certain destination points. They may be concerned with physical aspects, or be time-related. Some of the more detailed ones can only be applied if computer routeing is used because of the difficulty of taking so many complicated variables into account at the same time. The most common customer and service constraints are:

- specified times for delivery (eg 8 am);
- specified delivery windows (eg between 10.15 and 11.00 am);
- early closing days;
- lunch breaks;
- access restrictions (eg only vehicles of a certain size can deliver);
- unloading restrictions (eg no fork-lift truck available to unload pallets);
- drop size limitation (eg only a certain number of packages/pallets can be received);
- parking problems (eg cannot park or unload in the main road);

- paperwork problems (eg all goods must be checked by the driver and signed for).

Certain *vehicle restrictions* will also need to be taken into account. Typical examples might include:

- the type of vehicles available;
- the number of vehicles available;
- the need to pre-load trailers;
- mixed fleets (ie rigid and articulated vehicles);
- vehicle capacities (in weight or volume);
- use of compartmentalized vehicles.

Driver constraints will also be relevant, the major ones for consideration being:

- drivers' hours legislation;
- shift patterns and hours of work;
- the number of drivers available;
- different types of licence and training;
- the need for a mate to assist with deliveries.

Route factors refer to the different constraints that apply to the make-up of individual vehicle routes. These include:

- the road infrastructure;
- maximum number of calls per route;
- multiple trips (ie more than one journey in a day by one vehicle);
- two-day trips (ie vehicle and driver do not return to the depot every night);
- simultaneous delivery and collection.

There are a variety of factors that may need to be considered with reference to the *product or unit load* that is being distributed. Typical examples are:

- the weights and dimensions of the different products;
- the weights and dimensions of the different unit loads;
- variable unloading times (different products or unit loads may vary in the time it takes for their unloading);
- separation of products within a vehicle because of potential contamination or fire hazard;

- the need to collect empty containers;
- a requirement for special handling equipment.

MANUAL METHODS OF VEHICLE ROUTEING AND SCHEDULING

In this section different examples of vehicle routeing and scheduling procedures are described. Because of the detailed nature of such an exercise only a broad picture of what actually takes place will be painted. Bearing in mind the objectives and major characteristics that were described in the previous section, however, it should be possible to get a good general understanding of what is required.

The examples include a manual system for day-to-day scheduling and a manual system for long-term planning.

A daily (manual) scheduling system

This example describes the daily routeing and scheduling system and procedure undertaken by a load planner for a depot situated in London. The company is a contract haulier with a few large and several small clients for which it undertakes delivery. This particular depot covers London, East Anglia and the south-east of England. Although some locations are visited quite often, there are no regular deliveries made and new locations occur quite frequently.

Procedures at the depot are relatively straightforward. The majority of orders are received from the head office by fax, although some may come directly to the depot. The orders give information relating to the delivery address, deliver-by date, product, quantity, packaging, gross weight and any special delivery instructions. The deadline for receipt of orders is midday. This leaves the afternoon for the load scheduling and preparation of order picking notes for the following day's work. It also provides for some time allowance for the adjustment of the existing planned loads to take account of urgent orders that are required for delivery the next day.

On the day following the receipt of order, the goods will be picked and marshalled by the warehouse staff and then loaded on to a vehicle by the driver on returning in the late afternoon. Delivery takes place the next day.

A copy of every order is date-stamped, and then order types are categorized according to delivery status. These different categories are as follows:

- *Forward orders* (ie delivery required at a later date) – these are placed in a forward-order tray one week ahead, two weeks ahead, etc.

- *Normal delivery* – these are to be delivered according to the company's standard service level (say within five days). These orders are used as the prime basis for making up loads.
- *Urgent orders* – these occasional orders are for delivery within 24 hours. They are also used for making up full vehicle loads, but outside contractors are brought in if this is not feasible.

Orders are accumulated in a system of pigeon-hole racking, which is arranged on the basis of geographic areas in a formalized layout. The aim is to have a number of main delivery areas spread around the depot. The depot should be near the centre of the system. For the East London depot, the pigeon-hole racking is arranged as shown in Figure 27.2.

	Beds	Cambs	Norfolk	
Oxford	E Bucks	W Herts	E Herts	Suffolk
W Bucks	NW	N	NE	N Essex
Berks	W	C	E	S Essex
	SW	S	SE	
N Hants	W Surrey	E Surrey	W Kent	E Kent
	S Hants	W Sussex	E Sussex	

Figure 27.2   Pigeon-hole racking

After the orders are placed in the pigeon-holes, the load scheduling and routeing exercise takes place. As already indicated, the loads are assembled with urgent orders as a priority when forming the basis of a load. The planner schedules so that the furthest drops in each area are chosen first. The full load is then made up from other drops within that pigeon-hole that are relatively close, and from drops that can easily be made *en route* from or to the depot. These additional drops can be readily selected using the pigeon-hole system because of its geographical format. Using a system such as this, it is easy, on a daily basis, for a load planner to develop 'petal-shaped' routes that have the depot as their central point. This can give very efficient vehicle routeing.

Manual scheduling for strategic purposes

Manual vehicle scheduling can also be undertaken for strategic or long-term planning. The procedures that are used are somewhat similar to the scheduling system that has just been described, but they are in much greater detail. The results are used to plan fleet schedules that may be used as the basis of a delivery operation for a given period of perhaps up to about six months.

The main information and data requirements are the same as those characteristics of road transport delivery that were outlined in the previous section on data. Within these different categories there are many detailed items of information that need to be collected and then used when the scheduling procedure takes place. The main data sources for this information may be as follows:

- historical records of a company (eg sales orders);
- special surveys that are undertaken specifically for the scheduling exercise (eg vehicle loading and unloading times);
- 'standards' of performance that are accepted within an industry or by union agreement;
- legal specifications and regulations (eg driving hours, lunch breaks, etc);
- tachograph records (for vehicle speeds);
- customer surveys (delivery windows and access restrictions).

The different data requirements for any one schedule can vary for several reasons, eg type of product, type of company, type of vehicles, etc.

A DETAILED APPROACH TO MANUAL SCHEDULING

In this section the steps to undertake a detailed strategic manual routeing and scheduling exercise are described. The key elements are shown in Figure 27.3.

The basic *delivery data* describes the operational parameters from a depot near Northampton in the UK. The depot is used by an FMCG distribution company and deliveries are made from the depot to customers in an area largely to the north of Northampton. The depot closes at the weekend. All deliveries in this very basic example are to be scheduled for a single day. The parameters and constraints are:

- Two vehicle types are available. These are 16-tonne rigid vehicles (type 1), each with a carrying capacity of 700 cases, and 32-tonne articulated vehicles (type 2), each with a carrying capacity of 2,100 cases. Volume capacities are not used.

Establish delivery data & parameters

Determine geographic area (map/grid)

Determine demand

Determine customer drop constraints

Allocate demand to geographic area

Decide on geographic 'rules'

Plan trips

Plan routes

Calculate vehicle requirements & mileage travelled

Calculate the delivery cost

Calculate vehicle utilization

Figure 27.3 Steps taken to undertake a manual routeing and scheduling exercise

- Order sizes are represented as the number of cases.
- The acceptable times at which deliveries can be made vary amongst customers. There are six groups of delivery time window codes:

Code		
1	All day	9.00 am – 6.00 pm
2	Lunchtime closing	9.00 am – 1.00 pm and 2.00 pm – 6.00 pm
3	Early closing	9.00 am – 1.00 pm
4	Early am only	9.00 am – 11.00 am
5	Lunchtime only	12 noon – 2.00 pm
6	Late pm only	4.00 pm – 6.00 pm

- Drivers work an 11-hour day. Drivers must take a 45-minute break after driving for 4 hours and 30 minutes. Maximum driving time is 9 hours a day.
- The average road speeds are:

	Urban	Rural
Motorway	44.0 mph	56.0 mph
Dual Carriageway	27.5 mph	35.0 mph

| A Roads | 22.5 mph | 31.0 mph |
| B Roads | 17.5 mph | 25.0 mph |

- The time taken to unload goods at customers' premises varies as a result of access problems and unloading equipment available. There are three main groups. Each group has a fixed time (which is incurred regardless of the quantity delivered) and a variable time related to the size of the delivery. The groups are as follows:

	Fixed (minutes per drop)	Variable (minutes per case)
1	10	0.025 (1.5 seconds)
2	20	0.050 (3 seconds)
3	25	0.075 (4.5 seconds)

- The drivers are able to leave the depot at any time after 6.00 am. The latest return time of a vehicle to the depot is 7.30 pm.
- Vehicles are pre-loaded for delivery.
- Second trips in a day are allowed. If a vehicle does multiple trips in a day, the time required to reload vehicles at the depot is 10 minutes fixed time and a variable time of 0.015 minutes (0.9 seconds) per case. The minimum time that must be available for a further trip is 2 hours.

Demand data is given for each of the locations to which a delivery is to be made. Any delivery constraints need to be identified. Demand and constraints are indicated in Table 27.1.

A suitably detailed map should be used and the drop points indicated accordingly. An example of a computer-generated map is given in Figure 27.4.

A process of *measuring distances* needs to be established. This might be according to the actual roads that are used during the delivery run, although this can take a lot of time if there are some complicated routes developed. A simplified approach is to measure any distance as a straight line and then multiply this up by a 'wiggle factor' that is representative of the way that roads twist and turn. A factor of 1.2 is appropriate. Sometimes motorways are measured directly and other roads estimated using the straight-line approach.

Once the basic data is identified and recorded, then the actual *route-planning procedure* can take place. The overall objective for such an exercise is likely to be to 'find the best routes that will minimize the numbers of vehicles and minimize delivery mileage – within the set demand and delivery constraints'. Routes are planned based on what is known as the principles of 'maximum drop density' (drops that are close together are scheduled on the same vehicle) and the full use

Table 27.1 Demand data for the FMCG distribution company

Number	Name	Location	Number of Cases for Delivery	Fixed Unloading Time (mins)	Total Variable Unloading Time (mins)	Vehicle Type Restriction	Delivery Time Window Code	Grid Reference
E046	GOMM	DERBY	40	25	3	both vehicles	1	4350,3360
F450	BROWN	BURTON-U-TRENT	240	25	18	both vehicles	1	4240,3230
F251	LOW	BURTON-U-TRENT	180	10	5	16-tonne only	1	4240,3230
E248	BULL	SWADLINCOTE	180	20	9	both vehicles	1	4300,3200
A508	ANDERSON	COALVILLE	50	20	3	16-tonne only	1	4425,3140
F353	ASKEW	RUGBY	320	10	8	both vehicles	1	4524,2766
A502	ALEXANDER	RUGBY	300	20	15	16-tonne only	6	4485,2730
B416	TOMLINSON	WARWICK	278	10	7	16-tonne only	1	4280,2640
G460	BRICKWOOD	KENILWORTH	30	10	1	both vehicles	1	4290,2710
C420	CHARLESWORTH	COVENTRY	130	10	3	both vehicles	3	4330,2790
C322	WATTS	COVENTRY	170	10	4	both vehicles	1	4330,2790
B717	TATE	PETERBOROUGH	150	10	4	both vehicles	1	5190,2980
A204	RAWLINSON	PETERBOROUGH	285	20	14	both vehicles	5	5190,2980
F058	LANCY	STAMFORD	75	10	2	16-tonne only	1	5025,3080
D334	MARSDEN	UPPINGHAM	160	10	4	both vehicles	1	4865,3000
C328	MARSHALL	WIGSTON	140	25	11	both vehicles	4	4610,2990
B711	EVANS	LEICESTER	220	25	17	both vehicles	3	4590,3050
D939	MANDERS	WEST BRIDGFORD	810	10	20	both vehicles	3	4580,3370
E341	BOSWORTH	NOTTINGHAM	60	10	2	both vehicles	5	4570,3415
A409	DAVIES	NOTTINGHAM	360	20	18	both vehicles	1	4570,3415
D838	COOK	BEESTON	105	25	8	both vehicles	1	4530,3360
D636	BURNS	LONG EATON	110	25	8	both vehicles	1	4480,3320
C624	WILLIAMS	BEDWORTH	310	25	23	both vehicles	1	4360,2870
A307	SAUNDERS	NUNEATON	125	25	9	both vehicles	1	4360,2920
C325	HOPKINS	TAMWORTH	1200	20	60	both vehicles	3	4210,3040
A401	WATSON	HINCKLEY	100	20	5	both vehicles	2	4430,2940
C626	WILSON	HINCKLEY	200	10	5	both vehicles	1	4430,2940
D430	HOWARTH	BEDFORD	1950	10	49	both vehicles	1	4935,2539
B319	TAYLOR	RUSHDEN	230	25	17	both vehicles	1	4960,2670
A703	ALLRED	HUNTINGDON	280	25	21	both vehicles	1	5240,2720
F359	BULL	OUNDLE	450	10	11	both vehicles	1	5030,2885
F055	GRAHAM	KETTERING	70	10	2	both vehicles	1	4870,2790
A906	JORDAN	KETTERING	215	25	16	both vehicles	2	4870,2790
F654	ROBERTS	ROTHWELL	140	10	4	both vehicles	1	4810,2810
B818	BEATTIE	WELLINGBOROUGH	200	25	15	both vehicles	1	4900,2680
	DEPOT	COLLINGTREE						4760,2550

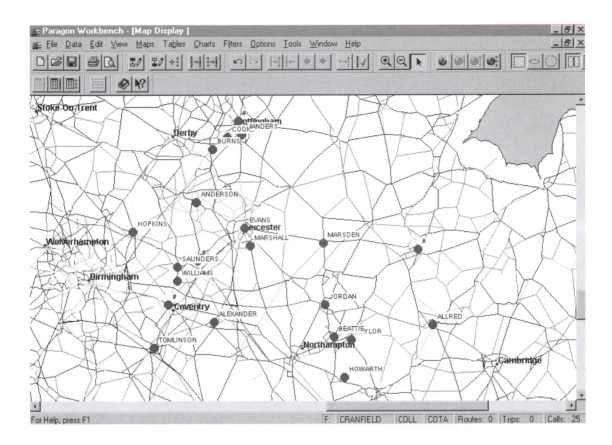

Figure 27.4 Digitized map of drop points and depot (courtesy of Paragon Software Systems www.paragon-software.co.uk)

of vehicles (use as much vehicle load capacity and vehicle time as is possible). The basic steps are thus:

- Identify drop points on the map.
- Identify demand and constraints by drop point.
- Decide on distance measurement rules.
- Identify drops that can provide a single drop trip and schedule these.
- Form clustered trips as follows:
  - Start with the drop that has the most constraints or that is the furthest from the depot.
  - Form trips by combining adjacent drops until there is a full vehicle load.
  - Identify a suitable vehicle (by its capacity).
  - Record the total time taken (travel time plus delivery time).

436 | Freight Transport

- Final trips are short ones near to the depot.
- Combine trips into routes where possible (ie two trips per vehicle day).
- Determine fleet requirements (number and type of vehicles) and mileage travelled.

The procedure is straightforward, but very time-consuming if there is a large number of deliveries to be scheduled.

The final stage is to *cost the operation* by calculating the fixed cost, based on the number of vehicles used, and the variable cost, based on the mileage travelled by the fleet. In addition the respective utilization factors can be calculated. For the small problem outlined here, the results are as follows:

Costs and utilization factors for the vehicle fleet

Vehicle costs (calculated on a daily basis):

2 rigid vehicles @ £75 per day	£150
634 kilometres @ 20 pence per kilometre	£127
3 articulated vehicles @ £146 per day	£438
662 kilometres @ 31 pence per kilometre	£205
Total cost per day	£920
Annual cost	£220,800

Cost per case delivered	(£920/9,863 cases)	9.3pence/case
Cost per kilometre	(£920/1,296kms)	71.0pence/km

Vehicle utilization:

Time utilization: $\dfrac{\text{actual hours}}{\text{available hours}}$ $\dfrac{44\text{hours 13 minutes}}{55 \text{ hours}}$ 80%

Load utilization: $\dfrac{\text{actual cases}}{\text{maximum cases}}$ $\dfrac{9,863 \text{ cases}}{11,200 \text{ cases}}$ 88%

Examples of the routes are given in the next section – although these have actually been derived by using a computer routeing and scheduling package!

COMPUTER ROUTEING AND SCHEDULING

As discussed earlier in this chapter, there are four main uses to which computer vehicle routeing and scheduling packages may be put – strategic, tactical, day-to-day operational and planning. Some computer packages are designed to address a particular one of these aspects, but most are likely to cover more than one. Most packages that have digitized road databases to support their scheduling capability will be capable of undertaking all of these approaches.

The general aim of computer routeing and scheduling packages is to 'optimize' vehicle usage whilst providing a given service level for a given level of work. This may be achieved in a variety of ways – maximize vehicle time utilization, maximize capacity utilization, minimize mileage, etc, and will be constrained by the many factors that have already been highlighted – vehicle capacities (weight and volume), time restrictions, etc. Note that the majority of packages do not, in fact, provide an optimum solution to a problem. They provide the best answer within a given set of constraints and demands.

The computer provides the transport planner with the ability to go into even greater detail than is possible with a manual system because it can undertake many more calculations; and many more alternatives can be investigated than when using a manual system.

There are a number of different routeing and scheduling computer packages available. New ones are brought on to the market periodically, and existing ones are continuously developed and updated. The scheduling procedures used in computer packages vary according to the nature of the answers that are required, but the basic system is quite similar to that used for manual scheduling, albeit a lot more sophisticated. A relatively simple system is now described.

Information is recorded in a data file for each individual delivery point. For each delivery point the exact location, quantity of goods to be delivered, delivery access restrictions and any time constraints are noted. In addition there will be a series of data files that record all the other relevant constraints, such as vehicle capacities and numbers, hours of work, legal restrictions, speeds for different road types, loading and unloading rates, and depot information. The computer program will calculate for each individual delivery location the time it takes to travel from the depot, using the speeds and distances applicable to the type of road used.

Individual locations are then linked together to form vehicle routes. The algorithm used will select the most difficult drops first of all (those that have the most difficult constraints and those that are furthest from the depot) and will then form trips by combining drops until an acceptable vehicle load has been put together. An appropriate vehicle is then identified for the load. Trips are, of course, constrained by vehicle capacity, time available, early closing days, vehicle access restrictions, etc, all of which are tested by the program as each practical route is found.

The principal advantage of using the computer for planning is that it can take account of many more constraints, and measure many more alternatives, than can ever be done manually. Computer systems incorporate advanced scheduling methods (algorithms) that can generally be relied upon to provide very efficient solutions. Used interactively, a computer package can enable the scheduler to make fundamental changes to existing routes to allow late or urgent orders to be planned into the schedule whilst the computer checks for any implications (missed delivery windows, legal infringements, etc).

Typical computer output includes extremely detailed vehicle routes that indicate the precise order of delivery drops, the locations, the drop sizes, summary results (see Figure 27.5), visual maps of the trips (see Figure 27.6), bar charts to show route summaries (see Figure 27.7), etc. The visual output makes it much easier to interpret and understand the results, and the detailed delivery schedules can be used by the drivers.

Some of the main routeing and scheduling packages are shown in Table 27.2. Additional information on these and other packages can be found in several annual guides to logistics software. Some of the advantages claimed for computerized vehicle routeing and scheduling systems are as follows:

- decreased standing costs as the vehicle establishment can be minimized;
- decreased running costs as efficient routeing reduces mileage;
- less need to hire in vehicles;
- increased customer service through consistent and reliable schedules;
- less chance of breaking transport regulations through the ability to program in legislative constraints;
- savings in management time as schedules can be calculated quickly; and
- increased level of control because more accurate management reporting is possible.

OTHER COMPUTER APPLICATIONS

There are other types of planning undertaken using different types of computer package. One example is for *single vehicle routeing* – these computer packages are based around very detailed computerized road databases. By indicating origin and destination points, and any intervening points to be visited on the route, the program will construct routes based on the real road network. Routes can be

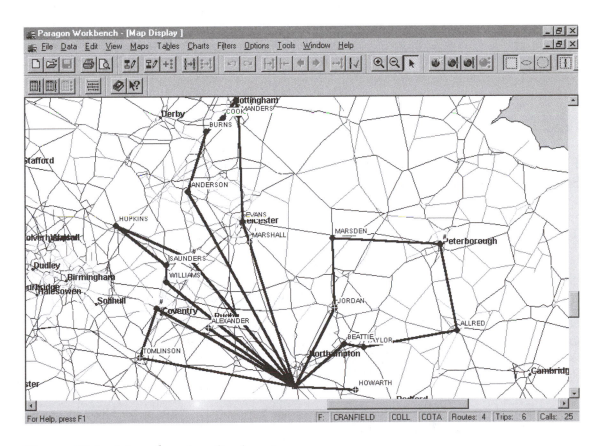

Route No.	Trip No.	No. of Calls	Distance (Mls)	Duty Time	Delivery Weight	Delivery Wt. Util.	Delivery Vol. Util.	Vehicle Group Name
1	1	3	86	3:06	578	82.6	0.0	16T
1	2	1	47	1:57	300	42.9	0.0	16T
2	1	5	110	7:14	1,935	92.1	0.0	32T
2	2	1	32	2:48	1,950	92.9	0.0	32T
3	1	8	150	9:09	1,855	88.3	0.0	32T
4	1	7	122	8:41	1,520	72.4	0.0	32T
4	6	25	547	32:55	8,138	78.5	0.0	

Figure 27.5 Summary results of Paragon run (courtesy of Paragon Software Systems www.paragon-software.co.uk)

Figure 27.6 Map showing final routes

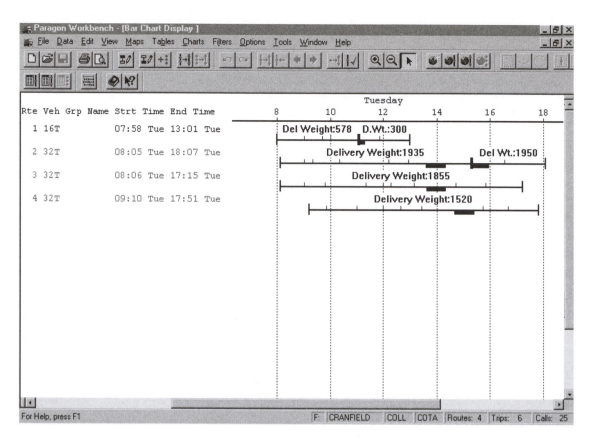

Figure 27.7 Bar charts showing the recommended routes (courtesy of Paragon Software Systems www.paragon-software.co.uk)

Table 27.2 Main vehicle routeing and scheduling packages

	UK	Users Europe	Outside Europe	First Developed	Origin Country
Dayload	31	1	–	1982	UK
Optrak 3	35	79	?	1992	UK
Paragon	390	32	?	1979	UK
Roadshow	60	150	800	1987	USA
Routemaster	30	7	5	1967	UK
Trandos	220	45	330	1983	USA
Truckstops	80	100	200	1983	USA

Source: Andersen Consulting and Cambridge Marketing Intelligence (1998)

determined on the basis of shortest, quickest, cheapest, etc. Very detailed parameters can be user-input, such as road speeds, costs, etc. Output is provided by a detailed description of the route, giving instructions on when to change from one road to another, together with the times and distances between these road links. As with routeing and scheduling packages, these packages provide colour screen maps of the chosen routes, enabling visual comparisons to be made.

There are several recent developments in *vehicle-based computer systems*. These systems and applications are generally aimed at monitoring the driver and the vehicle. Included are:

- data loggers, for monitoring fuel, etc;
- local monitors, for monitoring security, weight, etc;
- diagnostics, for measuring vehicle conditions such as stress factors on engines, suspension, etc;
- in-cab display, for providing driver information on preferred routes, road conditions, etc;
- the tracking and tracing of vehicles.

SUMMARY

In this chapter the emphasis has been on the means of undertaking planning and resourcing for road freight transport. The reasons for this were outlined at the outset.

The prerequisite for successful fleet resourcing is to identify, understand and analyse the basic detailed work requirements for the fleet, hence the use of routeing and scheduling techniques. It was shown that routeing and scheduling problems can be categorized in four different ways:

1. strategic;
2. tactical or operational;
3. interactive; and
4. planning.

As well as the basic demand data, routeing and scheduling require data that reflects the different characteristics of road transport delivery. The major data requirements were identified as:

- demand data;
- distance factors;

- customer and service constraints;
- vehicle restrictions;
- driver constraints;
- route factors;
- product or unit load constraints.

A daily (manual) scheduling system was described, and then a manual approach to scheduling for strategic purposes was outlined. A particular approach to manual routeing and scheduling was used as an example. Finally, an identical analysis was undertaken using a computer package, and these results were reviewed. The basic steps were as follows:

- Establish delivery data and parameters.
- Determine geographic area.
- Determine demand.
- Determine customer constraints.
- Allocate demand to the geographic area.
- Determine the geographic transport 'rules'.
- Plan trips.
- Plan routes.
- Calculate vehicle requirements and mileage travelled.
- Calculate the delivery cost.
- Calculate vehicle utilization.

Finally, the use of a computer routeing and scheduling package was considered and some typical output was reviewed.

Part 6

Information and the supply chain

28

The monitoring and control of logistics and distribution operations

INTRODUCTION

Recent advances in information technology have focused attention on the importance of good information systems to support logistics and distribution activities. This requirement for information has always existed, but the computer has enabled the development of more sophisticated means of data storage, processing and presentation.

Information can be seen as the 'lifeblood' of a logistics and distribution system. Without the smooth flow and transfer of information it is impossible for a distribution system to function adequately and effectively. To this end, it is important that a company develops an appropriate corporate strategy for its information requirements. This plan will need to take account of a number of different objectives, from strategic planning through to operational control.

A typical framework illustrating the planning and control cycle is shown in Figure 28.1 (previously shown as Figure 2.3). This framework emphasizes the cyclical nature of the planning and control process, starting with the question 'Where are we now?' where the aim is to provide a picture of the current status of an operation.

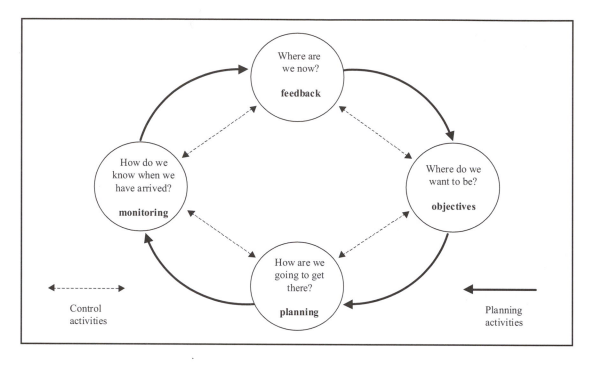

Figure 28.1 The planning and control cycle

This might be through an information feedback procedure and / or through the use of a distribution audit. The second stage is to identify the objectives of the distribution process. These should be related to such elements as customer service requirements, marketing decisions, etc. The third stage in the cycle is the process that includes the development of appropriate strategic and operational plans to achieve these objectives. Finally, there is a need for monitoring and control procedures to measure the effectiveness of the distribution operation compared to the plan. The cycle has then turned full circle and the process is ready to begin again. This emphasizes the dynamic nature of distribution, and the need for continual review and revision of plans, policies and their operations. This must be undertaken within a positive planning framework to ensure that continuity and progress are upheld.

This chapter begins with the consideration of the need to monitor logistics operations. The importance of identifying clear business objectives as the basis for setting up appropriate operational measures is emphasized. A formal approach for monitoring and control is outlined and the major comparative standards are discussed. The basis for a clear operational planning and control system is outlined.

Companies can be categorized according to the sophistication of their approach to the monitoring and control of their operations. These different categories are outlined. Some specific areas of good practice are considered. Although based on sound common sense these factors are essential to the development of an effective monitoring system. In addition, several influencing factors are highlighted. These are used to help explain the differences that occur when systems are monitored for comparative purposes. Finally, a number of detailed and key monitoring and control measures are indicated.

WHY MONITOR?

To establish an effective system for cost and performance monitoring and control there is a need to identify some overall guidelines or aims that the system is designed to fulfil. These are likely to reflect major business objectives as well as more detailed operational requirements. Thus it is important to be aware of the role of logistics and distribution within the context of the company's own corporate objectives. It is also essential that the control system reflects the integrated nature of logistics within an organization.

Typical aims might be:

- To enable the achievement of current and future business objectives – where these are directly linked to associated logistics and distribution objectives.
- To facilitate the effective and efficient provision of logistics services, thus enabling checks to be made that the distribution operation is appropriate for the overall objectives ('doing the right thing'), and also that the distribution operation is run as well as it can be ('doing the thing right').
- To support the planning and control of an operation, so that any information can be fed back to the process of planning and management.
- To provide measures that focus on the real outputs of the business – this enables action to be taken when the operations are not performing satisfactorily or when potential improvement to the operation can be identified. This will generally be linked to some form of productivity improvement or better use of resources.

In addition, some fairly specific objectives need to be identified that relate to the logistics operation itself. A major feature is likely to be to measure actual progress against a plan. Typically this will be to monitor the budget in a way that identifies if some change from plan has taken place but also to provide a usable indication of *why* actual performance or achievement does not reflect what was originally planned.

Another feature may well be to highlight specific aspects or components of the system that need particular attention.

Care needs to be taken in identifying these broader objectives. They need to be meaningful. Examples that fail the test include:

- *'The aim for distribution is to minimize costs.'* Is this to be at the expense of customer service? There needs to be a clearly identified relationship between cost and service requirements.
- *'The level of service is "as soon as possible".'* What does this really mean? Are all orders treated as urgent?
- *'Everything is to be delivered on our own vehicles.'* Does this mean resourcing the fleet to cover peak demand all year round? This is almost certainly not a cost-effective approach for determining transport requirements.

An example of carefully prepared objectives comes from a manufacturer and distributor of soft drinks:

> Overall objectives
> To provide accurate, timely and useful information on distribution cost and operational performance to enable:
>
> - the business to monitor progress towards set objectives at the total distribution level;
> - the operational departments within distribution to measure their performance against their objectives and targets, and to make operational adjustments as necessary;
> - the regular provision of information to other internal operations and functions to help assess wider trade-off opportunities;
> - a solid database of information for use in strategic and operational planning.
>
> Overall the information must be quantitative and comparative wherever possible, relating to set objectives.

MONITORING AND CONTROL: A GENERAL APPROACH

The monitoring and control of logistics and distribution operations are often approached in a relatively unsophisticated and unplanned way. Control measures are adopted as problems arise, almost as a form of crisis management. It is important to adopt a more formal approach, although this should not necessitate a complicated format. A simple and straightforward approach is as follows:

1. Determine scope of logistics activities.
2. Identify organization and departmental objectives.
3. Determine operating principles and methods.
4. Set productivity and performance goals (using standards, etc).
5. Measure and monitor performance (develop MIS).

The *scope* of distribution and logistics activities will, of course, vary from one company to another as will the extent of integration. Because of this, it is impossible to identify a standard system that can be adopted generally. A company must first determine the scope of activities that need to be considered, taking into account the overall logistics requirements and objectives as well as the traditional components of the functional sub-systems (trunking, depot operations, local delivery, etc).

More detailed *departmental objectives* should be defined. These will include such areas as stock-holding policies by individual line or product group, customer service levels by product, by customer type or by geographical area, delivery transport costs, utilization and performance, etc.

Operating principles and methods need to be clarified with respect to the different logistics components, such as trunking and delivery transport, warehousing resources and usage, together with implications for seasonality, etc. These factors will provide the basis for establishing realistic and relevant measures.

Productivity and performance goals should then be set in relation to the detailed operational tasks that are performed and with respect to the overall output requirements for the integrated logistics system as a whole. These should cover all the essential aspects of the physical distribution system. It is often easier to categorize these under the major sub-systems of warehousing (order picking performance, labour utilization, cost per case, etc); transport (vehicle utilization, cost per mile, fuel consumption, etc); and administration/stock-holding (customer orders received, stock-outs, percentage of orders fulfilled, etc).

Goals should be set based on some acceptable standards or comparative information. There are several different approaches used by organizations, and these are discussed below. They include:

- measuring cost and performance against historical data;
- measuring against a budget plan;
- developing physical or engineered standards;
- using industry standards;
- benchmarking against 'best practice'.

Finally, *key indices and ratios* need to be developed to allow for appropriate monitoring and control to be undertaken (eg actual work against planned work, cost per case, cases per hour, tonnes per journey, etc). These need to be representative of the distribution operation, and they should be capable of clearly identifying *why* a deviation has occurred as well as *if* a deviation has occurred.

WHAT TO MEASURE AGAINST?

As already indicated, there are a number of different approaches that can be adopted to determine appropriate goals. These range in sophistication from very simplistic internal 'year on year' comparisons to quite detailed externally related engineered standards. Most well-developed systems are internally budget-oriented, but are also linked to external performance measures.

Historical data

Systems that merely compare overall activity costs on a period-by-period basis may not be providing any useful information that can be used to monitor operational performance. As an example, a measure may indicate that the cost of distribution for a company has reduced as a percentage of total revenue for this year compared to last year. Without any background to this measure it is impossible to be sure whether or not this is an improvement *in terms of distribution performance*.

Budget

Almost all companies will have a budget plan, and this should include a breakdown of the logistics costs in appropriate detail – an activity budget. A traditional means of monitoring an operation is, therefore, to evaluate the cost of the logistics operation in relation to the expectations of the budget plan.

The budget approach has been developed in a variety of ways to enable more sophisticated and more meaningful measures to be created. The 'activity' concept means that the budget – and the respective measurement process – can identify and differentiate between functional activities (warehouse, transport, etc) and, more importantly, across core business-oriented activities. This might, for example, be by product group or by major customer, thus allowing for very detailed measurements reflecting the integrated nature of the logistics activities under scrutiny.

An additional development is the concept of flexible budgeting, which recognizes one of the key issues of monitoring – the need to be able to identify and take account of any changes in business volumes. This is particularly important in the logistics environment where any reductions in volume throughput can lead to the under-performance of resources. The concept is based on the premise that budgets are put together with respect to a planned level of activity. The fixed, semi-variable and variable costs appropriate to that level of activity are identified, and form the basis of the budget. If activity levels fluctuate, then the planned budget is flexed to correspond with the new conditions. Thus semi-variable and variable costs are adjusted for the change. In this way the change in cost relationships that results from a change in the level of activity is taken into account automatically, and any other differences between planned and actual cost performance can be identified as either performance or price changes.

This approach is particularly applicable to logistics activities as there is very often a high fixed cost element, and any reduction in levels of activity can increase unit costs quite significantly. With a fixed (ie non-flexible) budget system it can be difficult to identify the essential reasons for a large variance. To what extent is there a controllable inefficiency in the system, and to what extent is there under-utilization of resources due to falling activity? A typical example is the effect that a reduction in demand (throughput) can have on order picking performance and thus unit cost. A flexible budget will take account of the volume change and adjust the original budget accordingly.

Finally, an effective budget measurement system will incorporate the idea of variance analysis. In the context of logistics activities, variance analysis allows for the easier identification of problem areas as well as providing an indication of the extent of that variance, helping the decision process of whether or not management time should be assigned to solving that particular problem. As indicated earlier, an effective system will indicate if a variance has occurred, the extent of that variance and also why it has occurred with respect to performance/efficiency change or price/cost change (or a mixture of both). Variance analysis is best used within the context of a flexible budget because the flexible budget automatically takes account of changes in activity.

Engineered standards

A number of companies use internally derived measures for certain logistics activities through the development of engineered standards. This involves the identification of detailed measures for set tasks and operations. The means of determining these measures is a lengthy and often costly process involving the use of time and work study techniques.

When suitable and acceptable standards have been agreed for specific tasks, then a performance monitoring system can be adjusted to allow for direct measurement of actual performance against expected or planned performance. The advantage of using engineered standards is that each task is measured against an acceptable base. A monitoring system that measures against past experience alone may be able to identify improved (or reduced) performance but it is always possible that the initial measure was not a particularly efficient performance on which to base subsequent comparisons.

Apart from cost, a potential drawback with engineered standards is that the initial time or work study data collection is difficult to verify. There is no certainty that an operative who is under scrutiny will perform naturally or realistically (whether consciously or subconsciously).

Many logistics tasks do lend themselves to the application of engineered standards. Most warehousing activities fall into this category – goods receiving, pallet put-away, order picking, etc, as well as driver-related activities – vehicle loading, miles travelled, fixed and variable unloading. An outline example is given below:

Developing standards for delivery transport: an example
Standard costs can be related to measured or standard times. These should cover the three main operations:

1.   running/driving time (speeds related to road types);
2.   selection and delivery time (fixed and variable);
3.   depot/loading time.

Standard time journeys can then be built up. These can be incorporated with standard costs to give a standard cost per minute. Thus, the planned and actual performance are linked, and variance analysis can be undertaken. This provides for a stronger system of control.

External standards and benchmarking

Another approach to cost and performance measurement is to make comparisons against industry norms. The intention here is that a company's performance can be compared to similar external operations and standards, making comparison more realistic and therefore more valuable. For some industries, such as grocery retailing, these measures are fairly readily accessible through industry journals and associations. Examples of typical measures include order picking performance (cases per hour), delivery cases per journey, etc.

A further development to this is the idea of 'benchmarking'. Here, the aim is to identify appropriate 'world-class' or 'best-in-class' standards across a whole range of different organizations and operations. This enables a company's performance to be compared with the very best in any industry. It is a broader concept than merely identifying variations in performance, the intention being to identify the reasons why a certain operation is the best and to establish ways and means of emulating the operation. A number of 'benchmarking' clubs have been formed to this end (see Chapter 29).

Recent surveys have shown that there is still significant room for improvement for many companies in the context of the use of appropriate monitoring systems. Figure 28.2, which is based on the results of a survey of logistics productivity carried out by A T Kearney, indicates that the majority of companies base their performance measures on past experience or have no set standards at all.

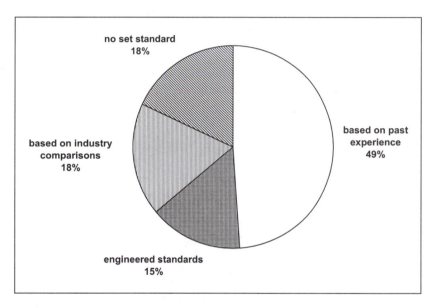

Figure 28.2   Goal-setting basis used in sample UK companies

AN OPERATIONAL PLANNING AND CONTROL SYSTEM

The budget should be used as the basis for providing quantitative objectives for the relevant elements to be monitored within the logistics operation. Linked to this should be any appropriate internal (engineered) or external standards that are deemed to be important measures of the business.

The operating plan should be drawn up based on the above factors to indicate the operational parameters or cost centres. This will show how costs are to be split by period (week or month), by functional element (eg fuel or wages), by logistics component (storage, local delivery, etc) and by activity (major customer, product group, etc). The plan should also show which key business performance indicators are to be used (eg tonne/miles delivered, etc) and demonstrate how they are linked to set standards.

The operating control system involves the process of identifying whether the operating plan has been adhered to – what deviations have occurred and why – so that remedial action can be speedily taken. Figure 28.3 outlines this process.

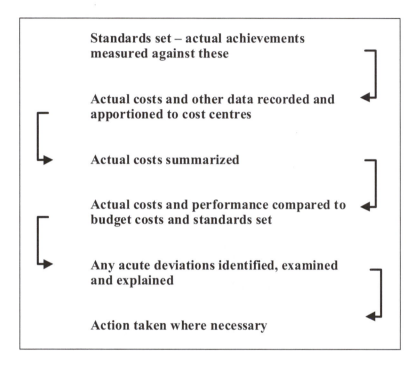

Figure 28.3   An operating control system

In measuring these deviations it is important to be aware of three major causes of deviation. These are:

1. changes in the levels of activity (ie less work is available for a fixed capacity – labour or equipment);
2. changes in efficiency or performance (ie the resource, labour or equipment has not performed as expected); and
3. changes in price (ie the price of an item, say fuel, has increased so costs will increase).

Activity level changes can, of course, be taken into account by the use of flexible budgets.

Key indices and ratios need to be developed to allow for appropriate monitoring and control to be undertaken (eg actual work against planned work, cost per case, cases per hour, tonnes per journey, etc). These need to be representative of the distribution operation, and they should be capable of clearly identifying why a deviation has occurred as well as if a deviation has occurred.

LEADERS AND LAGGERS

As with many aspects of business, companies vary in the extent to which they have developed the sophistication of their performance measurement. There are the leaders, which have adopted a very forward-looking approach to the monitoring and control of their operations, and incorporated ideas such as flexible budgeting, variance analysis, productivity standards and integrated control measures. There are also the laggers, which do little more than compare broad costs on a period-by-period basis.

It is possible to identify discrete categories of companies indicating the different approach to, and different level of use of, cost and performance monitoring techniques. The emphasis is very much one of 'attitude' to measurement and productivity performance. The consultants, A T Kearney, have suggested four company categories as follows:

- inactive;
- reactive;
- proactive;
- integrative.

Inactive companies have few clear measures and a tendency to react to crises as their sole means of monitoring. At the most they will isolate very broad costs and link these to macro outputs such as sales revenue, subsequently comparing these over long time periods.

Reactive companies have budget-based monitoring systems and tend to evaluate performance only against the budget. The approach is broadly one of historical cost accounting. Budgets are likely to be broken down to different functional activities, but will not reflect key core business activities. Companies in this category are positioned to pursue cost reduction programmes rather than productivity improvement programmes.

Proactive companies will incorporate measured/engineered standards as well as flexible budgets and variance analysis. The more sophisticated will have moved towards industry-based standards and may have begun some benchmarking programmes.

Companies in the integrative category will have adopted the same approach to measurement as the proactive companies but rather than identifying and measuring the different functional activities in isolation will have developed overall logistics-related measures. This will help provide the ability to monitor and plan in an integrated way, allowing trade-off opportunities to be identified and evaluated.

GOOD PRACTICE

There are a number of key areas of 'good practice' that need to be considered when developing the detail of an effective monitoring and control system. These are all fairly straightforward but bear discussion. They can be broadly categorized as:

- principles;
- content;
- output.

Most of the main *principles* associated with an effective system are based on sound common sense. They can be used to provide distinct guidelines for the development of an appropriate new control system as well as to help identify reasons why an existing system is not functioning satisfactorily. They include:

- *Accuracy.* The basic input data to the system must be correct. Inaccurate data will obviously produce incorrect measures, but will also undermine confidence in the system as a whole.
- *Validity/completeness.* The measures used must reflect a particular activity in an appropriate way, and must cover all the aspects concerned. For example, a broad carton-per-hour measure for order picking is clearly inappropriate if there is a substantial element of full pallet picking or broken case picking.
- *Hierarchy of needs.* Individuals within an organization only require certain pieces of information. To swamp them with unnecessary information is expensive and may diminish the usefulness of an information system. Typically, the higher the level of personnel within an organization, the more general or more aggregate is the information required. Figure 28.4 indicates this hierarchy, illustrating the relationship between what might be termed as command information and feedback/control information.

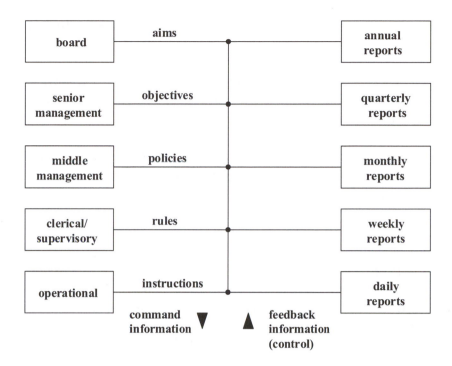

Figure 28.4 Hierarchy of needs showing the different information requirements at the different levels of an organization

- *Targeting of the correct audience.* Linked very much to the previous point is the need to ensure that the correct audience is identified and that all the key information is then directed to this audience.
- *User ownership.* The fault of many an information system is to impose information on individuals without first including them in the process of identifying and determining information requirements. This can be very demotivating. It is a very valid step to include potential users at the systems requirement stage, thus conferring user ownership of the information when the system is in place. The information should be useful and those who use the information should understand the detail.
- *Reactivity to changes in business activity.* Not a simple requirement to put into practice, but an effective control system will need to be dynamic and so take account of any changes in business activity. To a certain extent this is achieved through flexible budgeting.
- *Timeliness.* Reports must be available at the agreed time, and the frequency of reports should be such that suitable control action can be taken.

- *Ease of maintenance.* A fairly obvious comment is that an effective system must not be overly complicated to maintain and progress. Simplicity is certainly a virtue.
- *Cost-effectiveness.* Again, a fairly obvious but very relevant point is that a monitoring system should not cost more to set up and run than can possibly be saved through using the system.

The elements of good practice that come under the category of *content* have almost all been covered in previous sections, and they are as follows:

- the need for clear cost categories, with careful identification of fixed and variable costs;
- the use of flexible budgeting;
- the use of variance analysis;
- the clarification of controllable and non-controllable elements;
- the use of reference points against which the monitored elements can be measured – these might include
    - budget
    - forecast
    - trends
    - targets
    - comparative league tables.
    (Both the final two factors are useful for monitoring contractor operations and for setting up inter-depot comparisons.)

The final aspect of good practice concerns the type of *output* that the system produces. This is the information on which any form of action is based. It has already been emphasized that this information must be relevant and useful. The major output characteristics are:

- Reports can vary. They may be
    - summary (providing key statistics only)
    - exception (identifying the major deviations from plan)
    - detailed (including all information).
- Reports should be made to a standard format – especially important where any inter-depot comparisons are to be made.
- Data should be presented in whatever means is most appropriate to the eventual use of that data.

Different types of data output are as follows:

- *trend data* – based upon moving annual totals to identify long-term changes;
- *comparative data*
    - data analysis over a *short period* (eg this month against last month)
    - data analysed against a *target* (eg this month compared with budget)
    - data analysed against a *measured standard* (eg this month compared with standard)
    - comparative data analysis *also* identifies *variances* that indicate the degree of performance success;
- *indices* – data in statistical form compared with a base position over time;
- *ratio* – a combination of two or more pieces of meaningful data to form a meaningful figure for comparison;
- *graphs* – comparative trends in pictorial form.

What do companies see as being the most valuable characteristics of a good monitoring system? The example outlined below provides an indication.

An international manufacturer and supplier of computer equipment identified the need for a more adequate information system for monitoring and controlling performance in its three warehouses. The company set up a project team to investigate these requirements, and produced some interesting output.
Five key areas for measurement were identified:

1. *volume* – what is moving through the warehouse;
2. *efficiency* – how well the operation is being run;
3. *cost-effectiveness* – whether the cost is reflecting the work being done;
4. *quality* – how well the service levels are being met;
5. *stability* – what the staff turnover picture looks like.

Outline requirements were:

- overall business control;
- activity measures within the business area;
- trend indicators and productivity measures.

Factors for consideration were:

- *action* – the system should lead to a change in the current position, and should be used;

- *confusion* – the system should filter out the irrelevant information that confuses and diverts attention;
- *comprehensibility* – everyone who receives information must understand it;
- *defensiveness* – the defence reaction to figures, especially adverse ones, needs to be overcome;
- *timeliness* – the information has to be available in sufficient time for action to be taken;
- *validity* – actual changes in performance must be reflected by the system;
- *dynamism* – the system must be sensitive to the changing internal and external conditions, as tomorrow's problems cannot be solved with yesterday's measurement system.

INFLUENCING FACTORS

Many monitoring systems are developed with a view to using them to enable comparisons to be made between different depots. Some companies will do this across their own operations. It is also common practice for some of the major users of dedicated contract operations to compare how well one contractor is performing against the others.

If this is the major use of a monitoring system then *it is essential that there is a broad understanding of any different operational factors that might influence the apparent effectiveness or efficiency of one operation compared to another.* Thus, a number of operational influencing variables can be identified, and may need to be measured, to enable suitable conclusions to be drawn and explanations given for any comparative assessments.

Any number of these may be relevant, but typical examples are:

- throughput variability (by day);
- product profile;
- order profile;
- store profile;
- store returns;
- special projects (promotions, alternative unitization);
- equipment specification;
- RDC design (building shape, mezzanines);
- employee bonus schemes;
- methods (secondary sorts, etc);
- local labour market (quality, need for training, etc);

- regional cost variations (labour, rent, rates, etc);
- staff agreements (guaranteed hours, etc);
- unit definitions.

DETAILED AND KEY MEASURES

For most logistics operations it is possible to identify certain key measures that provide an appropriate summary measurement of the operation as a whole and of the major elements of the operation. Detailed measurements are likely to differ from one company to another, depending on the nature of the business.

Measures are generally aimed at providing an indication of the performance of individual elements within an operation as well as their cost-effectiveness. In addition, the overall performance or output is often measured, particularly with respect to the service provided, the total system cost and the return on capital investment.

Typical detailed and key measures used are summarized in three different case examples. These cover customer service requirements, a warehouse operation and a multi-depot delivery transport operation. Both the warehouse and the transport examples indicate adherence to the principle of the hierarchical nature of information requirements. Also, see Chapter 3 for customer service measurements.

Example 1
For a supplier of consumables, major customer service measurements are:

- percentage of orders satisfied in full;
- percentage of items supplied at first demand;
- percentage of overdue orders;
- numbers of stock-outs;
- orders delivered within set lead times; and
- percentage of deliveries outside fixed delivery windows/times.

Example 2
For a grocery multiple retailer, measures are designed to assess the performance of the delivery transport system. They are aimed at measuring the cost-effectiveness of the operation and also the quality of service. Note the hierarchical approach, and also that there are no cost-related measures at the lowest level. The levels and associated measures are:

- director/head office (strategic planning and control)
  - ROCE
  - cost/case (divisional)
  - cost/vehicle (divisional)
  - cost/value of goods delivered
  - cost as a percentage of company sales;
- depot managers (management control)
  - cost/mile
  - cost/vehicle
  - cost/roll pallet
  - average earnings/driver
  - maximum earnings/driver
  - maintenance costs/vehicle;
- transport manager (operational control)
  - cost/mile
  - cost/case
  - cost/vehicle
  - cost/roll pallet
  - cost/journey
  - roll pallets/journey
  - journeys/vehicle
  - damage repairs/vehicle
  - miles/gallon per vehicle
  - damages in transit and cases delivered
  - percentage cases out of temperature
  - percentage journeys out of schedule;
- supervisors
  - overtime hours as percentage of hours worked
  - contract vehicles as percentage of vehicles
  - percentage of vehicles off the road
  - percentage of drivers absent
  - percentage vehicle fill
  - percentage of vehicles over weight
  - percentage of breakdowns
  - average hours worked/driver.

Example 3

These are the information requirements for an FMCG manufacturer and supplier at three levels, related to the company's warehouse operations in terms of performance measurements and operating ratios:

- CEO
    - profit
    - return on investment
    - growth
    - stock turnover
    - distribution cost
    - sales value;
- distribution director
    - service achievement
    - cost-effectiveness
    - capital employed
    - stock turnover by depots
    - storage cost/unit
    - warehouse handling cost/unit
    - overall labour efficiency;
- warehouse manager
    - inventory level
    - stock availability
    - operating cost
    - operating productivity
    - actual hours
    - standard hours (stock receiving and location, order picking, packing, dispatch)
    - warehouse cost/unit (order)
    - stock turnover.

SUMMARY

An approach to monitoring logistics and distribution operations has been described in this chapter, linked wherever possible to actual company practice. The need for monitoring and control procedures to measure the effectiveness of actual distribution performance against a prescribed distribution plan has been identified within the context of the framework of a planning and control cycle. The need to establish clear, business-related objectives has been emphasized.

A formal approach for a monitoring and control system was outlined, but it was felt important that this should not be a complicated format. Several different means of identifying suitable goals were introduced. These were:

- measuring cost and performance against historical data;
- measuring against a budget plan;
- developing physical or engineered standards;
- using industry standards;
- benchmarking against 'best practice'.

The major factors related to these alternatives were discussed, together with the relative advantages and disadvantages of the different approaches. Finally, an operational planning and control system was described, with the emphasis on the need to identify and measure *what* deviations had occurred and *why* they had occurred. This should specifically consider changes in:

- levels of activity;
- efficiency or performance;
- price or cost.

It was noted that companies could be categorized according to whether they were leaders or laggers in the development of reliable cost and performance monitoring systems. One study was quoted, which identified four main company categories:

1. inactive;
2. reactive;
3. proactive;
4. integrative.

A number of key areas of good practice were considered. These were deemed essential in developing the detail of an effective monitoring and control system. These were considered under the heading of principles, content and output. In addition, a number of influencing factors were highlighted as being important to help explain the differences that occur when systems are monitored for comparative purposes.

Finally, a series of key and detailed cost and performance measures were considered. These were drawn from a number of specific case examples.

29

Benchmarking

INTRODUCTION

Benchmarking is the process of continuously measuring and comparing one's business performance against comparable processes in leading organisations to obtain information that will help the organisation identify and implement improvements.

(Benson, 1998)

The continuous process of measuring our products, services and business practices against the toughest competitors and those companies recognised as industry leaders.

(Xerox definition of benchmarking)

The process known as benchmarking is quite straightforward to explain but is extraordinarily difficult to conduct successfully in practice. The reason for including this chapter is that benchmarking or comparison lies at the heart of performance measurement.

As with many approaches to improving performance, benchmarking has its enthusiasts and its detractors. There is no doubt that, conducted sensibly, a benchmarking project can be of benefit to an organization, not least because it forces the participants to look closely at their own organization's processes and question them.

It is worth sounding a note of caution at this stage. Benchmarking partners need to be chosen carefully because no two organizations are *exactly* alike. This may sound obvious but it is remarkable just how different organizations are even when they are engaged in the same business, never mind a completely different industry. This tends to lead to the participants having to examine generic areas of operations, which can dilute the power of the exercise.

Another point to note is that benchmarking partners may, for their own reasons, not be strictly open and honest with others involved in the exercise. For example, competitors would fit into this category. All information derived from the process should be carefully weighed and considered in the light of corroborative evidence. Do not take everything as the absolute truth as it could send your organization off on a path that is not fruitful.

It is worth pointing out that some detractors suggest that benchmarking only serves to make the organization aspire to be average rather than to lead the field. This may be true in certain areas of the business but it is also the case that organizations can learn from one another, and benchmarking is one way of facilitating this learning process.

Benchmarking by definition forces an organization to change its focus from the internal to the external environment by attempting to compare its performance with that of the best-in-class companies.

WHY SHOULD AN ORGANIZATION ENGAGE IN BENCHMARKING?

The simple answer is to remain competitive. Institutionalized benchmarking leads to the organization having a better understanding of its competitive environment and its customers' needs. Table 29.1 neatly sums up the main reasons for benchmarking.

HOW TO CONDUCT A BENCHMARKING EXERCISE

This section will describe a framework for conducting a benchmarking project. Given the diversity of organizations and processes it will not be possible to go into great detail. The Japanese are credited with starting the benchmarking approach to continuous improvement. At a very simple level employees are seconded to other companies in order that they may learn new ways of working. This practice is called Shukko.

Table 29.1 Reasons for benchmarking

Objectives	Without Benchmarking	With Benchmarking
Becoming competitive	Internally focused	Understanding of competition
	Evolutionary change	Ideas from proven practices
Industry best practices	Few solutions	Many options
	Frantic catch-up activity	Superior performance
Defining customer requirements	Based on history or gut feeling	Market reality
	Perception	Objective evaluation
Establishing effective goals and objectives	Lacking external focus	Credible, unarguable
	Reactive	Proactive
Developing true measures of productivity	Pursuing pet projects	Solving real problems
	Strengths and weaknesses not understood	Understanding outputs
	Route of least resistance	Based on industry best practices

Source: Camp R C (1989)

The following sections illustrate benchmarking approaches developed by two companies, Xerox and Alcoa.

The Xerox approach to benchmarking is as follows:

Planning
1. Identify what is to be benchmarked.
2. Identify comparative companies.
3. Determine data collection method and collect data.

Analysis
4. Determine current performance 'gap'.
5. Project future performance levels.

Integration
6. Communicate benchmark findings and gain acceptance.
7. Establish functional goals.

Action
8. Develop action plans.
9. Implement specific actions and monitor progress.

10. Recalculate benchmarks.
Maturity
1. Leadership position attained.
2. Practices fully integrated into processes.

The Alcoa approach to benchmarking is as follows:

1. Decide what to benchmark – what is important to the customer, mission statement, business needs, etc.
2. Plan the benchmarking project (choose a team leader and team members, submit the project proposal).
3. Understand own performance (self-study in order to examine factors that influence performance positively or negatively).
4. Study others (identify candidates for benchmarking, short-list, prepare questions of interest, conduct the study).
5. Learn from the data (identify performance gaps and which practices should be adopted).
6. Use the findings (for the benefit of the organization and its employees).

(Source: Zairi, 1994: 11–12)

The following is a step-by-step guide to conducting a benchmarking exercise. Naturally each organization will have its own special needs and circumstances that will dictate how they will conduct their own projects, therefore this is only an example of how it may be undertaken.

Step 1

As with any major project, senior management commitment to the exercise must be secured at the outset. This is necessary not only to ensure that resources are made available for the project but also because any potential improvements identified by the benchmarking team will need senior management support to progress them satisfactorily. Ideally a senior management champion should be identified who can take ownership of the project. This will ensure that any useful outcomes are presented at the highest level in the organization. If senior management commitment is not secured then progress to a satisfactory conclusion is unlikely. Middle managers may feel threatened by change and quietly bury the results.

Step 2

Objectives need to be set for the project. It is a mistake to attempt to do too much immediately. These types of project can generate huge amounts of data. The trick is to be able to identify the useful information buried in all this data. It is much easier to identify a specific process or activity and concentrate on this one area before moving to the next one. Therefore a list should be prepared of specific processes and performance criteria that the company wishes to benchmark first.

Step 3

The next stage involves deciding whom to benchmark against. There are several options.

Internal colleagues

This is the easiest form of benchmarking to conduct as the information should be readily available and accurate. Different divisions in the same organization may be compared easily. The problem with this approach is that if performance is generally poor in the company then any benchmarking project will not improve competitive performance.

Industry benchmarking

Benchmarking against competitors can be fraught with problems. Firstly, it seems unlikely that a competitor would wish to engage in an exercise that may lead to a loss of competitive advantage but some organizations are very open with their information so it is not impossible. Secondly, information provided by a direct competitor without corroborative evidence should be treated with scepticism. Finally, trade associations do produce industry statistics but these are likely to be non-specific and based on averages. This information will be of little use if the benchmarking organization is already exceeding these standards. The statistics may provide some comfort through the knowledge that the company is not below average but it will not be helpful if offshore competitors are exceeding these standards significantly. The desire of many companies is to be the best in class or world class for their industry.

Non-competitive benchmarking

This type of benchmarking involves benchmarking against other companies in different industries. This has the advantage of excluding market competition from the process of comparison. By the same token it does make it more difficult to identify specific areas of comparison between non-competitive benchmarking partners. For example, a retailer is unlikely to have areas of operations that are similar to a manufacturing company. However, what they will have in common are areas such as purchasing or supplier appraisal. It is through examining in detail the processes used by the different partners that areas of improvement will be identified.

Many companies see the advantages of continuing benchmarking activities on a regular basis and so they have set up benchmarking clubs as a forum to continue the activity.

Other benchmarking activities

Obtaining competitors' products or services and dismantling them (reverse engineering) is one way of comparing the organization with its direct competitors. Published accounts, trade conferences, articles in the trade press and employees recruited from competitors are all sources of useful information about competitors. It must not be forgotten that the organization's customers are a good source of competitive information. Through asking the customer questions about the organization's performance it is possible to glean information about competitors' performance in key areas also. This should help to forge stronger links with major customers.

Step 4

Having decided on objectives and benchmarking partners it is necessary to decide on what disciplines are required in the team. Clearly, one member of the team should be intimately acquainted with the process to be benchmarked. Other useful disciplines might include an accountant for financial information or an information systems expert, if that is appropriate. Apart from relevant related disciplines it may be worth including one member of the team who is simply there because they know the business and where it is going, but are not aligned to the process under review. This approach can often prompt the naïve question: 'So why do we do it this way?' It is a well-used idiom, which says that sometimes individuals are so intimately involved in a process that they find it hard to question fundamental principles. Being unable to 'see the wood for the trees' is as common as it ever was.

Next it is essential that any available information is identified and located. Information is unlikely to be forthcoming from the benchmarking partner in a format that matches the company format. Time will have to be spent configuring and sifting the information from both sides to allow meaningful comparisons to take place. Mapping out the steps in a process by producing a process flow diagram is also very useful by way of preparation. Information may flow between the partners even at this stage by means of questionnaires, company literature or informal meetings.

In some cases confidentiality agreements are exchanged between the participating companies. If required these need to be in place at an early stage and are useful if a long-term relationship is envisaged.

Step 5

It is highly likely that a number of visits and meetings will be required as requests for information from both sides are processed after each round of meetings.

Early meetings are likely to include tours of facilities. This helps set the scene for the visiting team. Establishing terms of reference will also be agreed upon.

If the planning and preparation have been carried out thoroughly then the process will move swiftly to exchanging information. The process will be iterative as partners return to their companies to digest the information they have received. In doing so many questions will emerge from this analysis. These must be logged for future meetings. Eventually, useful information will begin to emerge.

Step 6

Obviously not all the information gleaned from an exercise will be useful but it would be unusual if absolutely nothing of benefit emerged from the exercise.

If conducted with appropriate energy then the very minimum to be gained will be a better understanding of how the company functions in a given area. Some may throw their hands up in horror and say that a company should already know what is going on inside itself without going through such an elaborate process. The truth is that many companies do not really know what is going on inside their organization. Where there are written operating procedures senior management (understandably) tend to assume that is how things get done. At the point where the operating procedures are supposed to apply, things may be very different. In the course of collecting information and possibly mapping the process in preparation for a benchmarking exercise these types of anomaly will be exposed. When and if this situation arises then an open-minded approach will be useful. It may well be that the way the job is really done, as compared to the way the procedure says it should be done, might be the most effective way of working.

If better ways of working or tighter targets have been identified through benchmarking as achievable then systematic plans should be made to implement the necessary changes. Assuming that senior management support for the process is in place then resources and responsibilities need to be allocated. Once this has been decided, the staff involved in the planned change need to be involved fully. They will already be involved to some extent as they will probably have participated in the preparation stage of the project.

As with any change in the management situation, there will be a measure of concern amongst the staff involved because change usually augurs (for them) a step into the unknown. If these fears are recognized and dealt with sympathetically by management, communication and involvement will generate commitment to the process of change.

The success of any improvements instigated as the result of benchmarking should show up in the relevant performance measures for that functional area. It could be in the business ratios such as return on capital employed or in something as straightforward as reduced picking errors in the warehouse.

Step 7

There are several ways of continuing the process:

- Allocate staff on a permanent basis to engage in continuous benchmarking activities. Obviously the organization needs to be large enough to justify this kind of action.
- Identify long-term benchmarking partners. Join a benchmarking club, for example the Best Practice Club. There is also a benchmarking exchange Web site on the Internet. Try to identify the best-in-class organizations for the area of operations that is being benchmarked.
- Use benchmarking as part of a continuous improvement culture. Measure and communicate performance improvements widely within the organization.
- Use industry-specific trade association figures. For example, the Freight Transport Association produce *The Manager's Guide to Distribution Costs* every year.
- Create a computerized database of benchmarking information. This will require constant updating in the light of the latest information.

FORMAL BENCHMARKING SYSTEMS

The following are some of the formal benchmarking systems that have been developed over the years:

- *Quality function deployment (QFD)*. This benchmarking approach has been developed by Japanese managers. It takes the customer's requirements as the starting-point and aims to improve performance by converting customers' perceptions of suppliers' performance into an improvement agenda.

- *ISO 9004.* As part of the ISO 9000 series of quality management frameworks ISO 9004 provides a framework of constant comparison for any type of business.
- *The Malcolm Baldridge National Quality Award benchmarking framework.* This is an award for quality awareness started in 1987 in the USA. The framework is based on four basic elements:
  - the role of senior managers in promoting quality excellence;
  - the processes used to achieve the objectives of the organization;
  - quality achievements;
  - customer satisfaction.

BENCHMARKING DISTRIBUTION OPERATIONS

This section outlines the major features of a benchmarking or auditing exercise for a group of companies involved in grocery distribution. The aim is to describe an approach to distribution benchmarking. In addition, some of the potential problems and pitfalls are identified, and some key issues are highlighted. The major emphasis is on the depot operations, but a similar approach can also be used for benchmarking transport operations.

The key elements described are:

- the main principles behind studies such as these;
- a typical format and approach;
- data collection and analysis;
- interpreting the results.

For this type of benchmarking, there is a recognized benchmarking hierarchy that can be summarized at four different levels:

1. *Single task* benchmarking – covering single distribution activities such as goods inwards, order assembly, etc.
2. *Function-wide* benchmarking – where all the tasks in a distribution function are reviewed with an aim to improving overall performance. This might, for example, include all the processes from goods receipt to vehicle loading in a given depot.
3. *Management process* benchmarking – covering broader cross-functional issues such as quality, information systems, payment systems, etc.
4. *Total operation* (logistics) benchmarking – where the complete logistics chain is reassessed, from procurement and supply through to end-user delivery.

The approach described here is for the quite specific function-wide benchmarking that applies to a distribution depot. The example used is based on an inter-firm comparison in the grocery industry. The major factor is that it is a single industry study. This helps to ensure that any comparisons between the different operations are drawn on a reasonably similar base.

The study broadly consists of a series of snapshot evaluations of the actual cost and performance derived for the different depots. This is undertaken through the detailed data collection and analysis of the key functions within the depots. Data is broken down according to various activities (goods receipt, reserve storage, etc) and various product groups (chilled, ambient, wines and spirits, etc). Other categorizations may be relevant in different circumstances – for manufacturers, customer classification may be important (national account, wholesale, independent, etc). Comparisons are made across different depots and/or companies according to a series of 'league tables' drawn up for all the key statistics. The cost and performance of an individual depot can then be assessed according to the position in the league table.

Such an audit procedure is likely to be a two-stage process: 1) an initial function-wide study to identify the key cost and performance drivers; and 2) subsequent, smaller and more directed studies to monitor the key drivers and identify any activity shifts and new drivers that might evolve. These might suggest a revision of certain operations or activities.

Format and approach

There are two main areas for data collection and analysis. The first includes all the major functional depot activities, costs and performance factors. These are likely to be fairly standard (cases picked per hour, etc). The second includes those other elements that may be essential to help *explain* the cost and performance indices derived. Why is depot X performing so badly in its order picking operation? Why does depot Y have such a high-cost goods reception facility? These are often classified as a part of the logistics 'environment' in which the distribution function operates. Typical examples of the essential elements within the logistics environment are:

- source of goods coming into the depot;
- product characteristics;
- sales characteristics;
- customer profile;
- inventory profile;
- returns, etc.

One additionally important element is the information system that supports the physical distribution operation. A clear understanding and measurement of this may help explain some of the audit results. Thus, information flows, hard copy versus paperless operations, software and associated systems, EPOS and other external systems may all need to be included within the audit structure.

Finally, the depot performance will be very dependent on the impact of service levels. The importance of these may vary from company to company, but they may include:

- levels required (and achieved!);
- lead time;
- stock availability;
- minimum drop/order size policy;
- order and delivery frequency;
- quality checks;
- full loads delivered on time.

The general approach to the distribution audit is outlined in Figure 29.1. It follows a logical sequence of data collection, collation, analysis and interpretation.

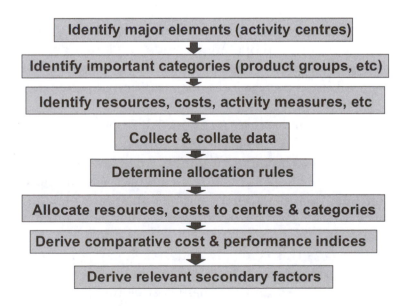

Figure 29.1 General approach

The steps are:

1. *Identify major elements.* These are the major activity centres that best represent the flow of product through a depot (see Figure 29.2).

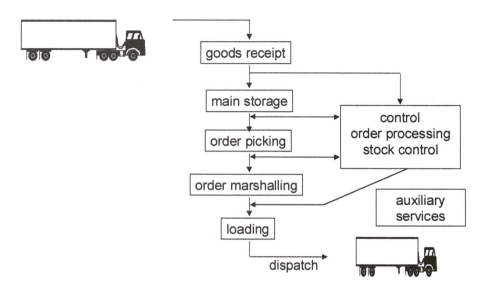

Figure 29.2   Typical activity centres

2. *Identify important categorizations.* These should consist of any major categories that are fundamental to the operations under review. Careful selection will enable some useful comparisons to be made of key elements within the business. For grocery distribution this typically means different product categorizations – chilled, ambient, fresh, etc.
3. *Identify resources, costs and activity measures.* All resources and their associated costs need to be included. A classic breakdown covers buildings, building services, equipment and labour. In addition, some key activity measures need to be made. These are likely to include throughput (in an appropriate unit of measurement, say receipts in outers, storage in pallets, picking in items, etc), the number of orders, the number of picking lists, the number of lines per picking list, etc.
4. *Collect and collate data.* This is ideally undertaken using a spreadsheet format. Such a format is outlined in Table 29.2. This shows the main activities across the top of the spreadsheet and the main cost elements along the side of the spreadsheet.

Table 29.2 Allocation matrix with costs (all product groups)

Averaged 'Weekly' Cost £	Unloading	Mainstore	Order Picking	Marshalling	Loading	Control	Aux. Services	Totals
Direct Labour	516	722	1,821	486	24	168	–	3,737
Supervision	247	180	180	180	43	138	–	968
Buildings	60	1,102	431	74	17	8	25	1,717
Bdg. Services	70	1,406	555	102	22	10	32	2,197
Equipment	475	1,558	346	76	10	–	46	2,511
Total	1,368	4,968	3,333	918	116	324	103	11,130
General Administration – Direct								1,906
– Supplementary								1,533

5. *Determine allocation rules.* This is an important aspect of the process. A typical example might be how to allocate main storage costs across a number of different product groups where products are randomly located. Most rules will follow a logical, common-sense approach – in this example, allocate main storage on the basis of the number of pallets stored per different product group.

6. *Allocate resources and their costs to centres and categories.* Use the allocation rules. Ensure that all the inputs (resources, costs, throughputs, etc) are double-checked for accuracy. An example of how this might look is also given in the allocation matrix in Table 29.2.

7. *Derive comparative cost and performance indices.* Many of these will be common to most depot operations (cases picked per hour, etc); others may be particular to one type of operation (units returned and reprocessed in a mail order depot, etc).

8. *Derive relevant secondary factors.* These are the elements of the logistics 'environment' that might help to explain the main results.

The key points to the approach can be summarized as:

● A formalized approach such as this should be used to ensure that all the appropriate costs are included in the analysis.
● There is a need for relevant support information. This concerns the 'logistics environment', and the information is essential to help explain the results.

- It is important to select the appropriate functional elements. These are the activity centres, and they should represent relevant elements of the distribution operation.
- Valid activity measures should be used to ensure that the costs are allocated correctly.
- The matrix structure provides a very suitable format for data analysis.
- 'Top down' costs should be collected as well as 'bottom up' costs. This allows for consistency checks to be made using costs derived from a different source.

Data collection and analysis

The collection of accurate and useful data is by far the most problematic aspect of a distribution audit. It is also, of course, essential to a successful auditing or benchmarking exercise.

Some of the major problems and potential pitfalls are:

- *Data availability.* It will always be necessary to compromise. The data required will never be available in its entirety. This is especially so where several companies are involved.
- *Sampling.* It is likely that some sampling will be required. Care must be taken to ensure that sample sizes are sufficient and that samples are adequately representative.
- *Data consistency.* Again, especially where cross-company analysis is to be undertaken, care must be taken that allocation rules and procedures are common. Most companies have different accounting practices, so there is ample opportunity for error due to inconsistent classification. It is likely that a uniform or generalized allocation procedure will need to be designed and used.
- *Appropriate categories and groups.* Any categorization, such as for different product groups, needs to be relevant for all participating companies.
- *Time periods.* Clearly, these need to be common for all depots. Any sales cycles, seasonality, etc need to be taken into account. Data availability is likely to be a prime driver. Beware of the problem of calendar months compared to four-week months.
- *Units of measure.* These may differ from one company to another, and will be especially important when comparing across industry sectors.

Interpreting results

The grocery distribution audits produced a series of results that could be interpreted in a general context, as well as some that were specific to a particular depot as it was compared to the others in the study. In general terms, there were two key drivers identified as being crucial to the understanding of depot efficiency in the context of grocery distribution. These are consistent with earlier studies.

Firstly, the results indicated that building costs could vary considerably from one depot to another. The extent of this variation, and the impact of these costs, meant that some depots that appeared to be operationally expensive were not in fact so, because the major cost element was a very high building cost. Thus, it was clear that building costs needed to be treated carefully when assessing operating efficiencies. It was possible, however, to identify economies of scale to the benefit of the larger depots. Also, a clear lesson to be learnt was the need to maximize space utilization within a depot. In particular, this applied to the full use of height in a building.

Secondly, the highest-cost operational area in all the depots was that of order picking. Clearly good picking performance was one of the keys to a cost-effective depot operation. There were obvious benefits to accrue through reviewing layout and reducing walking time, and through reviewing the information processing time spent by order pickers.

It is possible to produce a myriad of detailed results from a study of this nature. These can be represented in chart or histogram format. For comparative purposes the development of 'league tables' is also relevant. Some useful results from this study showed:

- the overall warehouse unit cost analysis broken down by main costs;
- the relative weekly throughputs for the different depots – these can help to explain some of the differences in cost and performance results;
- the breakdown of direct labour costs for the different depots;
- the range of picking performance for the different depots in cases picked per person-hour. Different handling and information systems as well as lines per order and picks per line will influence these results.

A number of general issues are relevant to the interpretation of results from such a study. These can be summarized as:

- It is useful to draw up a number of 'league tables' to compare individual depot positions.
- Even in a single industry study, major differences can be apparent. It is necessary to take special care in a cross-sector study when comparing operations that are very dissimilar.
- It can help to group common operations and concentrate comparisons on these.

● It is possible to identify key drivers from this type of study.
● It can be useful to compare the cost and performance implications for different product groups, etc.
● High-cost and low-performance areas can be readily identified, allowing significant improvements to be made.
● It is very important to identify and select suitable measures that help to explain any major differences in the results (the logistics environment). Typical variables that might influence operations are
  – volume forecast accuracy
  – throughput variability (by day)
  – product profile
  – store profile
  – store returns
  – special projects (promotions, alternative unitization)
  – equipment specification
  – RDC design (building shape, mezzanines)
  – employee bonus schemes
  – methods (secondary sorts, etc)
  – local labour market (quality, need for training, etc)
  – regional cost variations
  – staff agreements (guaranteed hours, etc)
  – unit definitions.

It can be useful to differentiate between controllable and non-controllable elements and costs. An expensive building may lead to a relatively high cost operation overall. The actual operation itself (that is without a consideration of the cost of the building) may be very cost-effective. There is little a manager can do to affect the cost of a building.

Regional differences may impact on results. Scale effects may be relevant – that is, economies that result from large-scale operations.

Other logistics audit types

The example described above demonstrates in some detail an audit for a distribution depot. Similar approaches can be used for transport and other logistics operations. In addition, quality audits can be undertaken. Example elements for a transport audit are as follows:

- groups
  - by vehicle type
  - by vehicle make
  - by depot/site
  - by job type;
- costs
  - cost per vehicle type
  - cost per kilometre
  - cost per kilogram/case/etc;
- utilization
  - weight
  - time;
- service
  - next day delivery;
- others
  - maintenance costs
  - cost of hired vehicles and drivers.

An example of a quality audit for a wines and spirits manufacturer using a contractor is summarized in Figure 29.3.

- general warehouse condition
  - cleanliness: depot and stock
  - condition and storage of stock

- check on aged stock

- check on stock
  - labelling/pallet build/bar-coding accuracy/lot marking

- review security on site

- random stock checks

- review depot equipment

- review systems
  - procedures/pallet tracking/date coding

- transport
  - cleanliness of vehicles
  - delivery personnel
  - general condition of the order

Figure 29.3   Quality audit for a wines and spirits manufacturer using a contractor

SUMMARY

This chapter has covered benchmarking. Two working definitions of benchmarking were reproduced. The usual reasons why benchmarking is undertaken were discussed. This comparative process forces organizations to look outside at competitors' performance or the performance of companies in other industries. The idea is to aid the process of continuous improvement and increase competitiveness.

A framework for conducting a benchmarking exercise was described in some detail and formal benchmarking systems were briefly covered.

Finally, a section on benchmarking distribution activities was included. The detailed description covered:

- the main principles behind these studies;
- a typical format and approach;
- data collection and analysis;
- how to interpret the results;
- other types of logistics audit.

30

IT in the supply chain

INTRODUCTION

There can be no doubt that the availability of cheap computing power has led to dramatic developments in the science of logistics management. The ability to handle vast amounts of data quickly and accurately has in the last 30 years literally transformed the way business is conducted. It has been described, with good cause, as the second Industrial Revolution. The ability to pass information between supply chain partners via electronic data interchange is being exploited by more and more companies daily. The advent of mass access to the Internet has sparked off a boom in home-/office-based shopping to say nothing of the use of e-mail as a means of communicating with friends and business colleagues around the globe.

Information systems and associated hardware used in supply chain management fulfil different roles. They may aid the decision-making process, help to monitor and control operations, create simulated systems, store and process data, and aid communication between individuals, companies and machines.

A great deal has already been written about this vast area, therefore it is not the purpose here to go into any great detail. What is intended is to highlight the most common features with respect to distribution and logistics, and to explain briefly what they are and how they work.

BASIC COMMUNICATION

Electronic data interchange (EDI)

EDI has been defined as: *computer-to-computer exchange of structured data for automatic processing*. EDI is used by supply chain partners to exchange essential information necessary for the effective running of their businesses. These structural links are usually set up between organizations that have a long-term trading relationship. For example, some multiple retailers will supply electronic point of sale (EPOS) data directly to suppliers, which in turn triggers replenishment of the item sold. As a consequence of this type of strong link, suppliers will be able to build a historical sales pattern that will aid their own demand forecasting activities. In this context, EDI has many benefits. It is providing timely information about its customers' sales, it is highly accurate and it is very efficient because it does not require staff to collate the information manually. EDI is used to send invoices, bills of lading, confirmation of dispatch, shipping details and any information that the linked organizations choose to exchange.

UN/EDIFACT is the standard that ensures that information may be sent and retrieved in an appropriate format by trading partners. The initials stand for: United Nations/Electronic Data Interchange for Administration, Commerce and Transport.

The main advantages of using EDI are:

- information only needs to be entered on to the computer system once;
- speed of transactions;
- reduced cost and error rates.

Bar codes

A bar code is the representation of a number or code in a form suitable for reading by machines. Bar codes are widely used throughout the supply chain to identify and track goods at all stages in the process. Bar codes are a series of different width lines that may be presented in a horizontal order, called ladder orientation, or a vertical order, called picket fence orientation.

For example, goods received in a warehouse may be identified by the warehouse management system and added to stock held in the warehouse. When put away, the bar code is used to associate the storage location with the bar-coded stock, and on dispatch the stock record is amended. The use of bar codes can speed up operations significantly. Problems can occur if bar codes are defaced or the labels fall off in transit.

Order processing

Customer order processing is often not the direct responsibility of a logistics department. However, the consequences of order processing in terms of the allocation of stock and the construction of picking lists are very important.

The main developments have occurred in two specific areas. The first of these is the information now provided by order takers. This includes the visibility of stock availability, which allows the order taker to identify immediately whether or not stock can be supplied 'off the shelf' to the customer. Also, the order taker is often required to provide the customer with an agreed delivery date at the time the order is taken. This means that delivery schedules must be clear and reliable. These developments help to allow a much better service to be offered to customers, but also, of course, pose a new discipline on logistics operations.

Secondly, there has been an increase in the ability to place orders automatically and directly through EDI. This has been extended in some instances to allow customers to have automatic access to their order status, so as well as placing orders remotely via EDI they can then track their progress through the supply chain.

SUPPLY CHAIN PLANNING

Enterprise-wide information systems

An important development for many major companies has been the introduction of enterprise-wide information systems, often known as ERP or enterprise resource planning systems. These are transaction-based information systems that are integrated across the whole business. Basically, they allow for data capture for the whole business into a single computer package, which then gives a single source for all the key business information activities, such as customer orders, inventory and financials.

Proprietary names such as SAP, Baan, J D Edwards and Peoplesoft feature strongly whenever these systems are discussed and many companies are using them to their advantage. It must be remembered that installation of such systems will entail widespread change within the organization and must not be entered into lightly. It will have implications in terms of organizational structure as well as of the way in which individuals work. It is not a question of simply computerizing an existing paper-based system (with all its current flaws) but rather a matter of installing a completely new system. This must take place while the rest of the organization tries to keep the business running. It must be thoroughly planned and executed, which will require significant extra resources to achieve a successful outcome.

Many companies have benefited from using these systems whilst some have experienced severe problems with their application. Generally, they are very expensive to purchase, require a lot of tailoring for each user company, take a lot of expensive consultancy time to implement and a high degree of training for use at the operative level. It is a logical extension of the principles of supply chain management to have one overarching computerized system that allows for the organization and support of the planning of the whole enterprise. Currently ERP systems do not do this. They need to be linked to appropriate supply chain management and network strategy software so that the relevant planning can be undertaken.

In the future these linked systems are likely to be commonplace. For today, apart from implementation problems, it is necessary to be aware that IT is developing at such a speed that provision must be made for systems to be easily updated. Ideally, they should be 'open' systems, which are linked to suppliers and customers alike to ease the flow of information up and down the supply chain. Significant provision must be made for disaster recovery in the event of system failure because effectively all of a company's eggs are placed in the one basket.

Supply chain management

Supply chain management systems are, very broadly, decision support and operational planning tools. They enable a company to plan and manage its logistics operations through the use of an integrated system-wide package. Such tools will use information such as real-time demand and/or forecasting, linked to production capacities and run rates, inventory holding levels and locations, supplier lead times, associated costs, etc to help determine operational production and inventory requirements.

To be effective these systems rely on the accuracy and real-time nature of the data that is fed into the system. They are often transaction-based, similar to ERP systems. They also rely on the appropriate algorithms embedded in the system to arrive at useful solutions. Typical packages include Manugistics, i2 and Numetrics. Such supply chain management software is now being associated much more directly with some of the major ERP system providers.

Network strategy

Network strategy systems consist of a variety of different strategic rather than operational decision-making tools. Typical of this type of package is the depot location package, which attempts to optimize the number and location of depots within a company's distribution network.

These systems allow for the analysis of data using various algorithms to arrive at an optimum solution for a given situation. For example, the problem may be to establish the optimum location to make a product within a network of production sites, which themselves are spread across a wide geographical area. The system will enable the analysis of the costs of sourcing raw materials, the costs and availability of production capacity, and transport costs, to arrive at the optimum location.

Amongst the main packages are CAPS Logistics and Cast DPM. A more detailed discussion of the use of network strategy modelling is given in Chapter 8.

WAREHOUSING

Warehouse management systems

This type of computer system controls all the traditional activities of warehouse operations. Areas covered usually include:

- receipt of goods;
- allocation or recording of storage locations;
- replenishment of picking locations;
- production of picking instructions or lists;
- order picking;
- order assembly;
- stock rotation.

Some systems are used in conjunction with radio frequency (RF) communications equipment. This equipment can be mounted on fork-lift trucks. The warehouse management system communicates via the RF system and directs the activities of the warehouse staff. For example, when picking it will provide the tasks for the operative to carry out. Once the task is complete the operative updates the system and is directed to the next task. This has the advantage of updating the stock-holding in real time.

There are also highly sophisticated systems that control the operations of fully automated warehouses. This may include automated storage and retrieval systems (AS/RS), automated guided vehicles (AGVs), and the many other devices that are relatively common in today's modern warehouse: conveyors, carousels, sortation systems, etc.

A number of computer models have now been developed to assist in the planning of warehouse design and configuration. These are generally very sophisticated 3D simulation models that provide a graphic, moving illustration on the computer screen of the layout of the warehouse. They enable different design configurations to be simulated, depending on varying demand requirements, etc.

INVENTORY

Forecasting and inventory management systems

The area of forecasting future customer demand and associated inventory carrying requirements has been revolutionized by the use of customized computer packages. These packages contain many different algorithms that allow the forecaster to use various techniques, such as regression analysis, exponential smoothing and moving averages. These systems may be fed with information directly from sales order processing and inventory management systems to allow them to assess very quickly how customer demand is developing by individual stock keeping unit.

Inventory management systems provide the ability to run the day-to-day detailed management and control of stock within a company. They are absolutely essential for the location of stock and in their ability, if used effectively, to control the levels of stock within a system. This type of expertise allows organizations to reduce their inventory carrying requirements, which improves stock turn and return on capital invested. Customer service is also maintained through the use of these systems by reducing the incidence of stock-outs.

TRANSPORT

Vehicle fleet management

These types of system assist transport managers in the task of monitoring the effectiveness of their vehicle fleet. Information regarding vehicle activities will be collected, such as:

- mileage travelled;
- vehicle details – age, gross vehicle weight, type of body, axle configuration, engine capacity, etc;
- tonnes carried;
- idle time;
- maintenance details;
- fuel used;

- driver details;
- tachograph details and analysis;
- details of deliveries made.

This information may be manipulated to produce key performance indicators for the vehicle fleet. These are likely to include:

- miles per gallon;
- vehicle utilization in terms of time in use and vehicle fill;
- tonnes per mile;
- average drop size;
- average drop miles;
- costs per mile;
- tyre costs;
- maintenance costs;
- fuel costs;
- costs per tonne;
- whole life costs of the vehicles.

Very often computerized fuel monitoring equipment controls and records fuel dispensed to each vehicle. This information may be transferred automatically into the fleet management system. In a similar way tachograph records can be analysed and the information downloaded into the main system.

Many modern heavy vehicles are equipped with engines that are controlled by computerized engine management. This information can provide a great deal of detailed information about the vehicles' activity. Also, re-programming can enable some of these engine management systems to change the horsepower rating of the engine itself.

It is the intention of the European Union to introduce an electronic tachograph that will be fitted with a smart card rather than the existing system of recording drivers' activities on a wax-covered disk. One of the advantages of this development is that it will allow the smart card information to be easily downloaded into the fleet management system.

Computerized routeing and scheduling

This is covered in detail in Chapter 27.

OTHER APPLICATIONS

Electronic point of sale (EPOS)

Now a common sight in most large retail sites in the developed world this facility has revolutionized the process of paying for goods purchased. Equipment includes scanning equipment, electronic scales and credit card readers. Goods marked with a bar code are scanned by a reader, which in turn recognizes the goods. It notes the item, tallies the price and records the transaction. In some cases this system also triggers replenishment of the sold item.

One of the major advantages of an EPOS system is that it provides an instant record of transactions at the point of sale. Thus, replenishment of products can be co-ordinated in real time to ensure that stock-outs in the retail store are avoided.

Another advantage of this system is that it has speeded up the process of dealing with customers when large numbers of items are purchased. It reduces errors by being pre-programmed with the selling price and avoids staff having to add up purchase prices mentally.

Many retailers offer loyalty card systems, which offer customers small discounts for continuing to shop with a given retailer. The advantage to the retailer is that loyalty cards with customers' personal details are linked to their actual purchases, which allows the retailer to obtain vital marketing information about these customers.

Manufacturing planning and control systems

These have been dealt with in Chapter 11. It is worth pointing out that systems such as materials requirement planning (MRP) and manufacturing resource planning (MRPII) would not be possible without access to cheap computing power.

Many production plants use computers extensively to control and monitor operations.

General applications packages

It is easy to forget that it was not many years ago that desktop computers were not as common as they are today. This development has provided the business world with applications at their fingertips that have allowed them to be far more self-sufficient and flexible. For example, spreadsheets have allowed managers to manipulate information in a way that suits their individual needs. Word processing packages allow staff to produce letters and documents very quickly and to a high standard. Internal and external electronic mail has facilitated rapid communications between organizations and individuals across the globe. Most if not all these applications are virtually standard specifications for desktop computers.

These standard tools, along with faxes and electronic calculators, contribute to creating fast, effective and flexible logistics operations.

The Internet and 'e-commerce'

As more and more individuals and organizations become connected to the Internet the possibilities for creating business opportunities seem almost endless. By the same token this phenomenon has created even greater challenges for the supply chains that support this type of commerce. Some of the implications of trading via the Internet are outlined in Chapter 34.

A particular example to illustrate the extent of the implications for logistics is the opportunities for shopping from home. Home shopping is creating a need for deliveries of small quantities of goods to domestic premises. These goods may have different product characteristics, such as frozen and ambient goods. The consignee may very well be a busy individual who is only at home after 7 o'clock in the evening or in the early morning. Customers are likely to return unwanted goods with a much higher frequency than is normally expected when goods are delivered. All of these problems are not new, as the catalogue and domestic furniture delivery services know. What is different is the scale and scope of home shopping that is being facilitated by use of the Internet. Specialist vehicles and drivers with good interpersonal skills will also be required.

The recipe of small delivery quantities, limited time windows, specialist small vehicles, poor vehicle utilization and returns adds up to an expensive mix. Distribution systems are currently being developed to cope with this new phenomenon.

SUMMARY

This chapter has outlined the main areas where information technology has an impact on logistics. Brief descriptions were provided, as follows:

- Some of the basic elements of communications were considered first, including electronic data interchange (EDI), bar codes and order processing.
- Key developments in supply chain planning were considered to be those involving enterprise-wide information systems, supply chain management and network strategy.
- Looking more closely at the basic logistics components, the IT-related aspects of warehousing, inventory and transport were reviewed.
- Finally, some other important aspects were considered, including electronic point of sale (EPOS) systems, general applications packages and the use of the Internet and e-commerce.

Part 7

Associated factors

31

Outsourcing: the selection process

INTRODUCTION

One of the most fundamental developments in distribution and logistics has been the growth in the use of third-party service providers, or the outsourcing of logistics operations. Some of the main features of this development were introduced and discussed in Chapter 4. An important consideration concerns the need for the careful selection and management of service providers. This chapter puts forward an approach for the selection of service providers and explains the detailed steps that are required.

APPROACH

An approach to the contractor selection process is outlined below, and described in detail in the rest of this chapter. It is a step-by-step guide to the different stages that must be followed to ensure that all of the important elements are considered. It is typical of the approach that would be used by any major company contemplating the use of a third-party service provider to undertake all or part of its logistics operation. It is important to adopt a clearly defined process that is well planned, has clear objectives and is adequately resourced, so that the many key stages can be successfully carried out.

As well as the main identification and selection of a contractor, also included are the important topics of contract development and contractor management.

The approach to the selection process will be considered under the following headings:

- Identify type of service required.
- Broad strategic review of likely distribution structure.
- Identify potential service providers.
- Request for information process (RFI)and then short list.
- Preparation of invitation to tender (ITT) or request for proposal (RFP) or request for quotation (RFQ).
- Tender evaluation and comparison.
- Contractor or partner selection.
- The contract.
- Implementation plan.
- Contractor management.

Identify type of service required

Having made the decision that all or part of the business is to be outsourced, the next step is to determine which of the many services offered by third-party providers are likely to be required. The main types of service were described in detail in the second part of Chapter 4. A major question is whether the user company should choose a dedicated operation or join a multi-user operation where resources will be shared with other user companies. For some companies this may not be a clear-cut decision and they may decide to ask the short-listed service providers to quote on the basis of both of these different types of operation. The most important factor is that the providers are clear on what basis they should be quoting for the work, so that they don't base all of their effort and analysis on determining a solution that is inappropriate to the user.

Broad strategic review of likely distribution structure

At a very early stage in the selection process it is sensible for a company to undertake a broad strategic review of the likely distribution structure that it will be looking for. Many companies might complete this as a matter of course when taking their initial decision over whether they should continue as own account or go the third-party route. It might be argued that this is an unnecessary step because the service providers will be expected to devise their own recommended structure. Although this will be the case, it is still a good idea for the user company to go through this review for the following reasons:

- *To provide a clearer idea of what the main requirements are.* It is far easier to assess the different quotations made by the third-party companies if the user already has a good understanding of what the operation should look like.
- *To help in the eventual preparation of the invitation to tender.* In requesting the third party to quote, it will be necessary to provide a great deal of data and information on which it can make its analysis. It is useful to use this data to undertake a strategic review to identify likely solutions.
- *To clarify key activities.* Certain activities will be outsourced, whilst others will be kept in-house. A strategic review will help to identify those elements of the business that should be considered by the third party. It will also help to clarify exactly where the line is to be drawn between outsourcing and own account. Clarification of these areas of interface is crucial at an early stage.
- *To enable a 'long list' of potential contractors to be drawn up.* The information from a strategic review will help to identify which contract companies are the most appropriate for consideration in the selection process. This will help to ensure that time is not wasted holding preliminary discussions with companies that are unlikely to be able to offer appropriate services.

Identify potential service providers

As already indicated, a 'long list' of potential contractors should be drawn up. The aim behind this is to identify a large list of service providers that are capable of undertaking the business, and then to draw up a short list of those that are the most interested and the most likely to provide a cost-effective and service-proficient solution. There is no point in contacting companies that specialize in small parcels delivery if it is a full trailer load service that is required. It is neither feasible nor sensible to have a large number of potential contractors provide a full tender because the entire process is a very time-consuming one for both the contractor and the user company. Information on contractors can be obtained very readily from the trade press, where there are many articles to be found that review the service providers and comment on the latest contracts. A typical list might have 20 to 30 contract companies.

Request for information process (RFI) and then short list

Each potential contractor that appears on the long list should be contacted with a brief description of the likely requirements. This is to ascertain whether the contractor would be interested in tendering for the business and to identify whether or not it would be appropriate to include the company on the short list of contractors. This description is often known as the request for information (RFI). The RFI should be a concise document consisting of key information, as follows:

1. introduction and confidentiality clause;
2. description of the company – operation and product overview;
3. description of opportunity
   - overview of strategy and likely requirements
   - contractual relationship;
4. the selection process
   - procurement process
   - key selection criteria;
5. content of response;
6. format of response.

Responses to the RFI and other factors should be evaluated against key selection criteria to enable the short list to be drawn up. Selection of the key potential providers might be on the basis of:

- written response to RFI;
- assessment of supporting documents;
- current client list;
- contact with current clients;
- assessment of broad capability;
- financial probity of the company.

Preparation of invitation to tender (ITT) or request for proposal (RFP) or request for quotation (RFQ)

The major part of the contractor selection process revolves around the provision of detailed data and information to the short-listed companies, which they then use to develop a plan and cost the proposed operation. These responses are then compared by the user company to enable them to identify a limited number of companies with which to complete the final negotiations. This process is based on a very important document, known as the invitation to tender (ITT), the request for proposal (RFP) or the request for quotation (RFQ). There are two main objectives for the ITT: 1) to provide a specification of business requirements to selected vendors in a standard format to facilitate objective comparison of proposals; and 2) to maintain equitable flow of information across all tenderers and establish total confidentiality rules.

More specific uses from the point of view of the contractor are to:

- design a distribution system to perform the task and meet the service requirements;
- determine the resources required (personnel, property, vehicles, plant and equipment);
- estimate the costs and hence decide on the structure and level of the rates to be charged;
- be clear which distribution components are to be provided by the contractor and which by the user company;
- be clear which information systems need to be provided and specify them in detail.

A great deal of detailed data and information must be included in the ITT. A typical ITT structure might be as follows, but the precise content will vary according to the company, operation and contract requirements:

1. introduction including confidentiality clause;
2. background to operating company;
3. business description;
4. data provided with the invitation to tender;
5. physical distribution specifications;
6. information systems;
7. distribution service levels and performance monitoring;
8. assets currently employed in distribution operations;
9. risk assessment and transfer;
10. industrial relations;
11. business relationship – contract type and contract management relationship;
12. charging structure;
13. terms and conditions;
14. environmental issues;
15. the selection process including key selection criteria;
16. response format.

The data to be provided with the ITT should be at a sufficient level of detail to allow the contractor to undertake adequate analysis to calculate the resources required to run the operation and to identify all the associated costs. As might be imagined, this is a lot of data! Again this will vary depending on the services required, but typical distribution data is likely to include those elements outlined in Figure 31.1.

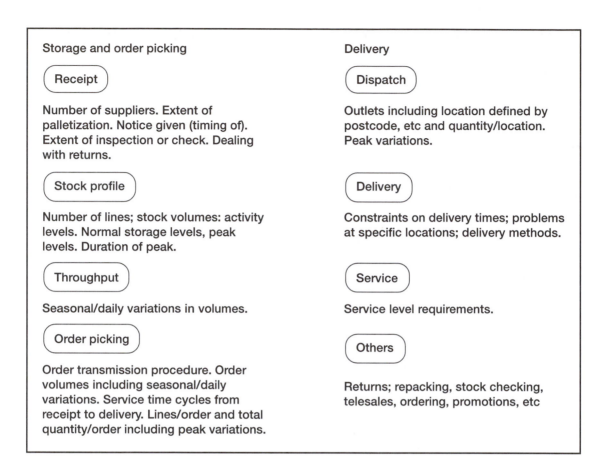

Figure 31.1 Typical distribution data

There are several different types of pricing or charging structure that might be adopted. The choice of these is the prerogative of the client, but in some instances low volumes of business that have to fit into a multi-user operation may offer less scope for some of these to be used. They can be broadly categorized as follows:

- *Unit price or fixed price agreements.* An agreed unit price is paid for the services provided. This might be cost per case, cost per mile, cost per drop, etc, or a combination of these costs, depending on the services being offered. This is the traditional method of third-party payment and is common for low-volume business.
- *Hybrid unit price agreements.* These are based on a unit price but also include guarantees for specified volume throughput, resource usage, etc. This ensures

that the contractor is not penalized by seasonal effects or unexpected demand fluctuations when the contractor may have resources that are underutilized. This approach allows for reducing unit price steps as throughput increases.

- *Cost-plus arrangements.* These provide for the payment of an agreed fee for the facilities used and the services provided. A pre-set profit margin for the contractor is added to this. One major criticism of cost-plus is that it offers no incentive for the contractor to improve the operation. Indeed, any trimming of costs would lead to a reduction in payments to the contractor.
- *Open book contracts.* As it suggests, an open book contract is where the client company pays for the entire operation plus a management fee to the contractor. This type of arrangement can only be used for completely dedicated operations. Performance is monitored against a budget that is agreed between the contractor and the client. The danger with this type of arrangement is that it may compound any inefficiencies that are built into the original agreement. It is now common to include cost reduction or performance-related incentive clauses to provide a shared benefit where the contractor identifies improvements.

Response pro formas should be included in the ITT to ensure that contractors respond in such a way that comparisons can easily be made. These can then be evaluated against set goals, business metrics, costs and any other particular selection criteria. It is extremely difficult to make meaningful comparisons between tenders if all the responses are constructed to a different format. As well as a clearly defined format for the numerical response, many companies ask the service provider to identify specific elements on which they expect detailed information to be provided. These might include:

- the resources and facilities to be used;
- contract management and supervision;
- information systems – data processing and communications;
- security, insurance, stocktaking procedure, etc;
- structure and level of charges and procedure for price increases;
- penalties (if any) for premature termination of contract;
- invoicing and payment;
- draft outline contract, conditions of carriage or conditions of storage;
- project management/transfer/implementation.

Tender evaluation and comparison

Tender evaluation is usually undertaken with a view to identifying key data and information from the tenders submitted and then drawing comparisons between the different submissions, hence the importance of using a response format that is straightforward for the contractor to use. Comparisons are going to be quantitative – mainly assessing the relative costs of the different solutions, and qualitative – a consideration of all the non-quantifiable aspects that may be relevant. For a typical warehouse and delivery transport proposal, the main cost elements are the same as the standard ones, and they have been discussed in previous chapters. They would include the costs of storage, delivery transport, information systems, administration, overheads and management fee – depending on the extent of the logistics operation to be outsourced. Costs may be expressed as totals for the operation as a whole or as unit cost per pallet stored, case delivered, etc. Some key considerations are:

- Compare quotations on a standard basis.
- Be clear what has and what has not been included (eg 'other' work, collections, etc).
- It is likely that the quotation includes some qualifications (perhaps because of the interpretation of the specification). These need to be clarified or eliminated.
- Beware of imponderables such as 'likely future rent reviews'.
- Check that service levels are clearly going to be met.
- The lowest price may not be the best.

Non-quantifiable factors that might be considered could consist of a large number of different aspects. The ones to use are those that are seen to be important to the user company. For one company these might be environmental or people-related. For another they might be more concerned with ease of management and control. Such factors could include:

- the quality of the proposal;
- the extent to which the proposal meets the ITT requirements;
- views on the extent to which it is felt that the proposed physical system can perform the required tasks;
- views on the extent to which it is felt that the proposed resources are appropriate to the task and the system;
- whether levels of utilization, productivity and cost are realistic;
- how appropriate the cost is to the recommended design;
- the overall design of the information systems;
- strategies for future enhancement of the operation;
- environmental policy;
- the culture of the company – whether it fits with that of the user company;

- the quality of the contract management team;
- staff training.

A useful approach is to adopt a structured assessment of the contractors' tender submissions. Each major factor can be listed and given an appropriate weighting that reflects its importance to the company. The tenders are then scored against all the different factors. An overall total for each tender will then provide a comparative measure to help differentiate between the various tender submissions. These structured assessments can be categorized between, say, operational, financial and contractor-related factors. An example of how a part of one of these might look is shown in Table 31.1.

Table 31.1 Example of approach to structured assessment

Contractor-related factors	Weighting (%)	Score (1 to 5)	Total (%)	Comments
1. Financial standing				
2. Experience/client base				
3. Management structure and resources				
4. Understanding of requirements				
5. Flexibility and innovation				
6. Initial presentation				
7. Implementation plan				
8. Long-term strategic support				
9. References (existing clients)				
10. Site visits				

Contractor or partner selection

The use of a structured approach for the assessment of the different tenders makes the final selection process a distinctly simpler task because the main points for comparison are much clearer. The most favoured contenders can then be investigated further through visits to reference sites and through preliminary negotiations. For large dedicated contracts it is likely that two or three preferred service providers will be identified. These can then be taken forward for much more rigorous negotiation to ensure that the detailed elements of the proposal are satisfactory and to identify further opportunities for enhancing the contract arrangements. The entire process can now enter the final stages.

For this final negotiation it is important to be aware of the different phases that a dedicated contract relationship might take. These are often termed the 'development cycle'. The development cycle reflects the evolutionary process of many dedicated contract arrangements. There are three different stages:

1. *Initial set-up.* The contractor takes over an existing operation with all its inherent problems and physical assets. The major aim is to keep the operation running efficiently during the change-over period.
2. *Medium term.* Here, the two parties enter into a more clearly defined agreement over three to five years. The operation remains a dedicated one.
3. *Longer term.* In the longer term, the contractor may wish to take on additional third-party work in association with the existing operation. This will occur as market opportunities arise and as scope for cost reduction by better asset utilization becomes apparent. It is essential that any benefits that arise are mutual to the contractor and the original user, and that the user is protected in terms of service and cost, as well as market competition. This stage of the cycle has become known as the development of shared-user opportunities. It is unlikely to arise with very large dedicated operations.

The complete development cycle may not occur for all dedicated contract arrangements, but it has occurred for some. It is important that the opportunity for potential future developments of this nature are borne in mind and are taken into account during the preparation of any initial contract.

Another important element in the change to a new contractor is the question of responsibility for existing staff. Legislation exists, particularly the Transfer of Undertakings: Protection of Employees (TUPE) legislation, whereby care must be taken to respect the employment rights of current staff. The TUPE UK regulations grew out of the Acquired Rights Directive, which is European legislation. The real implications of this legislation are at times unclear because periodically it has been reinterpreted. The main requirement is that if employees are transferred to a new contractor, the new contractor must honour the existing terms and conditions of employees – if it is a relevant transfer. The key question is – what is a relevant transfer? A relevant transfer is broadly one that is 'the same business in different hands'. Thus, whenever a new contractor takes on an operation, it must be clear where the responsibility lies for any redundancy payments that may have to be made.

Risk assessment may be undertaken with a view to identifying any elements that might be a major issue either at the time of the change-over to contract distribution (such as the loss or transfer of personnel, facilities, etc) or during the operation of the contract (such as delivery failure, etc). There are three main categories of risk in outsourcing that are often considered. These are service risks – relating to the provision of services; business risks – relating to the operating company's business requirements; and external risks – relating to external changes that might affect the contractor's business.

The final selection process needs to be undertaken by an experienced team that has all the relevant negotiating skills. Thus it should include representatives with legal, procurement, human resource and logistics operational skills. Negotiations are likely to be a fairly long and drawn-out process because they entail the review and agreement of all the detailed aspects of the operation and the associated business arrangements, as well as the development of the contract. The results of all the negotiations need to be documented and agreed by all parties.

The contract

The contract contains a large amount of detailed information and requirements. It will include a comprehensive specification of the services that are to be provided, the associated tariffs and the obligations of the parties concerned. Some of the detailed points from the key areas are considered under the four headings of initial contract, cost-related/tariff structure, service-related, and administrative and others.

Initial contract points include:

- take-on of warehouse sites
  - which are acceptable/unacceptable
  - procedures for take-over;
- take-on of vehicles and capital equipment
  - which vehicles and equipment are included
  - how they are valued, etc;
- take-on of personnel
  - which, if any, are transferred
  - the financial basis
  - terms of employment
  - pension rights
  - etc;
- redundancy agreement – that agreement will be negotiated as necessary by the client, the basis of this agreement, etc.

Cost-related/tariff structure points include:

- capital/investment costs (vehicles, warehouse equipment, hardware, etc) and return on investment;

- operational costs (rent, building services, staff, transport running costs, administration, insurance, etc) and cover for operational costs;
- management costs and expenses (proportion of contractor head office cost – diminishing short to medium term, and including project work and time related to contract);
- cover risk / make profit – should be taken into account by return on investment and operational cost cover and length of formal contract.

Service-related points include:

- service requirements
  - definition of service to be provided
  - indication of main areas, including delivery zones and service levels (eg once a week), delivery / collection times at stores, cut-off points for receipt of information at depots, special orders and how to deal with them, emergency orders and how to deal with them, etc;
- service-related aspects
  - preferred vehicle specification
  - vehicle livery
  - driver uniforms;
- service / performance measurement
  - measures, report format, etc
  - damages, late delivery, refusals, etc.

Administrative and other points include:

- information systems
  - formal means of communication
  - operating requirements (order processing systems procedures, stock control, store liaison, etc);
- administration / liaison
  - head office (planning)
  - regional (liaison)
  - specific feedback (PODs, stock control, etc);
- 'prospective' agreement
  - regular sight of client's business plans (with respect to the distribution operation)
  - one- to three-year horizons
  - store openings and closures, product mix, etc;

- 'retrospective'/inflation clause – to allow for regular (annual) readjustments where estimates are sufficiently different from actual to warrant financial adjustment (demand levels, product mix, etc);
- penalty/termination clause
  - in the event of premature termination by either party
  - to cover, for example, the risk of 'unusable' assets specially taken on for the operation.

The specification will necessarily be very detailed. Typical components that need to be considered are shown above, although within a contract they would be to a greater level of detail. These will vary considerably from one contract to another, depending on the breadth of the operational coverage and the type of contractual arrangement. It is common practice to include the tender response from the contractor, as this contains a description of the operational elements. The measures by which operational performance is to be assessed may also be included.

A service level agreement will be an important part of the contract. It will identify all the key performance measures related to the provision of customer service and will indicate the levels of service that have been agreed.

A cost and tariff structure will be indicated. This may take a variety of forms and will, of course, depend on the precise payment method that has been agreed. Those elements that need to be covered are indicated above. Important considerations will be the costs of any additional activities that are to be included as exceptional payments (eg product returns), costs that are beyond the control of the contractor (eg fuel price increases and inflation) and any productivity targets or opportunities.

The length of a contract can vary from six months to five years. Three- to five-year contracts have become the norm for dedicated operations because of the amount of capital required for investment in depot and transport facilities and equipment.

Implementation plan

As with any large business project it is essential to identify and agree a project plan to ensure that responsibilities are clear and that there is a feasible timetable for implementation. A typical implementation plan will need to identify the tasks for both the user and the contractor organization, including contingency planning. The aim is to effect a smooth transition from the old to the new contract. From the user perspective it is vital to ensure that there is clear visibility of the implementation process. A team that includes both user and contractor staff needs to be established, and this team needs to meet on a regular basis to monitor and discuss progress. Detailed project plan activity charts should be used.

Part of the implementation process is likely to include the preparation of new administrative, safety and service procedures, which will be incorporated in an operations manual.

Contractor management

The final part of the outsourcing process is to ensure that the contractor is adequately managed. This is a key consideration that is sadly neglected by some users. The signing of the contract should not be seen as the end of the outsourcing process. It is vital to continue to control and monitor the contractor to ensure that the overall business and operational objectives are achieved.

There are a number of different means of controlling and monitoring the contractor with respect to the usual twin goals of cost and service performance achievement or improvement. The main activities are likely to include:

- the contract;
- budgetary control;
- management information and metrics;
- review meetings;
- audits through open book;
- incentivization of the management fee.

Typically, a manager is nominated from within the user organization to be responsible for the management of the contract. The manager's objectives might be to ensure that cost and service targets are met and to develop opportunities and initiatives for continuous improvement. This will be achieved through the use of suitable metrics. The use of a nominated manager brings both focus and accountability to the outsourcing arrangement, as well as providing the contractor with a main point of communication. This manager is likely to meet with the contractor for regular reviews. As well as reviewing cost and service performance, these meetings should consider any operational difficulties that are at issue and look forward to future forecasts of changes in activity that might impact on the operation. As already indicated, the relationship that is developed should not just consider how well the contractor is complying with the contract arrangement, but should also look to identify opportunities for the continuous improvement of the operation through better service performance at lower costs. This is often associated with the use of incentives linked to the management fee.

There are many examples of good and bad contract arrangements, and it is clear that the safest way to ensure success is to follow a clearly defined process of contractor selection. This is the only way to make certain that all the important aspects have been covered. It is also important to include all the steps within such a process, right through to the requirement to monitor and manage the contractor. Many successful relationships reflect the need to treat outsourcing more as a partnership than as a strict contract-driven arrangement. The experience of one large user company shows this. Its first foray into outsourcing was on the basis of a cost-plus contract that provided for no input from its managers. This led to problems such as:

- lack of encouragement for the contractor to innovate or improve;
- lack of recognition of the need to manage the contractor;
- poor management structure – the managers were demotivated;
- loss of in-house distribution expertise.

In the renegotiation of a subsequently successful contract, the key areas for success were seen to be:

- an active role in implementation by the user company;
- communication with the contractor – a partnership approach was adopted;
- the fee was a partly incentivized management fee, *not* cost-plus;
- a detailed cost budget and monitoring system were included;
- management responsibilities were clearly defined;
- relevant management information systems were developed and used.

SUMMARY

This chapter has described an approach to the contractor selection process. As discussed throughout the chapter, it is very important that a carefully structured process is carried out to ensure that all essential considerations are made. The main task is to put together a detailed invitation to tender, which can be used by the contract companies to prepare a suitable proposal for their running of the operation to be outsourced. Tender proposals are then carefully evaluated and compared so that a short list of suitable contractors can be drawn up. After the final selection is negotiated, a detailed contract should form the basis for a provider–user relationship that is closely managed by the user, but allows opportunities for continuous improvement.

32

Security and safety in distribution

INTRODUCTION

Unfortunately crimes against vehicles and property have become almost an everyday feature of life in distribution and logistics management. In the 12 months prior to September 1998, one in five operators in the UK suffered at least one incident of load or vehicle theft. Forty per cent of these thefts were from the operators' own depots and the value of the unrecovered losses was £130 million (FTA, 1998). These findings by the FTA bring this problem into sharp focus. What is not included in these figures are the costs associated with the disruption caused by these events. Management time, replacement vehicles, service failures and general upheaval are difficult to quantify but are all too real to the victims.

The aim of this chapter is to provide an outline of the measures that should be considered when planning security. The most common areas and equipment will be described but any specialist requirements will not be covered. Vehicle, depot and personnel security are the three main areas that will be examined. A section on safety in distribution centres has also been included.

VEHICLE SECURITY

Vehicles may be attacked because the thieves wish to steal the load, the vehicle itself or both. In recent years commercial vehicles have been targeted by thieves either to dismantle or to sell on intact. Sometimes vehicles are dismantled, loaded into containers and shipped abroad with extraordinary speed. In this type of situation speed of response is essential. On other occasions vehicles are simply driven away, sold in countries where checks on ownership are lax and never seen again. Therefore when specifying vehicles, one should consider security of the vehicle, the load carrying area and the driver.

The vehicle

The keys

Obviously if a thief has access to the vehicle's keys then the job is made very simple. Never leave keys in the ignition and ensure that keys are securely locked away in the office when vehicles are at base. Only issue keys to known drivers or those with clear authority. A common ploy is to pose as an agency driver in the early hours of the morning, request keys and drive away with valuable vehicles and loads.

Windows

Windows should be etched with the registration number of the vehicle. It is worth remembering that rubber surrounds to windows may simply be cut away allowing access. Small panel vans with glass in the rear doors should be replaced with vans with complete steel door panels. Existing windows may be protected by grilles or bars if necessary.

Where vehicles have a walk-through arrangement between the driving area and the load area, a bulkhead should be installed that hinders easy access to the load.

Immobilization

The aim of this type of security is to prevent the vehicle being driven away or at least to buy time. It does not prevent the vehicle being unloaded where it stands. There are many types of immobilizer to choose from but these are the more common varieties:

- *Steering locks.* These are fitted as standard by manufacturers but sadly they offer little protection from the professional thief. They will deter the opportunist or casual thief. They will also buy time and slow the criminals' progress.
- *Air brake immobilizers.* Many modern commercial vehicles use spring brakes as part of their braking system. These brakes require air to release the brakes. When

there is no air supply the brakes remain firmly applied by a powerful spring mechanism. An extra air valve is fitted to the air brake system, which ensures effective immobilization.

- *Starter motor immobilization.* The starter motor is rendered ineffective through a system that jumbles up the electrical wiring unless the right key is inserted.
- *Fuel valve immobilization.* This prevents fuel being pumped to the engine, although it does not prevent the thieves gaining access to the vehicle, releasing the handbrake and towing the vehicle away.
- *Wheel clamps.* These may be fitted to the wheels of small vehicles and trailers but are generally too cumbersome for larger wheeled vehicles.
- *Kingpin locks.* These are metal clamps that are locked to the kingpin of articulated semi-trailers. They prevent another tractor unit coupling to the trailer.

Vehicle alarms

As with immobilizers, there are several different types of alarms for different circumstances. An alarm system will either be manual or automatic. The manual system relies on the driver to activate it before leaving the vehicle, and the automatic system sets itself. The manual system's weakness lies in the fact that if the driver fails to activate it then it is of no use. The use of automatic systems overcomes this problem.

Depending on the level of security required alarm systems may require an independent power source, which is housed in a secure area of the vehicle. Commercial vehicles that have their batteries exposed would be vulnerable to the power supply being cut and the alarm deactivated. Even cars that have their batteries secure under the locked bonnet are not immune to someone cutting the power supply from beneath the car. A four-hour back-up requirement is specified by the British Standard BS6803.

This standard also specifies a minimum 115 dB (a) for audible warning alarms but often the output is higher. As with the power supply the audible alarm should be housed in a secure area of the vehicle to avoid the wires to the sounder being cut by a would-be thief.

The alarm wiring system may be of the single or twin circuit variety. Single circuit wiring may be suitable for cars but twin circuit wiring is required if the driver's compartment needs locking whilst the loading area is open. Most security specialists recommend that the wiring is closed circuit, which means that the alarm is activated if the circuit is broken by someone cutting the wires. Monitor loops are another way of protecting the wiring from attack. Open circuit wiring does not provide this type of protection.

Alarm contacts should be fitted to all points of access into the vehicle. Some urban delivery vehicles have been robbed whilst they are stuck in slow-moving traffic. If this is a possibility then consideration should be given to fitting a rear door ignition alarm. This alarm will sound if the rear doors are tampered with whilst the engine ignition system is still running, thus alerting the driver and hopefully warning off the criminals.

The internal spaces inside the vehicle may be protected in several ways listed below. However, it is important to note that commercial vehicle bodies that have glass fibre roofs are vulnerable to being cut open and may need protection through the addition of steel mesh. Similarly tautliner curtains are vulnerable to being cut by sharp knives. Neither the glass fibre roofs nor the curtains will be protected by internal space detectors.

Internal space detectors include:

- *Ultrasonic detectors.* These work by emitting and receiving high-frequency sound-waves. They are activated by air movement inside the space being monitored.
- *Inertia sensors.* These sensors work by monitoring vibration levels. Vibrations caused by someone attempting a break-in will trigger the alarm system.
- *Break glass detectors.* These clever devices recognize only the sound of breaking glass and work if a window is broken (but not if the rubber surround is cut out).
- *Dual tec sensors.* These work by using two different types of sensors that only trigger if they both detect something is amiss. These types of sensor obviously reduce false alarms.

When the driver is away from the vehicle the alarm system can be fitted with a pager that alerts the driver if the alarm system is activated. Alternatively a radio panic alarm allows the driver to activate the alarm system remotely if he feels the need to do so. If required, the driver's personal security may be enhanced through the fitting of a panic button that sounds an audible alarm when pushed.

The driver's behaviour whilst going about his daily duties can help avoid many opportunist-type crimes. The following is a list of dos and don'ts produced by the FTA:

- Lock your vehicle and its load space whenever it is left unattended – even when making a delivery.
- Do not leave windows open when away from the vehicle.
- Lock the doors while sleeping in the cab; back the vehicle up against a wall or other barrier to prevent access to the rear doors; remember the top of the vehicle will remain vulnerable.

- Remove the ignition keys and lock the door when you go to pay for fuel. Also remember to lock the fuel cap when you put it back on.
- If anti-theft devices are fitted to your vehicle – use them!
- Never leave the vehicle unattended in a secluded area or, at night, in an unlit area. Try to keep your vehicle in sight if you leave it unattended.
- Never leave vehicle keys hidden for collection by a relief driver.
- Don't leave trailers unattended in lay-bys. Where possible use pre-arranged secure parking areas for overnight stops. Particularly, avoid using insecure casual parking places as a routine practice.
- Don't chat about your load or your intended route in public or over the radio. Avoid asking unknown people for advice on local off-road parking facilities. Remember that the first breach of security occurs when the existence of the target becomes known to the thief.
- Do not carry unauthorized passengers in your vehicle.
- After a driving break or other stop where the vehicle is left unattended, look out for signs of tampering with doors, straps or sheets – someone may be back to finish the job later.
- Be vigilant and cautious when returning to the vehicle alone. Check for other suspicious vehicles nearby or persons in the immediate vicinity, particularly if seen taking undue interest in the vehicle. Note descriptions, registration number, etc. Get assistance from other drivers if seriously concerned or telephone the police for advice.
- In the event of a breakdown, consider the possibility of tampering or sabotage. Always take into consideration the security of the load if it is necessary to leave the vehicle.
- Treat unsolicited offers of assistance from unknown persons with caution and treat signals from other drivers that something is amiss with your vehicle with extreme caution.
- If you make the same journey frequently consider whether the route/schedule can be varied, if this is possible or permitted.
- Where high-value loads are carried, travel in convoy with other known and trusted drivers if possible. Beware of bogus officials or staff – ask for identification. Carry a 'vulnerable load' card for production if stopped by the police – if in doubt keep going to the nearest police station!
- On arrival at your delivery destination, do not allow yourself to be persuaded to leave your vehicle in charge of anyone else or to deliver to any other location unless certain that such action is legitimate.
- Never leave valuables on view in your cab, whether these are loose equipment or your personal belongings.

- Look out for and report any security defects on your vehicle – faulty locks, bolts, straps, anti-theft devices, etc. Report unserviceable security equipment at once and insist on prompt rectification.
- Keep documentation about the load in a secure place. This can be used as authority to collect goods.

(Source: FTA, 1994: 57–58)

As mentioned in the list above, maintenance of anti-theft equipment is extremely important and should be included as a regular service item when vehicles are being maintained. Any vehicle-based equipment will be exposed to the elements to a far greater extent than static equipment and will require a higher level of maintenance as a consequence.

THE DEPOT

The very nature of distribution depots presents many headaches from the point of view of security. Access for large vehicles 24 hours a day requires large access gates that may be left open most of the time. Company employees, visiting drivers, customers, suppliers' representatives, contracted maintenance staff such as tyre fitters, and agency staff will all require access to the depot at different times of the day. Most will be going about their business in a diligent fashion but this freedom of access also allows criminals similar freedom. Stories of commercial vehicles being driven away in broad daylight under the eyes of the depot staff are all too commonplace. The following are some suggested actions that will help reduce or eliminate this.

Depot location

Insurance companies are able to categorize different areas of the country into those that are more or less likely to suffer from criminal activity. The same will be true for different areas within a region. Depots are located, by and large, in the best location to service their customers cost-effectively. In many cases the opportunity will not exist to relocate the depot but where it does it may be worth considering, along with all the other factors, the level of crime in the target location.

Fencing

Perimeter fencing should create an effective barrier to the would-be criminal. Security experts recommend that palisade fencing topped with barbed wire and at least 2.4 metres high should be used. The top of this fencing should be angled outwards and all the links in the fencing should be welded to minimize the possibility of the fence being dismantled from the outside.

It is most important that vehicles are not parked next to the fencing. The vehicles could aid the criminals in their endeavours either by shielding them from view or acting as a platform for them to gain access to the depot. Do not stack pallets or other materials against the fencing as these too could be used in a similar fashion. Once fencing has been installed, ensure that it is well maintained.

Gates

There is little point in having good fencing if the gates to the depot are left wide open at all times. Electric sliding gates are expensive but very effective. If the price of electric gates is prohibitive then any gates that are fitted should have their hinges and bolts secured to prevent them being lifted off.

Pedestrians will require access and this could involve them having to pass through a secure gatehouse where they are booked in and out by a competent security guard. Regular employees could be issued with swipe cards or identification cards complete with photographs to speed their access. The close control of visitors will discourage all but the boldest criminal but it also helps from a health and safety point of view.

Some high-security establishments photograph all visitors every time they visit, and in some cases a video of all people and vehicles visiting the site is made and retained for a given period, say four weeks.

Road blockers that raise and lower may also be used to protect entrances but these are very expensive as well as being very effective.

Closed circuit television (CCTV) and intruder alarms

The security of perimeter fencing can be enhanced through the use of intruder alarms that are activated when the beam is broken. In the same way CCTV can help improve security but again it is expensive. There are some shortcomings with CCTV. They are:

- The monitors need to be constantly viewed for them to be effective.
- Tapes need to be managed carefully to ensure that they do not get taped over or wear out.
- If the criminal is dressed in dark clothing at night with the face disguised, the tapes are of little value for identification after the event. If the monitors are being watched constantly then immediate action can be taken.

- If the equipment is not turned on then its value is compromised.
- The positioning of cameras needs to be well thought through. This is not only to ensure that they have a good field of vision but also to ensure that they can be seen but not attacked and put out of action. The sight of CCTV cameras can have a deterrent value in itself.

Where intruder alarms and CCTV are used, advertise the facts prominently through the use of signs to aid the value of the deterrent.

Security guards

Employing your own guards will be expensive if seven-day/24-hour cover is required. However, employed guards of the right calibre will know your business and your staff and can be an asset. Contract guards who visit the site on a mobile basis are an alternative but the danger is that they fall into a routine visiting time that the criminals simply avoid. In this area you get what you pay for and the decision must be made in the light of the level of security required.

Lighting

Criminals in general don't like to operate where the area is well lit. Ensure that there is sufficient lighting to deter would-be thieves. In residential areas lighting may also be a nuisance so this must be borne in mind when positioning lights. Lights that are activated by heat or movement are an alternative to full-time lighting.

PERSONNEL

Extreme care should be taken when recruiting new staff. Criminals have been known to insinuate themselves into the organization either by applying for jobs as direct employees or through employment agencies. The following useful advice regarding recruitment was prepared by the FTA:

1. Take references for all previous employers.
2. If possible speak person to person with the previous employer and discuss the applicant's work record and character.
3. When checking references by telephone, obtain the number you need from a telephone directory. Any number supplied by the applicant could be that of an accomplice.

4. Do not accept open references, such as 'To whom it may concern'.
5. Beware of unexplained gaps in the employment record – query them.
6. Avoid employing anyone with a known record of alcohol abuse, extreme habitual gambling or serious financial irresponsibility. A stable domestic background is to be preferred.
7. Insist on seeing the applicant's original birth certificate, not a photocopy.
8. Check driving licences thoroughly. Compare the date of birth against the birth certificate. An ordinary licence will expire the day before the holder's 70th birthday.
9. Examine the licence closely in a strong light for signs of alteration, discolouration or erasure. Ensure that the pink or green background is intact. Be suspicious of stained or damaged licences. Check for endorsements, photocopy the licence and retain this on file.
10. Be suspicious of duplicate licences, which usually have 'duplicate' printed on them. Most duplicate licences are issued for quite legitimate reasons but disqualified drivers have been known to apply for and receive a duplicate licence before their trial and use this to gain employment.
11. Obtain a photograph of the applicant and get the applicant to sign it in your presence.
12. Exercise special care when recruiting temporary drivers, unless they are personally known to you.
13. Agency drivers should be employed only from reputable agencies whose staff are vetted and ideally fidelity bonded. In any event, all agency drivers should be photographed before being allowed to drive any company vehicle. Driving licences should be examined, as described above. Do not rely on the agency to do this for you.

(Source: FTA, 1994: 23–24)

USEFUL PUBLICATIONS AND SOURCES OF INFORMATION

These include the following:

- Home Office Public Relations Branch (1994) *A Load on Your Mind?*
- Maple, J *A Guide to Commercial Vehicle Security*, 2nd edn, Maple Commercial Vehicle Security
- FTA (1994) *Theft Prevention Guide*, FTA, Tunbridge Wells
- Road Haulage Association *Hands Off Our Freight*

- BS6803, parts 1, 2 and 3, British Standards Publications
- Police crime prevention officers are generally only too willing to provide help and guidance on security matters.

SAFETY IN THE DISTRIBUTION CENTRE

The very nature of warehousing and distribution centre operations implies the handling of goods, and the use of mechanization and automation to facilitate and speed up handling has not eliminated the hazards from handling operations. Walk into many so-called 'automated' warehouses and you will see fork trucks working on vehicle loading and unloading, and considerable manual handling associated with order picking and packing.

The traditional potential hazards of collisions, vehicle overturns, load collapse, falls, equipment malfunction and manual handling injuries are still with us, sometimes exacerbated by a less-than-ideal working environment and the pressure to move goods quickly to meet customer service and other time constraints.

The causes of industrial handling accidents can be many and various, from unsafe stacking of goods, unsafe truck driving practices, the condition and maintenance of handling and storage equipment, equipment overload and poor manual handling techniques. To these physical factors can be added safety management, and factors such as poor safety supervision and discipline, inadequate training, and pressure to meet tight deadlines.

Despite greater safety awareness and training, it is still true that in handling and storage operations there are many more manual handling injuries than for truck and other equipment-associated accidents, although the consequence of equipment-centred accidents can be much more serious than manual handling injuries.

Safety should be a fundamental and integral part of management and company operations. Prerequisites for success include the attitude and example of senior management being seen to require safe working, willingness to invest in training for all levels in the organization, supervision and where appropriate discipline to ensure safe working, and channels of communication on safety matters within the organization.

Safe practices

In this text it is not appropriate to give detailed lists of good practice for handling and storage, but some examples may illustrate the sort of considerations when setting up and managing such activities:

- *working areas* – visibility and lighting levels, floor strength and condition, separate truck and pedestrian aisles, housekeeping (no spillages), unobstructed movement routes (no protruding pallets), adequate and marked working and turning aisles, ventilation;
- *fork trucks* – head guard and safety lights, use of horn, secure and stable load within capacity of truck, safe speed, no passengers, load at front when going up a slope and truck in reverse when descending a slope, drive with load lowered, appropriate servicing and maintenance;
- *racking and stacking* – racking designed to meet codes of practice, racking damage repaired, safely loaded pallets of the right size and in good condition, adequate aisle widths.

Other particular issues may have to be considered when handling and storing chemicals. These include the toxicity, flammability and corrosive properties and their impact in the event of spillage. Facilities for ventilation, emergency showers, eyewashes or other antidotes, etc may be required, and the use of special protective clothing such as gloves and goggles. Some materials may require special or separate storage, or may only be permitted to be held in specified maximum quantities. The actions necessary in the event of leakage should be clearly displayed and understood by the staff. Legislation governs the handling and storage of certain specific chemicals and flammable materials.

The other major potential hazard in warehousing is fire, and some of the losses incurred in warehouse fires have been very high. This is an aspect covered by legislation, and in addition is subject to the advice and requirements of local fire officers and the company providing insurance for the facility. Measures to satisfy fire safety are usually considered at the design stage of a facility, and will require some or all of such features as in-rack sprinklers, fire-resistant dividing walls between sections of the facility, emergency lighting, fire exit doors and possibly fire escape tunnels.

Legislation and regulation

Recent years have seen an increasing amount of national and international legislation and regulation designed to minimize hazards and make for safer working, and managers need to be aware of the extent of such legislation.

In the UK, the Health and Safety at Work Act has been with us since 1974, and has served a vital purpose in ascribing responsibilities for safe working, whilst encouraging a co-operative approach to safety by all concerned parties – employers, employees, designers, manufacturers and suppliers.

Specific directives that have appeared include:

- Machinery Safety Directive (89/392/EEC) – prevents risks to operators through safe design and construction, and incorporates mobile and lifting equipment as amended 91/368/EEC;
- Use of Work Equipment Directive (89/391/EEC) – to ensure that employers buy equipment and machinery that complies with relevant directives;
- Manual Handling Directive (90/269/EEC).

SUMMARY

This chapter has outlined areas of concern in respect of vehicle and depot security, and the means of dealing with them. Specific areas covered included:

- vehicle immobilization;
- vehicle alarms;
- a guide to dos and don'ts for drivers;
- depot location;
- depot fencing and gates;
- closed circuit television;
- personnel and security guards;
- a list of useful publications.

Safety should be taken into account when designing any facility, and it should be an integral part of good management practice.

The extent and detail of legislation and guidance relating to safety in warehousing are very considerable and beyond the scope of this text. The authors commend a 1992 Health and Safety Executive publication, *Health and Safety in Retail and Wholesale Warehouses* (ISBN 0 11 885731 2).

33

Logistics and the environment

INTRODUCTION

It is not the purpose of this chapter to lay out in detail current and planned environmental legislation. However it is inevitable that people involved in logistics, whether in an active operational role or in a strategic planning role, will at some stage have to consider the environmental effects of their actions.

What is meant by the environment? Broadly speaking it can be divided up into the internal environment, ie inside the organization, and the external environment, which encompasses everything that is outside of the organization.

The internal environment will be concerned with health and safety issues such as noise levels, handling of dangerous substances and occurrences, as well as risk assessments and safe systems of work. Naturally, some issues will be of concern to both the internal and the external environment, such as noise pollution or emissions of substances into the atmosphere or watercourses. This chapter concentrates on issues relating to the external environment.

National governments and the European Union (EU) as a whole have produced a great deal of legislation relating to environmental issues over the last few years. Increasingly it is being recognized that environmental issues are everyone's responsibility and that 'the polluter must pay'. It is no longer sufficient to design, introduce and sell a product into the chosen market. Now manufacturers must consider the long-term effects of their products. Is it possible to recycle all or part of the product?

What will happen to the packaging after delivery has been effected? Do the processes involved in manufacture cause unacceptable levels of pollution? Which mode of transport will be used to deliver the goods?

Those involved in logistics will increasingly have to deal with used products being brought back through the system for recycling or disposal. Waste packaging will most likely also follow the same route or at least arrangements will have to be made for a third party to discharge the organization's legal obligations in this regard. The choice of transport system will have to be carefully considered because of the adverse effects of transport fuel emissions and congestion. Congestion and fuel emissions apply particularly in the case of road transport but the other modes of transport are not immune to these problems. The location of manufacturing and distribution sites will have to pay due regard to environmental issues.

THE EUROPEAN UNION AND ENVIRONMENTAL LEGISLATION

The European Commission's White Paper, 'Growth, competitiveness and employment' (1993), sets out the main thrust of the EU's approach to environmental policy. Further to this publication, the EU's Fifth Environmental Action Programme, 'Towards sustainability', sets out five areas of economic activity that may affect the environment. They are:

1. tourism;
2. energy;
3. transport;
4. agriculture;
5. industry.

A number of major environmental issues to be confronted are also identified within the programme. They are:

- management of waste;
- biodiversity and the protection of nature;
- urban environments;
- coastal zones;
- water resources;
- acid rain and air quality;
- climate change.

The five areas of economic activity and the major environmental issues to be confronted will apply to those involved in logistics to a greater or lesser extent. For example, locating manufacturing or distribution sites may be restricted by some of the above issues. Similarly the choice of transport mode for trunking and final delivery could be affected. Almost certainly the packaging used and provisions for its recycling or disposal will have to be considered.

Areas of EU environmental legislation, both current and under consideration, are concentrated in the following areas:

- *Carbon tax.* This proposal is aimed at limiting greenhouse gas emissions by imposing a tax on the inefficient use of energy resources.
- *Waste.* The programme proposes targets of 50 per cent recycling or reusing of glass, paper and plastics (all used in packaging materials). It is also proposed that by 2000 no waste will be exported from the EU for final disposal.
- *Waste transportation.* In 1993 an EU regulation controlling the transportation of waste both inside and outside the EU set up a control system for handling and disposal of hazardous waste.
- *Waste and landfill.* This is an area where the EU wish to enact legislation.
- *Packaging waste.* In 1994 the EU introduced the Packaging and Packaging Waste Directive. The directive requires member states to set up return, collection and recovery systems for waste packaging. It also requires the setting of targets for recycling and recovery. This is an area that will greatly affect those involved in logistics management.
- *Integrated pollution, prevention and control.* This legislation will set up an EU-wide licensing system that will set limits on emissions to atmosphere, water and soil.
- *Vehicle emissions.* Standards have been set on the amount of carbon monoxide, oxides of nitrogen and hydrocarbon emissions that new vehicles over 3.5 tonnes gross vehicle weight can produce. These have come to be known as Euro 1, Euro 2, Euro 3 and Euro 4. Standards relating to fuel quality and exhaust after treatment complete the picture.

The above list does not make any mention of the huge amount of Health and Safety legislation that mainly covers the internal environment. The main thrust of this legislation has moved in recent years from descriptive to prescriptive legislation. The principles of managing health and safety through risk assessment force management to create an agenda for corrective actions. Risk assessments are undertaken for given work activities. In the course of conducting the risk assessment, hazards are identified and an evaluation made of the likelihood of that hazard creating an accident. Having identified both the hazard and the risk, management are then obliged to undertake corrective actions.

In many ways, following best environmental and health and safety practices can make good business sense. After all, is it not the objective of logisticians to optimize the performance of the whole organization? Elimination of wasteful activities can be environmentally friendly and make good business sense. Maintaining a safe and healthy internal environment for its workforce will ultimately benefit the organization. Time lost to industry because of accidents, illness and management time in dealing with these issues alone is breathtaking in its scale.

Hand in hand with lost time go the additional costs created by accidents, associated with consequential loss, and replacement assets and people. Criminal and civil legal actions will also be avoided by following best practice.

LOGISTICS AND ENVIRONMENTAL BEST PRACTICE

This section is designed to highlight some of the key areas that should be considered when dealing with the management of environmental issues. Given the complexity of many environmental issues and their ability to generate intense public interest, this section should only be seen as an introduction to the area. Specialist help should always be sought by management if any doubt exists as to the proper course of action in a given set of circumstances.

Environmental management systems

As we have seen, logistics and transport activities have been identified as having a major impact on the environment in which we all live. Consequently they have attracted significant legislation at both the national and international level. Targets for improving environmental performance have been set by the international community via the Rio and, more recently, the Kyoto summit meetings. At the level of the organization it has been recognized that a formal system for the management of environmental matters would be useful. The ISO 14000 series of standards outlines such a system.

This standard provides a framework for managing environmental issues rather than establishing performance requirements. The approach is defined in the introduction of the standard's specification. It is seen as an iterative process that starts with the creation of an environmental policy by the organization. This leads on to planning how the organization will meet its legal obligations as well as any targets it wishes to set, which in turn leads to implementing and operating the plan. Implementation will pay due regard to the organizational structure and allocation of responsibilities. Training and communicating with staff, control of relevant documentation and operational controls must all be covered in the implementation.

Having set up the system it is then formally monitored through an auditing process, which will identify corrective actions that will need to be carried out. Top management are required to review the performance of the system formally on a regular basis. This review may lead to the policy or objectives being changed or updated in the light of auditing reports or changing circumstances. This process should encourage a commitment to continuous improvement in environmental management as well as ensuring that the organization is not exposed by failing to meet its legal and moral obligations.

Environmental checklist

The following checklist was published in 1991 by the UK Department of Trade and Industry in a useful document entitled *Environment: A challenge for business*. In a series of questions it helps focus attention on the key areas for consideration:

- What environmental risks do your firm's activities pose?
- Do your processes and materials pose any danger?
- Do you know what impact your products (including their disposal) and services have on the environment?
- Do you know what quantity and type of waste you produce?
- Do you know how it is disposed of and what the cost is?
- Is your firm operating the most cost-effective method of controlling or eliminating pollution risk?
- Are there hidden benefits (for example, greater production efficiency) – or even straight business opportunities (for example, commercial utilization of waste) – from adopting alternative methods of controlling or eliminating the pollution risk?
- Can you meet the consumer demand for environmentally improved products?
- Are you aware of existing environmental standards and legislation in the UK and overseas?
- What arrangements do you have for monitoring compliance with environmental legislation?
- Is senior management actively involved in ensuring that proper weight is given to environmental considerations throughout the firm?
- Could you improve your environmental image to the public and your employees?
- Are you highlighting your environmental performance to private investors, financial institutions and shareholders?

Packaging

Packaging is important to logisticians for a number of reasons. Its shape may define how effectively the products can be loaded into transport containers in the form of either cartons or vehicles. For example, a cylindrical-shaped product is unlikely to fill a given cubic capacity as well as a rectilinear shape. This has implications for how much product can be stored or transported in a given space and, as all storage and transport resources have a finite size and weight restriction, filling these spaces effectively is extremely important. The more product stored or transported in a given cubic capacity the more the associated unit costs, as well as the environmental impact, can be reduced.

Packaging is also important in protecting the products from damage in transit and even pilferage. Packaging in the form of unitized containers, whether they are pallets or reusable containers, will often require transportation back to the point of origin to facilitate reuse.

Many industries have developed forms of packaging that do all that is required of them whilst in transit between the point of origin and the end user but that do not warrant the expense of returning them to the point of origin. Therefore the packing is only used once and then consigned to the rubbish tip. This principle goes all the way down to the level of the single tin or carton of food. In this case the consumer transports the container from the retail outlet to the point of use and then simply discards the container.

It is this type of packaging, in all its forms, that the environmental legislation aims to control. For logisticians the problem manifests itself in the form of reverse logistics. Waste packaging needs to be brought the opposite way up the supply chain or at least the obligation to do this needs to be dealt with. It is possible under the UK regulations to join a compliance scheme that helps discharge the organization's obligations in this regard.

The Producer Responsibility Obligations (Packaging Waste) Regulations (1997) came into force in March 1997. These regulations implemented the EU Directive 94/62/EC on packaging and packaging waste and required each member state to comply with the following by 2001: 1) to recover between 50 and 65 per cent of packaging waste; and 2) to recycle between 25 and 45 per cent of packaging waste with a minimum of 15 per cent by weight of each packaging material used.

The responsibility for executing these regulations is shared by all the parties in the packaging chain, described as the 'producers'. These 'producers' are legally obliged to do the following:

1. Register with the Environment Agency or the Scottish Environmental Protection Agency.

2. Arrange for the recovery and recycling of packaging waste.
3. Supply a certificate of compliance to the Environment Agency to demonstrate that waste has been reprocessed.

'Producers' may either discharge their responsibilities themselves or register with a 'compliance scheme', which will discharge their obligations on their behalf.

Companies with a turnover of less than £5 million (before 2000) or £1 million (from 2000) are exempt from the regulations. Any company that handles less than 50 tonnes of packaging or packaging materials annually is also exempt.

Waste transport and disposal

The Environmental Protection Act 1990 created responsibilities for all those involved in the production, keeping, treatment, transport and disposal of waste. All parties involved were charged with a 'duty of care', which covered the escape of waste, the transfer of waste only to persons authorized to receive it and documentation describing the waste and parties involved in its disposal. Waste management licences were required by those involved in keeping, treating or disposing of waste. Waste transfer notes had to accompany the waste on its journey from producer to final disposal. The Environment Act 1995 transferred waste regulation authority to the newly formed Environment Agency for England and Wales and to the Scottish Environment Protection Agency for Scotland from April 1996.

Performance measures

As with any management exercise, performance measures are useful for evaluating the progress or otherwise of a given initiative. Most business managers will be concerned with costs and benefits because businesses are concerned with making a healthy return on investment. Very often best environmental practice will result in financial benefits in return. For example, investment in driver training may deliver savings in the form of reduced accident figures and better fuel consumption.

However, some environmental projects may have to be undertaken because of legal requirements, and will not generate commensurate cost savings for the business. For example, a noise abatement order generated because local residents have objected to the noise emanating from a distribution centre at night may result in the installation of noise screens, landscaping or restrictions on operating hours. Clearly any of these measures will simply add cost and no financial benefit to the business concerned, although some public relations benefits may accrue. Obviously it would be desirable to avoid this kind of problem by selecting operating sites carefully, but some sites, through no fault of their own, have over time been slowly surrounded by residential dwellings. Unfortunately, being there first is not enough to make them immune from this kind of problem.

Organizations with environmental management systems, whether formal or informal, will attempt to monitor their performance in certain areas of their operation. Simple measures might include:

- miles per gallon of fuel used;
- percentage of fleet using less polluting fuels;
- percentage of truck fleet in the Euro 1/Euro 2/Euro 3 and Euro 4 emission regulation bands;
- average life of tyres expressed in miles;
- percentage of tyres remoulded or regrooved;
- amount of waste lubrication oils generated by the operation;
- utilization of vehicle load space expressed as a percentage;
- percentage of miles run by vehicles empty;
- targets for reducing waste packaging;
- targets for reducing noise levels.

The contribution of road vehicles to the production of harmful emissions has generated a great deal of attention from governments, the press, environmental pressure groups and many other concerned parties. For those organizations operating very large fleets of vehicles the following formula may prove useful in measuring performance: *1 litre of diesel fuel produces 3 kilograms of CO_2 or 1,000 litres of diesel fuel produces 3 tonnes of CO_2.* This formula may be used in practice by simply identifying the number of litres of diesel fuel saved through the implementation of a given initiative and multiplying the saved fuel figure by 0.003 to arrive at the number of tonnes of CO_2 emissions that have been avoided. Other commercial vehicle emissions may be calculated using Table 33.1.

Noise levels are measured using decibels (dB (a)). The problem with measuring improvements in noise levels is that sound-waves are reflected by different surfaces. Measurement of the effect of noise attenuation on, say, a piece of vehicle ancillary equipment – such as the blower used in the discharge of powder tankers – would be affected by any surrounding buildings or the position of the person in relation to the blower itself. However, providing that these limitations are recognized and accounted for then it is possible to compare different blowers in the same location and arrive at an indication of improvement.

Table 33.1 HGV emissions by vehicle age

Age of vehicle	Emissions per 1,000 litres of diesel fuel (kg)			
	CO	HC	NOx	PM
1982 to April 1991 (Euro 0)	12	2	37	5
April 1991 to October 1996 (Euro 1)	12	1	21	2
From October 1996 (Euro 2)	11	1	18	1

CO = carbon monoxide
HC = hydrocarbon
NOx = nitrogen oxide
PM = particulate matter
Source: ETSU, FTA (FTA calculations based on ETSU data and EU directive limits)

Possible areas for improvement

For the depot, consider these areas for improvement:

- location;
- vehicle access/egress;
- noise reduction by
  - landscaping
  - erecting noise screens
  - moving noisy operations away from local residents
  - restricting noisy activities to certain hours
  - restricting visiting vehicles to certain hours
  - using noise-attenuated equipment where possible
  - turning vehicle engines off when not in use
  - insisting on drivers turning off radios when working in the depot at night;
- reduction of visual intrusion through landscaping and a generally neat and tidy approach;
- reduction of water wastage by the use of water recycling on vehicle washes;
- avoidance of pollution of the watercourse with run-off from fuel dispensing areas through the use of interceptor tanks;
- consideration of the use of a computerized fuel dispensing system;
- careful management and monitoring of other hazardous chemicals on site (paying due regard to the Control of Substances Hazardous to Health (COSHH) regulations);

- keeping pallet stacks tidy and out of sight if possible;
- fitting particulate traps to diesel fork-lift trucks to reduce emissions;
- consideration of the use of electric or gas-powered fork-lift trucks;
- better management of the production, collection and disposal of waste.

For the vehicles, consider these possible areas for improvement:

- Driver training reduces accidents and improves fuel consumption. Use on-board vehicle technology to monitor driver performance. Computerized engine management can provide a wealth of information.
- Consider less polluting fuels.
- Monitor fuel consumption.
- Monitor vehicle utilization in terms of both payload and empty running.
- Use speed limiters on smaller commercial vehicles that don't require them by law.
- Follow preventative maintenance programmes because slipping clutches, blocked air filters, fuel leaks, poorly inflated tyres and binding brakes all use fuel unnecessarily.
- Consider the use of aerodynamic kits on the vehicles to improve fuel consumption.
- Specify the most appropriate driveline (engine, gearbox and drive axle) for a given vehicle duty cycle.
- Consider the use of synthetic oils as their use may reduce the overall use of oil in the vehicles.
- Lubrication oils in the engine, gearbox and driving axles all impose drag on the driveline. Consider using different oils to produce fuel savings.
- Use computerized routeing and scheduling packages to reduce overall vehicle mileages run.
- Instigate better tyre management through the increased use of recutting and remoulding of tyres to extend useful life.
- Dispose of used tyre casings responsibly.
- Use low rolling resistance tyres to improve fuel economy.
- Muffle vehicle body noise where possible.
- Use self-tracking (or positively steered) steering axles on trailers to reduce tyre wear and tear.
- Specify attenuated ancillary equipment such as refrigeration units, discharge blower units and tail-lifts.
- Specify air brake silencers.
- Use quiet floor materials in vehicle bodies.

- Use asbestos-free brake linings and clutch plates.
- Use air suspension on vehicles to reduce road damage and prolong the life of vehicle components.
- Use chlorofluorocarbon-free body insulation materials.

A further area of consideration for possible improvement is the transfer of some freight to rail or other mode of transport.

Main legislation

The main legislation in respect of the external environment is as follows:

- Control of Pollution Act 1974;
- Single European Act 1986;
- Control of Pollution (Amendment) Act 1989;
- Environmental Protection Act 1990;
- Controlled Waste (Registration of Carriers and Seizure of Vehicles) Regulations 1991;
- Controlled Waste Regulations 1992;
- Water Resources Act 1991;
- Water Industry Act 1991;
- Environment Act 1995;
- Special Waste Regulations 1996;
- Trans-frontier Shipment of Waste Regulations 1994.

The main legislation in respect of the internal environment is as follows:

- Health and Safety at Work Act 1974;
- Management of Health and Safety at Work Regulations 1992;
- Occupier's Liability Acts 1957 and 1984;
- Control of Substances Hazardous to Health Regulations 1994 (COSHH), revised 1999;
- Employers Liability (Compulsory Insurance) Act 1969;
- Reporting of Injuries, Diseases and Dangerous Occurrences Regulations 1995;
- Management of Health and Safety at Work Regulations 1992, revised 1999;
- Workplace (Health, Safety and Welfare) Regulations 1992;
- Health and Safety (Display Screen Equipment) Regulations 1992;
- Manual Handling Operations Regulations 1992;
- Personal Protective Equipment at Work Regulations 1992;

- Provision and Use of Work Equipment Regulations 1992, revised 1998;
- Offices, Shops and Railway Premises Act;
- Factories Act.

This list must not be regarded as exhaustive. It is meant only as a guide to the major legislation in this complex field. For example, there is hardly an area of organized commercial endeavour that does not have its own specific health and safety regulations. In fact, any field that may be excluded is usually covered by the imposed 'duty of care' with regard to the health, safety and welfare of employees laid down by the Health and Safety at Work Act 1974. After all it would always be wise to adopt a health and safety approach in the workplace whether or not there were specific regulations in place. Accidents in the internal or external environment will cost the organization dearly.

Reverse logistics

For the most part logistics management is about moving materials from raw materials through production and onward to the end customer. Usually going in the opposite direction from the end customer through production planning to raw material suppliers is information about customer requirements. However, there are occasions when it is necessary to move materials in the other direction as well. These circumstances are usually:

1. product recall for quality or safety reasons;
2. the return of unwanted goods;
3. used packaging for recycling or disposal.

Moving materials back through the distribution channel presents organizations with many challenges because the system is primarily designed to move goods in one direction only, ie from the organization to the customer and not the other way round. However, there are businesses where reverse logistics is a part of the fabric of their organizations. For example, the mail order / catalogue companies can experience return rates on dispatched goods of up to 50 per cent, especially where fashion items are concerned. The increase in shopping via the Internet or other media will clearly affect this phenomenon. The postal services and parcels carriers also specialize in systems that both collect and deliver goods.

For those companies that are not set up to deal with reverse flows through their systems, there are many obstacles to overcome. The following is a brief outline of what should be considered:

1. *Is there a strategy for reversing the flow of materials in the system?* Responsibilities should be allocated in advance and any resources unavailable internally should be identified in advance. Cost elements should also be identified in advance. Cost elements involved in a product recall fall under four headings: communication costs, documentation costs, replacement costs and disposition costs. Communication costs include
   - registered and certified mail
   - return receipts
   - instructions
   - telephone, telegrams (and faxes)
   - messenger service.

   Documentation costs include
   - filing of receipts of notices for recall
   - estimates for disposition and replacement
   - plans of item recalled
   - plans for replacement item
   - instructions for replacement/repair
   - authorizations for work to be performed
   - receipts for items replaced/repaired.

   Replacement costs include
   - manufacture and installation
   - employee visits
   - shipping, packing and warehousing
   - testing and retesting
   - identification of product
   - identification of carton
   - identification of shipping carton
   - temporary personnel
   - invoicing
   - overtime of employees.

   Disposition costs include
   - locating all items
   - inventory of items
   - removal from customer's property
   - packaging and unpacking
   - labelling
   - shipping
   - inspection
   - repair or replace

- discard or salvage
- instruction pamphlet
- refunding
- allowances for time used
- repurchase of item
- compensation for loss of use
- warehousing: storage.

NB: item in brackets added by author
(Source: Gattorna, 1990: 470)

2. *What is the urgency associated with this reverse flow?* Clearly, in the case of malicious contamination of food products, which usually are life-threatening in nature, speed is of the essence. These particular situations may be further complicated by police insistence on secrecy if blackmail is involved. Even if this is not the case, very often the perishable nature of the goods has ensured that they were distributed very quickly across a large geographical area. In these circumstances, hours and minutes can be critical to success or failure. If goods are defective in some way that is not life-threatening but the consumers' enjoyment of the products may tarnish the company's reputation in the market-place, then a rapid resolution of the matter may even enhance the standing of the company in the consumers' eyes. Naturally the opposite is also true. Used packaging or unwanted goods need to be dealt with efficiently and professionally, but they will not attract the same level of urgency as either malicious contamination of food products or defective goods.

3. Having established the relative urgency of the reverse flow it is then necessary to establish where the goods are in the distribution channels. It can be easily understood that the more links in the distribution channel that exist the more complex and costly it will be to both locate and return the goods. This is where a good product traceability system will come into its own.

4. Assuming that the goods have been located, the next task is to collect them. If the goods are in the hands of the consumer then this is the most difficult situation of all, as the manufacturer's distributors may not know the identities of these consumers. This situation will require some form of publicity campaign but even then consumers may not choose to respond. In this situation limited success is very likely. Associated transport costs will be higher than usual because consignments are likely to be smaller and more widely dispersed.

5. When the goods are returned, care will have to be taken to isolate and quarantine them to avoid the possibility of their being inadvertently dispatched again. This is especially important where the reason for collection is not immediately obvious to the casual observer. The potential for salvage and reworking of the products will also need to be established.

This list has concentrated on product recalls as they can be very complicated, costly and have disastrous results. In the case of material moving back up the distribution channel for recycling the need for urgency is likely to be reduced unless the material is hazardous in some way. As stated earlier in this chapter the disposal and handling of waste have attracted a great deal of legislation and media attention, which means that this process cannot be approached in a half-hearted way.

Many manufacturers are designing their products with recycling in mind. Scania AG, the Swedish truck manufacturer, is a case in point. It produces heavy trucks that are virtually completely constructed of materials that may be recycled. It also produces annually an environmental report, which lays out the company's progress against stated environmental objectives. In future the challenge for manufacturers will be to retrieve and recycle their own products.

Instances of reverse logistics can also be seen in the service sector. For instance, a holiday tour operator may need to repatriate its clients at short notice due to disease, civil unrest or severe weather conditions. The principles are very similar.

SUMMARY

This chapter has looked at the area of environmental law and best practice with specific reference to the impact on logistics management. Broadly the subject matter was divided between the internal and the external environment. Environmental legislation tends to deal with the external environment while the internal environment is covered by health and safety legislation.

The direction and content of EU environmental legislation was outlined, as was the environmental management system – ISO 14000. A useful environmental management checklist was reproduced.

Packaging was highlighted as an area singled out for special attention by the legislative authorities. The main requirements under these regulations were outlined. Waste transport was also covered.

Useful performance measures were suggested to aid the process of monitoring improvements in environmental best practice. Specific points regarding environmental best practice for both vehicles and depots were listed. Reverse logistics and its implications for logistics management were briefly discussed.

34

New concepts in logistics

INTRODUCTION

As the discipline that has come to be known as logistics develops and matures it seems that hardly a day can go by without some new acronym or theory appearing. Very often these apparently 'new' ideas are simply refinements of existing concepts. Home delivery, for example, has been in existence for many years. However, what is new is the potential scale of operations and not the basic idea. On the other hand, buying and selling using the Internet is a genuinely new medium for trade. Despite the highly technical method by which trading is conducted across the Internet, it still requires traditional methods of distribution to complete the transaction, ie delivery of the goods or services.

Efficient consumer response (ECR) and 'lean' principles applied to production planning and control fit more into the category of refinement of existing principles, as does the idea of the 'agile supply chain'. Some would argue that ECR has nothing new to offer and is nothing more than clever marketing on the part of the US management consultants Salmon Brothers. Others would contend that it is a wholly new approach.

As with any new ideas, they are eventually refined and modified, both through practical application and debate. The purpose here is to outline some of the most recent developments that are likely to have an impact on business in general and logistics in particular.

TRADING USING THE INTERNET

Connections to, and use of, the Internet is growing on an unprecedented scale. It is with good reason that it is often referred to as the second Industrial Revolution. Daily, more and more organizations and individuals are connecting their computer systems to the Internet. Not only does this open up access to vast amounts of information but it also presents the opportunity of trading on a global scale. One side-effect has been to generate a whole new subset of logistics terms. Most, if not all, would fit into a single generic category called 'e-commerce'. The 'e' stands for electronic and is an obvious reference to the use of digitized information being transferred between computer systems. Where the prefix 'e' is used, it is a fair bet that Internet trading is involved.

It is useful to be aware of the difference between what is known as business-to-consumer (B2C) and business-to-business (B2B) e-commerce. B2C Internet commerce is concerned with the direct interaction and commercial relationship between a business and the end consumer. This can be either the traditional retailer dealing privately with a member of the public, or a manufacturer or supplier dealing with a member of the public who is an end user. B2B Internet commerce is concerned with the interaction and commercial relationship between businesses. These may be any type of business trading raw materials, components, spare parts, finished goods or routine office items.

Initial attention has been concentrated on the opportunities for developments in B2C e-commerce, but there are significant opportunities and implications for B2B e-commerce.

E-tailing refers to the multiple retailers using the Internet as another channel to market. In this particular case the retailer produces a Web site, which allows it to display its wares to all those potential customers who possess a computer linked to the Internet. Customers make their selection, pay using their credit card and the groceries are delivered. What is significant, in this example, is that whereas before customers effected the final delivery by transporting the goods to their homes, now final delivery will require another goods vehicle. This has environmental implications with regard to traffic congestion. It also calls into question the future size of retail outlets, the range stocked in them and logically their very existence in the longer term. When every household has a terminal will all groceries be delivered directly from a distribution depot? Given our current perspective this is unlikely, as many people enjoy the social process attached to visiting a shop, but it must have some effect.

Trading on the Internet offers businesses and consumers alike a much more sophisticated approach than simply buying and selling. Companies are able to publish details of their goods and services on their Web site, which saves them from having to produce masses of printed material. This obviously reduces costs for the organizations concerned but consumers can also benefit through the use of customization. If consumers provide information about their particular preferences then whenever they log on to a given site only those preferences are displayed as a matter of course.

As the Internet is a global facility it opens up new geographical markets to businesses. It must be remembered that the Internet may open up these markets but if goods or services have to be physically delivered then this can present considerable challenges. For example, the whole world does not benefit from the standard of transport infrastructure that may be found in the United States or Europe. On the other hand if the goods themselves can be digitized then they may be delivered via the Internet. Examples include music, films, television, photographic services, computer software, telephone calls and video conferencing. These goods do not require any further infrastructure to complete the transaction.

E-fulfilment is a term that has been developed to emphasize the need to ensure that the physical delivery of products ordered via the Internet is carried out effectively. Although Internet access provides a direct and instantaneous link from the customer to the selling organization, the actual physical fulfilment of the order must still be undertaken by traditional physical means. Very often this may even necessitate the introduction of a new means of physical distribution, because traditional channels are set up to distribute to shops rather than direct to the home. This is likely to necessitate a major change in the distribution strategy of many companies. Some of these issues are discussed in the next section on home shopping.

E-procurement refers to the development of electronic means of undertaking purchasing on a company-to-company basis, so this is an area of opportunity for B2B e-commerce. There are likely to be particular opportunities for the simplification of the purchase of low-value, routine items and the development of online catalogues.

There are a number of other logistics-related developments evolving from Internet applications. From a supply chain management perspective, the Internet provides many opportunities. Companies such as Tesco, the UK multiple retailer, are allowing their suppliers access to their computer systems to keep them updated on sales demand, current inventory carrying and promotional activity.

Parcels companies allow their customers to access their track-and-trace systems so that they can check on the progress of consignments easily. This type of initiative allows supply chains to be much more responsive and agile than ever before.

HOME SHOPPING

One phenomenon associated with Internet trading is home shopping. Home shopping has been around for many years in the shape of catalogue and television selling. What is new is the scale and scope of the growth in this area. Furniture and white goods have traditionally been delivered to customers' homes because of their bulky nature and difficulty in installation. Many famous department stores deliver customers' purchases to their homes, regardless of the size of the item, as part of their overall customer service package. The mail order catalogue companies have been delivering direct to their customers and collecting unwanted items for many years.

It is important to differentiate between home shopping and home delivery. Home shopping refers to the different ways of shopping for and ordering products from home. This includes mail order catalogues and also the use of Internet shopping. Home delivery refers to the physical delivery of the product to the home. Now, more often than not, goods that are ordered from home are indeed delivered directly to the home. There are, however, many occasions when goods are viewed and ordered in shops but are then delivered to the home – some department store purchases, white and brown goods, furniture and frozen foods can all fall into this category.

With the enormous growth in communications ability, through television, telephones, facsimile machines and the Internet, possibilities that were once only the stuff of dreams have been realized. For some years now in the USA it has been possible to purchase goods by watching dedicated television programmes. Admittedly these usually involve high-value items. As described above, the Internet has made it possible for all manner of companies to sell using this medium. This has created particular problems for the distribution companies that have to effect the final delivery.

Various estimates have been made as to the take-up of home shopping facilities but one thing is certain: for some members of society this service is very useful. For example, it is easy to see how the disabled, the elderly, parents with small children, and working people with hectic schedules would all benefit from such a facility. It is also easy to see how the elderly would not be happy about opening their doors during the hours of darkness and how working people would only be able to receive deliveries at this time.

Possible solutions that have been suggested are the provision of secure boxes outside the property where goods may be left, but this in itself would not be wholly satisfactory. The average grocery delivery is likely to contain some chilled, some frozen and some ambient goods. Delivery facilities would have to deal with this problem. Those distribution companies involved in these types of deliveries have developed specialist vehicles that have compartments for all three types of groceries.

Some problems have already been identified with the early trials of grocery home deliveries. These are very familiar issues, such as the number of mis-picks that occur in this type of single item picking operation, damage to the product and the less-than-perfect quality of the fresh food items. This latter problem may be due to poor picker selection or to the degradation of the product in its final journey to the customer.

Alternative points of delivery such as the place of work or the petrol station have been suggested as a way of overcoming some of these problems. Picked and packed goods would be delivered there to await the customer collecting them at a later time. Operations using these approaches have already been tried with varying success.

Another headache is the problem of returns. Catalogue companies have lived with returns running at a rate as high as 50 per cent. Typically, shoppers may not be exactly sure of the size of clothes they require so they order two and keep only one. Most distribution systems are designed for goods flowing in one direction, ie from the manufacturer to the consumer.

Delivery staff will have to have very good interpersonal skills, as they will be dealing face to face with customers, often in the customers' own homes. This will have implications for recruitment and training. If the goods being delivered require installation then the drivers will need appropriate training.

Home shopping will also affect the size and diversity of retail outlets and the distribution centres that service them. It is unlikely that many organizations will continue to pick goods for home delivery from a retail outlet. They will probably prefer that the goods are picked and delivered directly from a distribution centre. In turn this will have an effect on the design of these distribution centres as well as on their location. Will some manufacturers attempt to circumvent the retailer altogether and trade directly with the end consumer? Will groups of manufacturers join together to provide such direct services?

From the environmental point of view home shopping will create numerous extra road journeys by delivery vans. This must raise questions about congestion, as many customers may well still visit the retail outlets for the social experience while having their goods delivered to their homes later. Shared user distribution services are a possible way to mitigate these unwanted effects.

EFFICIENT CONSUMER RESPONSE (ECR)

ECR is a technique that originated in the USA and has been developed within the grocery industry specifically. In the 1980s Wal-Mart (a large US retailer), Procter & Gamble and Kurt Salmon Associates worked together to develop the ideas that are now called ECR.

Many logisticians find it hard to draw a distinction between supply chain management and ECR. Some feel that it is merely the same ideas parcelled up by consultants in a different format. The Director General of the Institute of Logistics in the UK attempted to draw a distinction in the following piece:

Efficient Consumer Response

Not surprisingly then, there has been confusion caused by the emergence of another tool, or technique, called Efficient Consumer Response (ECR). ECR has emerged, glossily packaged and 'consultant assisted', from America. It has quickly gained support. It seems very similar to logistics. So, what is it?

ECR started in America as a co-operative initiative in the food industry to reduce supply-chain costs in response to competitive pressure. In its current form it is specifically tailored to the food industry and concentrates on specific aspects of the supply-chain such as Efficient Replenishment, Efficient Introduction of New Products, Category Management and others. All these aspects are addressed using well known logistics techniques and tools and there seem to be no completely novel techniques introduced. So, if ECR is nothing new in principle, why has it gained such recognition and been taken up by so many large companies?

The answer is that ECR is not a new technique, or a replacement for logistics. ECR is a co-operative initiative amongst companies, mainly in the food sector at the moment, to apply some aspects of logistics in a focused way. The significant thing about it is a co-operation initiative, supported at a senior management level, by companies that are trading partners. Therein lies its strength and its potential.

For most companies the first, and most important, step in supply-chain optimization and integration is to introduce the logistics concept, and supply-chain thinking, throughout the company itself. When the maximum optimization has been reached inside the company then extending the concept outside the company to suppliers and customers has been shown to deliver further benefits. Various studies have shown that, usually, only companies that have integrated internally can integrate successfully externally. This is not surprising since forming supply-chain 'partnerships' requires a degree of openness, trust and transparency of information which is not easy to develop.

(Canadine, 1998)

ECR is often described as having four pillars that support a lintel known as category management. The four pillars are:

1. *efficient replenishment* – which uses techniques such as vendor-managed inventory (VMI), co-managed inventory, continuous replenishment and cross docking;
2. *efficient introductions* – which covers the development of new products and their introduction;
3. *efficient assortment* – which covers the management of the range and number of products available to the customer;
4. *efficient promotions* – which covers the management of promotional activity.

A fifth pillar, known as *efficient alignment*, seeks to cover areas such as benchmarking, the use of common terminology and the eradication of duplication of effort in the supply pipeline.

Additional information concerning some of the concepts behind ECR, together with a review of the main benefits and an approach to implementation, is given in Chapter 13.

LEAN THINKING

The results of a world-wide benchmarking programme in the automotive industry were published in a book called *The Machine that Changed the World* in 1990. It identified huge opportunities for closing the gap between the best in the world and other manufacturers. The lean approach uses the Toyota system of production management as a model.

The five principles of lean thinking have been derived by the Cardiff Business School. They concentrate on the elimination of waste. The principles are as follows:

1. Specify what does and does not create value from the customers' perspective and not from the perspective of individual firms, functions and departments.
2. Identify all the steps necessary to design, order and produce the product across the whole value stream to highlight non-value-adding waste.
3. Make those actions that create value flow without interruption, detours, back-flows, waiting or scrap.
4. Only make what is pulled by the customer just in time.
5. Strive for perfection by continually removing successive layers of waste as they are uncovered.

Lean thinking concentrates on the elimination of waste in all its forms. The seven wastes as listed in Chapter 11 are used as a menu for creating a 'lean' enterprise. Lean thinking owes a lot to the philosophy of just-in-time and is an extension of this type of approach.

THE AGILE SUPPLY CHAIN

A development of lean thinking is the concept of the agile supply chain. The emphasis is on the need for companies to work together across the supply chain in order to fulfil customers' requirements, and to be flexible in the way that they are organized for production and distribution. This will allow them to be responsive to any changes in customer requirements. The concept is one that recognizes the key importance of the final customer for a product and strives to set up a system and structure that can service these customer requirements in the most effective way.

Agility is, therefore, about the development of a strategic structure and operation that allows for the rapid response to unpredictable changes in customer demand. Two dictionary definitions serve to emphasize the difference between lean thinking and the agile supply chain:

lean: *having no surplus flesh or bulk*
agile: *quick in movement, nimble*

These ideas on agility have been developed at the Cranfield School of Management, where the Agile Supply Chain Research Centre has been established.

Some of the reasons for this need for a rethink in the way that companies are set up to respond to changes in customer requirements include:

- the dramatic shortening of product life cycles – PCs have about a six-month life cycle, and mobile phones become outdated in even shorter periods;
- the rapid increase in the variety of final products in terms of colour and style refinements;
- the build-up of stock, which can quickly become obsolete as demand requirements change so rapidly, in traditional supply chains;
- developments in direct selling and buying – notably via Internet shopping – that mean that customer expectations of acquiring the most up-to-date products have become even greater.

A number of techniques are now used to try to identify opportunities to increase agility within a supply chain. Many of these are already established techniques, but have been adapted to provide a different perspective. Some of the main ones are:

- to identify inventory at all the different levels within a supply chain, from raw material supplier to retailer;
- to identify value-adding time (activities that create benefit) and non-value-adding time (activities that do not create benefit, such as stock-holding) in the supply chain;
- to identify measures of throughput efficiency (the relationship between total lead time and value-adding time);
- to review the processes in the supply chain and identify which ones create unnecessary inventory or unnecessary delay;
- to map the supply chain to identify, graphically, positive process time (which will be value-adding and maybe non-value-adding time) and negative idle time (which is normally time spent as inventory and will be non-value-adding);
- to identify the extent of variety in the supply process.

The agile approach to supply chain management aims to create a responsive structure and process to service customer demand in a changing market-place. Key characteristics of an agile approach are:

- Inventory is held at as few levels as possible.
- Finished goods are sometimes delivered direct from factory to customer.
- Replenishment at the different levels in the supply chain is driven by actual sales collected at the customer interface.
- Production is planned across functional boundaries.
- Supply chain systems are highly integrated, giving clear visibility of inventory at all levels.
- Minimum lead times are developed and used.
- The principles of the postponement of production are practised.
- The majority of stock is held as work in progress awaiting final configuration, which will be based on actual customer requirements.

FOURTH-PARTY LOGISTICS

In recent years there has been some concern expressed by the users of third-party service providers that they are not being given the expected levels of service and business benefits. Users have also indicated that service providers are insufficiently proactive in their approach to the contracted operations – that they only aim to provide the minimum and fail to enhance the operations they are responsible for. On the other hand, service providers claim that they are seldom given the opportunity to develop new ideas and offer improvements, because users are not prepared to give them adequate information of their complete supply chains. One consequence of this has been the idea of using an additional enterprise or organization to oversee and take responsibility for all the outsourced operations a user might have. This has become known as fourth-party logistics.

Some of the typical failures that have been claimed for some third-party contracts include:

- Contracts and arrangements require substantial senior management time to co-ordinate and review.
- There is an inability to broaden the service offering.
- Increasing customer service requirements cannot be maintained.
- There is limited service flexibility, and an emphasis on scale economies and asset management.
- There are limited skills in the planning and replenishment processes (eg demand and inventory planning). The focus is mainly on transactional and execution processes (eg order picking, warehousing and transportation).
- There is a lack of network (re)design and management capabilities on a global and even continental level (eg the European Union).
- There is a lack of IT and change management capabilities.
- Contractors are often activity-driven (eg invoicing for space occupied or shipments delivered), as opposed to being value-driven (eg management of the total supply chain costs).
- They often provide one-off savings with limited on-going reductions.

One of the major reasons for these problems is said to be the traditional use of the RFQ (request for quotation) or ITT (invitation to tender) process. This is described in Chapter 31. This process is said to prevent the development of useful strategic partnerships and co-venturing initiatives. It is outdated and inappropriate for such arrangements because:

- It ignores total costs.
- Its aim is to drive down suppliers' margins.
- It is an over-engineered process, which doesn't allow for innovative solutions.
- It has an over-rigid format.

- It has extensive legal phrasing.
- It is a very expensive process for the contractor.
- It doesn't allow for total supply chain solutions.

The need to take a total supply chain approach means that a different type of service provider and a different type of RFQ/ITT approach are required. The idea is to aim to provide solutions, not just services. It is important to recognize that there are often several different organizations or participants in a supply chain, that there is a need to develop partnerships and that there should be opportunities to integrate and rationalize along the supply chain.

Thus, solutions can be developed by the co-venturer or fourth-party service provider to offer:

- a total supply chain perspective;
- visibility along the supply chain;
- measurement along the supply chain (cost and performance);
- open systems;
- technical vision;
- flexibility;
- tailored structures and systems.

Andersen Consulting have defined a fourth-party logistics service provider as 'an integrator that assembles the resources, capabilities, and technology of its own organization and other organizations to design, build and run comprehensive supply chain solutions'.

In his book, *Strategic Supply Chain Alignment*, John Gattorna discusses a number of different ways in which fourth-party logistics can solve some of the main problems of third-party logistics. These can be summarized as:

- addressing strategic failures
  - minimizing the time and effort spent on logistics by the user
  - a fourth-party organization is a single point of contact for all aspects of logistics
  - the management of multiple logistics providers is handled by a single organization
  - allows for provision of broader supply chain services (IT, integration strategy, etc)
  - a fourth-party organization can source different specialists with best-in-class credentials;

- addressing service and cost failures
  - the freeing of the user company's capital for core/mainstream use by selling assets
  - the continuous monitoring and improvement of supply chain processes, performance and costs
  - the benchmarking of different supply chain processes against world-class companies
  - the continuous monitoring and reassessment of service level achievements
  - the development and use of core expertise from all logistics participants;
- addressing operational failures
  - a new entity makes it easier to eradicate old industrial relations issues
  - a new entity should enable the transfer of selective personnel
  - a new and more flexible working environment can be established
  - a new company 'culture' can be created;
- additional benefits
  - provision of 'knowledge management', 'the bringing together and effective sharing of knowledge among the identified stakeholders'
  - provision of supply chain accountability for achieving desired performance
  - the provider assumes risk on behalf of the user in return for a share of the profit.

ALTERNATIVE FUELS

With the increasing concerns about global warming, attention has inevitably been focused on the causes of this phenomenon. One of the major culprits identified by scientists has been the emissions created by burning fossil fuels in transport vehicles, with special emphasis on road vehicles.

This area of science is extraordinarily complicated in itself. However, it is made even more incomprehensible to the layperson when the scientists themselves do not seem to agree on the extent or the degree of this problem.

It is not just the macro-environment (global warming and greenhouse gases), but the effects of road vehicle emissions on human health in the micro-environment such as a city street that concern many people. Fossil fuels tend to produce what is called particulate matter (PM), which is, amongst other things, unburnt fuel. Diesel engines are particularly prone to producing this type of emission. Medical studies have raised concerns about what has come to be known as PM10s and their effect on sufferers of respiratory illnesses such as asthma. PM10s are particulate matter smaller than 10 microns in size. An effective method for reducing these emissions is exhaust after-treatment. A device called a particulate trap is fitted to the vehicle exhaust system, which effectively prevents the PMs being discharged into the atmosphere. It is not a straightforward matter to fit this equipment to existing vehicles because of the effects it may have on engine performance and the space required to accommodate the equipment.

The internal combustion engine also produces other emissions that are a cause for concern. The main culprits and their effects are:

Emission	Main Effects
Carbon monoxide	Toxic
Carbon dioxide	Implicated in global warming
Oxides of nitrogen	Photochemical smog and ozone formation
Volatile organic compounds	Photochemical smog
Sulphur dioxide	Acid rain
Particulate matter	Respiratory problems

Reading the above table it is little wonder that attention has turned to finding an alternative fuel to power road vehicles. Before discussing alternative fuels it is worth explaining that the quality of road fuels and engines has been dramatically improved in the last 10 years. In the main this has been achieved by:

● reducing the sulphur content in diesel fuel;
● fitting catalytic converters to all new cars sold after 1 January 1993;
● high-pressure fuel injection systems;
● the use of computerized engine management systems.

Unfortunately much of this good work has been nullified by the increase in road congestion and the number of private cars on the roads.

There are many alternative fuels being developed currently. This section will briefly outline the fuel and highlight any particular points of interest.

Compressed natural gas (CNG)

Natural gas is mainly methane and is to be found in most homes in the UK where it is used for domestic purposes. Natural gas is used in a combustion engine in the same way as petrol, that is to say it requires a spark to ignite it rather than compression.

One obvious problem with this fuel is the lack of refuelling infrastructure, therefore vehicles will either have to return to their base at the end of their journey or at least go to another point where they may be refuelled. This is all the more frustrating when one understands that this gas is already widely distributed via the existing domestic gas infrastructure. Should the vehicle run out of fuel then it will have to be towed back to base, as currently there is no alternative.

CNG-powered trucks require roughly five times the volume of fuel storage that a diesel-powered truck requires. The weight of fuel tanks will obviously be increased and detract from the payload capacity of the vehicle. The actual process of refuelling can be achieved in two ways – either fast-fill or slow-fill. The fast-fill method requires a compressor to compress the gas after taking it from the main supply network. The compressed gas is then stored in tanks ready for vehicles to draw the fuel. Using this method, vehicles may achieve a refuelling time comparable with fuels such as diesel. The slow-fill method uses a smaller compressor and no intermediate storage tanks. This option is a low-cost alternative to fast-fill provided there is a gas supply to the vehicle's base. Its major drawback is that the vehicle will have to be coupled to the refuelling system overnight.

From a financial point of view, CNG engines will cost more than standard diesel engines but there are currently grants available from the government to help with the additional cost. The excise duty on natural gas is also currently attractively lower than on traditional road fuels.

From an emissions point of view natural gas performs very well and is increasingly seen as a viable alternative for commercial vehicles working in urban areas. This is mainly due to the range and refuelling limitations of the fuel but also because of its beneficial exhaust emission performance.

Liquid natural gas (LNG)

This is the same fuel as CNG, the only difference being in the way it is stored and supplied. LNG is stored at a temperature of -162 degrees Celsius but in many other respects behaves like diesel fuel. Refuelling times are very similar, although the person refuelling will have to use protective equipment for safety reasons.

The use of both CNG and LNG has been steadily growing in recent years as operators of commercial vehicles, especially in urban areas, have become convinced of their advantages.

Bi-fuel or dual fuel options

Bi-fuel systems are designed so that the vehicle is running exclusively on either one fuel or the other. Dual-fuel options are designed so that the vehicle can operate on a mixture of fuels at the same time or revert to operating on only one fuel if necessary.

These types of hybrid vehicles have been developed to overcome operating range or operational difficulties. Usually the vehicle will have a choice of fuel. This could be CNG and diesel or petrol and electric power. The problem with these vehicles is that they are not only more complex in design but also do not necessarily deliver the full benefits of one option or the other.

Liquefied petroleum gas (LPG)

This is a mix of propane and butane gas. It is a by-product of the petroleum and natural gas production process. It requires a spark ignition engine and is popular as an alternative to petrol. It benefits from an existing refuelling infrastructure especially in continental Europe.

Bio-diesel

This is a fuel that is refined from various vegetable-based oils such as rapeseed oil. It performs much like diesel fuel and is currently used in a limited way.

Electric power

Vehicles powered by electricity have existed for many years. The use of electricity has been confined to smaller vehicles due to the weight and volume of batteries required. Recent developments in battery and fuel cell technology have made electric power for light transport a viable alternative. These vehicles benefit from low emissions and are very quiet.

Fuel cell technology is likely to provide the motive power for light transport in the future. This technology exploits the electricity produced by hydrogen and oxygen atoms when they combine together to form water. Fuel cells usually require a hydrogen-rich fuel such as methane. The resultant electricity drives an electric motor, which in turn provides the motive power. Fuel cells produce low emissions.

SUMMARY

In this chapter a number of new concepts and ideas in logistics have been considered. The first of these was the development of trading on the Internet. A number of new and very different ways of conducting business were reviewed, and it is clear that most of these will have significant implications for logistics. The major implications should come from e-tailing, e-fulfilment and e-procurement.

The phenomenon of home shopping was also discussed. It was noted that it is important to differentiate between home shopping and home delivery because these are related but very different developments. Once again it is clear that there will be some significant implications for distribution and logistics as these concepts become more established.

The important development of ECR (efficient consumer response) was briefly described. This concept serves to emphasize the need to take a supply chain approach to serving customers, and this type of approach necessitates companies working together across company boundaries. Linked to the ECR approach, the ideas of lean thinking and the agile supply chain were outlined. These techniques promote the need for supply chains to be cost-effective, but also to be responsive to the fast-changing requirements in today's market-places.

The move to a more sophisticated format for outsourcing logistics operations was discussed with the idea of fourth-party logistics. Some of the drawbacks currently to be found with third-party arrangements were shown to be the reason for the development of fourth-party logistics.

Finally, some of the characteristics of alternative fuels were reviewed.

References

Andersen Consulting and Cambridge Marketing Intelligence (1998) *Logistics Software Guide*, Institute of Logistics, Corby

Benson, R (1998) Benchmarking lessons in the process industries, *Manufacturing Excellence*, May, Haymarket Business Publications, London

Bicheno, J (1991) *Implementing Just-in-time*, IFS

Camp, R C (1989) *Benchmarking: The search for industry best practices that lead to superior performance*, ASQC Quality Press, Milwaukee

Canadine, I C (1998) in *Members Directory*, Institute of Logistics, Corby

Christopher, M (1997) *Marketing Logistics*, Butterworth Heinemann, Oxford

Datamonitor (1999) *European Logistics 1999: Opportunities in a consolidating market*, Datamonitor

Department of the Environment, Transport and the Regions (1998) *Focus on Freight*

Department of Trade and Industry (1991) *Environment: A challenge for business*

FTA (1994) *Theft Prevention Guide*, FTA, Tunbridge Wells

FTA (1998) *The Manager's Guide to Distribution Costs*

FTA (1998) *Vehicle and Load Theft Survey*

Gattorna, J L (1990) *Handbook of Logistics and Distribution Management*, 4th edn, Gower, Aldershot

Gattorna, J L *Strategic Supply Chain Alignment*

Hesket, J L, Glaskowsky, N and Ivie, R M (1973) *Business Logistics*, Ronald, New York

Scott, C and Westbrook, R (1991) New strategic tools for supply chain management, *sIJPDLM*, **21** (1)

Stone, C A (1968) *The Logistics Review*, **A** (16)

Szymankiewiez, J (1996) The changing role of third party logistics, *Logistics Focus*, October, Institute of Logistics

Van Den Burg, G (1975) *Containerisation and Other Unit Transport*, Hutchinson Benham, London

Zairi, M (1994) *Competitive Benchmarking*, Stanley Thornes, Cheltenham

Index